Political Culture in the Nineteenth-Century South

Political Culture in the Nineteenth-Century South

Mississippi, 1830–1900

Bradley G. Bond

Louisiana State University Press
Baton Rouge and London

Manufactured in the United States of America
First printing
04 03 02 01 00 99 98 97 96 95 5 4 3 2 1

Designer: Amanda M. Key
Typeface: Sabon
Typesetter: Moran Printing, Inc.
Printer and binder: Thomson-Shore, Inc.

Library of Congress Cataloging-in-Publication Data
Bond, Bradley G., 1963—
Political culture in the nineteenth-century South : Mississippi, 1830–1900 / Bradley G. Bond.
p. cm.
Includes bibliographical references and index.
ISBN 0-8071-1976-8 (alk. paper)
1. Mississippi—Politics and government. 2. Political culture—Mississippi—History—19th century. 3. Mississippi—Social conditions. I. Title.
F341.B76 1995
306.2'09762'09034—dc20 95-11134
CIP

The author is grateful to the *Journal of Mississippi History* for permission to quote from his previously published articles: "Edward C. Walthall and the 1880 Senatorial Nomination: The Politics of Balance in the Redeemer Era," L (February, 1988), 1–20; and "Habits of Foodstuff and Market Production: A Look at Mississippi," LVI (August, 1994), 211–31.

The paper in this book meets the guidelines for permanence and durability of the Committee on Production Guidelines for Book Longevity of the Council on Library Resources. ♾

For my grandparents

Contents

Tables

Acknowledgments

While working on this book, I received assistance from numerous individuals and institutions; I am pleased to acknowledge their favors.

The Department of History at Louisiana State University, through its T. Harry Williams Fellowship, made available invaluable financial aid to conduct research. The graduate school awarded a travel grant. At the research facilities I visited, numerous archivists and librarians assisted me, but none were more supportive than Bill Erwin of the William R. Perkins Library, Duke University.

Since this study started as a doctoral dissertation, my initial critics were graduate school advisors. William J. Cooper, Jr., in every way an exemplary mentor, weathered my earliest drafts without complaint. His advice has never failed me. Charles Royster, Gaines M. Foster, and Veronica Makowsky commented on later drafts, and I benefited as well from the critical insight of William K. Scarborough. Paul Paskoff cheerfully tolerated my intrusions on his time. Sam Hyde, Robert Page, and Kevin Yeager allowed me to test ideas on them; Mary Jane Smith did that and more; and Clay Holland assisted in the final preparation of the manuscript. For the wise counsel that they each shared, I am forever grateful.

To the following family and friends, I owe a word of thanks: Max Draughn opened his home to me for a long period and made my stay in Jackson, Mississippi, a pleasant one; Richard and Shannon James welcomed me during a long journey; and M. E., Ione G., and Deborah W. Bond never doubted that I would one day complete the task.

Finally, I wish to thank the Louisiana State University Press, especially Margaret Dalrymple and John Easterly, who guided me through the process of turning a manuscript into a published volume. Nicola Mason has been an expert editor.

I dedicate this book to Xina Pearl and Lemuel Hugh Ginn, Jr., and to Retha Naomi and Murphy Ambrose Bond: salt of the earth.

Abbreviations

LSU	Louisiana and Lower Mississippi Valley Collection, Hill Memorial Library, Louisiana State University, Baton Rouge.
MDAH	Mississippi Department of Archives and History, Jackson.
MSU	Mitchell Memorial Library, Mississippi State University, Starkville.
NL	Illinois Central Archives, Newberry Library, Chicago.
SHC	Southern Historical Collection, University of North Carolina, Chapel Hill.
UM	Special Collections, University of Mississippi, Oxford.
WRP	William R. Perkins Library, Duke University, Durham, North Carolina.

Political Culture in the Nineteenth-Century South

Mississippi Regions
1880
Northern Bluffs
Marshall
Panola
Pontotoc
North-
Central
Hills
Delta
Washington
Lowndes
Black Prairie
Noxubee
Leake
Warren
Copiah
Jones
Southern Bluffs
Piney Woods
Wilkinson
Harrison

Introduction

As pioneering interpreters of the South, Wilbur J. Cash and C. Vann Woodward outlined the contour of a debate that has animated southern historiography for nearly fifty years. Published within a decade of each other, their seminal works (Cash's *The Mind of the South* and Woodward's *Origins of the New South*) articulated contrasting understandings of the region.[1] In Cash's South, time stood still. The features that lent the region its antebellum distinctiveness persisted into the twentieth century, while in Woodward's South the Civil War and Reconstruction ushered in a period of change. Neither interpretation entirely satisfies, and neither sufficiently accounts for the complexities of the nineteenth-century South. Whereas Cash failed to consider the fullness of the postbellum transformation, Woodward neglected to explain the continuation of certain attitudes common among white southerners.

No state offers historians a better view of the transforming-yet-persisting South than Mississippi. Between 1830 and 1900 the state followed a familiar pattern of evolution from sparsely settled wilderness to prosperous part of the cotton kingdom, only to emerge from the 1860s impoverished and in search of industrial-commercial development; political, social, and economic changes in the late nineteenth century, however, failed to alter prevailing concepts of racial identity. Neither does any state offer historians such an uncrowded field of study. Although existing works on Mississippi collectively and admirably cover the nineteenth century, none attempts to tell the story of Mississippi's tumultuous passage from Old South to New South.[2]

My object is to examine over a broad period of time white southerners'

1. W. J. Cash, *The Mind of the South* (1941; rpr. New York, 1969); C. Vann Woodward, *Origins of the New South, 1877–1913* (Baton Rouge, 1951). For a different but nonetheless grand approach to the New South, see Edward L. Ayers, *The Promise of the New South: Life After Reconstruction* (New York, 1992).

2. Included among the studies that focus on aspects of Mississippi history are: John Hebron Moore, *The Emergence of the Cotton Kingdom in the Old Southwest: Mississippi, 1770–1860* (Baton Rouge, 1988); John Bettersworth, *Confederate Mississippi: The People and Policies of a Cotton State in Wartime* (Baton Rouge, 1943); William C. Harris, *Presidential Reconstruction in Mississippi* (Baton Rouge, 1967); Harris, *Day of the Carpetbagger:*

social ethic, a collection of ideas, at times contradictory, about the nature of a good republic and good citizenship. As such, the book can be read as a narrative that attempts to synthesize extant literature while making slightly revisionistic arguments about specific phenomena. But a variety of subtexts also course through the study: the interaction of race-consciousness and class-consciousness, the competing ideologies of market production and self-sufficiency, and the influence of perceptions upon reality (and vice versa). It should also be noted that the book deals with the predominant social ethic as espoused by white males, who for half of the time covered in the study acted alone in political culture, though not without making reference to others; as autonomous players, white females and blacks occupy a minor role in the story told. In recognition of the fact that white women perhaps possessed visions of a good republic contrary to the predominant one and that blacks loathed the principal idea undergirding southern political culture, the phrase "the social ethic" should be understood to mean "a social ethic."

Briefly, I propose that the social ethic as envisioned by white southern males, particularly as reflected in ideal notions of liberty and virtue, informed the political culture, which is defined as the "obvious and universal" facets of political life that "every one sees and no one is astonished at." Political culture is what Ronald Formisano has called the "taken-for-granteds" of politics. It is a fashionable description of what was formerly known as ideology.[3] In this study, the terms *political culture* and *social ethic* are practically used as synonyms. For at the base of the southern social ethic lay concerns about preserving liberty and virtue, the chief concepts that the political culture sought to preserve. The primary difference between the two concepts resides in the fact that the social ethic was a body of ideas,

---

Republican Reconstruction in Mississippi (Baton Rouge, 1979); Michael Wayne, *The Reshaping of Plantation Society: The Natchez District, 1860–1880* (Baton Rouge, 1983); Vernon Lane Wharton, *The Negro in Mississippi, 1865–1890* (1947; rpr. New York, 1965); Robert L. Brandfon, *Cotton Kingdom of the New South: A History of the Yazoo Mississippi Delta from Reconstruction to the Twentieth Century* (Cambridge, Mass., 1967); James C. Cobb, *The Most Southern Place on Earth: The Mississippi Delta and the Roots of Southern Identity* (New York, 1992); Albert D. Kirwan, *Revolt of the Rednecks: Mississippi Politics, 1876–1925* (1951; rpr. New York, 1965).

3. All quotes derive from Ronald Formisano, *The Transformation of Political Culture: Massachusetts Parties, 1790s–1840s* (New York, 1983), 4, who is quoting John Stuart Mill and Louis Wirth. Compare the definition of *political culture* offered herein with the definition of *ideology* suggested by Eric Foner, *Free Soil, Free Labor, Free Men: The Ideology of the Republican Party Before the Civil War* (New York, 1970), 5.

while political culture was more tangible. It was the expression of deeply held beliefs. Put another way, ideal notions of good citizenship and a good republic, founded as they were on concepts of liberty and virtue, shaped political culture, though as happened after the Civil War, the consequences of defeat altered political culture and obliged white Mississippians to amend some of their ideals.

The emphasis on liberty and virtue as vehicles for conducting an exploration of political culture stems from recent developments in American historiography, specifically from the debates that appear in the literature on the early republic and that pit historians who see republicanism as key to understanding political culture against those who see liberalism as most important. During the past three decades, scholars have undertaken rewarding labors tracing the pedigree of American political thought, and even though disputes have arisen over the sway that one writer or another enjoyed among the Founding Fathers, students of the subject agree that the young nation construed notions of liberty and virtue from diverse schools of Western thought. By 1830 a curious combination of Enlightenment-era ideas, refracted through nineteenth-century democratic reform, modeled concepts of liberty and virtue.

One version of liberty and virtue embraced by Mississippians stemmed from country republican thought. As embodied in the nation's early national history, the chief tenets of country republican thought concentrated on citizens' freedom to pursue their own affairs under the protection of the law and to participate in the process of governing. Unlike their nineteenth-century heirs, country republican thinkers, when defining good citizenship, referred less to "the people" than to a natural aristocracy of talented men. Self-sacrifice and service to the commonweal, they believed, qualified the talented few to claim liberty and virtue as their unique possession.[4] Another school of thought molded Mississippians' notions of liberty, too. In recognition of the revolutionary changes that occurred in commerce and politics after 1688, Thomas Hobbes and John Locke remodeled English notions of liberty and virtue. Taking their cue from the merchant

4. Works important to my understanding of country republican thought include: Bernard Bailyn, *Ideological Origins of the American Revolution* (Cambridge, Mass., 1967); Robert Shalhope, "Toward a Republican Synthesis: The Emergence of an Understanding of Republicanism in American Historiography," *William and Mary Quarterly*, 3rd ser., XXIX (1972), 49–80; Gordon S. Wood, *The Creation of the American Republic, 1776–1787* (1969; rpr. New York, 1972); J. G. A. Pocock, *The Machiavellian Moment* (Princeton, 1975); Dorothy Ross, "The Liberal Tradition Revisited and the Republican Tradition Addressed," in *New Directions in American Intellectual History*, eds. John Higham and Paul Conkin (Baltimore, 1979).

class, Hobbes and Locke downplayed the significance of participating in civic life as a means of ensuring personal liberty; instead, they argued, liberty and virtue could best be achieved through individual economic success and the jealous protection of property rights. According to J. G. A. Pocock, by the late eighteenth century, "a right to things became a way to the practice of virtue." In the United States, the liberties associated with the Bill of Rights granted citizens without the leisure or capacity to govern rights identical to those enjoyed by folk who possessed such attributes.[5]

Both versions of liberty and virtue fashioned white Mississippians' social ethic and in turn their political culture. The combination owed to previous southerners' facile unification of competing schools of thought. Historians of the early national period have concluded that influential country republican thinkers, Thomas Jefferson and James Madison especially, fused republican and liberal ideas when faced with the reality of governing a population less virtuous than they had imagined. As a result, they left their southern admirers an ambiguous legacy. The original Jeffersonian vision, which apotheosized yeoman farmers who shunned the market and intrusive governmental power, evolved into a vision of an active federal government concerned with securing agricultural and industrial markets abroad. While they maintained the goal of fostering a society both free and virtuous under the tenets of Arcadian simplicity, Jefferson's and Madison's mature social vision endorsed market-oriented behavior, too.[6] As the cotton frontier expanded, Mississippians found meaning in the revised vision. They continued, just as had the statesman from Monticello, to believe the good republic susceptible to self-serving attitudes, but they nevertheless pursued material success in the market. Semiconscious of their truncated view of good citizenship in a good republic, residents found salvation from the contradictory ideology they had inherited in another idea, an idea that surmounted the tension between Arcadian and market-oriented values by proclaiming white liberty dependent on the presence of an enslaved class of

5. Quoting J. G. A. Pocock, *Virtue, Commerce, and History: Essays on Political Thought and History, Chiefly in the Eighteenth Century* (Cambridge, England, 1985), 50. On liberalism in the United States, see John Patrick Diggins, *The Lost Soul of American Politics* (New York, 1984); Diggins, "Comrades and Citizens: New Mythologies in American Historiography," *American Historical Review,* XC (1985), 614–38, as well as Diggins' "Reply" to Paul Conkin, *ibid.*, 647; Joyce Appleby, *Capitalism and a New Social Order: The Republican Vision of the 1790s* (New York, 1985); Appleby, *Liberalism and Republicanism in the Historical Imagination* (Cambridge, Mass., 1992).

6. On Jefferson's and Madison's epiphanies, see two works by Drew McCoy, *The Elusive Republic: Political Economy in Jeffersonian America* (New York, 1980); *The Last of the Fathers: James Madison and Republican Legacy* (Cambridge, England, 1989).

laborers, too poor and beholden to claim liberty and virtue as their own. Thus, the institution of black slavery made possible the union of disparate notions of liberty and virtue, and permitted too the creation of white cultural homogeneity based on popular support for slavery.[7]

Some of the ideas that informed the social ethic, then, derived from traditional schools of thought (communitarian, Arcadian, and pastoral values), while others derived from modernity (market participation). Sociologists, political scientists, and historians have long employed modernization theory, a holdover from the positivism of the early twentieth century, and Marxism, its ideological opposite, to describe societies and the changes that they undergo. Where modernization theorists see a natural and healthy progression from traditional to modern social structures, scholars writing from a Marxist perspective view the transition as an augury of exploitation and alienation experienced under capitalism. According to modernization theory, all civil entities are built upon complex systems of social relationships and organized along traditional or modern principles. Traditional societies secure their structure from communitarian values, ascriptive status, and the ownership of the tools of production by the producer, while modern ones, generally those that have undergone an industrial revolution, eschew communitarian values, emphasize individuals' achieved status, and divorce producers from the means of production. Modern societies possess a high degree of political participation, not simply that measured by voter turnout, but that indicated by the appropriation of a society's political symbols and goals by those at the periphery of political power.[8] Briefly stated, modern societies are democratic and capitalistic, industrialized and urbanized.

The traditional-modern dichotomy inherent in modernization theory

7. On southerners' fusion of country republican and liberal strains of thought and the influence of slavery, see Robert E. Shalhope, "Thomas Jefferson's Republicanism and Antebellum Southern Thought," *Journal of Southern History,* XLII (1976), 555–56. Charles Sellers, *The Market Revolution: Jacksonian America, 1815–1846* (New York, 1991), 396–427, more forcefully contends that slavery shaped economic liberalism in America. On the transformation of a free state's concepts of liberty in the early nineteenth century, see Christopher Clark, *The Roots of Rural Capitalism: Western Massachusetts, 1780–1860* (Ithaca, 1990), 230–43, 317–29. On the notion that southerners believed liberty could only be claimed if one strove to possess it, see Michael Kammen, *Spheres of Liberty: Changing Perceptions of Liberty in American Culture* (Madison, 1986), 95–98. Such an idea allowed southerners to think of slaves as unfit for liberty.

8. Richard D. Brown, *Modernization: The Transformation of American Life, 1600–1865* (New York, 1976), 8–14; S. N. Eisenstadt, *Modernization: Protest and Change* (Englewood Cliffs, N.J., 1966), 2–15.

may be easily applied to Mississippi, but doing so wrongly suggests certain progress and minimizes the importance of early signposts of modernity, especially the maturation of a market economy. The sixteenth-century commercialization of England's economy fostered the development of political centralization, stimulated the expansion of the market, and sent the nation's redundant children to work in factories or to live in the New World; two centuries later, the descendants of those transatlantic immigrants continued the process of adaptation to a market society and filled the public lands of the Deep South.[9] They left their former homes not as refugees from modernity, however, but as acquisitive searchers, looking to make a place for themselves in the market economy. Scholars who ignore settlers' motivation in moving to the old southwestern frontier miss the beginning of the long process of modernization. Although immigrants arrived with two ideas characteristic of traditional societies (the institution of slavery and a disdain for strong central authority), they nevertheless sought to augment their status in the market.[10] Just as surely as early America was the child of Europe's commercial revolution, the market ethos was always present in the Deep South; it was the midwife at Mississippi's birthing.[11]

9. On the application of modernization theory to Mississippi history, see Lester Milton Salamon, "Protest, Politics, and Modernization in the American South: Mississippi as a 'Developing Society'" (Ph.D. dissertation, Harvard University, 1971). On the commercialization of England and changing attitudes, see Joyce Appleby, "Modernization Theory and the Formation of Modern Social Theories in England and America," *Comparative Studies in Society and History,* XX (1978), 259–62, 265.

10. Two reasons have been advanced to explain colonial whites' embrace of slavery: a low man-to-land ratio in the South Atlantic states during the colonial period, and racial prejudice. See Peter A. Coclanis, *Shadow of a Dream: Life and Death in the South Carolina Lowcountry* (New York, 1989), 61; Edmund S. Morgan, *American Slavery, American Freedom: The Ordeal of Colonial Virginia* (New York, 1975). On market orientation in colonial America, see Carole Shammas, "How Self-Sufficient Was Early America?" *Journal of Interdisciplinary History,* XIII (1982), 247–72.

11. Alternative views of southern social development might be found in Eugene Genovese, "Yeoman Farmers in a Slaveholders' Democracy," *Agricultural History,* XLIX (1975), 336; Genovese, *The Political Economy of Slavery: Studies in the Economy and Society of the Slave South* (New York, 1965), 13–40; Steven Hahn, *The Roots of Southern Populism: Yeoman Farmers and the Transformation of the Georgia Upcountry, 1850–1890* (New York, 1983); Hahn, "The Yeomanry of the Non-plantation South: Upper Piedmont Georgia, 1850–1860," in *Class, Conflict, and Consensus: Antebellum Southern Community Studies,* eds. Orville Vernon Burton and Robert C. McMath, Jr. (Westport, Conn., 1982), 45; Hahn, "The 'Unmaking' of the Southern Yeomanry: The Transformation of the Georgia Upcountry, 1860–1890," in *The Countryside in the Age of Capitalist Transformation: Essays in the Social History of Rural America,* eds. Steven Hahn and Jonathan Prude (Chapel Hill, 1985), 141–79; Michael Merrill, "Cash is Good to Eat: Self-Sufficiency and Exchange in the Rural

As long as a prevailing devotion to the institution of slavery obfuscated competing aspects of Mississippians' complex notions of a good republic, the political culture of the state remained open to all white citizens equally, if they avoided becoming, like slaves, poor and dependent upon others. But when the federal government determined that African Americans should be incorporated into the political and economic life of the South, Mississippi's antebellum social ethic seemed imperiled to contemporaries. Later, white southerners' conscious efforts to spark commercial progress exacerbated the danger presented the ethic. For between 1865 and 1880, Mississippi not only obtained the appurtenances of modernity (railroads, broadened political participation, industrial development), it also entered a period of ideological evolution. Communitarian values slowly disappeared, and the commercial world lured some citizens into its web. Furthermore, to meet the exigency created by the emergence of African Americans from slavery, white citizens altered their concepts of liberty and virtue. No longer did they think of the political culture as open to all whites; instead, liberty and virtue were unique possessions of whites who followed the Democratic party. In the last twenty years of the nineteenth century, the social changes precipitated by Civil War and Reconstruction appeared in competing notions of liberty. On one hand, the beneficiaries of the commercial order considered wealth and respectability signs of virtuous living. But on the other, agrarians retained their love for the Jeffersonian ideal: only tillers of the earth might claim to be the children of God, the possessors of liberty. Although these two visions of a good republic and good citizenship conflicted, the differences were subsumed, just as they had been in the antebellum period by an overarching devotion to the racial division of society.

Two significant conclusions are advanced in this study. First, between 1830 and 1900 Mississippi experienced great social and economic changes. Second, despite such transformations, anxieties about fostering white cultural homogeneity and preserving African Americans as an underclass of non-citizens, prompted Mississippians to mask all other concerns behind the veil of race.[12] Mississippi's transformation from frontier into a

Economy of the United States," *Radical History Review,* IV (1977), 42–66; Morton Rothstein, "The Antebellum South as a Dual Economy: A Tentative Hypothesis," *Agricultural History,* XLI (1967), 373–82; Joseph P. Reidy, *From Slavery to Agrarian Capitalism in the Cotton Plantation South: Central Georgia, 1800–1880* (Chapel Hill, 1992), 245.

12. The "other concerns" submerged by white Mississippians' affinity for elevating racial prejudices included primarily class conflict. The interaction of race and class is a perennial

small part of the late nineteenth century's commercial order failed to alter substantively the race-conscious underpinnings of the social ethic. To facilitate a systematic treatment of the evolution of Mississippi's social ethic, the work has been divided into three parts.

In the first part, "The Way Things Were," I offer an initial definition of the ethic.[13] Chapters One and Two alternately portray the state as tradition-bound and modern, influenced by both communal and individualistic values. Communitarian values, nourished in Mississippi's rugged environment, gave residents a sense of shared suffering and bolstered their belief that they acted independent of governmental authorities. Yet Mississippi was not merely a state on the frontier. The environment that gave Mississippi its backcountry aura made possible the production of staple crops and the conduct of a variety of other market-oriented activities. Oddly, however, immigrants brought to the cotton frontier concepts of liberty that demanded self-sufficient production, too. As self-described independent men who also produced for the market, antebellum Mississippians asserted their command of liberty and virtue as defined by citizens of Arcadia and by citizens who experienced the sixteenth-century commercial revolution. In matters of politics, the ability to participate in the process of governing and the willingness to perpetuate African-American slavery permitted white southerners to formulate a consensus that skirted over their competing ideals and that formed the core of the social ethic. The antebellum ethic, then, demanded that the possessors of liberty and virtue practice self-sufficiency within the context of market production; it also required the creation of an underclass that could neither produce for the market nor participate in politics. The presence of that underclass allowed white residents to submerge class tensions and thus to foster a sense of white cultural homogeneity that led them to embrace secession as the only available method for protecting their concepts of liberty.

The second part of the study, "Agencies of Change," examines the influence of Civil War, Reconstruction, and the commercial order upon the social ethic and society. One of the first victims of the war was the social ethic itself. The concepts of liberty and virtue that white southerners fought

---

topic for historians of the South, but no one handles it better than Charles L. Flynn, Jr., *White Land, Black Labor: Caste and Class in Late Nineteenth-Century Georgia* (Baton Rouge, 1983), though he dwells more on the planter class than do I.

13. The titles of the first two parts of the study are taken from Eugen Weber's *Peasants into Frenchmen: The Modernization of Rural France, 1870–1914* (Stanford, 1976), and the title of the final section is a slightly altered version of Weber's third section title.

to protect quickly faded as the Confederate and Mississippi governments enacted policies contrary to prewar ideals. Furthermore, during the second phase of the war to defend the social ethic, the war against free labor, the federal government and ex-slaves attempted to disrupt whites' closely held notions of liberty. The appearance of three postwar amendments to the federal constitution testify to their success; the emergence of the crop-lien law, however, testifies to the failure of the amendments to destroy the race-conscious foundation of the social ethic. Under the sway of the crop-lien law and political violence, white citizens recreated aspects of their antebellum ethic, denying freed persons the full measure of economic and political liberty promised by the northern social ethic. They continued to define claims to liberty and virtue by the presence of a black underclass that represented the antithesis of their ideals. Even though they preserved some of their notions of the social ethic based on African-American subservience to whites, they could not completely halt the transformation of the postbellum South. The emergent commercial order, epitomized in Mississippi by railroads, the lumber industry, and country merchants, destroyed former notions of economic liberty as the agencies of commercial development demanded economic dependence, the antipode of the antebellum social ethic.

Part III of the work, "Accepting and Rejecting Change," discusses Mississippians' responses to the New South commercial order. While both middle-class whites and agrarians refused to relinquish aspects of the ethic, the former attempted to protect the new order, and the latter sought to alter it. To refashion the homogeneous social order of the prewar South as they envisioned it and to remove from society those left behind by the state's advance, middle-class reformers advocated prohibition and disfranchisement, as well as the eradication of disease and ignorance. Agrarians, on the other hand, advocated the creation of a homogeneous order founded on antebellum notions of an egalitarian economic and political order for whites. Returning to the ideal of self-sufficient production within the context of market participation and the broad participation of plain folk in the process of governing promised to restore the values cherished by their predecessors. Neither the middle-class nor agrarian versions of the social ethic triumphed during the nineteenth century. The political rednecks who ascended to power in the early twentieth century curiously combined middle-class affection for the commercial order with agrarian class-conscious rhetoric denouncing the new order.

By the early 1900s the social ethic had been redefined. Where once citizens who wished to proclaim themselves possessors of liberty and virtue believed that they had first to practice self-sufficiency and market production, postbellum claimants were clerks and farmers, planters and industrial boosters. All would admit, with joy or sadness, that they lived in a world different from the one their parents had known. Yet despite changes in the state's political culture and subtle alterations to the social ethic, white citizens insisted, as had their ancestors, that good citizenship belonged exclusively to members of their race. African Americans, their economic and political gains notwithstanding, could not claim liberty as their own in southern political culture.

Part I

The Way Things Were

For all of us there is a twilight zone between history and memory; between the past as a generalized record which is open to relatively dispassionate inspection and the past as a remembered part of, or background to, one's own life.

—Eric Hobsbawm

On a cool, crisp January day in 1840, Andrew Jackson visited the Mississippi city named after him. Three years into retirement and no longer a maker of others' political fortunes, he was nonetheless greeted at the outskirts of the city by fawning admirers vying to escort the former president to Governor Alexander G. McNutt's residence; later, revelers ushered Jackson to a ball staged in his honor. On the following day, a Saturday, townspeople and farmers from the countryside joined state legislators at the capitol to cheer as local dignitaries sang the general's praise. Pomp and "the usual strain of exaggeration" were the order of the day.[1] Anxious to hear a denunciation of the political opposition, the crowd, which flowed onto the hillside grounds of the state house, heard only perfunctory and courteous remarks. Jackson seemed old. His voice was weak, hardly befitting a man known for vitriolic outbursts. Yet despite his physical frailty, few who saw him considered the day a disappointment.

At the time of his visit, Mississippians counted Jackson a champion of common folk and an exemplary citizen. His war against the power accorded banks resonated with the people, who had only recently embarked upon a struggle to repudiate state debts accrued in support of two financial institutions; in the face of other forms of institutional power, his enthusiastic posturing as the guardian of personal liberty appealed to Mississippians. They regarded critics of the great man's legacy as contemptuous of democracy. Even after his death, Jackson's reputation endured. Having ob-

1. Woodville *Republican*, January 23, 1840.

served the political uses to which "the *soverigns* [*sic*]" put their memories of Jackson, one Alabama wag, writing in the early 1850s, observed that "it is somewhat dangerous to tell them that the Jin'al is not a candidate this election, or they would consider it a reflection upon the old Gen.'s democracy."[2] In the collective remembrances of many white southerners, Jackson was the fountain of personal liberty and egalitarianism.

Besides glorifying the ex-president as their defender, Mississippians admired as well his progress from humble origins to the White House. He was the patron saint of ambitious fathers and their children. Like many of his admirers who had migrated to the Deep South, Jackson exhibited a frontiersman's desire for material success. Possessed of high aspirations and a keen eye for judging the future value of property, he secured substantial land- and slaveholdings before bursting upon the national scene. To Deep South men-on-the-make, his preservation of what historian Mary Elizabeth Young has designated the *Zeitgeist* of the age ("freedom, frugality, and equality of opportunism") extended to future generations the promise that they too might achieve some tangible measure of economic and political independence.[3]

In 1861, no less than in 1840, Mississippi was a product of its history. The actual events that had occurred in the past, as well as myths about the past, informed citizens' concepts of liberty and virtue in a good republic. Jackson, who at once represented success in the market economy and the independent man of the frontier, embodied the contradictions of the social ethic. Mississippians' apotheosis of him signaled their refusal to recognize the inherent conflict between their myths and the realities of life in the Deep South. Their concept of political and economic liberty, based as it was on the perpetuation of African-American slavery, allowed them to obfuscate the incongruence between their ideals and reality and to create in the process a sense of cultural homogeneity among whites as a means of assuring political and economic liberty.

Three competing forces, all of them suggested by the celebration of Jackson as an exemplary citizen, combined in the antebellum period to produce white Mississippians' complex and contradictory social ethic. First, communitarian values, the product of rural custom and a rugged environment, nurtured illusions of the state as Arcadia. Based on their affection for com-

2. William S. Powell to Cordelia Powell Mansfield, July 28, 1853, in John Lipscomb Johnson Papers, SHC.

3. Mary Elizabeth Young, *Redskins, Ruffleshirts, and Rednecks: Indian Allotments in Alabama and Mississippi, 1830–1860* (Norman, Okla., 1961), 193. Robert Remini's *Andrew Jackson* (1966; rpr. New York, 1969) provides insight into Jackson as a man-on-the-make.

munitarian values, citizens demanded that the state play a restricted role in their lives. They placed the burden for maintaining roads, river channels, and levees on communities, safeguarding, they believed, the version of liberty that belonged to isolated, rough, and autonomous folk. Second, a thirst for material success that citizens evinced by producing for the market economy contradicted the Arcadian ideal. Through the strict maintenance of frontier notions of economic independence, particularly those that demanded responsible economic behavior and the avoidance of debt, citizens thought they could preserve their liberty even though they were entangled in the market economy. Finally, institutional forces allowed whites to found notions of liberty and virtue in their identification of an underclass composed primarily of African Americans. A broad-based consensus on the place of slavery in society obscured the contradictions inherent in Mississippians' retention of communal and market-oriented values; and the central place assigned slavery in the social ethic in turn complemented and informed other values, particularly the overarching desire to unite all deserving citizens in a good republic.

Whatever internal conflicts individual citizens might have experienced when considering which version of liberty and virtue (the Arcadian or market paradigm) to pursue, all agreed on the fundamental necessity of slavery to secure their independence. Taken together, these forces created a social ethic that revered both white liberty and black enslavement, market production and self-sufficiency, traditional values and modern ones. In 1861 white Mississippians occupied a twilight zone in their history, willing neither to surrender their mythological past nor to reject firmly the modern world they strove to invent.

Chapter 1

Vagaries of the Backcountry

"I suppose dirt and rags are always in part the emblem of this wild state of society," observed the dyspeptic English traveler Margaret Hall upon her arrival in Natchez. Freshly washed by a shower, the city appeared new in 1827, but the rain transformed the streets into a dough-like muck that claimed one of Hall's shoes. More disturbing to her than Natchez's streets were its children: "The children are not in rags and their outer garments, altho' of the worst make and most unbecoming fabric are still whole. All that is below the upper part of the apparel is dirty and slovenly to a degree that the lower classes in England would scorn to allow their families to wear." [1]

One need not turn to travelers' accounts of the 1820s to find portrayals of Mississippi as backcountry: isolated, poor, and dangerous. A variety of eyewitnesses testified that frontier conditions, bordering occasionally on savagery, prevailed until the twentieth century. Bears, panthers, and wolves prowled pine forests and canebrakes; irregularly maintained roads and river channels made travel difficult, at times impossible; dysentery, malaria, and yellow fever touched, in varying degrees, most of Mississippi; and levees, if built at all, rarely performed according to design.

Few residents, not just the ill-clad children that Hall observed, knew the feel of silk. Even at Natchez, the epicenter of planter-class culture, folk "common as hell" outnumbered grandees.[2] Such an observation is not intended to suggest that slaveholders, especially that rarefied group known as planters, failed to wield in political matters leverage far greater than their numbers justified, or that those outside the planter class looked contemptuously upon their neighbors who worked vast tracts of land with slaves. Instead, the proliferation of just such conditions that so alarmed Hall suggests that for the majority of Mississippians life was, in Hobbesian terms,

1. Una Pope Hennessy, ed., *The Aristocratic Journey: Being the Outspoken Letters of Mrs. Basil Hall Written During a Fourteen Months' Sojourn in America, 1827–1828* (New York, 1931), 268.

2. The reference to folk "common as hell" derives from William Alexander Percy, *Lanterns on the Levee: Recollections of a Planter's Son* (1941; rpr. Baton Rouge, 1973), 62.

truly nasty, brutish, and not infrequently short. Wealthy residents insulated themselves from some of the vagaries of the backcountry, but regardless of the assets an antebellum planter or a postbellum businessman acquired, never mind his sophistication, the perils of the backcountry could suddenly rise up and take his property, perhaps his life.

By 1840 Mississippi's frontier line of settlement had been erased, and with its disappearance, some of the backcountry's perils began slowly to diminish.[3] Forty years later, progress in removing vestiges of the backcountry was readily apparent. In some ways, however, little had changed. Crevasses continued to tear through the levee line, as yet incomplete; exotic diseases borne by foul water, mosquitoes, and ignorance claimed scores each year; and travel by common roads and waterways, though greatly improved since the antebellum period, remained burdensome. Despite manifest signs of progress, Mississippi was backcountry through most of the nineteenth century.

Faced at every turn by the vagaries of the backcountry, residents formulated concepts of good citizenship and a good republic that celebrated as liberty-loving and virtuous the rough-and-tumble pioneer, who carved from the wilderness a homogeneous society of independent, like-minded white folk, long-suffering pioneers all. Based on their civic identity, they invented a social ethic that rejected as oppressive governmental intrusion into private and communal life. For most of the nineteenth century, the autonomous individual, who turned not to governments for assistance in conquering the backcountry but to neighbors, remained the quintessence of good citizenship. Yet like the backcountry itself, which withered after 1880, habits of mind informed by the backcountry underwent a transformation in the last decades of the period. The gradual disappearance of communitarian values, in fact, was more significant than the limited gains made in controlling frontier qualities of life and the natural forces that threatened residents; but the two events (the amelioration of the backcountry's vagaries and the transformation of the social ethic) were related. As Mississippians constrained deleterious aspects of the frontier, they began relieving individuals and communities of the onus for constructing and maintaining internal improvements. The appearance of the signposts of modernity spurred the devolution of backcountry features of life and, in symbiotic fashion, prompted citizens to redefine concepts of good citizenship and a good republic.

* * *

3. For an introduction to frontier Mississippi, see Thomas D. Clark and John D. Guice, *The Old Southwest, 1795–1830* (Albuquerque, 1989).

"Let us begin by discussing the weather, for that," according to Ulrich B. Phillips, "has been the chief agency in making the South distinctive." Employing assumptions that would later be identified with the Annales school of historical study, Phillips, in the first chapter of his *Life and Labor in the Old South,* ascribed to southern environmental peculiarities a host of political and economic contingencies: the cultivation of staple crops, the plantation system, the importation of slave labor, the sectional crisis. Additionally, "the tedious heat" of the region explained, at least to Phillips, characteristics associated with southerners such as indolence and slow, slurred speech. Wilbur J. Cash agreed that the physical world, "itself a sort of cosmic conspiracy against reality in favor of romance," bred into southerners a carefree temperament. Where, to his mind, a lack of arable land and harsh winters molded New Englanders into a severe and disciplined people, southerners found subsistence easy, materials to construct shelter plentiful, and leisure, because of the torpid heat, an exercise in hedonism.[4] Although Phillips and Cash overstate the influence of climate, they properly accord the environment a fundamental role in providing a foundation for the state's agricultural society, a building block important to the construction of the social ethic.

Lying within a latitudinal belt given to warmth and humidity, Mississippi developed (due to climatic conditions, not to mention good soil quality) a market economy based on, though not limited to, the cultivation of a staple crop.[5] The prominence of the market economy, especially the cotton market, promoted the formation of the plantation system and the institution of slavery, in each of which the southern social ethic germinated. Environmental forces that made possible the state's agricultural economy also sustained a fierce physical world that fostered backcountry habits of

4. Ulrich Bonnell Phillips, *Life and Labor in the Old South* (1929; rpr. New York, 1937), 3; Cash, *The Mind of the South*, 48. For an overview of environmental determinism in southern historiography, see A. Cash Koeniger, "Climate and Southern Distinctiveness," *Journal of Southern History,* LIV (1988), 21–44. Other historians have seen forces besides environmental ones as influential in creating southern distinctiveness. See Grady McWhiney and Perry D. Jamieson, *Attack and Die: Civil War Military Tactics and the Southern Heritage* (University, Ala., 1982); Forest McDonald and Grady McWhiney, "The South from Self-Sufficiency to Peonage: An Interpretation," *American Historical Review,* LXXXV (1980), 1095–118; John Hope Franklin, *The Militant South, 1800–1861* (Cambridge, Mass., 1956); Bertram Wyatt-Brown, *Honor and Violence in the Old South* (New York, 1986).

5. On climatic conditions, see Sam Bowers Hilliard, *Atlas of Antebellum Southern Agriculture* (Baton Rouge, 1984), 14–17; B. L. C. Wailes, *Report on the Agriculture and Geology of Mississippi: Embracing a Sketch of the Social and Natural History of the State* (Jackson, 1854), 305–308. On soil quality, U.S. Department of Agriculture, Forest Service, *A Forest Atlas of the South* (1969), 7.

living. If white residents wished to reap the benefits of good soil and climatic conditions, they had first to beat back native canebrakes and forests and the wild animals that dwelled within them. While undertaking the arduous task of controlling the physical world, they invented a collective identity reflective of the ruggedness of the land. Like the world in which they lived, they were resistant to intruders and resilient when confronted.

To the eyes of some visitors to the interior, Mississippi resembled more a land of pastoral splendor than one of harshness and peril. Yet for all its beauty, the physical world offered a bounty only to those who would conquer it. And in a land that required a full day's hard labor to clear a quarter acre of canebrake, conquer it they must. Mississippi's environment favored not only cotton and corn but thick forests and native animals; leaving bottomland fallow for several seasons invited self-sown cottonwoods and canebrakes to reassert their natural dominance. In the mid-1840s, when A. J. Paxton visited his brother, a Jackson lawyer turned Washington County planter, bear-infested canebrakes three miles wide and thirty miles long greeted him.[6]

The area through which Paxton passed, however, differed from the rest of the state. By 1840 the pioneering work of controlling the environment had been initiated in most of Mississippi. Wholesale ecological change had taken place. Desoto would not have recognized mid-nineteenth-century Mississippi as the same ecological wilderness he had known, nor would have Pushmataha, the Choctaw chieftain who died in 1825, five years after ceding tribal lands to the United States. Even in the wilds of the thinly populated Piney Woods, farmers and herdsmen had stamped on the region's ecological system a record of their presence. Traveling between Columbia and Hobolochitto, Benjamin L. C. Wailes remarked that the land was "barren of trees, which were formerly reed brakes, which have been destroyed

6. On Mississippi's landscape as idyllic, see A. De Puy Van Buren, *Jottings of a Year's Sojourn in the South . . . and Reminiscences of Distinguished Men* (1859; rpr. Louisville, 1960), 35; Henry Tillinghast Ireys, "Autobiography," in *Memoirs of Henry Tillinghast Ireys: Papers of the Washington County Historical Society, 1910–1919,* eds. William David McCain and Charlotte Capers (Jackson, 1954), 12; John H. Napier III, "Piney Woods Past: A Pastoral Elegy," in *Mississippi's Piney Woods: A Human Perspective,* ed. Noel Polk (Jackson, 1986), 15. On the ruggedness of the land, see A. J. Paxton, "Recollections of Deer Creek," in *Memoirs of Henry Tillinghast Ireys,* eds. McCain and Capers, 104; Evelyn Hammett, "Pioneer Days in East Bolivar," in *History of Bolivar County, Mississippi: Compiled by Florence Warfield Sillers and Members of the Mississippi Delta Chapter, Daughters of the American Revolution and the County History Committee,* ed. Wirt A. Williams (Jackson, 1948), 174; John Milliken to [?], December 26, 1844, in George Wilson Humphreys and Family Papers, MDAH.

by the herds of cattle, and by the firing of the woods."[7] As farmers put the plow to virgin soil, they initiated what would become a constant struggle to beat back the wildness of the land and to control native animals and diseases common to the backcountry.

On the eve of the Civil War, substantial numbers of forest animals (predators and game) still occupied Mississippi alongside humans. Although white settlers had tried since their arrival to eliminate some species, they fell short of their goal because of their relatively small numbers and scattered pattern of occupation. A population boom that began in the 1830s funneled settlers into the wilderness, but even as late as 1860 only the areas around Natchez, Vicksburg, and Columbus supported a population density over thirty persons per square mile. By 1880 a postbellum stampede of newcomers elevated the population density to that level over a significant portion of the state.[8] Bringing in their wake railroads and industries, New South citizens accelerated the process that began in the antebellum period: they decimated native species, especially those deemed detrimental to human enterprise. Between 1830 and the turn of the century (but most successfully after the war), Mississippians waged constant warfare against wild animals. The killing served several purposes. Hunting placed game on farmers' tables, and through communal hunts the activity drew isolated farmers into closer union. As an ever-increasing human population found uses for the land and its products, habitat for native animals became so diminished and their numbers so depleted that the importance of hunting faded. By the late nineteenth century, Timothy Dwight's assessment of colonial New England could be applied to Mississippi with only slight hyperbole: "Hunting with us exists chiefly in the tales of other times."[9]

7. Quoting B. L. C. Wailes Diaries, August 13, 1852, Microfiche, MDAH. Recent historians have pointed out that Native Americans altered the North American environment before Europeans arrived; white farmers accelerated the pace of change by cutting more timber, burning more forests, and instituting European notions of property rights. See William Cronon, *Changes in the Land: Indians, Colonists, and the Ecological History of New England* (New York, 1983), *passim*; Albert E. Cowdrey, *This Land, This South: An Environmental History* (Lexington, Ky., 1983), Chapt. 1; J. P. Coleman, *Choctaw County Chronicles: A History of Choctaw County, 1830–1973* (Ackerman, Miss., 1973), 35. In response to increased settlement, restrictions on the firing of forests became law in the 1820s. See *Laws of the State of Mississippi*, 1824–38, pp. 159–61, 530.

8. For maps of population density, see Hilliard, *Atlas of Antebellum Southern Agriculture*, 26; *Statistics of the Population of the United States at the Tenth Census* (1883), following p. 56.

9. Timothy Dwight quoted in Cronon, *Changes in the Land*, 116. On the importance of game in the southern diet, see Sam Bowers Hilliard, *Hog Meat and Hoecake: Food Supply in the Old South, 1840–1860* (Edwardsville, Ill., 1972), 13, 73–75, 78–80, 92; Hilliard, "Hog

Among the great variety of indigenous animals that lived in Mississippi, squirrel, rabbit, opossum, bear, turkey, waterfowl, and deer appeared regularly on rural folks' tables.[10] A taste for venison made deer the most popular game, but families could expect only one deer kill each year. To have a chance at killing a deer, farmers needed simply to arm themselves when inspecting corn and vegetable patches. But as generally practiced in Mississippi, killing deer was also a complex affair that involved aspects of manly sport and communal ritual. During the early 1800s hunters, working with groups of neighbors and kin, slaughtered deer by the dozens when they burned forests to flush animals through a gauntlet of gunmen. Such tactics ceased, however, as farmers occupied once-vacant public land and requested state protection against woods fires lighted by hunters. Hunters responded to prohibitions against firing the woods by introducing trained dogs to their hunts. Thomas Bangs Thorpe, the antebellum humorist, recalled that on one Louisiana deer drive his party shot six animals but retrieved only five. Searching for the dogs, Thorpe sardonically noted, took most of the day. Night hunters, who carried torches to illuminate deer's eyes, may have had the best luck of all; Charles Lanman reported that a hunting party in 1850 bagged one hundred deer in a single night. So thorough were hunters in their pursuit of deer that the southern herd (estimated to number between six and ten million in 1860) reached its nadir of one million by the turn of the century.[11]

Meat and Cornpone: Food Habits in the Antebellum South," *Proceedings of the American Philosophical Society,* CXIII (1969), 1–13; Royce Shingleton, "The Utility of Leisure: Game as a Source of Food in the Old South," *Mississippi Quarterly,* XXV (1972), 429; Shingleton, "The Republic of Porkdom," *Proceedings of the American Philosophical Society,* CLXII (1968), 407–10.

10. On the variety of game hunted, see Greene Callier Chandler, *Journal and Speeches of Greene Callier Chandler* (N.p., 1955), 51; David C. Estes, ed., "Opossums and 'Possum Hunting," in *A New Collection of Thomas Bangs Thorpe's Sketches of the Old Southwest* (Baton Rouge, 1989), 145–49; Ireys, "Autobiography," in *Memoirs of Henry Tillinghast Ireys,* ed. McCain and Capers, 15–16. The practice of allowing hogs to roam in the forests and swamps offered hunters another species of game to hunt. For an account of one planter who killed five domestic hogs-turned-wild, see Walter Wade Plantation Diaries, December 26, 1850, MDAH.

11. On hunting practices, see Joseph B. Lightsey Diary, November 31, 1847, January 14, 1848, February 24, 1846, February 25, 1850, MDAH; Edward Stuart to Annie E. Stuart, May 26, 1860, in John Bull Smith Dimitry Papers, WRP; Estes, ed., "Sporting in Louisiana," in *A New Collection of Thomas Bangs Thorpe's Sketches,* 110–11. The state first outlawed the firing of woods for the purpose of hunting in 1822. See *The Statutes of the State of Mississippi of a Public and General Nature. . . .* (New Orleans, 1840), 207–208, hereinafter cited

While Mississippians hunted some species for food, they sought merely to eradicate others considered dangerous to livestock, agriculture, and humans. Fear as much as sport motivated them to kill large native mammals, and their success might be measured by the near annihilation of the wolf population before 1850. Mobile pack hunters and scavengers with a taste for hog meat and beef, wolves looked upon humankind's initial encroachment into their territory as an invitation to feast. Cattlemen, who allowed their livestock to graze untended on public lands, quickly learned that eliminating wolves should be their first order of business. Throughout the countryside they dug deep pits covered by a flimsy door and baited with meat to trap them; they also organized parties to hunt the animals. In response to an increase in human and domestic animal encounters with wolves, the legislature in 1837 and 1838 authorized several counties to pay five-dollar bounties for wolf scalps. By 1841 the bounty system had so effectively driven residents to kill wolves that the legislature abrogated the laws. Even though the threat of wolf attacks lessened as the Civil War approached, the creature's howl and its pack nature continued to stir fear among rural folk and to inspire instructive folk tales. Every child in the state, perhaps the nation as well, knew that stripping off clothes would temporarily distract pursuing wolves. Of course, fiddle music lulled the animals to sleep, provided the musician first found a perch safely above the ground.[12]

One species alone provoked more acute fear and trepidation than the wolf: the black bear. In the popular imagination the black bear, whose territory at one time included every canebrake in the state, was unmatched for its ferocity and appetite. In reality bears were docile, even lethargic, unless provoked. Primarily because of the species' reputation for meanness, hunters viewed a bear kill as proof of superior skill and courage; killing bears, especially during communal hunts, served as an expression of individual masculinity. (According to B. L. C. Wailes, a single hunting expedition into the country between Natchez and the Homochitto River slaughtered one hundred bears for the sake of doing so.) But bears were also hunted

---

as *Code,* 1840. On estimates of the size of the deer herd and the average number of annual kills, see Hilliard, *Hog Meat and Hoecake,* 77–78.

12. Wailes, *Report of the Agriculture and Geology of Mississippi,* 345; Robert J. Baxter, "Cattle Raising in Early Mississippi: Reminiscences," *Mississippi Folklore Register,* X (1976), 6–7. For the bounty laws and their repeal, see *Laws of the State of Mississippi,* 1824–38, pp. 756–819; *Laws of the State of Mississippi,* 1841, p. 125. For folklore about evading wolves, see J. F. H. Claiborne, "A Trip Through the Piney Woods," Mississippi Historical Society *Publications,* IX (1906), 533–38.

for their meat and other by-products. In the spring, before the animals put on a layer of fat for the winter, Delta hotels served bear meat. Hides and oil, too, were highly prized as accouterments for the home: in youthful exuberance, Amanda Worthington looked forward to "slicking up" with bear lard upon the return of a household hunting party; rural folk regarded bearskin rugs and chair backing as conversation pieces. Generally, however, Mississippians killed bears as a preventive measure to protect corn and stock. For a brief period prior to 1860, Bolivar County hunters killed on average eight bears a day, but their excessive bloodletting failed to deter bear raids. As settlers decreased bear habitat to open more and more land to cultivation, pilfering in corn cribs and hog pens occurred with increasing regularity. A postbellum outbreak of grain thieving by starving bears prompted farmers to forego corn cultivation for two years.[13] Accounts of bears taking corn from cribs and carrying slain hogs under their arms suggest the damaging effect that farming and clear-cutting forests had on wild animals and also the hardships, however temporary, farmers suffered when they transformed wilderness into improved acreage.

Prior to 1900 the population of native wildlife evinced the consequences of human settlement. In the struggle to contain the dangers of the backcountry, humankind won. Once-predominant canebrakes, swamps, and forests declined in number, and the days of communal hunts disappeared with them. All that endured was the solitary farmer jealously guarding his crops and family against depredations less real than imagined. Johnny Parrott, a lumberman and hunter, noticed the dwindling wildlife in the Delta of the late 1880s; only burning canebrakes in preparation for cutting timber brought out the small numbers that persevered. As much as his lumbering operations, Parrott's style of hunting suggested another reason for the decrease in the wildlife population. Every animal that fled his fires became a target. Fortunately for the animals, he was not a particularly accurate shot.[14] Notwithstanding the poor aim of some hunters, the total ef-

13. Quoting Amanda Worthington to Albert D. Worthington, October 27, 1857, in Amanda Dougherty Worthington Papers, SHC. Wailes, *Report on the Agriculture and Geology of Mississippi,* 317; Baxter, "Cattle Raising," 8; Hammett, "Pioneer Days in East Bolivar," 179–80, and Mrs. L. A. Little, "Sketch of Life in Bolivar County," both in *History of Bolivar County,* ed. Williams, 165–67; Ireys, "Autobiography," in *Memoirs of Henry Tillinghast Ireys,* eds. McCain and Capers, 12. On the masculinity of the hunt, see Ted Ownby, *Subduing Satan: Religion, Recreation, and Manhood in the Rural South, 1865–1920* (Chapel Hill, 1990).

14. Johnny Parrott Diary, November 24, 1887, October 31, 1888, MDAH. Some species completely disappeared before 1880. According to J. C. Burrus, "My Recollections of the Early Days of Bolivar County," in *History of Bolivar County,* ed. Williams, 104, wild pigeons made their last flight into the Delta about 1870.

fect of an unrestrained slaughter conducted over a century was plain. By 1900 so barren of large mammals had the forests become that a single sighting of a predator created a stir in communities. Overnight the animal would obtain legendary size. But in reality bears, wolf packs, and panthers ten feet long lived almost exclusively in legend and in areas of the nation that retained more of their backcountry past than Mississippi.[15]

Clearing canebrakes and forests and draining swamplands in preparation for agricultural and commercial pursuits impinged on creatures other than native wildlife. The very destroyers of the environment felt the ill effects of the world into which they trod. Mississippi had always been a sickly society, "a land primed for fatality and already cursed with it," as William Faulkner once said, and Johnny Parrott, who lived in the part of the world that Faulkner later portrayed in his fiction, agreed that death seemed to stalk at every turn: "It takes a man with the constitution like an alligator to stand this old bottom." Throughout the nineteenth century settlers suffered a variety of illnesses, many of them directly related to a physical world more akin to Latin American jungles than to the environment of states north of the Mason-Dixon line. Plagued by an abundance of mosquitoes and dank swamps, the state annually experienced the perils of typhoid fever, malaria, and yellow fever. The regular appearance of other ailments (intestinal parasites, smallpox, measles, dysentery, and whooping cough) marked a general ignorance of epidemiology and sound sanitary practices.[16] Before 1900 the qualities of life that made the state fecund ground for diseases remained outside the realm of human control or even human understanding. Ironically, as the backcountry milieu and the modes of thought that it nurtured ebbed, new diseases incubated in modernizing Mississippi struck.

15. Several folktales originating in the early twentieth century celebrate exceedingly large wildcats. See Beulah M. D'Olive Price, "The Legendary Panther of the Forks of Hatchie," *Mississippi Folklore Register,* V (1971), 15–18; Ovid S. Vickers, "The Stratton Booger," *Mississippi Folklore Register,* IV (1970), 92–93; Burrus, "Recollections of Early Days of Bolivar County," in *History of Bolivar County,* ed. Williams, 104.

16. Quoting William Faulkner, *Absalom, Absalom!* (1936; rpr. New York, 1964), 24; and Parrott Diary, March 7, 1887. Contrary assessments of the state's environment as restorative can be found in Daniel Kelly to James Kelly, February 29, 1845, in John N. Kelly Papers, WRP; William Bullock, *Sketch of a Journey Through the Western States of North America . . . in 1827* (London, 1827), 250; Claiborne, "Trip Through the Piney Woods," *passim;* [?] to Samuel Smith Downey, February 27, 1836, in Samuel Smith Downey Papers, WRP. On the variety of deadly diseases, see William D. Gale to Mrs. Dudley Gale, May 16, 1845, in Gale and Polk Family Papers, SHC; Chandler, *Journal and Speeches,* 53.

An absence of medical knowledge and technology, deficiencies that existed in New England and New York as well as the South, exacerbated environmental conditions that made Mississippians particularly prone to sickness, and that ignorance was not the unique property of sufferers.[17] Self-proclaimed medical professionals, who propounded a baffling array of cures, exhibited an inadequate command of pathology and treatment. Anyone desiring to advertise himself or herself as a healer could do so without formal training or challenge. Traditional doctors who administered large doses of drugs, homeopathic practitioners who preferred small doses, and steam doctors (Thomasonians) who prescribed botanical cures and steam baths laden with cayenne pepper, practiced their vocations without real supervision. In a tentative effort to oust bogus practitioners, the state in 1824 implemented regulatory practices, requiring physicians to be licensed, but the law neither imposed standards for admission to the medical profession nor demanded that doctors undergo training. With the approval of the state, fraudulent and deadly physicians continued to practice. Considering the hit-or-miss nature of medical treatment and the state's open-armed approach to practitioners, it is no wonder that many Mississippians believed "the fool of the family must be a doctor."[18]

Epidemiology and the treatment of disease were at best improperly understood. Unlike forest-dwelling predators, which bolted at the sight of gun-toting men and obligingly fell victim to hunters' traps, diseases appeared despite the barriers erected to halt their progress. Typically, remedies native to Mississippi and other rural societies showed a dearth of etiological understanding and represented little more than wishful thinking informed by superstition and a strong belief in Providence: a buckeye car-

17. Failure to arrest disease owed not only to shortcomings in doctors' diagnoses and treatment but also to ordinary citizens, who looked upon even commonplace ailments as being as mysterious as their cures. Joseph B. Lightsey mourned the loss of a young nephew who died of an unfamiliar disease: pneumonia. Lightsey to Cornelius Lightsey, September 1, 1853, in Lightsey Diary. Educated members of the planter class lived with a similar medical befuddlement and uncertainty. See Wailes Diaries, June 4, 5, 1853.

18. Quoting *Biennial Report of the Mississippi State Board of Health, 1886–1887* (Jackson, 1888), 4. On physicians in Mississippi, see Chandler, *Journal and Speeches*, 53. *Laws of the State of Mississippi*, 1824–38, pp. 24, 109; Marshall Scott Legan, "The Evolution of Public Health Services in Mississippi, 1865–1910" (Ph.D. dissertation, University of Mississippi, 1968), 81. On Thomasonian treatments, see Drew Gilpin Faust, *James Henry Hammond and the Old South: A Design for Mastery* (Baton Rouge, 1982), 78–79; Thomas Shackleford, *Proceedings of the Citizens of Madison County, Mississippi and Livingston, in July 1835, in Relation to the Trial and Punishment of Several Individuals Implicated in a Contemplated Insurrection in the State* (Jackson, 1836), 21.

ried in the pocket warded off rheumatism; a stand of pine trees near one's home absorbed wind-borne malaria germs; the blood of a freshly killed bull or warm milk from a heifer, preferably one with its first calf, cured tuberculosis; quinine bottles hung from trees and shrubs warned evil spirits that a household had been protected from malaria; liberal doses of alcohol cured many sicknesses.[19]

Until the turn of the century, medical advances proceeded at a snail's pace, and residents exhibited little enthusiasm for embracing even the most rudimentary preventive measures. Dr. G. W. Purnell reported that, although innumerable ailments struck Hazelhurst, townspeople contentedly looked upon their neighbors' deaths and sicknesses as inexorable occurrences: "Everyone seems lithargic [*sic*], and as long as there are no rumors of yellow fever, are willing to go in the old beaten track, trusting in Providence until an epidemic threatens, and then thinking to their powers of locomotion." Yet the popularity of miracle cures (among them Winslow's Soothing Syrup for infants and a variety of bottled cures for female ailments) attests that Mississippians did not wait idly for illnesses to strike.[20] The prevalence of such cures also points out the gullibility of a population dumbfounded by the sicknesses they suffered.

Due in part to inadequate statistical data, no research has been undertaken to estimate the toll exacted by native diseases. Using the mortality schedules of the United States census, however, a rough estimate of deaths attributable to particular causes can be calculated, though it should be remembered that errors in attribution of the cause of death likely occurred frequently. On the eve of the Civil War, Mississippians most often died of pneumonia, typhoid fever, diarrhea, dysentery, consumption (tuberculosis), scarlet fever, measles, and whooping cough. Pneumonia killed

19. Perry A. Snyder, "Remedies of the Pineywoods Pioneers," *Mississippi Folklore Register,* VII (1973), 11–14; Frank E. Smith, *Yazoo River* (New York, 1954), 244–49; Ellen Orr, "The Bottle Tree," *Mississippi Folklore Register,* III (1969), 109–11; Kathryn Tucker Windham, *Count Those Buzzards! Stamp Those Grey Mules!* (N.p., 1979), 27–28. On the use of alcohol in the treatment of disease, see Marshall Scott Legan, "A Nineteenth Century Treatment of Yellow Fever," *Mississippi Folklore Register,* VI (1972), 91–93.

20. Purnell quoted in *Biennial Report of the Mississippi State Board of Health, 1880–1881* (Jackson, 1882), 37. For an account of the "electioneering medicine vendor" and his products, see *Biennial Report of the Mississippi State Board of Health, 1896–1897* (Jackson, 1897), 71; Legan, "Evolution of Public Health Services," 80. Patent medicines, especially treatments for female complaints, made amazing claims. Paxtine's Toilet Antiseptic advertised itself as a "local treatment of female ills, curing all inflammation and discharges, wonderful as a cleansing vaginal douche, for sore throat, nasal catarrh, as a mouth wash, and to remove tartar and whiten the teeth." See Batesville *Weekly Panolian,* November 13, 1902.

by far more Mississippians than any other ailment, 178 per 100,000 people. By comparison, typhoid fever, a communicable disease and the second leading cause of death, claimed nearly half as many victims, 93 people per 100,000; consumption, diphtheria, and croup (the latter two primarily childhood diseases) took just over 60 per 100,000. For a variety of reasons, southerners had long been concerned with the purification of their digestive tracts as a means of regulating their health. Poor sanitary conditions and tainted water supplies drawn from open cisterns surely contributed to anxieties about intestinal biliousness, as did the concomitant prevalence of diarrhea and dysentery. In 1860 the former affliction killed 48 persons per 100,000 and the latter 31. The good news for Mississippians in 1860 was that deaths attributable to measles, scarlet fever, and smallpox were on the wane, though they continued to kill a small number each year.[21]

After the war mortality rates for most diseases fell sharply. Scarlet fever as a cause of death, for instance, had almost disappeared by 1914, and deaths due to typhoid fever diminished by two thirds. The death rate attributable to whooping cough decreased by 60 percent to 13 per 100,000; in 1914 diphtheria and croup claimed a fraction of the lives (10 per 100,000) as they had in 1860. Better medical diagnosis and treatment decreased the number of deaths due to pneumonia to 78 per 100,000. Data gathered from the Deep South indicate that fewer Mississippians died of the above-mentioned diseases than did their nearby contemporaries.[22]

These cheery figures, however, somewhat belie the serious health problems that plagued Mississippi in the postbellum era. While deaths attributable to diseases of the backcountry fell off, the diseases themselves often persisted. Furthermore, social changes brought about by industrialization and the concentration of population exacerbated some health problems. Outbreaks of smallpox and cholera struck the state in 1866; one-half of the population of Natchez, Jackson, and Byram caught yellow fever in 1867; smallpox returned to Vicksburg in 1870 and prompted the city to offer indigents free vaccinations; yellow fever returned in 1871; a cholera epidemic accompanied the 1873 Delta flood; smallpox and yellow fever landed a double blow in 1878; epidemics of yellow fever appeared sporadically until 1897.[23] The worst epidemic to strike Mississippi occurred in

21. The mortality rate for various diseases was based on data found in *Statistics of the United States, (Including Mortality, Property, Etc.), in 1860* (1866), 35.

22. For the 1914 mortality rate, see *Report of the Board of Health, 1913–1915* (Memphis, 1915), 61–63.

23. On epidemics, see Legan, "Evolution of Public Health Services," 2–16, 109–20; *Report of the Mississippi State Board of Health for the Years 1878–1879* (Jackson, 1879),

1878 and 1879 when yellow fever swept the state. The fever apparently broke out in New Orleans in May, 1878, and by mid-July Mississippi reported its first cases. Contemporaries believed that sufferers unwittingly transported the yellow fever germ from New Orleans, a city prone to outbreaks, but the prevalence of lowlands, poorly maintained drainage ditches and privies, and open-air cisterns with their stagnant pools of water—prime breeding grounds for the vectors of the disease (mosquitoes)—deserve credit for its visitations.[24]

Across the South the 1878 and 1879 epidemic was a watershed event. Over the succeeding two decades state governments and physicians, ignoring the backcountry's animus toward intrusions into matters purely personal and communal, undertook campaigns to eradicate conditions that bestowed upon the region its infamous sickliness.[25] Notwithstanding gains achieved in controlling infectious diseases that traditionally afflicted backcountry Mississippi, some ailments that had previously barely touched the state gained a toehold after 1890. The proliferation of urban centers contributed to the spread of these diseases. Deaths per 100,000 caused by influenza, a bacterial infection of the lungs, increased about 85 percent between 1860 and 1914. The mortality rate for tuberculosis almost doubled. Syphilis caused almost eleven times more deaths in 1914 than it had in 1860.[26] In cities like Jackson, Vicksburg, Greenville, and Natchez, crowded quarters occupied by transients and working-class families served as incubators for disease. Prostitution and the illegal liquor trade flourished in

---

4–5, 9–19, 37, 41–45, 59–64, 76–79; Marshall Scott Legan, "Mississippi and the Yellow Fever Epidemic of 1878–1879," *Journal of Mississippi History,* XXXIII (1971), 199–218; Mrs. W. A. Anderson, "A Chapter in the Yellow Fever Epidemic of 1878," Mississippi Historical Society *Publications,* X (1909), 223–36

24. On contemporaries' understanding of the cause of yellow fever, see *Report of the Board of Health, 1878–1879, passim;* Margaret Humphreys, *Yellow Fever and the South* (New Brunswick, N.J., 1992), 17–22. On sanitary conditions prior to the 1878 epidemic, see James Robertshaw, "Greenville in its Early Days," in *Memoirs of Henry Tillinghast Ireys,* eds. McCain and Capers, 85–89. Besides killing hundreds, the fever caused great social disruption. See J. H. Campbell to John M. Stone, September 21, 1878; Campbell to Stone, September 24, 1878; Dr. J. D. McRae to Stone, September 19, 1878, in Record Group 27, Governors' Papers, MDAH.

25. See John H. Ellis, *Yellow Fever and Public Health in the New South* (Lexington, Ky., 1992), 1, 37. For a discussion of medical reform in Mississippi, see Chapter 7 herein.

26. *Report of the Board of Health, 1913–1915,* 61–63. For an instance of "modernity" leading to illness, see Dr. B. A. Vaughn's report in *Biennial Report of the Mississippi State Board of Health, 1882–1883* (Jackson, 1883), 78–79, in which he traces two cases of diphtheria to improperly installed indoor plumbing.

the areas, as did, according to some accounts, the use of cocaine and opium. While the health of residents living on the respectable side of towns benefited from drainage and street improvements, those trapped in filthy working-class neighborhoods rarely enjoyed the fruits of expanded city services and spread their illness into respectable neighborhoods. Dr. Benjamin F. Ward observed that the maladies of the working poor became the maladies of all: "Out of these hot beds of syphilis, scrofula and consumption, come the cooks, nurses, chamber-maids, washer-women and carriage drivers for the white person."[27]

Poor living and working conditions, chiefly the result of unsound sanitary practices, contributed to the sickliness of lower-class city residents, but all were subject to illness. One of the most striking examples of backward sanitary practices causing illness occurred in the meat preparation industry. Abuses in the industry attracted the nation's attention at the turn of the century, and in Mississippi conditions resembled the well-known ones in Chicago's meat-packing factories. According to the state Board of Health, slaughterhouse operators discarded carcasses in streams that provided water to poor neighborhoods, and the meat itself received improper care during processing. Offal and disease originating at slaughterhouses easily made their way into communities. A slaughterhouse near Arcola carried on so many practices detrimental to the health of the community that townspeople sought recourse through the Circuit Court. Ironically, and perhaps not surprisingly, the circuit judge had for some time been too ill to conduct proceedings.[28]

As the twentieth century approached, concerns about unsanitary practices increased among physicians and reformers. Attitudes toward health common to the general population, however, made eliminating unhealthy practices a never-ending struggle, even as Mississippi took on the trappings of the modern world. With the assistance of the state, which funded physi-

27. Ward quoted in *Biennial Report of the Board of Health of the State of Mississippi from September 30, 1903, to September 30, 1905* (Nashville, 1906), 6. On the relationship between industrial development and the proliferation of some diseases, see John Duffy, *The Sanitarians: A History of American Public Health* (Urbana, Ill., 1990), 10–51, 66. On the development of separate and unequal housing and services, see W. W. Woollard, "History of the Liquor Fight in the Early Days of Bolivar County," in *History of Bolivar County*, ed. Williams, 215–17. On the spread of typhoid fever in a tenement house and the drug use by all classes of people, see *Biennial Report of the Board of Health, 1880–1881*, 65–66, 94; Henry Waring Ball Diary, September 6, 1906, MDAH. On outlawing cocaine, see Legan, "Evolution of Public Health Services," 130.

28. For an account of sanitary conditions in the meat-packing industry, see *Biennial Report of the Board of Health, 1884–1885* (Jackson, 1885), 116–17, 119.

cians' campaigns to educate the public about hygiene and sanitary procedures, progress was made in eliminating some of the most pernicious diseases. Much remained to be done, but just as the decimation of native wildlife suggested humankind's triumph over a backcountry environment, so too did quantitative changes in health reflect another way in which Mississippi advanced beyond its days as a frontier state.

Despite the postbellum success realized in regulating native wildlife and disease, reminders of Mississippi's backcountry past, chiefly communitarian values, survived longer than did backcountry conditions. While frontier conditions ameliorated, collective remembrances of them permitted residents to identify themselves with the courageous souls who had formerly battled the dangers of the backcountry. Liberty-loving and virtuous citizens had once taken on bears, wolves, and canebrakes; their children appropriated such experiences as their own so that they might keep alive the fiction of the independent and tightly-bound community. As the vagaries of the backcountry diminished after 1880, residents continued to embrace communitarian values, but the values too waned in importance over the next two decades. The persistence of communitarian values recalled the state's backcountry heritage and testified to citizens' reluctance to surrender their past even as they trudged into modernity.

In nineteenth-century Mississippi communitarian values appeared in two guises. First, they undergirded corporate activities. House raisings, hog killings, corn shuckings, hunting expeditions, quilting bees, and assistance with crops—in part ways of life transplanted from other regions of the country and in part a response to dispersed settlement—informed the rhythm of backcountry life.[29] Those rituals disrupted the monotony of day-to-day existence and gave white residents a sense of shared experience. Second, and perhaps more importantly, communitarian values defined individuals' relationship with the state, for they held that citizens, working in league with their neighbors, could best build roads, clear river channels, and construct levees. Communitarian values thus strengthened the bond that cemented all white citizens in the great battle to control the environment and to secure backcountry notions of individual autonomy.

29. On communal rituals, see Nicholas P. Hardeman, *Shucks, Shocks, and Hominy Blocks: Corn as a Way of Life in Pioneer America* (Baton Rouge, 1981), 58. Colonel Thomas Dabney, a Virginian by birth, offended two of his neighbors before learning the importance of communal rituals. First, he arrived at a house raising with twenty slaves; then, he directed from horseback a retinue of slaves laboring to save another neighbor's cotton from weeds. See Susan Dabney Smedes, *Memorials of a Southern Planter* (Baltimore, 1888), 67.

In a competitive market economy it is a wonder that communitarian values survived. Their protracted career reflected the lure of tradition and Mississippians' fear of appearing beholden to markets or governments. Yet communitarian values slowly ceased to direct the progress of internal improvements as Mississippians, increasingly concerned with material progress rather than protecting frontier notions of autonomy, came to question their worth. Even before the Civil War, initial signs that residents would forsake communitarian values in exchange for material advancement appeared: Delta planters were the first to relinquish some of their communal responsibilities when they called for the state to build a levee system, and after 1865 they increasingly sought federal assistance for protection of their land against floods and in clearing river channels. By 1900 the last vestiges of communitarian values vanished from laws addressing the construction and maintenance of common roads as well. When communities resigned the responsibility for internal improvements, the death knell of backcountry habits of mind sounded, for with their demise the feature of the social ethic that had previously apotheosized the hardy and independent frontiersmen locked in combat with the environment and wild animals died, too.

Environmental forces that nurtured Mississippi's antebellum agricultural wealth also lent a wildness to the land that made travel along the state's highways nightmarish. Until the twentieth century roads remained little more than mud bogs and dust bowls. Their notorious reputation made them the subject of tall tales. According to one popular story, a traveler, seeing a hat in the road, discovered beneath it a rider astride his horse. The rider, after thanking the man for his concern about the apparently misplaced hat, expressed his pleasure in having found a good stretch of road, one covered with mud only ten feet deep. With slightly less hyperbole, another old adage suggested much the same: if mud did not seep over the top of a mounted horseman's boot, the road was judged "a middling good" one. Contemporaries verified that travel along common roads was difficult. Samuel Agnew noted in his diary that it took two bone-jarring days of riding in a wagon to travel from his father's Tippah County farm to Holly Springs. Such progress was fair, Agnew believed, though the time consumed may explain why rural folk infrequently went to town. Stagecoaches offered a smoother ride than common wagons but were poor protection against all dangers since they traveled the same ill-kept roads. George Rogers, traveling from Washington, Mississippi, to Woodville, found little comfort in a coach. As water passed through the vehicle, Rogers sat on his feet to preserve his shoes. Fearing for his life, he also opened the windows to allow himself an escape route if the coach overturned on the boggy road. Gustavus A. Henry likewise experienced a tedious, wet journey while traveling on a road near the Bogue Chitto River. Distracted by having to ride with his feet on the seat, Henry's inattention permitted a thief to steal a trunk of clothes attached to the back of his rented carriage.[30]

As Rogers and Henry attested, conditions on common roads owed much to environmental forces, but concepts of a parsimonious and limited state government prohibited development of good roads, too. In 1822 the essential elements of nineteenth-century road-building law entered the state's legal code. The law, apparently taking its cue from federal legislation designed to facilitate the movement of troops, required that county courts appoint within each militia captain's district a Board of Commissioners to supervise roadwork. A clerk hired by the commissioners handled administrative tasks, and an overseer monitored actual labor. The overseer, according to the law, had at his disposal for up to six days each year all males between the ages of sixteen and fifty, excluding ministers, students, teachers, and mill and ferry operators. Failure to answer a call to work resulted in a six dollar fine; failure to serve as overseer when requested carried a forty dollar fine. The law provided overseers few instructions and expected little in return. Roads had to be at least twenty feet wide and causeways sixteen feet; mile posts and directional signs had to be placed at regular intervals; roots and stumps had to be leveled to within six inches of the roadbed. Although the state demanded slight effort from Boards of Commissioners, few followed the law to the letter. When building one of the first roads in Bolivar County, commissioners gave their overseer no instructions other than to make it "well blazed."[31] The requirements of the law notwithstanding, many roads were, in fact, merely well-worn paths that farmers sporadically maintained with their scrapers and mules.

During the antebellum era this system of road building served the state adequately. Yet with roads constructed by untrained hands and designed mainly to provide transportation for staple crops, the best roads were of-

30. Quoting Smith, *Yazoo River,* 47. While mud ten feet deep might have been an exaggeration, sand "fetlock deep" on the road between Ellisville and Augusta was not; see Claiborne, "Trip Through the Piney Woods," 518; Samuel A. Agnew Diary, January 12, 1853, Microfilm, SHC; George Rogers, *Memoranda of the Experiences, Labors, and Travels of a Universalist Preacher* (Cincinnati, 1845), 275; Gustavus A. Henry to Marion Henry, November 25, 1849, in Gustavus A. Henry Papers, SHC.

31. Quoting Cordelia McNees West, W. B. Roberts, and Florence S. Ogden, "Roads in Bolivar County," in *History of Bolivar County,* ed. Williams, 63. For road-building laws, see *Code,* 1823, pp. 350–57.

ten private ones leading to planters' homes. Recalling the roads around Greenville, James Robertshaw agreed that once one traveled away from planters' homes the quality of roads diminished. Backcountry byways were only "clefts in the foliage." Except for tending the roads immediately surrounding their property, planters rarely pitched in themselves, opting instead to pay the small fine for not doing so or, as generally happened, sending their slaves to answer the overseer's call to labor, another method of skirting the communitarian sentiment of the road-building law. County courts complied with planters' wishes by assigning them administrative positions as road commissioners and overseers, but even these small tasks proved irksome to a few. Their inattention to community service angered poorer folk and occasionally others of their own status, too. Writing in the Natchez *Mississippi Free Trader* in 1846, "R" chastised his fellows for failing to do their part and for allowing yeomen to construct roads better suited to their common wagons than to fine carriages and well-bred horses. Some planters did their civic duty without comment. Robert B. Alexander of Marshall County answered the road overseer's call in February, 1854, and worked a part of the road near his home. In May, a busy month for planters, the road overseer returned to the neighborhood and called for all of Alexander's slaves, as well as his father's, to work the road.[32]

According to state law, ultimate responsibility for road building rested with county Boards of Police (later Boards of Supervisors), who responded to requests made by road commissioners and overseers. Commissioners, of course, chose to improve the paths that farmers most often used in their never-ending search for land and markets. Predictably, a comparison of two maps, one circa 1830 and one dated 1852, suggests that centers of trade formed hubs out of which roads extended into the backcountry. In the early 1830s few highways traversed the eastern half of the state; those that existed led to Natchez and to New Orleans via Jackson, Monticello, Columbia, and Madisonville, Louisiana. When the small number of farmers who lived in the eastern counties wished to send their wares to market, they less often depended on roadways than the Tombigbee and Pascagoula Rivers.

32. Quoting Robertshaw, "Greenville in Its Early Days," in *Memoirs of Henry Tillinghast Ireys*, eds. McCain and Capers, 81–82; Natchez *Mississippi Free Trader*, October 14, 1846. Robert B. Alexander Diary and Account Ledger, January 30, 1854, May 10, 1854, MDAH. For accounts of planters working roads, see Susan S. Darden Diaries, February 29, 1860 (Typescript in Darden Family Papers), MDAH; Robert and James Gordon Diaries, January 21, 1853, MDAH; and for a planter who tried to convince county officials to appoint his plantation overseer to the Board of Commissioners in his stead, see Wailes Diaries, June 20, 1856.

Both maps indicate that New Orleans, Memphis, Natchez, Jackson, and Columbus were the largest centers of trade, but by 1852 Vicksburg and Mobile, too, served as major hubs. During the late antebellum period, the goal of connecting rural farmers with markets took on added urgency as the population expanded; to meet farmers' demands the number of roads increased exponentially. The 1852 map hints at the fact that the market economy, not unlike a giant spider web with strands stretching to distant objects, extended its influence into previously remote areas. As these areas, connected as they were to centers of trade—Memphis for farmers in the Northwest, Mobile for those in the East, New Orleans (the dream market) reigning over all—fell into the market economy, Boards of Police authorized more highways to serve their growing needs. One consequence of the increased number of roads was that small towns such as Monticello and Columbia, which had once served as minor markets and way stations for farmers en route to New Orleans, were bypassed when new roads opened direct routes to larger centers of trade.[33]

While communitarian values lay at the heart of road-building laws, an inherent conflict between such values and a desire to achieve personal financial success entered into the road-building process during the population boom of the 1830s. Individuals and companies occasionally eschewed the communitarian values that undergirded road-building laws by constructing byways and charging user's tolls. The builders of these roads evinced more interest in making money than in communitarian values, an attitude that the state sanctioned when it approved the toll pikes; the Holly Springs and Mississippi River Turnpike Company even received state authorization to sell stock. The speculative boom of the 1830s, however, ended in an economic depression, and in the following decade the state curtailed the number of charters granted road-building companies. With the exception of taxing privileges occasionally offered Delta counties, the state's involvement in road building ended, and Mississippi returned to the plan inherited from its days as a frontier state.[34]

33. On development of roads along geographic features such as dry river beds and ridge lines, see Claiborne, "Trip Through the Piney Woods," 510–11; Robert Baird, *View of the Valley of the Mississippi: Or the Emigrants and Traveller's Guide to the West. . . .* (Philadelphia, 1832), 247. Maps used include that by Thomas Cowperthwait and Company, "A New Map of Mississippi with Its Roads and Distances," 1852, MDAH; and the foldout map in Samuel Augustus Mitchell, *Mitchell's Traveller's Guide Through the United States. . . .* (Philadelphia, 1836). On the powerful sway that the New Orleans market held over Mississippians, see Mrs. H. B. Theobald, "Reminiscences of Greenville," in *Memoirs of Henry Tillinghast Ireys,* eds. McCain and Capers, 54, who recalled that men "spoke of going 'to town' as if New Orleans was only a mile distant."

34. *Laws of the State of Mississippi,* 1824–38, pp. 719–20, 802–805, 821–22; *Laws of*

For thirty years road construction took shape under the system established in 1822 with few alterations. Yet even the minuscule antebellum changes legislated bespoke Mississippians' willingness to exchange their communitarian values for better roads. Prior to 1848 specially designated road districts in each county replaced militia districts as units of organization, indicating that the state ceased to view roads as primarily for the use of the military. The 1848 law code recognized as well a long-standing practice that allowed individuals to avoid calls to work if they provided farm implements and slaves to operate them.[35]

The most substantive changes to road-building law came about between 1871 and 1892. While men who previously refused to work on the roads had been subject to small fines, the amended law code of 1871 established a guilt-free method of avoiding road work: a five dollar commutation fee could be paid directly to road overseers. Adopting the policy of commutation permitted wealthy planters and businessmen to escape their communal responsibilities without being stigmatized as slackers or foes of communitarian values. Additionally, the office of road commissioner was eliminated and commissioners' duties turned over to Boards of Supervisors, the chief administrative body of each county. Boards of Supervisors received the privilege of entering contracts with construction firms for two-year periods, according to the 1892 code, and in a curious combination of communitarian ideals and concern for middle-class interests, contractors might demand that individuals join in roadwork and collect from others the commutation fee. If the amount of labor and money thus raised proved insufficient to meet a county's needs, then for the first time state law allowed the separate counties to levy a tax for road construction not to exceed one mill. Finally, by 1892 the law forbade road builders to use county convicts in conjunction with communal road workers.[36]

---

the State of Mississippi, 1840, pp. 206–208, 297–303; *Laws of the State of Mississippi,* 1841, pp. 163–73. For laws granting specific Delta counties taxing privileges to build roads, *Laws of the State of Mississippi,* 1857, p. 9.

35. *Code of Mississippi: Being an Analytical Compilation of the Public and General Statutes of the Territory and State from 1789 to 1840* (Jackson, 1848), 252–54, hereinafter cited as *Code,* 1848.

36. *The Revised Code of the Statute Laws of the State of Mississippi of a Public and General Nature. . . .* (Jackson, 1871), 511–20, hereinafter cited as *Code,* 1871. *The Revised Code of the Statute Laws of the State of Mississippi of a Public and General Nature. . . .* (Jackson, 1880), 245–61; hereinafter cited as *Code,* 1880. *The Annotated Code of the General Statute Laws of the State of Mississippi* (Nashville, 1892), 866–71, hereinafter cited as *Code,* 1892.

In the postbellum period, as the vagaries of the backcountry subsided and as professional men began their rise to prominence, the communal responsibilities that had once informed the rhythm of life in Mississippi dissipated. Responsibility for building roads passed from the control of communities and into the hands of local bureaucracies, a process accelerated in the early 1900s by the Good Roads movement and federal highway legislation.

Until the arrival of the motor car and a city-dwelling professional class, Mississippi failed to revamp dramatically its system of road building; after all, because of the availability of river packets and railroads for transporting crops to market, residents lacked an urgent need for accessible transportation facilities. Keelboats, flatboats, and steamers traveled innumerable Mississippi streams, and for road-weary travelers, added excitement and danger to journeys. Bandits in the early days, drifting timber capable of rupturing vessels' hulls, and steamer explosions created great anxiety about journeys by boat. River transportation, especially steamboating on the Mississippi River, attracted adventurous souls and ne'er-do-wells. Feeding the fears of travelers, the state press relayed in prurient detail reports of steamboat explosions occurring between New Orleans and Pittsburgh. William H. Allen, passing from Cincinnati to New Orleans in 1832, recalled "the dreary and tedious recurrences" of Mississippi River travel that bound all steamboat passengers. Floating ice—a rarity on the lower river—explosions, groundings, and most of all, "mist, fog, dark nights . . . storms, the suddenness and terrific force of which no one who has not witnessed would hardly realize or credit" kept travelers in an excited state.[37]

While some steamboats offered passengers posh accommodations, most primarily served the cotton trade. During the 1840s, according to E. W. Gould, ten steam packets owned jointly by planters and commission merchants and capable of carrying up to 1,500 bales ferried goods between New Orleans and Vicksburg. Four others operated exclusively between New Orleans and Natchez. Built with shallow drafts, packets could negotiate low water on the Mississippi and smaller streams.[38] The Mississippi

37. Quoting William H. Allen, "Shadows of Steamboat Life," *Knickerbocker Magazine,* XL (August, 1852), 156. For an interesting description of the Natchez wharf and travelers, see William Henry Holcombe Books, January 24, 1855, SHC. On the perils of river transportation see Michael Allen, *Western Rivermen, 1763–1861: Ohio and Mississippi Boatmen and the Myth of the Alligator Horse* (Baton Rouge, 1990), 140–69.

38. E. W. Gould, *Fifty Years on the Mississippi: or Gould's History of River Navigation* (1899; rpr. Columbus, Oh., 1951), 277.

was the main waterway that cotton planters used to ship their crops, but traffic on the Tombigbee River, and to a lesser extent on the Pearl, was also notable before the Civil War. Between 1839 and 1854 packets departing Aberdeen on the Tombigbee carried on average each year some 4,400 bales of cotton, making it a bustling center of the cotton trade in northeast Mississippi. Because of a consortium of commission houses and packet captains, the majority of cotton was shipped to Mobile. After the war, Aberdeen's share of the river trade plummeted, however, as Columbus, a city that achieved prominence as a trading center during the Civil War, employed its position on the river and the Mobile and Ohio Railroad to augment its importance to cotton producers and brokers. In 1869 Columbus shipped by river 25,000 bales of cotton, and Aberdeen sent only 800. Elsewhere, too, river trade, though never totally dead, stagnated after the war as railroads spun branch lines into remote places formerly not served by steam packets. Trade on the Pearl River, a shallow stream at the edge of the Piney Woods, never blossomed as it did on the Tombigbee largely because of competition from the Mississippi. Nevertheless, efforts were made to keep the channel clear, since lumbermen sent timber, charcoal, and pitch downstream to New Orleans. After the war the Pearl's importance as a route to markets diminished when the Illinois Central Railroad, which ran parallel to the river, captured most of the local trade with New Orleans and Jackson.[39] Maintaining channels on these and other rivers obviously benefited all who shipped goods to distant markets, but cotton cultivators in the main enjoyed the greater profits afforded by readily available and cost-effective river transportation. Not surprisingly, state law provided for the protection of river channels.

Unlike smaller rivers, which needed human assistance to keep their channels clear of traffic-stopping obstructions, the Mississippi River's swift current tended to whisk away debris. On other rivers though, as with roads, responsibility for maintaining their free flow devolved upon people living near them. State laws required that the legislature or county road commissioners, after an extensive survey, declare rivers and creeks navigable. Once so declared, they fell under state protection, making illegal the un-

39. John E. Rodabaugh, *Steamboats on the Upper Tombigbee* (Hamilton, Miss., 1985), 3–5, 39–41; Baird, *View of the Valley*, 250. See also W. A. Evans, "Steamboats on the Upper Tombigbee in the Early Days," *Journal of Mississippi History*, IV (1942), 216–24. For an account of cotton shipped on the Pearl River, see Dr. Philip Marshall Catchings Diary, January 29, 1885 (MS in Catchings Collection), MDAH. Small rivers like the Pearl and Tombigbee more severely suffered the effects of droughts than did the Mississippi; see Maria Dyer Davies Diary, January 25, 1855 (MS in Davies Papers), WRP.

tended transportation of timber downstream. To maintain open channels, commissioners appointed hands from a "convenient distance" to clear obstructions and to fell any trees that might fall into the river. Although laws affecting the maintenance of river channels were classified in the various law codes with road-building laws and drew heavily upon well-established communitarian values, the state cast aside such values where rivers were concerned long before it amended road-building laws. In the late 1860s the federal government, at the insistence of Delta planters, proffered funds to clear wartime wreckage from waterways, and Mississippi accepted with alacrity, testimony to the fact that anxieties about securing inexpensive transportation of crops to market supplanted communitarian values and sectional animosity.[40]

The improvement of the Yazoo River system illustrates the influence that federal assistance exerted over river trade and the sway that Delta planters had upon the federal government. In the antebellum period the Yazoo was navigable by steam packet to the Tallahatchie River, but during the war Federal and Confederate troops literally filled the channel with debris and sunken vessels, attempting to block river traffic. After 1865 planters, natives as well as northerners who sought their fortunes in the Delta, wanted the channel cleared so that they could advantageously send cotton to market, and the national government began removing vessels from the channel; in 1873 the Mississippi River and Yazoo Packet Company began operating on the river. Preceding by a decade the Delta boom precipitated by construction of the Yazoo and Mississippi Valley Railroad, these efforts initially opened the Delta to investors and accelerated settlement. By the late nineteenth century, navigation on the Yazoo River system, including Tchula Lake, the Tallahatchie River, and the Coldwater, reached 375 miles above Vicksburg. High water allowed packets even greater range. Along the way, over four hundred landings, many of them nothing more than wood stops, dotted the river. The extension of navigation on the Yazoo system not only allowed planters and lumbermen convenient access to markets, it fostered the development of small towns and linked to the commercial order timber cutters who sold cordwood to packet captains.[41]

40. *Laws of the State of Mississippi,* 1824–1838, pp. 70, 112–13, 175–76, 308–309; *Laws of the State of Mississippi,* 1840, p. 118.

41. Harry P. Owens, "Steamboat Landings on the Yazoo and Tallahatchie Rivers (1875–1882)," *Journal of Mississippi History,* XLVII (1985), 267–69. For accounts of wood stops on the Mississippi and Tombigbee rivers, see James Wistar Metcalfe Diary, January 27, 1843 (MS in Metcalfe Papers), SHC; Charles Cobb, *American Railway Guide and Packet Companion for the United States* (New York, 1851), 122; Rodabaugh, *Steamboats on the Upper Tombigbee,* 7; *Directory for the City of Mobile, 1859* (Mobile, 1859), 27.

Although the arrival of the Yazoo and Mississippi Valley Railroad opened the Delta to settlement and trade faster than the river system could have in twice the time, river transportation remained an important feature of Delta life throughout the nineteenth century.

Life in the Delta was also defined by overflows of the Mississippi River and its tributaries. The costly and deadly recurrence of Delta floods hindered development of the region more than any other natural cause. To control floods individuals erected private levees, and when their efforts proved incapable of restraining the free flow of the river, they turned to local, state, and federal governments. Only in the 1880s, as the levee system funded by the federal government was constructed, did the Delta, long advertised as the South's fertile crescent, begin to live up to its billing. Nineteenth-century failures of the levee system affirm the difficulty that planters had in controlling environmental forces; the effective cajoling of the federal government to aid in the construction of a levee system signaled their substantial political authority and their willingness to abandon communitarian values and states' rights (if only for the sake of building levees) to ensure economic progress.

While the Delta's rich soil remained a secret but a few years, the difficulty of draining swamplands and protecting them against seasonal overflows continued. Antebellum planters and politicians had long imagined the Mississippi Delta a regional, if not a national, asset and called upon the federal government to manage the river's flow. The combination of communitarian rhetoric and market-oriented values at times caused them to assume uncomfortable positions. In 1845, at a Memphis convention of southern and western states, John C. Calhoun laid bare a glowing inconsistency in his political thought when he argued against federal aid to internal improvements and in the same breath pleaded for the national government to construct a levee system. Disregarding the illogic of Calhoun's remarks, latter-day proponents of government aid to levee builders echoed his reasoning: Charles Ellet, Jr. in 1853 and Benjamin G. Humphreys in 1914 prophesied that protecting Mississippi's rich cotton lands from overflows would bring great wealth to the nation, the Mississippi Valley, and, of course, the planter class. Typical of that class's boosterism, Ellet claimed that the Mississippi Delta was "destined to bloom, the garden-spot of this great valley, if her skill, finances, and fortitude prevail, or to be known only as a desolate swamp if she falter and yield to the force of the flood."[42] Marshal-

42. Quoting Charles Ellet, Jr., *The Mississippi and Ohio Rivers. . . .* (Philadelphia, 1853),

ing the technology and finances necessary to control the river proved as burdensome as bearing with the floods.

Despite the much-ballyhooed benefits of levees, the persistence of communitarian values hamstrung citizens in their efforts to guard against floods. Until 1858 levee legislation in Mississippi followed a precedent instituted in an 1819 law that addressed the matter on a county-by-county basis. A Warren County Board of Levee Commissioners, chartered by the 1819 law, received special powers (and an eight thousand dollar state appropriation) to construct a levee. Fourteen years passed before another act regarding levees made its way through the legislature. In the interim, authority to construct levees passed by default into the hands of local residents, who employed black slaves and Irish laborers in the building of private levees. Designed to protect single plantations, the hodgepodge of privately erected embankments often spared one plantation at the expense of another by redirecting the flow of water onto unprotected lands. Some leveeless planters, acting out of self-interest, blasted their neighbors' work in order to save their own property. Private levees were unsatisfactory also because of their size (they averaged about four feet) and the methods used to construct them. Since excavating clay from beneath the thick layer of Delta topsoil was nearly impossible, levee cores consisted of stumps and trees, at best temporary expedients. Between 1833 and 1838 laws intended to correct the shortcomings of the levee system empowered Boards of Supervisors to take an active role in constructing levees in the individual counties. Under the new laws counties hired levee inspectors, compensated landowners for the use of their slaves to construct levees, and raised taxes. All went to little effect. The 1844 overflow, arriving after rainwater had filled the swamps, convinced the legislature that riparians could not construct an adequate system.[43]

The state's predisposition to leave levee construction entirely in the hands of those most affected by floods ended with the passage of the federal Swamp

---

224. See, too, Benjamin G. Humphreys, *Floods and Levees of the Mississippi River* (Washington, D.C., 1914), 90; John A. Fox, *A National Duty: Mississippi River Flood Problems: How the Floods Can Be Prevented* (Washington, D.C., 1914), 28.

43. Robert W. Harrison, "Levee Building in Mississippi Before the Civil War," *Journal of Mississippi History,* XII (1950), 63–69. For an account of levee blasting by flooded planters, see Smith, *Yazoo River,* 306. The state reacted slowly to the 1844 flood, and perhaps would not have acted at all had the Swamp Act of 1850 failed in Congress. Delta residents responded without waiting for the goverment to protect them. In 1840 prominent Washington County citizens formed an association to coordinate their efforts at flood prevention. See Vicksburg *Tri-Weekly Whig,* January 13, 1849.

Act of 1850, which allowed Mississippi to build levees with the proceeds from sales of some 3.29 million acres of swampland. In order to offset negligible sales of these uncultivated lands, counties issued land scrip that functioned as transferable bonds to pay contractors for their levee work. More so than any previous piece of state legislation, the introduction of state-paid contracted labor signaled the demise of community control over levee construction. Yet the difficulty of controlling the river was not ended, for the river was not a static force in this drama. Four substantial Delta floods occurred in the 1850s. The 1858 flood, by far the worst of the antebellum overflows, covered nearly 6,800 square miles to an average depth of three feet and prompted the legislature to permit counties broad taxing powers to build levees. Most of the counties received authorization to tax land in the floodplain up to ten cents per acre for five years; some were allowed to tax up to twenty-five cents per acre. In 1861 James L. Alcorn, a Delta planter employed by the state to survey the levee, found an almost complete system stretching from the Tennessee border to near Vicksburg. The levees had been constructed for slightly less than $1.3 million, though several hundred miles that remained under contract, Alcorn estimated, would almost double the cost. The protection offered by the levee, however, was at best uncertain, and the taxes raised to construct it, some planters complained, more ruinous than overflows. (In 1859 Buckner Darden, an adventurous but hard-luck planter, lost one-half of his crop to floodwater, saw his property value drop 20 percent, and had his taxes raised to rebuild the levee.)[44] Relinquishing their authority over levee construction allowed planters to gain greater control over the environment, an exchange that most favored.

The Civil War, however, wiped out antebellum progress in controlling the river, returning the levee system to its pre-1848 condition. Federal troops blasted sections of the levee, and miles of neglected embankments fell into the river. At the war's end, planters once again clamored for the state to address the problem of levee construction. But the state, saddled with its own enormous pecuniary difficulties, could not pursue the matter vigor-

44. Robert W. Harrison, "Levee Building in Mississippi Before the Civil War," *Journal of Mississippi History*, XII (1950), 69–95. The Swamp Act not only affected the Delta, farmers from the interior received loans and state credits to construct levees around swamps. See *Laws of the State of Mississippi*, 1857, pp. 96–99, 105. On Alcorn's activities, see Lillian A. Pereyra, *James Lusk Alcorn: Persistent Whig* (Baton Rouge, 1966). A. A. Humphries and H. L. Abbot, *Report Upon the Physics and Hydraulics of the Mississippi River . . . Based Upon Surveys and Investigations* (Philadelphia, 1861), 87–90, 172–76. Darden Diaries, August 15, 1859 (in Darden Papers).

ously until the late 1860s, when it impaneled two boards—one to fund the reconstruction of the levee, the other to liquidate $1.5 million in debt amassed to build the antebellum levee. The achievements of the levee boards were of dubious value to established farmers in the Delta. In fact, by 1874 taxes raised to fund levee construction and to pay antebellum debts sent one-half of all Delta lands to the state's unpaid tax rolls. Lacking titles to their lands and pressed by floods to abandon their plantations, planters mustered their political pressure to force the federal government to build a levee system. In 1879, as the sectional tensions of Reconstruction abated, Washington consented and formed the Mississippi River Commission. The commission's work was largely limited to surveying until 1882, when technical and financial assistance arrived.[45]

Seemingly in defiance of the commission's effort to protect the lowlands, the river regularly flooded and created problems familiar to backcountry Mississippi. The 1882 flood of the Mississippi, the Yazoo, and their tributaries caused by far the most suffering. During the flood, which lasted from March until May, cities like Greenville disappeared underwater. Benevolent societies from around the country sent clothing and food to the state; the federal government supplied rations and tents to help refugees stay alive, if only barely. Unlike Washington politicians whose favor planters could curry, the unrestrained river offered wealthy farmers no special consideration. Planters and tenants alike suffered. Writing to Governor Robert Lowry, a black farmer, Jacob Jackson, summed up the desperation that spread with the floodwaters: "Me & my family & my stock will die in a few days unless you Send us Some meat & meal & rice, & some hay & oats for my horses." As with other late-nineteenth-century floods, crevasses ranging in length up to one mile sent waves of water crashing over homes and crops. In 1882, 284 breaks undermined the levee system, and in the two succeeding years, 408 crevasses further weakened it. According to engineers who examined the levee following the floods of the 1880s, midwestern drainage projects exacerbated flooding in the postbellum era as more water than usual passed down the river and placed antiquated levees (some with cores of rotting timber and others weakened by crayfish holes) under extraordinary pressure.[46]

45. Humphries and Abbot, *Report upon the Physics and Hydraulics of the Mississippi,* 96–97. For accounts of the levee system during the Reconstruction period, see Harris, *Presidential Reconstruction in Mississippi* (Baton Rouge, 1967), 186–93; Harris, *Day of the Carpetbagger,* 42–45, 245–46, 283–89, 486–92; Humphreys, *Floods and Levees,* 42, 54–57. On planter influence in creating the river commission, see Cobb, *The Most Southern Place on Earth,* 79.

46. Jacob Jackson to Robert Lowry, April 4, 1882, in RG 27, MDAH. A host of letters

With the assistance of the federal government, efforts at flood control and levee construction prevented for thirty years the recurrence of disasters similar to the 1882 overflow. The 1912 overflow, however, swept across the Delta with catastrophic ferocity: pilings supporting houses washed away, whole towns disappeared underwater, and thousands of livestock floated downriver. But because an early warning system had been established by the National Weather Bureau at Vicksburg, the toll on human life was light compared to earlier floods. Convinced by the damage wrought by the 1912 flood and by Delta politicians, who complained that the warning system, despite its benefits, provided insufficient protection, Congress appropriated for levee construction and repair the largest sum to date, $4 million. Where levees were concerned, communitarian values ceased to play a role by 1913, though the continuation of such institutions as the levee guard, a corps of volunteers that patrolled the system during high water to detect potential weak points, permitted the illusion of community control over levees to persist.[47]

In the backcountry milieu of Mississippi, placing effective controls on the environment and its exigencies took decades; finding suitable ideas to replace the habits of mind inherited from the frontier took longer still. Even though the isolation and danger of the early nineteenth century had largely disappeared by 1900, aspects of the backcountry endured. Native animals and diseases, however less evident than in 1840, lingered. Delta floods occurred despite the levee system. Poorly maintained roads and river channels continued to slow travel. The persistence of such phenomena in part verifies the difficulties of manipulating the environment without sophisticated science and technology. They also persisted for so long because Mississippians as a whole surrendered their backcountry habits of mind only after the Civil War, when signposts of modernity

---

from other flood victims exist; see also A. H. Brenham to Lowry, March 11, 1882; A. E. Anderson to Lowry, April 7, 1882; E. F. Walker to Lowry, June 1, 1882, all in RG 27, MDAH. For accounts of the 1882 flood, see Humphreys, *Floods and Levees,* 24, 28; Walter Sillers, "Levees of the Mississippi Levee District in Bolivar County," in *History of Bolivar County,* ed. Williams, 84, 88–89.

47. Humphreys, *Floods and Levees,* 55–60; H. C. Frankenfield, *The Floods of the Spring of 1903 in the Mississippi Watershed* (Washington, D.C., 1904), 3–21; William Starling, *The Floods of the Mississippi River . . . with a Particular Account of the Great Flood of 1897* (New York, 1897), 41, 47, 51–52; Fox, *A National Duty,* 28, 40, 47, 55; Sillers, "Levees of the Mississippi" in *History of Bolivar County,* ed. Williams, 94. On the levee guard, see Ball Diary, September 5, 1890; Percy, *Lanterns on the Levee,* 242–69.

and new ideas about the role of government in society found eager defenders in the state.

Until such ideas and phenomena arrived in Mississippi, residents contentedly plodded along in their familiar ways of living. They happily supported a parsimonious and limited government and took comfort in the knowledge that the self-sacrifice demanded by communitarian values assured the long life of their civic identity as a folk united by their plain living. Shared conflicts with the environment and a distaste for governmental authority bolstered that identity. Yet, increasingly after the Civil War, the physical frontier and its related backcountry habits of mind diminished in direct relation to the rise and expansion of the commercial order. As these habits withered, society lost the values that had once bound all white citizens, causing the civic identity and social ethic that sprang from Mississippi's frontier days to change, even if only in an evolutionary fashion.

Chapter 2

The Web of the Market Economy

Two lasting images of the backcountry South remain fixed in the popular imagination: the solitary matriarch reading from a volume of Shakespeare while churning butter in a quiet glen, and William Faulkner's gregarious Anglo-Saxon "roaring with Protestant scripture and boiled whiskey, Bible and jug in one hand and like as not an Indian tomahawk in the other, brawling, turbulent, uxorious and polygamous." Both were hardy types, victors in a frontier version of natural selection. Rough-and-tumble men and solemn, sturdy women could appear as daunting as the backcountry itself.[1] Even though conditions and attitudes born of the frontier indicated otherwise, Mississippi was not simply a wild country in which communitarian values alone reigned among a roughhewn folk.

In 1838 the Universalist minister George Rogers discerned a complex array of values at work in Mississippi. He, like other travelers, found the state barely advanced beyond an inchoate stage of development. Towns consisted of nothing more than a few poorly framed shacks, roads were quagmires, and savage animals awaited at every bend in the road. The wildness of the land and its people exercised such a powerful influence over all things that even the immigrant New Englander, Rogers worried, might be tempted to forsake "the steady habits of his native land" and adopt ones indigenous to the backcountry. Avarice was among the loathsome qualities evinced by Mississippians: "The people are characterized by that restlessness of habit which makes them impatient of every thing which does not tend either to their pleasure or worldly interest. Pleasure and gain are the deities at whose shrines every knee bows, and every soul does homage."[2] As Rogers recognized, Mississippi was a savage country, but not savage

1. Quoting William Faulkner, "Mississippi," in *Essays, Speeches, and Public Letters*, ed. James B. Meriwether (London, 1967), 14. For references to matriarchs reading Shakespeare, see Mrs. P. E. Metcalfe-Collins, "Sketches of Some of the Pioneers of Washington County," in *Memoirs of Henry Tillinghast Ireys*, eds. McCain and Capers, 13; Eleanor Percy Ware, "Agatha: A Tale of Romance" (MS in Eleanor and Catherine Ann Ware Papers), LSU, 7.

2. Rogers, *Memoranda of the Experiences*, 208, 210, 264–66, 269.

alone. Farmers moved their families into the wilderness and undertook the backbreaking work of controlling the environment not because they longed for the struggle but because they wished to plow for themselves a niche in the market economy. Just as communitarian values informed their civic identity as free men, so too did the desire to achieve material success.

In the mid-1830s, when the federal government opened to settlement the lands of the Choctaw and Chickasaw Indian cessions, a host of immigrants, largely southern-born, rushed into the state longing to enhance their economic status. Quantitative changes in the state's population, as well as a disproportionate increase in the state's annual cotton harvest, testified to the newcomers' intentions. Those who succeeded often remained, and those who failed typically left. Curiously, however, the broadly felt desire for success through market production that led immigrants to Mississippi did not preclude them from extolling backcountry values or regarding themselves as heirs of Arcadia. In their minds, participating in the market without surrendering personal autonomy seemed possible. Combining market-oriented values with those inherited from Arcadia's proponents, including communitarian ones and the self-sufficiency ideal, allowed them to fashion unique concepts of good citizenship and a good republic.

Notwithstanding widespread devotion to material success, its achievement was not certain. For the expansion of the Cotton Belt that vaulted Mississippi to its international influence in the market and permitted residents to obtain wealth ironically diminished farmers' autonomy. Whether a farmer sold to his Liverpool factor hundreds of bales of cotton or to a local planter his cotton in the seed, whether he sold livestock on the hoof or timber to coastal lumber mills, he confessed a dependence on the market to provide him cash for goods and services he could not command. The paradox of the market economy was that those who participated in it to ensure their material success, and thus freedom from poverty and dependence, became ensnared in its web of dependence. Like Robert Penn Warren's enormous spider web, which responded to the lightest touch (even on its furthermost extended strand) by entangling interlopers, the market wound antebellum Mississippians in its grasp, if only lightly.[3] Believing themselves insulated from the full effects of the market by their communitarian values and by their professed devotion to self-sufficiency, those who dabbled in it counted their participation inconsequential.

Joseph B. Lightsey thought of himself as a virtuous farmer. He not

3. Robert Penn Warren, *All the King's Men* (1946; rpr. San Diego, 1982), 188–89.

only participated in communal activities but helped secure his family's material success by raising foodstuffs and producing for the market. To Lightsey communitarian and market values coexisted without conflict. Likewise, producing for home consumption was not incongruent with market production. In many ways the Lightsey household resembled that of their neighbors. On their 200 improved acres they cultivated a variety of row crops, including cotton; large herds of stock roamed over their 520 unimproved acres, and they owned five slaves.[4] If the Lightsey household differed significantly from other Piney Woods families, Joseph, the Lightsey's third son, by keeping and preserving a diary, made it unique.

In 1850 Joseph B. Lightsey's world revolved around farm labor and a network of family and friends. Young Lightsey worked daily alongside his father's slaves in the forests and fields and received for his labor a rent-free plot of land and a monthly salary of ten dollars. Under his father's tutelage, Joseph learned the business of farming. During the winter he traveled with John, Sr. to Mobile for two days of trading. (Two years later, they drove steers and bulls to Mobile, loaded their wagons with goods on Christmas Day, and returned home.) As with farm families across the South, the season of the year determined the day's tasks and the intensity of the labor. In February Joseph split rails; in March he planted corn and dug new ditches around a rice patch; in April he planted cotton and hoed weeds from among young corn stalks. Ridges for potatoes were prepared in May, and oats were planted in June. The harvest began in August. The Lightseys first tackled the corn crop, pulling mature ears and removing the green blades to sun-dry as fodder. Then came cotton picking time. In January the cycle, with little variation, began anew. In a succinct two-sentence statement, which lacks any hint of melancholy or gloom, Lightsey reminds the twentieth-century reader that the routine of farm work, responding as it did to the ebb and flow of the seasons and the necessity of making a livelihood, determined the tempo of life: "This is my nineteenth birthday[.] I pulled fodder all day."[5]

Between his farm chores, Lightsey hunted and fished and assisted his neighbors with their work. He helped one build a chimney, another to clear

4. Manuscript Census, Mississippi, Jasper County, Schedule I: Free Population, Schedule III: Slave Population, and Schedule II: Agriculture, 1850. All Microfilm. *Seventh Census, 1850*, 447. The Lightseys owned four times more acreage than the average Jasper County farmer, but 60 percent of their neighbors held more slaves than did they.

5. Quoting Lightsey Diary, June 30, 1850. See, too, Lightsey Diary, January 5, March 4–8, April 9, 15, 20, 25, May 29, June 8, 27, August 8, 28, September 9–12, 21, 1850, December 2, 16–26, 1851.

a field of stumps, and yet another to pick his cotton. Opportunities to break the cycle of farm labor were welcomed, and Joseph regularly joined in leisurely communal activities. He attended a large community dinner hosted by an uncle; he took in the sights of a traveling menagerie and a circus; he swam with other young men in his future father-in-law's millpond; and in a spirit of communal conviviality, he made a few obligatory purchases at the Paulding Presbyterian Church bazaar.[6] Whether Lightsey turned to work or to leisure, the watchful eye of his network of family and friends greeted him.

As a young man without land of his own and reassured in his farming operations by a safety net of family financial support, Lightsey enjoyed a place in the market economy unknown to mature Mississippi farmers. His exceptional circumstances notwithstanding, his thoughts on farming suggest that living under communitarian values hindered not the development of a market-economy mentality. On the small plot of land that John, Sr. allowed him, Joseph planted watermelons, which he sold in Paulding, and cotton, which he sold to his father at market value. Joseph was an enterprising farmer. Between 1849 and 1852 he constructed an irrigation pond for his rice patch. Two bachelor farmers joined his venture in 1851, and together they cultivated six acres—four in corn, two in cotton. Working before breakfast and on Saturday evenings, they produced fifty bushels of corn and five hundred pounds of seed cotton, all of which they sold for eighty dollars. Despite the profits they achieved during the first year, the partners agreed that in 1852 they would "plant pretty well all corn and but little cotton."[7] Lightsey neglected to explain their decision, but likely the greater profit per acre offered by corn appealed to them.

Even though the Lightsey household looked for sustenance and income to sources other than Joseph's small crops, Joseph, like other farmers, counted on his crops to bring him cash. The best evidence of Joseph's devotion to the market economy appears in his diary at the close of 1850 when he recounted his "Gain" and "Expense" for the year. According to the running tally kept in the body of the diary, the year-end summary is incorrect. Failure to include some watermelon sales, however, matters less than the fact that a half-schooled, nineteen-year-old Piney Woods boy thought to keep a ledger. For to take stock of one's gains and losses is to adopt the attitude of a market-oriented producer.[8] One schoolboy's ledger,

6. Lightsey Diary, November 30, 1847, January 14, February 18, 1848, February 23, November 30, 1850, October 4, 1851.

7. Lightsey Diary, February 10, 1852.

8. Accounts at the end of the year 1850 in Lightsey Diary. His $38.90 income derived

however, hardly suffices as evidence of a prevailing market ethos in antebellum Mississippi; neither does it argue for the presence of an entirely modern manner of thinking about the market. But Lightsey's record-keeping practices suggest that the market ethos penetrated into the state's least likely region, the Piney Woods, which as late as 1860 remained on the periphery of the Cotton Belt.

For all of his dabbling in the market economy, Lightsey never ceased thinking of himself as an independent farmer, though his definition of the virtuous farmer differed significantly from the original Jeffersonian ideal of subsistence-oriented farmers as the children of God. Indeed, in an essay on farming Lightsey argued that tillers of the soil were not by definition virtuous. Some were lazy, practiced inefficient methods, and failed to set aside food crops and cash for a rainy day. He, on the other hand, ensured that he was among the virtuous by producing for home consumption and the market. Lightsey's ideal farmer in some ways resembled the one of Jefferson's Arcadian vision: "The farmer has though to be an honest industrious goaled kind of man to insur any degree of sucksess. . . . it is true Some men pretend to be farmers who lack all of these virtues but you may Set it down that they will not do much."[9] In rejecting the blanket application of the title "virtuous" to farmers, Lightsey suggested that the variety of self-sufficiency that made men poor was anathema to good citizenship. According to Lightsey, independent men worked hard, carefully planned their enterprises, and provided their households foodstuffs as well as cash.

Lightsey's story not only indicates that communitarian and market values coexisted, but it points out that visions of liberty and virtue underwent changes in the late antebellum period. Rhetorically, the self-sufficiency ideal remained important to farmers' claims to liberty and virtue; in practice, however, self-sufficiency was merely a way to shore up the farmer's bottom line. By 1860 material success had become a significant measure of individuals' achievement of liberty and virtue.

When Max Weber sought to illustrate the capitalistic ethos at work, he turned not to a prominent German businessman but to the Philadelphia

from selling shot and gunpowder, watermelons, and cotton. On bookkeeping techniques as an indication of a market ethos, see Peter A. Coclanis, "Bookkeeping in the Eighteenth-Century South: Evidence from Newspaper Advertisements," *South Carolina Historical Magazine,* XCI (1990), 23–31.

9. Lightsey Diary, December 29, 1850.

printer and statesman Benjamin Franklin, whose aphorisms ("Time is money," "Credit is money," "Money begets money") neatly fit Weber's concept of the spirit of capitalism. According to Weber, the capitalistic ethos valued labor, accumulation of money, and avoidance of hedonistic diversions.[10] He might as well have adopted any number of antebellum southerners (Lightsey among them) as a model, for ideas echoing Franklin's often spilled from the mouths of southerners, especially those who published in James D. B. De Bow's journal of commerce and planting. Chief among them was the ideal that all white farmers might ensure their material success and personal autonomy by adopting efficient methods and working diligently to produce for the market.[11]

For a brief time during the financial bonanza of the 1830s, Franklin-like ideas about the pursuit of virtuous living fell out of favor among Mississippians, but according to state Attorney General D. C. Glenn, the rupture of the speculative bubble served as a sobering tonic, restoring men of steady habits to their proper place in society. By 1849 farmers, now "earnest cultivators" all, labored at safe methods of accumulation. To the eyes of other contributors to *De Bow's Review,* Mississippians again took up the virtuous life too slowly. A "Southwestern Planter" with obvious ties to Mississippi accused his peers of pursuing fame and fortune through others' labor. He encouraged members of his class to implement their belief in the virtue of work by firing their overseers: "Let him [the planter] learn his sons that idleness is the 'road to ruin,' let him teach his daughters that they are not dolls or milliner girls, but that they are the future makers of manners of this beautiful republic." Those who bowed their backs at the plow and fertilized fields with their footprints, he promised, would receive great riches

10. Max Weber, *The Protestant Ethic and the Spirit of Capitalism,* trans. Talcott Parsons (New York, 1958), *passim.* Adam Smith likewise celebrated work and thrift as virtuous, but because of the institution of slavery, southerners had difficulty adopting the totality of Smith's thought to their place and time. Such difficulties notwithstanding, pamphleteers, including Matthew Estes of Columbus, argued that slavery fulfilled Smith's requirement that a division of labor exist in a capitalistic system. See Matthew Estes, *A Defense of Negro Slavery: As It Exists in the United States* (Montgomery, 1846), 145–68. The specious arguments that southerners engaged in to convince themselves that they were Smith's heirs serve mainly to point out that, though not themselves capitalists as defined by significant economic thinkers, they had assumed the attitude of capitalists. See Laurence Shore, *Southern Capitalists: The Ideological Leadership of an Elite, 1832–1885* (Chapel Hill, 1986), 6–8, 16–21.

11. On the importance of work, especially self-directed work, as a means of securing capital and independence, see the morality play in the Lightsey Diary, August 1, 1852. In the play, Dick Doolittle, a prodigal son, longs to return to his New Jersey home but refuses to work to buy his passage. Eventually, penury forces him to sign himself into a type of servitude (as a ship captain's cabin boy) for a free ticket.

and social acclaim. De Bow himself admonished planters to look inward, not to the federal government, when their financial conditions begged for redress. "Be industrious, be frugal, be circumspect," he implored in the fashion of Franklin, and the boundlessness of the region would overcome any short-term economic downturn. The agricultural reformer Martin W. Phillips offered the same advice in terms even the dullest farmer could comprehend: "Keep out of debt, and control your cotton." [12] Contributors to the *Review* intended that cultivators reading such instruction would adjust their cotton production to meet international demand and thus strengthen the economic and, indirectly, the political, power of the region. Yet Mississippi farmers needed little encouragement from their journals to pursue their economic best interest.

Underpinning maxims of thrift and efficiency lay the notion that through yeomanlike labor, the farmer who struck a balance between capital accumulation and economic independence deserved contemporaries' acclaim and the designation "free man." Contradictions in the simultaneous belief in personal economic autonomy and high regard for wealth obtained through market participation permitted the concurrent influence of traditional values, including communitarian ones, and the market economy. The conflict between corporate obligations and self-interest, however, seemed not to concern Mississippians: communitarian and individual concerns existed in separate spheres, and southern children learned at an early age the equal importance of corporate responsibility and self-service. Fathers, in their advice to their children, reiterated the message in *De Bow's Review* and encouraged their progeny to accumulate wealth, to obtain their educations, and to apply their talents with thrift and efficiency. In the process they imbued their children with what historian James Oakes has identified as a "materialistic ethos." [13] The importance that Mississippians attached to that ethos, a part of the social ethic, cannot be overstated, for fathers wished that their children would grow wealthy, not that they merely avoid debt.

One measure of southern fathers' emphasis on success can be located in their advice about education. According to fathers, formal education gave

12. D. C. Glenn, "Mississippi," *De Bow's Review,* VII (1849), 39; A Southwestern Planter, "True Remedy for the Embarrassment of Cotton Planters of the South and Southwest," *De Bow's Review,* I (1846), 436; J. D. B. De Bow, "Some Thoughts on Political Economy and Government," *De Bow's Review,* IX (1850), 262; M. W. Phillips, "Duty of Cotton Planters," *De Bow's Review,* VII (1849), 411. For a characterization of luxurious living as leading to ruin, see R. G. Dun and Company, Mercantile Agency Credit Ledgers, Marshall County, 25, Baker Library, Harvard University.

13. James Oakes, *The Ruling Race: A History of American Slaveholders* (New York, 1982), 69.

children basic skills for living and taught discipline, responsibility, and the value of hard work.[14] A Carroll County farmer directed that upon his death the family's field hands be sold to provide for his sons' education. He even instructed his wife to sell the plantation itself, if necessary, in order to educate and to fix them in a profession. When planters spoke of educating their children, they intended that their sons obtain practical knowledge such as writing and elocution—important skills for men-on-the-make. An understanding of arithmetic, too, might prove practical when it came time to design a cotton warehouse or to check the ledger. Planters wished their children to obtain the acumen necessary to improve their financial condition. During James Stuart's tenure at the state university at Oxford, his letters frequently garnered his father's wrath. Oscar J. E. Stuart, a planter and inventor, viewed James's correspondence as an opportunity to lecture on the virtues attendant upon grammatical precision. Care should be given to details, James learned, if he was to become a successful lawyer. So well did he learn his lesson that he took up his father's habit and chided a younger sister for clowning in school and making bad marks in arithmetic. Those planters who like the Worthingtons' Washington County neighbor, a Mr. Lashley, thought education a waste of time, became victims of private, if not public, criticism. Amanda Worthington informed her brother that Lashley foolishly believed his son capable of operating the family estate without benefit of a formal education. In regard to young Lashley she thought that "the more he has in his pocket the more he ought to have in his head, in order to keep his balance."[15]

Sometimes the direction fathers provided went unheeded. Sometimes the recipient of the advice failed to live up to expectations; sometimes fathers, by their examples, offered contradictory guidance. Children often

14. On the importance assigned education, by even plain farmers, see the morality play in Lightsey Diary, August 15, 1852. The play, really an extended dialogue, tells of a father resistant to the idea of schooling his son. The boy's teacher explains that book-learning is meant to produce a better farmer by making a better man, not to encourage foppish habits or to make lawyers of students. In the end the father decides himself to enroll to keep up with his son. Lightsey attended school for the first time at the age of twenty. See Lightsey Diary, July 19, September 31 [?], 1852.

15. Quoting Amanda Worthington to Albert D. Worthington, October 12, 1857, in Worthington Papers. See also Last Will and Testament of H. H. Weir, in Lockhart-Weir Family Papers, MDAH; James H. Stuart to Annie E. Stuart, January 15, 1855, in Dimitry Papers; John Hebron Moore, *The Emergence of the Cotton Kingdom*, 43–44. For others' thoughts about school, see Harry St. John Dixon Diary, June 28, 30, 1858 (MS in Harry St. John Dixon Papers), SHC; John P. Darden, *The Secret of Success, or Family Affairs: A Memoir in One Volume by a Mississippian* (Cincinnati, 1853), 29–30.

took to heart their fathers' advice about accumulating money and set aside admonitions about obtaining an education. During his first year of study at the university, James Stuart apparently remained focused on his goal of becoming a wealthy lawyer. Yet during his second year, he threatened in a letter to a female friend to follow in his father's footsteps, to marry at a young age, and then, as a famous Mississippi jurist had done, to set about making his fortune without a penny to his name. Albert Worthington acted on a similar temptation. Citing his poor preparation for academic work, terrible food, and family obligations, he dropped out of the University of Virginia. According to the younger Worthington, he preferred making money back in Mississippi to spending it in Charlottesville. It is not clear whether he intended to start his own farm or merely to help his father manage the family plantation, but Albert, well aware of the value his father placed on frugality and capital accumulation, made his appeal based largely on those points. Charley Adams, a West Point cadet and son of a newspaper publisher, likewise told his father he intended to quit school. At first the elder Adams refused Charley's request, only to discover near the end of the term that the resignation would be at the command of school officials.[16] The disappointment for father and son must have run deep.

Not only from their fathers did children learn to long for material success. Every member of the southern white family was expected to do his or her part in making the household prosperous. John Darden, a Franklin County planter, encouraged his children to live according to a code of honor, to keep their word, to associate with members of their class only, and to be wary of those with whom they would do business. The successful household that Darden envisioned, one which corresponded to the reality of many upper-class Mississippi families, placed the farmer's wife at her sewing, tending the vegetable garden, and supervising slaves in the making of soap and butter. A thrifty wife could be as much a boon to a Mississippi planter or businessman as one possessed of a large dowry. In 1858 James Roach, a Vicksburg banker and railroad developer, credited his wife, Mahalia, with enabling their household to achieve a nine thousand dollar cash surplus. While James displayed a penchant for betting imported cigars on

16. James H. Stuart to Ann L. Hardeman, December 4, 1856, in Dimitry Papers; Albert Worthington to "Father," November 7, 1857, in Worthington Papers. See, too, Simeon R. Adams to Willie Adams, December 20, 1857; Charley R. Adams to Simeon Adams, June 17, 1859; Simeon Adams to Charley Adams, November 30, 1859; Charley Adams to Simeon Adams, December 6, 1859; 1st Lt. S. B. Holabird to Simeon Adams, December 1859, all in Simeon Roe Adams Family Papers, MDAH. Also see, Absalom F. Dantzler to "Dear Brother," February 5, 1849, in Absalom F. Dantzler Papers, WRP.

changes in the cotton market, Mahalia felt the sting of her friends' gentle rebukes about "a woman's duty of dressing handsomely and visiting—for her Husband's sake." Ashamed of the sorry condition of her clothing, she wished to indulge her fashionable taste, but frugality prohibited her.[17]

If the sudden influx of folk into Mississippi is any indication, the advice that Mississippi fathers gave their children about making something of themselves resembled that espoused by their counterparts in other states. Animated by a desire to improve their financial well-being, immigrants during the 1830s initiated a population explosion. (See Table 1.) Even though the demographic revolution continued until the Civil War, the most dramatic increase occurred in the 1830s, when the population swelled by 175 percent: in 1833 the flood of acquisitive newcomers forced the state to organize twelve new counties north of Hinds, a territory that before included only three counties; in 1836 whites brought into the state an estimated 250,000 slaves.[18] There is no certain method for calculating how much of the population growth resulted from immigration, but estimates place the natural increase of the population (that attributable to births after taking deaths into consideration) at about 12 percent each decade. Assuming that 35 percent of residents in any given census year remained in Mississippi for ten years, a high percentage, more than one-half of the 1840 population might be counted as newcomers.[19] A good number of those who initially went to the state in the 1830s likely did not remain. In those hal-

17. Quoting Mahalia P. H. Roach Diary, July 23, 1856 (MS in Roach and Eggleston Family Papers), SHC. But see, too, James Roach Diary, January 9, 10, 1858 (MS in Roach and Eggleston Family Papers); Darden, *Secret of Success,* 13, 43, 51. For an example of Darden's ideal family in Mississippi, see Mrs. Jared Reese Cook Diary, January 3, February 12, April 9, 1855, April 24, 1857, typescript, MDAH. Cook sold farm produce in Vicksburg to pay for her daughter's dance lessons.

18. *House Document,* 22nd Cong., 1st Sess., No. 263, p. 36; *Compendium of the Enumeration of the Inhabitants . . . from the Returns of the Sixth Census. . . .* (1841), 56–58; *Seventh Census, 1850,* 440–47; *Population of the United States in 1860: Compiled from the Original Returns of the Eighth Census* (1864), 254–70. On the movement of slaves into Mississippi, see James L. Watkins, *King Cotton: A Historical and Statistical Review, 1790 to 1908* (New York, 1908), 171.

19. To determine the percentage of the population increase attributable to natural means the number of deaths recorded in the 1850 and 1860 censuses were subtracted from the number of births reported; the product was divided by the actual population. In the 1850s the population increased through natural means by approximately 1.2 percent; in the 1840s it was closer to 1 percent. Using the higher of the two figures, the natural increase of the population was assumed to equal 12 percent. *Seventh Census, 1850,* 448–49; *Statistics of the United States, (Including Mortality, Property, Etc.), in 1860,* 35.

cyon days of economic expansion, Mississippi's population was a highly mobile one, one that came in search of land and an opportunity to partake of the promise of the age: equality of opportunism and economic independence through market production. But when opportunities for achieving prosperity and independence diminished, residents left.[20]

TABLE 1 Percentage Population Change by Region, 1830–1860

Region	1830–1840	1840–1850	1850–1860
Southern Bluffs	47	17	23
Northern Bluffs	—	91	-5
Delta	373	44	69
Black Prairie	482	102	15
North-Central Hills	—	138	47
Piney Woods	61	35	88
State	175	61	31

Sources: *House Documents,* 22nd Cong., 1st Sess., No. 263, p. 36; *Compendium of the Enumeration of the Inhabitants . . . from the Returns of the Sixth Census,* I, 56–70; *Seventh Census, 1850,* 440–47; *Population of the United States in 1860: Compiled from the Original Returns of the Eighth Census,* 254–70.

The same could also be said of post-1840 Mississippians. Even after the initial rush to fill them, the fresh lands of north Mississippi continued for a decade and a half to entice settlers, though immigration slowed after 1837. (See Table 1.) The low price of cotton and the changed terms by which public lands were sold cured many cases of immigration fever, but the cure invited an outbreak of emigration fever. So unappealing had the state become, public land sales plummeted from a high of two million acres in 1836 to fifty thousand acres in 1840. Besides pulling out of the real estate market, immigrants during the depression years became more selective about the land they purchased. They concentrated on buying land in regions of the state known for their productivity. Throughout the 1840s land offices at Columbus and Grenada, which sold acreage in the Hill Country, the Northern Bluffs, and the Black Prairie, conducted more business than the other offices combined. Those regions also experienced the largest increase

20. For treatments of immigration, see James D. Foust, "The Yeoman Farmer and Westward Expansion of U.S. Cotton Production" (Ph.D. dissertation, University of North Carolina, 1967); Herbert Weaver, *Mississippi Farmers, 1850–1860* (Nashville, 1945).

in population. With the return to prosperity, immigrants determined to risk their future on the abundant but marginally productive lands of the Piney Woods. Between 1852 and 1860 the land office at Augusta led all others in sales, and the Piney Woods region recorded the greatest population increase.[21]

Coterminous to the demographic revolution, a prodigious change in the annual production of cotton occurred, too. As their fathers had instructed them, newcomers and old hands alike set about making something of themselves, and for the great majority, that meant cultivating cotton. By 1860 the Cotton Belt, an arbitrary designation reserved for counties producing 1,000 or more bales, included all but the counties in the southeastern corner of the state. On the eve of the Civil War, Mississippi farmers baled 148 percent more cotton than they had in 1850 (as production rose from 484,000 to 1.2 million bales). Not surprisingly, the Piney Woods and the North-Central Hills, two regions undergoing great demographic change, increased their production by over 75 percent and 67 percent respectively.[22] Yet the state's enlarged crop production reflected more than the expansion of the Cotton Belt, for the number of farmers cultivating the crop swelled, too. In a survey of farm-level production in twelve counties, 43 percent with less than fifty improved acres produced at least 1 bale of cotton in 1850. Sixty-nine percent did so in 1860. On farms larger than forty-nine acres, less than 19 percent in 1850 and 9 percent in 1860 failed to cultivate 1 or more bales. By the close of the antebellum period so many Mississippians produced cotton that the state annually sent to market more than 20 percent of the world's supply.[23]

21. The end of the depression and the availability of cheap lands also accounted for the population growth recorded in the Delta region. Describing the amount of land sold by the government in that region, however, is impossible, since no land office was located there. *Seventh Census, 1850,* 440–47; *Agriculture in the United States, 1860: Compiled from the Original Returns of the Eighth Census* (1864), 84–87. Records of public land sales by office may be found in the annual *Report of the Secretary of Interior* for the years 1840–1860.

22. Only the Northern Bluffs region, which saw an aggregate population decline, experienced less than 50 percent growth of its cotton production between 1850 and 1860. For a portrait of the Cotton Belt, see the maps in Hilliard, *Atlas of Antebellum Southern Agriculture,* 68–71. *Seventh Census, 1850,* 458; *Agriculture of the United States, 1860,* 85.

23. The survey was compiled from a random sample of 2.5 percent of farms (but not less than ten actual farms) listed in the manuscript returns of the census. Manuscript Census, Schedule II: Agriculture, 1850 and 1860, Copiah, Jones, Harrison, Leake, Lowndes, Marshall, Noxubee, Panola, Pontotoc, Warren, Washington, and Wilkinson Counties, Mississippi. Microfilm. All except Washington County were surveyed for 1860, as its census returns were destroyed. Hereinafter the samples will be identified as *Farm Survey* (1850) and *Farm Survey* (1860). Data about individual farmers selected was augmented by information located

Restless farmers testified to the prevalence of the desire to achieve material success by augmenting Mississippi's annual cotton production. Simply by going to the old southwestern frontier, they proclaimed a willingness to become entangled in the web of the market economy; after all, subsistence farming would not pay mortgages and taxes. Reports of their success encouraged others equally smitten with the idea of acquiring wealth, and thus economic independence, to move south. Just such families as Thomas Gale's Tennessee neighbors accounted for the post-1830 population and cotton booms. Enamored of the success that he had on his Yazoo River plantation, Gale, a native of Tennessee and part-time Mississippi resident, broadcast the news of his good fortune. Soon his neighbors prepared to move. "The spirit of emigration seems almost general," Gale reported. In 1836 James D. Davidson, while passing through Vicksburg, observed the effect that the boom times had on Mississippi. Vicksburg, he said, ran "mad with speculation." Inflation, combined with a dearth of specie, made cash purchases rare, but credit was widely available. The city bustled with men who fathomed the meaning of the Indian cessions, men-on-the-make who wished to improve their financial condition. Most of them, Davidson surmised, were "gentlemen adventurers who think they have nothing more to do than come South and be the Lord of a Cotton Plantation and a hundred slaves."[24] Others went to Mississippi with less lofty aspirations. Made wide-eyed by the sight of millions of acres of cheap public lands available on easy terms, men of moderate means saw an opportunity to purchase their own farm. The search for material success via that elusive cotton plantation and one hundred slaves, or realistically through more modest enterprises, drove southerners to purchase fresh lands and to produce for the market and to be seemingly forever on the move.

It took John Anthony Quitman, the son of a Pennsylvania Lutheran minister, only two changes of residence and ten years before he struck upon a course that propelled him to the pinnacle of Deep South success. Although he had in common with many who went to Mississippi a desire to succeed, Quitman, through his various roles (lawyer, planter, railroad builder, and government official), achieved a level of success about which most immi-

in slave and free population schedules of the census for the appropriate counties. For the 1850 data base, 231 farms were sampled; for the 1860 one, 217. Estimates of the state's share of the market derive from Watkins, *King Cotton*.

24. Thomas Gale to "Dear Sir," August 22, 1833, in Gale and Polk Papers; Herbert A. Kellar, ed., "A Journey Through the South in 1836: Diary of James D. Davidson," *Journal of Southern History*, I (1935), 356.

grants only dreamed.[25] In at least one other way Quitman differed from the vast majority of those who would later follow him into Mississippi. He was a northerner. A survey of households listed in the 1850 and 1860 censuses reveals that even though approximately 50 percent of the population recorded its birthplace as Mississippi, 23 and 17 percent, respectively, of household heads had been born in the state. Most heads of household (77 percent in 1850 and 72 percent in 1860) hailed from other slave states. Less than 10 percent were born in the northern states or in foreign countries.[26]

Particularly in the counties adjacent to the Mississippi River and the Gulf, northerners were not exactly a rare breed. As long as they tacitly or otherwise acquiesced to black slavery, they conducted their affairs without interference. Northern-born cultivators, such as Stephen Duncan and Quitman, in fact, succeeded in the market economy better than most southern-born ones.[27] Aspiring to "something more than a mere support" that the Lutheran ministry promised, Quitman, when he left Pennsylvania in 1819 bound for Ohio, escaped his father's plan for him to become a cleric. In the West he pursued a course often followed by young men longing for material success, studying law and working as a clerk in a land office. An acquaintance whose sons had found fame and fortune in Natchez convinced Quitman to abandon his new home for the South, and in late 1821 he moved to Mississippi. Quitman believed that the expansion of cotton production that followed the 1819 depression offered attorneys a broad field in which to practice their craft and boundless opportunities to become wealthy. His intuition proved correct. Despite a religious upbringing that stressed moderation, Quitman, who had always longed to dress the part of a dandy and to be welcomed in fashionable society, soon began ordering expensive suits from Philadelphia and attending soirees hosted by established planters.[28]

25. Robert E. May, *John A. Quitman: Old South Crusader* (Baton Rouge, 1985), 8–120.

26. Two and one-half percent of the households (but never less than twenty actual households) listed in Manuscript Census, Schedule I: Free Population, 1850 and 1860, Copiah, Harrison, Jones, Leake, Lowndes, Marshall, Noxubee, Panola, Pontotoc, Warren, Washington (except 1860), and Wilkinson Counties, Mississippi, Microfilm, were randomly selected for inclusion in the survey. In 1850, 319 households were sampled and in 1860, 347. Hereinafter these data bases will be cited as *Population Survey* (1850) and *Population Survey* (1860).

27. On the advantages enjoyed by northerners in the Delta, see Rothstein, "The Antebellum South as a Dual Economy," 379–81.

28. May, *John A. Quitman,* 8, 10, 17. On the importance of gaining entry in Delta high society via marriage, see Metcalfe Diary, February 22, May 28 to June 2, 1843 (in Metcalfe Papers). On the damning influence of a marriage outside one's social and economic class, see Darden Diaries, February 11, 14, 1861 (in Darden Papers).

The cotton market indirectly led Quitman to Mississippi, but his 1824 marriage to Eliza Turner, a Natchez orphan due a share of her father's plantation, placed in his hands a portion of Woodlands plantation on Palmyra Island. Two years later Quitman, who continued exclusively to practice the law while the courts settled the Turner estate, bought a two-story Federal-style mansion in Natchez. Borrowing heavily and forming a partnership with a planter, he purchased in 1828 a sugarcane plantation in Terrebonne Parish, Louisiana, and in 1834 a cotton plantation on the Mississippi near Natchez. More directly than ever, Quitman's livelihood depended on the cotton economy, and he reveled in his newfound role as a haughty patrician. But like many who signed their names for the sake of acquaintances' credit, the Panic of 1837 caught him unaware. Recovery came slowly. By 1842 he had rebounded sufficiently to assume the debts of his in-laws, and with a loan from a New Orleans commission house, he purchased the entire Turner plantation.[29] By the time of his 1859 death, Quitman had traveled a long distance from his Pennsylvania and Lutheran roots. He not only stood as lord over three plantations and hundreds of slaves, he had become one of the peculiar institution's staunchest defenders and a supporter of filibusters into Latin American slave nations. Caught in the web of the market economy, the austerity of his upbringing must have seemed irrelevant to the mature Quitman.

Quitman's good fortune was not shared by most immigrants. For them, moving to Mississippi required that they sacrifice familiar comforts in their pursuit of material success and accept, if only temporarily, a coarse existence. Even professionals, who like Quitman believed the Deep South an open field in which to practice their trades, found the road to success a rough one. The physician Edward Golladay complained that his profession scarcely provided a livelihood. If his financial status took a turn for the worse, Golladay jokingly remarked, he planned to exercise a squatter's claim to a cabin and a plot of land. Dogtrot cabins (floorless log structures) were the universal emblem of mobility and sacrifice. When hastily constructed, as they generally were, they might stand for a decade. Stick and mud chimneys, few, if any, windows, and dirt floors kept the labor and capital needed to construct dogtrots to a minimum, but comfort was sacrificed in the process. Ephemeral and uncomfortable, they suited a people willing to pull up stakes at every rumor of more fertile land at lower prices. In 1840 the idea of making something of himself prompted Benjamin L. Smith to resign his teaching post in Georgia, to purchase a few slaves,

29. May, *John A. Quitman*, 21, 26, 28, 111–12.

and to move to Lowndes County. After several years of cotton farming, Smith had little to show for it. During the mid-1850s, after almost completely forsaking cotton for stock raising, Smith realized his goal. The time for sacrificing had perhaps not subsided, but thirteen years of living in a floorless cabin ended when Smith erected a frame house. In 1839 Barrett Walthall, a failed businessman from Richmond, experienced another kind of sacrifice when he moved to Holly Springs: heirloom china and trunks of clothing shipped from Virginia disappeared at sea when the vessel transporting the items sank.[30]

Citing Gideon Lincecum's assertion that he had been "reared to a belief and faith in the pleasure of a frequent change of country," one historian has suggested that southerners owed their restlessness to cultural traits. Other historians posit that soil exhaustion in the South Atlantic region prompted farmers to seek out fresh lands. A more recent historian has suggested that native southerners, at least South Carolina's Piedmont farmers, migrated to Mississippi in search of material success.[31] Samuel Agnew's father, a farmer from Due West, South Carolina, moved to Tippah County determined to expand his farming operation; before leaving the Piedmont, he purchased two additional slaves. Within two years he had on hand enough grain to last eighteen months, and he had opened a grinding mill.[32] Agnew was a successful farmer by Old South standards. An overarching desire to obtain something more than he had previously known lay at the heart of this moderate farmer's restlessness.

Wealthier southerners also migrated to Mississippi with the thought of expanding their farming operations, and like their contemporaries of other classes, several moves often were required before they settled down. Patrick

30. Edward Golladay to George Golladay, January 12, 1860, in George S. Golladay Papers, MDAH; Benjamin Lafayette Smith, "Autobiography," MS in MDAH, 3–6. See also Seldon M. Burton to Samuel McCorkle, May 3, 1847, in Samuel McCorkle Papers, MDAH. On sacrifices made by immigrants, see Oakes, *The Ruling Race,* 87–89; Paul Douglas Hardin, "Edward Cary Walthall: A Mississippi Conservative" (M.A. thesis, Duke University, 1940), 10. On dogtrot cabins, see Beulah M. D'Olive Price, "The Dog-Trot Cabin: A Development in American Folk Architecture," *Mississippi Folklore Register,* IV (1970), 92–93; C. G. Parsons, *Inside View of Slavery: Or a Tour Among the Planters* (Boston, 1855), 107.

31. Gideon Lincecum quoted in Grady McWhiney, *Cracker Culture: Celtic Ways in the Old South* (Tuscaloosa, 1988), 32. The idea that soil exhaustion caused Upper South farmers to flee their homes is an old one. For correctives of that view, see Gavin Wright, *The Political Economy of the Cotton South: Households, Markets, and Wealth in the Nineteenth Century South* (New York, 1978), 17. On South Carolinians leaving the Piedmont, see Lacy K. Ford, Jr., *Origins of Southern Radicalism: The South Carolina Upcountry, 1800–1860* (New York, 1988), 39.

32. Agney Diary, December 15, October 25, July 14, 1852, June 29, 1854.

Henry was the first member of his family to move to the state. His brother Gustavus remained in Tennessee, where he loaned money to emigrants moving to Mississippi. Trying to convince Gustavus that he should come south, Patrick cautioned that loaning money to aspiring planters involved great risks, but cotton cultivation, on the other hand, paid his mortgage and provided enough cash to expand his slave force. Investing in land and slaves promised the highest return on investment and the safest course for men with capital. Not long after writing Gustavus, Patrick sold his plantation, purchased another in the state, and offered a third plot of land to his brother. Eventually, Patrick's pleas swayed Gustavus, who bought a 112-acre farm near Clinton, which he soon considered selling so that he might purchase a larger one. Traveling as far as southwestern Mississippi in search of a 500- to 600-acre plantation, Gustavus found none to his liking, but he remained determined to sell his slaves and farm for at least seventy thousand dollars. The cash brought by his 1852 and 1853 crops, he believed, would retire outstanding debts, and the money raised by selling real estate and chattel would allow him to invest in an ironworks or tobacco factory. His plans to become a captain of southern industry, however, were shelved when in 1854 he bought another Mississippi plantation.[33] Unlike the planter paternalists some historians have found in the South, Gustavus, knowing the market economy to be open to products other than cotton, invested in land and slaves for the sake of profit. Gustavus wanted something more than what he had known in Tennessee and cared not whether he achieved material success through usury, planting, or manufacturing.

As Gustavus Henry realized, obtaining material success in the Old South did not demand that one plant cotton. Other Mississippi immigrants also discerned that material success and liberty could be achieved without purchasing a plantation and a retinue of slaves. Merchants and attorneys, who conducted business for cotton producers, and even stock raisers and timber cutters, sought material success in the antebellum period, but none of them escaped the influence of the cotton market.[34] The latter two

33. Patrick Henry to Marion Henry, March 17, 1835; Gustavus A. Henry to Marion Henry, May 21, 1853; Gustavus to Marion, April 17, 1854, all in Henry Papers, SHC. On the toll that Henry's frequent moves exacted, see Elizabeth D. Henry to Marion, March 17, 1835, in Henry Papers, SHC.

34. On lawyers' role in the cotton economy, see Gail Williams O'Brien, *The Legal Fraternity and the Making of a New South Community, 1848–1882* (Athens, 1986), 79–90. On merchants as acquisitive immigrants, see Dun and Company, Harrison County, 54; Copiah County, 215; Leake County, 7; Warren County, 27.

groups of producers, though they generally neglected cotton cultivation, nevertheless found a market for the products of their labor in New Orleans and Mobile, as well as in local planters, who failed to produce all they consumed.

Better than some historians, travelers to the southern Piney Woods perceived that herds of cattle represented the hidden wealth of small farmers. Estimates place the number of cattle sent to market in the last twenty years of the antebellum period at one million, and the value of southern livestock stood at one-half billion dollars in 1860. Travelers also commented on the carefree tenders of the herds: "a peculiar race of petits Paysans," according to one; the breeders of "wild, half naked, unwashed, and uncombed" children who ran "through the woods and grass followed by packs of lean and hungry curs," said another. Some historians agree that those who chose to live in the pine barrens suffered from a deficiency of economic acumen and energy. In order to maintain their independence, they responded to a deeply ingrained call to live out their lives at a subsistence level. While isolated individuals surely existed in such bucolic settings, the post-panic population boom in the Piney Woods and North-Central Hills filled the forests with market-oriented producers ready to send products to market.[35] No less than the Delta planter, yeoman farmers and herdsmen depended on the market for cash and regarded their participation in the market as proof that liberty and virtue resided in them as surely as in cotton cultivators.

Travelers who observed a half-wild people haphazardly tending their herds formulated an accurate assessment of stock raisers' lifestyle. Yet even the least ambitious cattle drover occasionally draped traces over his shoulders and cultivated rice, corn, and sweet potatoes, if not cotton. He devoted his few improved acres to farming, since he likely sheltered and fed his stock on public lands or private range and woodlands. Under these conditions raising stock typically required a negligible capital investment in land; some stock raisers even built their herds without expending cash. When Thomas Leonidas Baxter migrated to Marion County, he procured a herd of cattle by managing on shares the stock of a Feliciana Parish, Louisiana, physician

35. Quoting Timothy Flynt, *Recollections of the Last Ten Years* (Boston, 1826), 317; W. H. Sparks, *The Memories of Fifty Years. . . .* (4th ed.; Philadelphia, 1882), 331–32. Forest McDonald and Grady McWhiney, "The Antebellum Southern Herdsman: A Reinterpretation," *Journal of Southern History*, XLI (1975), 156; McDonald and McWhiney, "The South from Self-Sufficiency to Peonage," 1115. On local markets, see Claiborne, "Trip Through the Piney Woods," 514–16, 522; Mrs. Arthur Turner, "Turkey Drives: South Mississippi, Greene County," *Mississippi Folklore Register*, III (1969), 31–32. On the absence of local markets in some parts of south Mississippi, see Adeline Russ Diary (MS in Henry Weston Family Papers), MDAH, 4.

and planter. In exchange for tending and driving the herd to Louisiana when demanded, Baxter received one-half of the calves born. Less is known about Pierre Saucier or how he amassed his herd, but by the early 1850s Saucier owned hundreds of head of stock, real estate valued at twenty thousand dollars, a slaughterhouse, a grocery, and several slaves. He rented his land at Pass Christian and butchered cattle for the local market; most he shipped on the hoof to New Orleans, where he traded on a cash basis for the goods sold in his store.[36]

Stock raising presented small landowners in the Piney Woods and elsewhere what cotton presented to planters, access to the market. Whether they sold their stock to planters or in the markets, stock raisers in the end fed cultivators who devoted their energy and acreage to cotton. By virtue of their propinquity to it and their reliance on cotton cultivators to purchase their stock, small farmers who dealt in cattle, as well as specialized herdsmen, developed a dependence on the cotton market for their material success.

Similarly, timber cutters depended on cash they received from cotton planters and market cities. Miles of virgin pine forests from just north of the coastal plain to the hill country and from the border with Alabama to the Delta attracted immigrant woodsmen. Even though the forest industries of antebellum Mississippi appear insignificant when compared to the industry that emerged after the Civil War, two trends often mentioned in connection with the postbellum lumber boom were rooted in the prewar period. First, substantial fortunes could be made in the lumber industry, and second, natives of New England and the Great Lakes states occupied a large number of skilled positions in the forest industries and owned a disproportionate share of mills. In 1847 Henry Weston, for example, arrived in New Orleans from the North, but finding no work in Louisiana's Piney Woods went to Logtown, Mississippi, where he labored as a sawyer for forty-five dollars a month. Before 1851 Weston's skills and experience earned him an even larger salary, and he spoke of saving sixty-five dollars a month. Working primarily in Logtown, Weston remained in south Mississippi for the rest of his life and came eventually to own a mill.[37] For sawyers

36. Claiborne, "Trip Through the Piney Woods," *passim*; Sparks, *Memories of Fifty Years*, *passim*; Baxter, "Cattle Raising," 3–5. On livestock raising in the late eighteenth and early nineteenth centuries, see John D. W. Guice, "Cattle Raisers of the Old Southwest: A Reinterpretation," *Western Historical Quarterly*, XIII (1977), 167–87. On Saucier, see Manuscript Census, Schedule I: Free Population, Mississippi, Harrison County, 1850; Dun and Company, Harrison County, 44. On stock raising in north Mississippi, see Smith "Autobiography," 3–9.

37. On the profitability of antebellum coastal mills, see Dun and Company, Harrison

and other full-time mill employees, living in the communities that sprouted up around the mills required that they, like urban laborers, depend on the market for their food and clothing.

Until the lumber boom of the 1880s timber was in the main a by-product of farmers' clearing land for cultivation. Outside the Piney Woods, cultivators floated cypress, pine, and oak down the Yazoo, Big Black, and Pearl rivers to local mills. When railroad companies entered the state, farmers went about cutting timber with more purpose. A contract to supply a railroad with crossties could keep a farm family busy after harvest time and provide a cash insurance against lean times in the winter. In the pine barrens, railroads played a less influential role in developing a lumber industry because timber had always found a market in coastal processing mills. So determined to sell timber were men of the Piney Woods that they overcame the lack of deep-water streams through ingenious methods. John Belchen, a former slave, recalled rolling timber into man-made, plank-lined ditches three and one-half feet wide and fifty miles long. During the dry winter months, woodcutters filled the canals with timber and stacked it nearby, awaiting spring rains that would transform the ditches into rivulets so their harvest could be shepherded to major streams and on to coastal mills. According to B. L. C. Wailes, timber floated from the north via canals turned the rivers and bays north of Biloxi into a sea of bobbing pine.[38]

County, 69. For a description of the virgin forests, see Claiborne, "Trip Through the Piney Woods," 523; Henry Weston to Levi W. Weston, January 7, 1847; Henry to S. W. Weston, December 15, 1851; Henry to Levi, August 23, 1857; Henry to Levi, July 15, 1860, in Weston Family Papers.

38. George Rawick, ed., *The American Slave: A Composite Autobiography, Supplement* (41 vols.; Westport, Conn., 1977), Ser. I, Vol. VI, 108–109, hereinafter, unless otherwise noted, all references will be to series I. Wailes, *Report on the Agriculture and Geology of Mississippi,* 349. See, too, Wailes Diaries, August 11, 1852. On farmers signing contracts to supply crossties, see Nathan Fox Diary, March 9, 1854 (Typescript in Nathan Fox Papers), MDAH. On the variety of mills found outside the Piney Woods, see John Hebron Moore, *Andrew Brown and Cypress Lumbering in the Old Southwest* (Baton Rouge, 1967), 73–111; George Young to James McDowell, November 1, 1843, October 3, 1842, all in James McDowell II Papers, WRP; Alexander Diary, January 5, 1859. On the rarity of craftsmen to install, operate, and repair mills, see [?] to Charles D. Fontaine, August 16, 1852, in Charles D. Fontaine and Family Papers, MDAH; Thomas Nesmith to Christopher Orr, November 21, 1847, in Jehu Amaziah Orr Papers, SHC. Skilled slaves in the lumber industry were not unusual. See Nollie W. Hickman, "Black Labor in the Forest Industries of the Piney Woods, 1840–1933," in *Mississippi's Piney Woods: A Human Perspective,* ed. Noel Polk (Jackson, 1986), 80. For an overview of the lumber industry, Hickman's *Mississippi Harvest: Lumbering in the Longleaf Pine Belt, 1840–1915* (Montgomery, 1962).

While travelers to the Piney Woods habitually expressed a prejudice in favor of plantation agriculture, the value and significance of the forest industries, even those conducted in the off-season months by farmers, rarely escaped them. Small enterprises around the state constructed wagons, staves, and fence rails that sold in local markets, though some of those commodities manufactured on the coast certainly made their way to New Orleans. Away from the coastal meadows, forest dwellers operated tar kilns, large rectangular fire boxes that consumed a hundred cords of wood in the process of making two barrels of tar, linking not only the owner but also local woodcutters to the market. The tar, according to Wailes, brought between a dollar fifty and two dollars per barrel. One storekeeper on the Hobolochitto River, a Mrs. Kimball, acted as a factor for local tar-makers, buying in one year approximately nine thousand barrels and shipping them to New Orleans.[39] Piney Woods residents developed industries for making pitch and charcoal and for extracting turpentine, too, enterprises they pursued in the hope of establishing for themselves a place in the market economy.

For every Gustavus Henry, John Quitman, Pierre Saucier, and Henry Weston who achieved success in Mississippi, countless residents failed to improve their material well-being. When the siren call of fresh lands quieted during the depression of the 1830s and 1840s, the rocky path to success appeared. At no time were the dangers of the market economy more apparent than in the years of the economic collapse. Farmers greeted news of the cotton market's apocalyptic decline with "dismay and panic," according to George Young; their baled cotton, which if sold at market prices would not pay transportation costs, accumulated on the banks of Mississippi rivers. Emotions ran to despair.[40] To many, the sacrifice that the depression required them to make was more than they could bear. With a haste equalled only by that which brought them to Mississippi, residents fled the state, bound for fresh lands at cheaper prices and a new start at improving their material condition.

Perhaps the greatest emigration from Mississippi occurred in the decade after 1837. On a trip to Jackson from northeastern Mississippi in 1845, Jehu Amaziah Orr noted the effects of the depression. Abandoned plantations ("bits of wreckage and flotsam marking the unseen graves of

39. On the other forest industries in the Piney Woods, see Wailes Diaries, August 13 to 15, 19, 27, 1852. Wailes, *Report on the Agriculture and Geology of Mississippi*, 349–53.

40. Quoting George Young to James McDowell, March 8, 1843, but see, too, Young to McDowell, January 15, 1845, all in McDowell Papers.

those who have perished there") fell into decay. Courts conducted a brisk business seizing property. Under the cover of nightfall, planters, pressed by their creditors, sent away their slaves, families, horses, and mules, "all in a double-quick march to Texas," which had become, according to another contemporary, the "stronghold of evil-doers." Although the rate of emigration caused by the economic collapse cannot be accurately calculated, the rate of persistence established for the 1840s indicates that the vast majority of white residents who migrated into the state during the 1830s fled before the depression ended. After the recovery, with the lessons of the depression in mind, Mississippians forsook their speculative ways and made themselves into what one booster called "a new and more prudent class" of farmers and businessmen. As a more cautious people, they found it unnecessary to take flight, and the rate of persistence in the 1850s rose. Almost 80 percent of Mississippi heads of household identified in a survey of the 1840 census failed to reappear ten years later in the same county or an adjacent one; roughly 73 percent of those identified in a survey of 1850 households likewise did not persist.[41] (See Table 2.) Mortality and errors committed in taking the census account for some of the unidentified, but most likely emigrated. The rates of persistence calculated for Mississippi favorably compare to those established for areas in the Midwest and Alabama. But, in fact, differences in the way the percentages were arrived at leave Mississippi with a comparatively low rate.[42]

41. Quoting J. A. Orr, "A Trip from Houston to Jackson, Mississippi, in 1845," Mississippi Historical Society *Publications,* IX (1906), 173–78; Duncan McKenzie to Duncan McLaurin, June 6, 1843, in Duncan McLaurin Papers, WRP; *The Southern Business Directory and General Commercial Advertiser* (2 vols.; Charleston, 1854), I, 141. On the burden of paying debts during the collapse, see John P. Stewart to Duncan McLaurin, May 17, 1837, in McLaurin Papers. The justification for including as persisters those who lived in a county adjacent to the one in which they were previously listed stemmed from two considerations: first, county boundaries were frequently redrawn, meaning that though a household's home county changed its name, the place of residence might have remained the same; second, relocating from one county to an adjacent one may have involved a move of negligible distance. Counting as persisters those whose place of residence changed to an adjacent county increases the rate of persistence by about 2 percent in the 1840s and 1850s. The survey of heads of household (2.5 percent, but not less than twenty heads per county) was drawn from: Manuscript Census, Schedule I: Free Population, 1840, Copiah, Jones, Leake, Lowndes, Marshall, Noxubee, Panola, Pontotoc, Warren, Washington, and Wilkinson Counties, Mississippi, hereinafter cited as *Population Survey* (1840). Harrison, which is included in *Population Survey* (1850) and *Population Survey* (1860), was not formed until after the 1840 census was taken. The rate of persistence for the 1850s was based on the sample included in *Population Survey* (1850).

42. On the difference in the way Mississippi's rate of persistence was determined, see note 41. Mildred Thorne, "A Population Study of an Iowa County in 1850," *Iowa Journal of His-*

TABLE 2 Rates of Persistence Among Heads of Household in Antebellum Mississippi, 1840–1860

Region	1840–1850 n = 50	1850–1860 n = 81
Southern Bluffs	19.0	34.6
Northern Bluffs	23.4	0.00
Delta*	2.4	25.8
Black Prairie	13.3	34.0
North-Central Hills	10.0	27.1
Piney Woods*	45.0	27.5
State Total	20.8	27.2

n = number of persisters

Sources: *Population Survey* (1840); *Population Survey* (1850); *Population Survey* (1860).

*The persistence rate from 1850 to 1860 for the Delta region includes only Warren County; the 1860 manuscript returns for Washington County are missing. The rate calculated for the Piney Woods from 1840 to 1850 includes only Jones County; Harrison County was not formed until 1841.

In a letter to Governor Tilgham M. Tucker, James Dickson of Columbus provided a clue to uncovering the reason for Mississippians' shallow roots. After trying to find work in Jackson, New Orleans, and Mobile, Dick-

tory, LVII (1959), 209–10, found that about 27 percent of males twenty years of age and over persisted during the 1850s; Don Harrison Doyle, *The Social Order in a Frontier Community, Jacksonville, Illinois, 1825–1870* (Urbana, Ill., 1978), 261–62, calculated the persistence rate for males aged twenty and over at 31 percent; and William L. Barney, "Patterns of Crisis: Alabama White Families and Rural Change, 1850–1870," *Sociology and Social Research,* LXIII (1979), 532, 540, established rates of persistence in four Alabama regions between 25 and 36 percent. Hal S. Barron, *Those Who Stayed Behind: Rural Society in Nineteenth-Century New England* (New York, 1979), 84, found that 63 percent of male heads of household living in a Vermont township in 1840 remained there in 1860. Persistence rates for the Carolinas as reported by Orville Vernon Burton (40 percent) and Robert C. Kenzer (52 percent) in the 1850s complement findings for Mississippi, as they suggest that the emigration out of the Carolinas and into the Deep South had subsided by 1850. See Burton, *In My Father's House Are Many Mansions: Family and Community in Edgefield, South Carolina* (Chapel Hill, 1985), 42; Kenzer, *Kinship and Neighborhood in a North Carolina Community, Orange County, North Carolina, 1849–1881* (Knoxville, 1987), 164. See, too, Myron P. Gutmann, *et al. Staying Put or Moving On? Ethnicity, Migration, and Persistence in Nineteenth-Century Texas* (Austin, 1990), Table 4, who asserts that approximately 35.9 percent of Texans in six counties persisted between 1850 and 1860.

son traveled to Natchez, where his bad luck apparently continued. Pleading with Tucker for assistance, he explained: "I left Home for the purpose of making something and I don't like to return until I do." Not unlike Quitman, and surely a host of others, the idea of acquiring something more than he had known and proving to his family that he deserved their respect as an independent man propelled Dickson to leave home. Often acquisitive young men like him, responding to the same motivation that drew immigrants to the state, left and never again returned. James R. Brumby, the son of a restless farmer who had been on the move for almost a decade prior to James's birth, was born in Holmes County in 1846. James's older siblings had been born in South Carolina, Alabama, and Mississippi, and the familiar pattern of moving continued during James's childhood. Twice before he reached the age of eight the Brumbys moved within the county. Then, in 1853, they relocated to nearby Yazoo County but returned soon afterwards when creditors seized the new farm. Hard times continued to keep the family on the move. Disappointed with farming, Brumby gave up on Mississippi altogether before 1860 and migrated to Marietta, Georgia, where he opened a tannery.[43] Individuals' inability to obtain material success, as suggested by the case of the Brumbys and Dickson, informed their decision to leave Mississippi.

The portrait of the emigrant resembles that of the immigrant. Most likely he was a farmer from a southern state; acquisitive and longing to find a place in the market economy, he wanted to maintain personal autonomy and freedom from debt, desires that might require him to flee. Participating in the market economy, if only occasionally and in a restricted manner, brought him to Mississippi. Greener pastures elsewhere, in conjunction with the inherent difficulties of achieving economic independence through market production, led him away.

The post-panic depression constituted one difficulty making southerners' quest for economic liberty rigorous. Even after the economy rebounded in the late 1840s, achievement of material success met with obstacles. Hardships stemmed from the structure of the cotton economy: methods used to finance and market the crop forced farmers into a role subordinate to the will of the market. They arose as well from southerners' attempts to retain diverse, even contradictory, definitions of economic independence. On one hand, citizens heralded the materialistic ethos that had originally driven

43. James Dickson to Tilgham M. Tucker, March 12, 1842, in RG 27, MDAH; James Brumby, "Autobiography" (MS in Brumby and Smith Family Papers), MDAH.

them to Mississippi in search of a plantation and one hundred slaves, while never surrendering the belief that virtue belonged to self-sufficient producers, especially those who labored in their own fields. The inconsistency demanded by allegiance to self-sufficiency and the materialistic ethos altered the original ideal of economic success inherited from preceding generations of Americans, so that by the late antebellum period southerners no longer sought to be mere self-sufficient farmers. Instead they strove for success in the market economy and pursued home production as much as they dared. Dallying in the web of the market economy imperiled their claims to economic liberty, as traditionally defined, and threatened to make them poor if they miscalculated the health of the market.

Practices employed to finance and market the cotton crop introduced into the South a variety of agents that hindered the search for economic liberty and made those who sought virtue through cotton cultivation subject to the market's fluctuations. In the South the cost of all commodities (specie, land, slaves, and staple items) rose and fell according to the price of cotton; and the price of cotton, always dependent on the demand of textile manufacturers in Europe and New England, eluded the control of producers. While individual farmers might adjust the amount of cotton they produced in order to meet expected changes in the market, the necessity of cultivating cotton for cash, even in the worst financial times, circumscribed farmers' ability to regulate the number of bales placed in the market. To make matters worse, geographic isolation and primitive communications networks compelled cultivators to rely on commission merchants for a host of services.

Planters, particularly northern-born ones with close ties to New York and Liverpool, maintained a distinct advantage over producers without such friends. But even they rarely received current information about cotton prices, and those who tried to watch the market themselves found it nearly impossible to direct their factors with precision. Proximity to New Orleans and Mobile commission houses, several of which opened branch offices in Mississippi, failed to secure for cultivators a significant advantage in marketing their crop. Typically, soon after ginning a share of the crop, a planter sent cotton to his factor, who then sold the crop at an agreed upon price, or at the best price possible. The factor applied profits from the sale of cotton to the planter's account and, during the following year, debited the account (and future earnings, if necessary) to cover the cost of plantation goods that the planter ordered. Cotton cultivators who used commission merchants depended on them for the commodities they needed, as well as the profits they realized. In the 1850s at least one planter, disgusted by the lack of control that he exercised over his bottom line, suggested that farmers form a cooperative to bypass commission merchants. Duncan McKenzie also wearied of his subordination to factors and the market after a New Orleans commission house sold his entire 1842 crop of twenty-one bales for 5.25 cents per pound—a price which, after deducting the cost of transportation and insurance, barely covered the amount of the advance he had received.[44]

Small-scale cotton cultivators, especially those in the interior of the state, had even less authority over their crop than did large planters. Commission merchants found the risks too great and the rewards too meager to justify dealing with small producers, forcing them to turn instead to local planters, country merchants, and itinerant speculators for the services that factors would not provide. In 1850 Peter Misso and Andre Monarcho, Italian immigrants operating a grocery in Macon, purchased from small farmers between two hundred and four hundred bales of cotton; Edward Jack of Warren County acted as a factor for small producers and eventually converted his general store into a commission house. Cultivators who could not secure the services of adventurous middlemen sold to planters their cotton in the seed at greatly reduced prices. In the Piney Woods cotton in the seed sold at four cents per pound before the panic struck; afterwards, in 1840, local planters paid one-half that amount. The mutually dependent relationship that developed among merchants and small producers resembled the one that factors and planters shared.[45]

44. On the relationship between farmers and commission merchants, see Harold Woodman, *King Cotton and His Retainers: Financing and Marketing the Cotton Crop of the South, 1800–1915* (Lexington, Ky., 1968), 3–60. Factors were particularly important in Mississippi, since banks were few in number; see Larry Schweikart, *Banking in the American South from the Age of Jackson to Reconstruction* (Baton Rouge, 1987), 23–27. On commission merchants in Mississippi, see *Kimball and James' Business Directory, for the Mississippi Valley, 1844* (Cincinnati, 1844), 416–19, 426, who counted three commission houses at Natchez and over twenty in Vicksburg during the mid-1840s. On the "Planters Chamber of Commerce," see Miles H. McGehee, "How Shall Cotton Maintain Remunerating Prices?" *De Bow's Review,* VII (1849), 74–75. Duncan McKenzie to Duncan McLaurin, June 6, 1843, in McLaurin Papers. On planters' dependence on commission merchants for services and advances, see the unattached "Account of John Darden [1860]," in Darden Papers. In the peak cotton-selling month of January, Darden had on balance with a New Orleans factor $371.11, one year's profits; the recent sale of seventy-five bales of cotton barely covered his 1859 advances for meat and molasses. See also accounts of George W. Humphreys with James Strideron, in Humphreys Papers.

45. On Misso and Monarcho, see Dun and Company, Noxubee County, 20. On Jack see Dun and Company, Warren County, 4. On the hazards of the commission business, see Dun and Company, Warren County, 29.

Besides operating in the cotton market through secondary agents, cultivators faced wide market fluctuations that checked their quest for material success. The Panic of 1837 taught hard lessons about the market's volatility: every bale of cotton that exceeded demand brought down the price. John Quitman's New Orleans factor perhaps best summarized the South's dependence on textile manufacturers: "If the Crop in the U.S. prove[s] a large one, it is generally thought prices [paid for cotton] in Europe will recede." While the reverse also proved true in some years, the amount of cotton on hand always determined the price. Stephen Duncan predicted a small cotton crop in 1844, but he doubted high prices would be paid. "With the stocks in Europe," he surmised, "the manufacturers can control the market."[46]

Other contingencies affected prices, too. Bad weather in a large area of the Cotton Belt would set speculators to work calculating the consequences for total supply, and the availability of specie determined how much of the crop could be purchased.[47] From 1837 until about 1848 the South, indeed the western world, experienced a dearth of specie. The devaluation of paper currency exacerbated by President Andrew Jackson's Specie Circular Act, which demanded repayment of debts owed the government in specie, contributed to the severity of the currency crisis. "Shinplaster" money that Mississippi bankers printed in the booming 1830s always lacked sufficient specie backing it, but the currency crisis devalued it more. The flush times that had served Joseph G. Baldwin's fictionalized Virginians so well abruptly ended as the price of cotton, outstripping the decline in the cost of consumer items, reflected the severity of the depression. In good times and in bad the relationship between the price of commodities and the price of cotton was, as Daniel Kelly noted, a direct one. In 1845 he said, "all necessaries are quite low in Mobile, all being governed by the price of cotton"; another resident of south Mississippi, R. A. Evans, observed that "every-

46. Quoting A. J. Denniston and Company to John Quitman, January 26, 1844, in Quitman Family Papers, SHC; Stephen Duncan to Charles P. Leverich, March 30, 1844, in Charles P. Leverich Papers, MDAH.

47. For an assessment of the effect that weather conditions had on prices, see Brown & Shipley and Co. to G. Caledonia, September 19, 1840, in Port Gibson Bank Papers, MDAH. On the scarcity of specie and the price of cotton, see W. Newton Mercer to Charles P. Leverich, May 25, 1843, in Leverich Papers. Other assessments of the cotton market may be found in: R. L. Adams and Company to S. T. Lockhart, November 18, 1858; Murphy, Sykes and Co. to Lucinda Lockhart, October 22, 1859, all in Lockhart-Weir Family Papers. On economic crises and their effect on currency supply and cotton, see Duncan McKenzie to Duncan McLaurin, November 1, 1857, in McLaurin Papers; Daniel Kelly to James and Ann Kelly, March 21, 1857; Daniel Kelly to James Kelly, November 8, 1857, in Kelly Papers.

thing [was] in proportion" to the price of cotton.[48] Until the late 1840s cotton and commodity prices remained low. For the crop years 1838–1839 to 1848–1849, average annual wholesale cotton prices in New York ranged from 5.63 to 9.5 cents per pound. Southern markets paid like prices: in Mobile the 1843–1844 crop sold for between 6.5 and 8.8 cents, and the following year prices ranged from 4.5 to 6.5 cents; in New Orleans low-middling cotton purchased between 1844 and 1846 cost wholesalers as little as 5 cents and as much as 9 cents. Cultivators, of course, received less for their crops than the wholesale price. Following the depression, except for the crop year 1851–1852, the average annual price of cotton at New York exceeded 10 cents per pound, and for a short time in the early 1850s the indexed price of cotton surpassed that of major consumer items.[49]

As long as specie remained dear and commodity prices low during the 1840s, the likelihood of farmers achieving economic independence remained doubtful. In response to the depression, farmers attempted to adjust their production by moving into and out of the cotton market, suggesting not only that they maintained in hard times their goal of obtaining material success but that they understood the supply and demand features of the cotton market. According to M. W. Phillips, cotton prices below 8 cents demanded that farmers living in the interior or on marginally fertile land scale back their production. (Some farmers, like Duncan McKenzie and Daniel Kelly, abandoned cotton altogether in 1845.) But, Phillips predicted, when the price reached 10 cents, as it did after 1848, farmers would again flood the market with cotton until the infusion drove down the price.[50] Except for missing the mark on the latter point, Phillips proved to be accurate in his augury. Once prices began to rise, more and more farmers, some of whom had taken advantage of low land and slave prices during the depression, reentered the cotton market convinced that the return to re-

48. Quoting Daniel Kelly to James C. Kelly, February 29, 1845, in Kelly Papers; and R. A. Evans Diary, July 21, 1857 (MS in R. A. Evans Papers), MDAH; Joseph G. Baldwin, *The Flush Times in Alabama and Mississippi* (1853; rpr. Americus, Ga., 1898), 72–108.

49. George F. Warren and Frank A. Pearson, *Prices* (New York, 1933), 25–27, 31–32. Watkins, *King Cotton,* 29–30, 145; Arthur Harrison Cole, *Wholesale Commodity Prices in the United States 1700–1861: A Statistical Supplement: Actual Wholesale Prices of Various Commodities* (Cambridge, Mass., 1938), 291, 296, 300; Emory Q. Hawk, *Economic History of the South* (New York, 1934), 367.

50. Phillips' ruminations on supply and demand can be found in U.S. Patent Office, *Report of the Commissioner of Patents for the Year, 1853* (1853), 199. See, too, Daniel Kelly to James C. Kelly, February 29, 1845, in Kelly Papers; Duncan McKenzie to Duncan McLaurin, December 28, 1845, in McLaurin Papers. Even though McKenzie ceased planting cotton, he attempted to remain in the market economy through corn production.

munerative prices cleared the way for a new boom and the accumulation of great riches.[51]

In addition to the methods employed to finance and sell the cotton crop, the search for economic autonomy ran up against another thwarting feature of the market economy: it tended to be greedy, to demand that farmers give most, if not all, of their attention to producing for it. The all-consuming character of the market economy placed Mississippians' ideals in conflict with the reality of their production habits. In traditional American country republican thought, the farmer who owed not his soul to another or to the market represented virtuous citizenship. He worked for himself and consumed only what he made at home. Such ideals might have been appropriate to the frontier, but after the economic boom of the 1830s residents discarded those pristine ideals. The return to economic stability during the last twelve years of the antebellum period persuaded Mississippi farmers to take up again their willful march into the web of the market economy and altered the original self-sufficiency ideal to meet with conflicting moral impulses that demanded pursuit of Arcadian simplicity and material success to achieve liberty and virtue.

While Mississippians spoke of self-sufficiency as an ideal to which they aspired, the meaning attached to it differed from that assigned under the original Jeffersonian-Arcadian paradigm. Unlike farmers enthralled by that vision, late antebellum–period citizens believed achieving maximum sufficiency while producing for the market ensured their financial well-being and thus their claims to economic liberty. Self-sufficient production was a proactive occupation that safeguarded prosperity; secondarily, if markets collapsed, home-raised foodstuffs could carry a family through a season, keeping them from indebtedness and poverty. An anonymous contributor to *De Bow's Review* captured the spirit of the amended self-sufficiency ideal when he cautioned farmers to consider the health of the cotton market, the fertility of their land, and the potential rewards of self-sufficiency when deciding what to cultivate. Planting cotton from one's back door to the

51. On the price of slaves during and after the depression, see Phillips, *Life and Labor in the Old South*, 175–81. See, too, Duncan McKenzie to Duncan McLaurin, March 24, 1841, in McLaurin Papers; I. T. Harris to Samuel McCorkle, March 26, 1841, in McCorkle Papers. Harris offered to sell two field hands and three children for $2,000; before the panic struck, a single field hand sold for $2,250 in his Covington County neighborhood. On the price of land and the easy terms at which it could be purchased during the depression, see [?] to James T. Harrison, July 27, 1834, in James T. Harrison Papers, SHC. On the rapid increase in land prices after the depression, see Samuel T. Nicholson to Blake Nicholson, December 13, 1853, in Samuel T. Nicholson Papers, MDAH.

most distant arpent promised in some cases a higher profit than attempting to raise foodstuffs; others might profit by planting diverse crops for home consumption and the market. Regardless of the decision, farmers needed to direct their energies toward finishing the year in the black: "The largest amount of nett [*sic*] money from a given amount of means invested, looking carefully and economically into all parts of the operation, is the part of wisdom and enterprise." The editor of the Woodville *Republican* went even further in assessing the validity of the self-sufficiency ideal. When chastising the Concordia (Louisiana) *Intelligencer* for encouraging farmers to pull out of the cotton market entirely and to produce foodstuffs instead, he attacked as antiquated the very notion of self-sufficiency. "The South did not owe her pristine prosperity to the policy recommended," the *Republican* said, "nor did she lose it by an opposite one, nor can it be regained by embracing it now."[52]

Keeping alive the idea of self-sufficiency in a world devoted to the market economy proved a challenge, but cultivators intended to grow as much as possible of what they consumed. J. W. Metcalfe, a farmer of moderate means, boasted that he planned to raise all that his household consumed: "I intend trying to raise all the meat that is used on the place and think without accident that I will succeed." Agricultural reformers, too, challenged farmers to cultivate sufficient foodstuffs: to stimulate home production, agricultural societies awarded cash prizes for achievements in fruit production and stock breeding. Despite such encouragement and their well-laid plans, post-depression farmers confronted rising cotton prices and became infected with a madness for the crop. A Franklin County planter observed that only "a few sensible old farmers" continued to raise livestock for meat. R. A. Evans, the Piney Woods farmer, intended to emulate such sensible men by raising enough grain and meat for his household, though he generally fell short because he devoted too many resources to cotton and oat production for the market: each year he made twenty bales and hundreds of bushels of oats. In January, 1858, Evans put up more than one-half ton of hog meat, but five months later his larder was depleted, compelling him to buy bacon in Jackson. Several weeks passed, and he also ran low on grain. He purchased from a Simpson County mill four hundred pounds of flour and stopped feeding his shoats, a practice that endangered his supply of meat for the following year.[53] The difficulty of achieving

52. Quoting "Cotton and the Cotton Planters," *De Bow's Review,* III (1847), 19; Woodville *Republican,* February 25, 1843.

53. Metcalfe Diary, March 31, 1843 (in Metcalfe Papers). The Franklin County planter is quoted in U.S. Patent Office, *Report to the Commissioner of Patents for the Year 1850*

self-sufficiency, of even planning to do so, endured as long as material success within the market economy animated farmers. Their dependence on others for farm implements and the allure of a healthy cotton market, which might drag even the most dedicated foodstuff producer deeper into the debt-producing cycle of buying more land and slaves to produce more cotton, complicated achievement of that goal. According to farmers themselves, they pursued self-sufficiency as a means of securing material success within the market and counted on feeding their families in the process. Because they geared their production toward the accumulation of cash and foodstuffs, with the primary emphasis on cash, self-sufficient production was strained.

Most historians who have studied southern agricultural production, however, contend that farmers undoubtedly achieved self-sufficiency. Variations in their conclusions exist, but they broadly agree that planters produced food enough for household consumption. Literary and census evidence, on the other hand, suggests that large farmers struggled to produce foodstuffs and not infrequently purchased grain and meat through commission houses. Historians also agree that cultivators with small landholdings adopted what Gavin Wright and Howard Kunreuther call "safety-first" production, which allowed them to concentrate on raising foodstuffs before cultivating staple crops in order to distance themselves from the market.[54] In reality, however, Mississippi farmers of all classes practiced what

---

(1850), 187–88. R. A. Evans Diary, January 16, May 25, June 18, December 25, 1858 (in Evans Papers). On the activities of agricultural societies, see U.S. Patent Office, *Report of the Commissioner of Patents for the Year 1858* (1858), 159. On the failure to achieve self-sufficiency, see Vicksburg *Weekly Whig*, December 22, May 22, 1852. For a similar view of self-sufficiency within the context of market production, see Bill Cecil-Fronsman, *Common Whites: Class and Culture in Antebellum North Carolina* (Lexington, Ky., 1992), 124–32.

54. The debate over southern self-sufficiency opened in the wake of Douglas North's, *The Economic Growth of the United States, 1790–1860* (1961; rpr. New York, 1966), 196–201, in which he argued that the South depended on Midwestern meat and grain for its sustenance. Economic historians who question his argument include: William K. Hutchinson and Samuel H. Williamson, "The Self-Sufficiency of the Antebellum South: Estimates of the Food Supply," *Journal of Economic History*, XXXI (1971), 591–612; Robert E. Gallman, "Self Sufficiency in the Cotton Economy of the Antebellum South," *Agricultural History*, XLIV (1970), 6; Raymond C. Battalio and John Kagel, "The Structure of Antebellum Southern Agriculture: South Carolina, A Case Study," *Agricultural History*, XLIV (1970), 36; Wright *The Political Economy of the Cotton South*, 63–64, 166; Hilliard, *Hog Meat and Hoecake*, 111. For arguments that seek to account for market and self-sufficient production, see David F. Weiman, "Farmers and the Market in Antebellum America: A View from the Georgia Upcountry," *Journal of Economic History*, XLVII (1987), 627–47; Mark D. Schmitz, "Farm Interdepen-

they preached: to secure their individual autonomy by avoiding poverty or even the appearance of poverty, they produced for the market; to ensure their liberty from the intrusive influence of the market, they produced for home consumption as much foodstuffs as they could without endangering their search for material success. Their habits of production, then, might be regarded as geared toward accumulation first—the accumulation of cash and foodstuffs.

Through the creation of two data bases constructed from random samples of the 1850 and 1860 censuses and through the application of certain assumptions and mathematical calculations to the data, a portrait of Mississippi farmers' accumulation-first methods of production reveals itself. Briefly, after constructing the data bases and collating data about production with household data, enumerated crops reported by the sampled population were converted into corn equivalents; the total grain output was subtracted from the grain needs of human and livestock consumers to render a surplus or deficit. The available supply of meat and demand for it was also calculated.[55] As might be predicted about a population imbued with the rhetoric of self-sufficiency, results of the calculations imply that Mississippi farmers produced enough foodstuffs to feed themselves. (See Tables 3 and 4.) But slight alterations in the formulas suggest that a majority of farmers lived on the edge, barely able to feed their families because of the attention they paid market production.

---

dence in the Antebellum Sugar Sector," *Agricultural History,* LII (1978), 93–103; Lacy K. Ford, "Yeoman Farmers in the South Carolina Upcountry: Changing Production Patterns in the Late Antebellum Era," *Agricultural History,* LX (1986), 17–37. On safety-first theory and its critics, see Gavin Wright and Howard Kunreuther, "Cotton, Corn and Risk in the Nineteenth Century," *Journal of Economic History,* XXV (1975), 528; Robert McGuire and Robert Higgs, "Cotton, Corn, and Risk in the Nineteenth Century: Another View," *Explorations in Economic History,* XIV (1977), 171.

55. The data bases used were *Farm Survey* (1850) and *Farm Survey* (1860). For a thorough discussion of the methods used to calculate foodstuff sufficiency, see Bradley G. Bond, "Habits of Foodstuff and Market Production: A Look at Mississippi," *Journal of Mississippi History,* LVI (August, 1994), 211–31. The assumptions and calculations derive largely from Battalio and Kagel, "The Structure of Antebellum Southern Agriculture," 26–29. Other historians employ different methods, see: Gallman, "Self-Sufficiency in the Cotton Economy," 3–23; Roger Ransom and Richard Sutch, *One Kind of Freedom: The Economic Consequences of Emancipation* (New York, 1977), Appendix E; J. William Harris, *Plain Folk and Gentry in a Slave Society: White Liberty and Black Slavery in Augusta's Hinterlands* (Middletown, Conn., 1985), 200–201; Robert William Fogel and Stanley L. Engerman, *Time on the Cross: Evidence and Methods: A Supplement* (Boston, 1974), 95–98.

TABLE 3 Agricultural Production:
By Farm-Size Cohort, 1850

Farm Size, Improved Acres	% Surplus (Deficit) Meat	% Surplus (Deficit) Grain	Average Bushels Grain	Average Bales Cotton	Average # Labor
1–19	52	(48)	136	.67	1.72
20–49	58	5	238	1.2	1.79
50–99	59	20	450	6.4	3.55
100–199	27	37	722	20.9	7.16
200–299	36	47	1914	37.5	17.05
300–499	31	63	1490	89.8	21.80
500 or More	(20)	41	5124	276.8	75.66

Source: *Farm Survey* (1850). "% Surplus (Deficit)" refers to the percentage by which each cohort achieved (or failed to achieve) sufficiency. "Average # Labor" refers to all labor within each household, including heads of household, white males over age fifteen, who do not list themselves as otherwise employed, and all slaves over age fifteen.

TABLE 4 Agricultural Production:
By Farm-Size Cohort, 1860

Farm Size, Improved Acres	% Surplus (Deficit) Meat	% Surplus (Deficit) Grain	Average Bushels Grain	Average Bales Cotton	Average # Labor
0–19	26	(33)	119	2.52	1.66
20–49	42	(6)	196	5.14	1.98
50–99	65	18	287	11.6	3.06
100–199	41	28	377	21.5	6.40
200–299	40	61	500	36.5	9.80
300–499	30	48	705	73.7	16.60
500 or More	11	45	1304	255	37.73

Source: *Farm Survey* (1860). "% Surplus (Deficit)" refers to the percentage by which each cohort achieved (or failed to achieve) sufficiency. "Average # Labor" refers to all labor within each household, including heads of household, white males over age fifteen, who do not list themselves as otherwise employed, and all slaves over age fifteen.

Besides suggesting that most farm-size cohorts produced sufficient grain and meat, as well as a sizable surplus, Tables 3 and 4 suggest that economies of scale dictated the cohorts' productivity. Farmers owning one hundred or more improved acres made significantly larger surpluses of grain than did those owning less land, while small farmers produced more meat than did their neighbors who worked substantial farms. Such observed economies of scale owed much to the availability of labor, the supply of which increased as farm sizes did. Because they enjoyed a favorable ratio of labor to household members (approximately 1.6:1 for both census years), large farmers believed themselves capable of producing grain enough to feed their households while also planting cotton. Their calculation to produce for the market and home consumption was aided by crop growth cycles. Corn, Mississippi's chief grain crop, reached maturity in mid- to late summer and cotton bolls neared the picking stage from late summer to early fall. If they planted both crops, farmers received the full value of their labor, and they occupied what might have been idle hours for laborers and made certain that workers produced a portion of the food they consumed.[56] In a similar fashion, the availability of labor adversely affected grain production on small farms. Laborers on farms smaller than one hundred acres had to produce grain to feed 1.3 household members, a ratio nearly equal to that reported for other farm-size cohorts. Considering the size of their holdings, small farmers needed to extract from their land relatively more bounty and from their labor more sweat in order to feed their families.

Common sense, then, dictated that farmers who commanded small parcels of land and relatively little labor focus on foodstuff production, but instead a majority sacrificed foodstuff production in order to plant cotton for the market. In 1850, 43 percent of farmers who owned less than fifty improved acres produced at least one bale of cotton; 69 percent did so in 1860. Among such cotton producers about one-third (in each census year) achieved sufficiency in both meat and grain production. Overall, 50 percent of farms smaller than one hundred acres produced too little grain; in 1860, 52 percent failed. Of farmers who had the most reason to follow safety-first habits of production (those with less than ninety-nine acres who neither owned slaves nor ginned cotton), 73 percent in 1850 did not make sufficient grain and 24 percent lacked the meat necessary to feed their families. For the 1860 survey group, 79 percent fell short of their grain needs and 24 percent produced insufficient meat for their households. Had safety-first methods motivated small farmers, more of them would have devoted their limited acreage and labor to foodstuff production.[57]

56. On the benefits of cultivating corn and cotton, see Gallman, "Self-Sufficiency in the Cotton Economy," 22–23.

57. It should be noted that of small farmers who achieved self-sufficiency in grain and meat over 70 percent in 1850 and 90 percent in 1860 also produced cotton. The highly efficient small farmers controlled no more labor than their peers who failed to achieve self-sufficiency while producing cotton. Soil quality, local variations in weather, and personal mo-

However suggestive the economies of scale and the broad trends outlined above, they neglect aspects of Mississippians' production habits. While Tables 3 and 4 suggest that farmers as a whole produced storehouses of surplus grain and meat, they tend to obscure the variety of production engaged in within each cohort. The percentage of farms harvesting insufficient grain reinforces the above observations: farmers on the smallest units had more difficulty producing grain than did their neighbors with large holdings. (See Table 5.) But subjecting the levels of self-sufficiency to a test of their sensitivity to changes in the prescribed rates of consumption indicates that individual farmers, if they fed their families at all, did so by observing the strictest pattern of distribution. Increasing by 25 percent the grain consumed by stock and humans on farms larger than ninety-nine acres results in a phenomenal rise in the percentage of those failing to feed their families. Reducing the amount of grain consumed on farms smaller than one hundred acres by the same percentage less dramatically (but significantly) alters the ability of cultivators to feed their families.[58] As displayed in Table 5, the changes caused by adjusting the formula are most dramatic among large farmers, suggesting that they could ill afford to modify their consumption habits upward. Where small farms are concerned, the changes suggest that yeomen (in lean years and in years they wished to produce row crops for the market) could avoid the appearance of poverty by slightly altering their consumption habits or depending more on unenumerated grains.

The previously cited broad pattern of the largest cohorts producing meat less efficiently than farmers in other cohorts reappears when examining individuals' habits of meat production. (See Table 6.) But just as in the case of grain crops, decreasing or increasing production levels significantly modifies the pattern, verifying once again that farmers with more than one hundred acres struggled to provide their households with foodstuffs. Such an observation is sustained by a body of literary evidence that indicates large

---

tivation likely accounted for these farmers' greater success in producing for the market and the household.

58. Justification for altering the formula lies in the fact that farmers with small landholdings depended less on grains to feed their stock than did large farmers and depended more on truck-garden vegetables. Large farmers, it is assumed, fed their stock and families better than did yeomen. On reliance on truck-garden vegetables, see Hilliard, *Hog Meat and Hoecake,* 172–73. Battalio and Kagel, "Structure of Antebellum Southern Agriculture," perform a similar test of their sampled population's susceptibility to changes in foodstuff demand, but their test produces no substantive change in the observed pattern of sufficiency.

TABLE 5 Percentage of Farms Producing Insufficient Grain:
25% Increase/Decrease in Grain Consumption

Farm Size (in improved acres)	1850	1860		1850	1860
0–19	67.4	65.9	**With 25% Decrease* in Grain Consumption:**	**55.8**	**47.7**
20–49	46.0	54.8		**25.4**	**46.4**
50–99	40.0	30.3		**31.1**	**18.2**
100–199	23.3	21.9	**With 25% Increase* in Grain Consumption:**	**60.0**	**62.5**
200–299	22.2	7.70		**55.6**	**38.4**
300–499	17.6	16.7		**29.4**	**50.0**
500 or More	00.0	4.30		**53.3**	**43.5**

Sources: *Farm Survey* (1850); *Farm Survey* (1860).

*While animal and human consumption requirements are altered by 25 percent, the meat produced under the amended formula is assumed not to have changed.

TABLE 6 Percentage of Farms Producing Insufficient Meat:
25% Increase/Decrease in Meat Consumption

Farm Size (in improved acres)	1850	1860		1850	1860
0–19	23.3	52.3	**With 25% Decrease in Meat Consumption:**	**20.9**	**38.6**
20–49	25.4	23.2		**20.6**	**12.5**
50–99	24.4	18.2		**17.8**	**12.7**
100–199	33.3	21.9	**With 25% Increase in Meat Consumption:**	**76.7**	**53.1**
200–299	27.8	23.1		**61.1**	**38.4**
300–499	17.6	16.7		**58.8**	**77.8**
500 or More	80.0	34.8		**93.3**	**73.9**

Sources: *Farm Survey* (1850); *Farm Survey* (1860).

farmers purchased meat from commission merchants and by the fact that small farmers, particularly those in the Piney Woods and North-Central Hills, excelled at stock raising. Small farmers' ability to produce surplus meat not only suggests that they employed their limited labor supply in a rational manner, but that they obtained access to the market economy despite their failure to cultivate large quantities of cotton.

The culmination of Mississippians' complex notions of liberty and virtue appeared in their habits of agriculture production. Instead of proving that safety-first and self-sufficient production were widespread, Tables 5 and 6 suggest that if farmers achieved sufficiency, they did so by the slimmest margin. Indeed, their habits of foodstuff production indicate that the idea of safety-first is a misnomer and that most farmers were calculating gamblers who sought not safety but the accumulation of cash and foodstuffs, in that order, knowing that when they failed to make sufficient food their market production provided cash to make up the shortfall.[59] Concepts of liberty and virtue mandated such behavior, for autonomous farmers produced for the market without becoming entangled in its web and consequently obtained material success while avoiding ruinous, speculative behavior. To planters, failure to make enough foodstuffs mattered little; their participation in the cotton market assured that they would, as long as prices remained high, achieve material success and supply their households with ample cash to purchase any necessaries not made on the farm. Similarly, small farmers' participation in the market economy (the cotton and secondary markets) assured their material success. In good market years profits protected them from falling into debt; in bad years they depended on their farm production to keep them from running up enormous debts. In short, farmers thought of self-sufficiency as a way to bolster their bottom line and concentrated on market production as a means of safeguarding their claims to material success, the idea that had propelled them to immigrate to Mississippi in the first place.

Through cotton cultivation, stock raising, and timber cutting, Mississippians consciously strove to touch the web of the market economy. Production for the market, if not conducted in a speculative manner or with disregard for foodstuffs, they believed, allowed them to avoid poverty and to be virtuous citizens. In varying degrees, however, participants in the market fell victim to it. Even timber cutters and stock raisers could not escape fluctuations in the cotton market as prices paid for all commodities reflected the price of cotton and their markets could at times run dry. Of all the market participants, cotton cultivators exposed themselves to the highest degree of dependence on the market. Large-scale cultivators were trapped in the numbing cycle of buying more land and slaves to raise more cotton

59. Wright and Kunreuther, "Cotton, Corn and Risk," 528, suggest that postbellum "institutional and historical developments" propelled farmers to become "gamblers." The argument here is that an overarching desire to achieve material success led farmers to engage in a risky kind of production.

and to pay off the debts incurred to purchase foodstuffs, land, and slaves, which they needed to produce more cotton; small-scale producers entered the same cycle to a lesser extent but nonetheless subjected themselves to the market's cruelties by cultivating the crop. Dependence on the cotton market rose in the last twelve years of the antebellum period as prices recovered from the depression and lured more and more farmers into the web of the market economy.

One irony of Mississippians' belief that personal autonomy could be achieved through market participation was that they developed a dependence on the market. Small farmers, too, though somewhat insulated from the exigencies of the market by their minuscule slaveholdings and their ability (if their debts were retired) to fall back into a subsistence mode of production, were still dependent on the market. By participating in it at all, they sacrificed to the market, perhaps unwittingly, and certainly with little thought as to the significance of their action, a measure of personal autonomy. And here the paradoxes are multiplied. For when it came time to decide in 1861 whether to secede or not, the great bulk of Mississippians came down on the side of traditional concepts of liberty and virtue and took up arms in a fight against the encroachment of modernity in a society wedded to its parent: the market.

CHAPTER 3

LIBERTY AND VIRTUE IN A "FALSE REPUBLIC"

As envisioned by whites in the antebellum period, liberty and virtue belonged to men who trod into the web of the market economy without becoming paralyzed by its entangling grasp. Besides proclaiming producers, who were resistant to the lure of single-minded service to the market, free and virtuous citizens, they accorded the same title to those who refused to submit to other forces. Those other forces included intrusive and overzealous governments, which Mississippians believed were preponderant during the repudiation and sectional crises of the late antebellum period.

Because of the controversy sparked by talk of repudiating state debts incurred in support of the Union Bank, a political party system evolved. One party fancied itself the champion of white common folk and opposed honoring the debts on the ground that doing so violated egalitarian principles and asked virtuous citizens to submit to the demands of immoral speculators; the other, believing, as did Ivan Golovin (a Russian traveler to the South), that without "honor and intellect" government by "the majority is that of dishonesty and stupidity," decried repudiation as a self-serving act supported solely by the degenerate multitude.[1] The class-conscious rhetoric bandied about during the repudiation controversy remained until the late 1840s, when sectional tensions relegated to obscurity the parties' competing views of good citizenship and a good republic. After 1848, with their political culture purged of divisive issues, white Mississippians refocused their energies on fostering cultural homogeneity, at the heart of which lay efforts to define black residents—free and enslaved—and undeserving whites as a submissive underclass. Building a homogeneous citizenry to stand against northern attacks on the social ethic empowered white southerners in their battle with abolitionism. By 1860 white citizens succeeded.

1. Ivan Golovin, *Stars and Stripes: Or American Impressions* (London, 1856), 112–13.

Twelve years of fervid insistence on unity in all things political killed the embryonic party system and deprived political culture of voices opposed to extreme reactions to every imagined slight to the social ethic.

Owing to white southerners' belief that preserving their notions of liberty and virtue demanded their resistance to foes who would undermine slavery, race-conscious politics prevailed over class-conscious politics. The mastery of the former convinced citizens that the social ethic could only be protected if they severed their ties to the Union. Southerners' object in secession was plain: to avoid the worst fate that could befall a man—becoming, like the enslaved, poor, lacking autonomy over their own lives, subject to others' will, and without access to markets—their only recourse was resistance. For if they remained in the Union, abolitionists would force them to submit to the northern social ethic that was founded on the premise of free labor and free men. Once the sectional crisis smoothed over divisions spawned by the debate over repudiation, whites united in defense of what the English novelist Charles Dickens called their "false republic," a republic that founded liberty on the existence of an underclass upon whose back all but the most woebegone white could stand.[2]

After several years of fits and starts, Mississippi's emergent second political party system found an issue, debt repudiation, that for a decade defined political discourse. Nascent parties, really nothing more than casually organized factions, had long existed in the state, but they remained facile, even amorphous, coalitions until the question of choosing Andrew Jackson's successor arose. In the mid-1830s national parties solidified behind their chosen candidates, and their affiliates in Mississippi assumed the look of formal parties, too. The economic collapse of 1837 and the ensuing debate over repudiation of state debts contracted in support of the Union Bank hastened their development and led the separate parties to espouse divergent notions of liberty and virtue.[3] By 1839 the Mississippi Democratic party had become political home to champions of egalitarian democracy and repudiation. Whigs stood for Henry Clay's American system, as well as payment of state debts.

Prior to the repudiation crisis, banking in Mississippi was an uncon-

2. Charles Dickens, *American Notes For General Circulation* (Leipzig, 1842), 283.

3. On party development in the 1830s, see Richard P. McCormick, *The Second American Party System: Party Formation in the Jacksonian Era* (Chapel Hill, 1966), 295–303. On the parties in the antebellum period, see David Nathaniel Young, "The Mississippi Whigs, 1834–1860" (Ph.D. dissertation, University of Alabama, 1968); and Edwin A. Miles, *Jacksonian Democracy in Mississippi* (Chapel Hill, 1960).

troversial subject. During the 1830s, when the number of banks exploded, neither political partisans nor citizens thought liberty and virtue jeopardized by the creation of banks. A dire need for credit on the cotton frontier made them popular institutions. To meet the demands of an expanding population, the state chartered twenty-seven banks between 1832 and 1837, twenty in 1836 and 1837 alone, and with the proliferation of such institutions, the speculative fever of the day consumed the conservative principles that previously guided bankers. Seeking to benefit from the freewheeling atmosphere of the cotton frontier, bankers obligingly printed quires of notes, which in turn fueled the growth of the cotton economy. The halcyon days of the southwestern cotton kingdom continued until 1836 when President Jackson's Specie Circular threw banks into disarray. Having printed more paper currency than their specie reserves could sustain, bankers fell victim to Jackson's policy, and their customers found that their notes exchanged at far less than par value. The onset of the worldwide depression in 1837 exacerbated the currency situation and revealed the extent to which bankers had overplayed their hands. In addition to lacking hard currency, they had made loans without sufficient collateral to back them, in some cases without collateral at all.[4] As banks foreclosed on unpaid loans, an air of doom swept over the state.

Chartered during the initial period of economic catastrophe, the Mississippi Union Bank, a quasi-official state institution, was first proposed in 1835, but received its charter only in February of the fateful year 1837. Both houses of the legislature passed the incorporating measure with little opposition, a fact that later came to haunt its Democratic supporters. Like other financial institutions chartered in the 1830s, the bank could make mortgage loans, receive deposits, and sell stock. Investors (required by law to be Mississippi property owners), who did not purchase their shares outright, could receive eight-year loans with which to buy stock as long as they had collateral—real estate or slaves—to cover the amount borrowed. Stock sales were to raise $.5 million capital, and Mississippi pledged its faith, through the issuance of $15.5 million in 5-percent gold bonds repayable by the bank, to provide the remaining start-up money. With the faith of the state backing it, the Union Bank, or so legislators thought, would draw specie into Mississippi and assist citizens in their attempts to retire personal

4. On banking in the early nineteenth century, see Robert Cicero Weems, Jr., "The Bank of the State of Mississippi: A Pioneer Bank of the Old Southwest, 1809–1844" (Ph.D. dissertation, Columbia University, 1952), 189, 593–95, 599–600; Schweikart, *Banking in the American South*, 204. On the advantages that the state believed it would receive in chartering a union bank, see Hawk, *Economic History of the South*, 351, 356.

debts.[5] In 1838 the charter returned to the body, as the state constitution required successive sessions to pass any bill that pledged the financial backing of the state. Legislators again voted to incorporate the bank, though this time with slightly more opposition from members who preferred that the state adopt parsimonious spending habits in light of the depression. Ten days after approving the 1838 law, Governor McNutt, in response to debt-conscious legislators, signed a supplement to the charter. The supplemental act called for the governor to purchase $5 million of bank stock, the money to be raised by the sale of semi-annual 5-percent state bonds, effectively altering the relationship between the bank and the state. No longer was the state simply the backer of the bank and its notes, it became a stockholder as well. Soon after signing the supplemental act, McNutt sent three commissioners to Pennsylvania to negotiate the sale of the bonds, and the bank opened its doors in 1838.[6]

According to R. W. Millsaps, a prominent late-nineteenth-century banker, the legislature intended the bank to relieve the state's economic distress, but it proved to be "prodigal in its loans, and lax in its securities." Millsaps rightly rested blame for the bank's failure on the incautious lending practices of the politicians charged with its management. Former governor Hiram G. Runnels (the bank's first president) and directors of the bank (including future governor and railroad entrepreneur John J. McRae) used the institution to serve their financial aspirations and those of their political friends: before 1840, twelve politically well-connected Mississippians, including Runnels and McRae, received loans equal to 7 percent of the bank's capital stock. While such unethical behavior, once revealed, diminished the bank's popularity, the directors pursued policies that more clearly expedited the institution's collapse. Believing the depression would be short-lived, they ignored the international dynamics of the economic downturn and lavishly loaned money in the hope that the bank would stimulate economic growth. The 1838 cotton crop, which the directors projected to sell at fifteen cents a pound, however, brought less than nine cents.[7] While true that restoration of the cotton and currency markets necessitated ac-

5. J. A. P. Campbell, "Planter's and Union Bank Bonds," Mississippi Historical Society *Publications,* IV (1901), 495–96. Weems, "The Bank of the State of Mississippi," 191; Schweikart, *Banking in the American South,* 180–81; R. W. Millsaps, "History of Banking in Mississippi," *Sound Currency,* X (March, 1903), 28–29; J. F. H. Claiborne, *Life and Correspondence of John A. Quitman, Major-General U.S.A. and Governor of the State of Mississippi* (2 vols.; New York, 1860), I, 196–97. For a history of the Union Bank, see Vicksburg *Tri-Weekly Whig,* June 17, 19, July 3, 1841.

6. Millsaps, "History of Banking," 28–30.

7. *Ibid.*, 31–36.

tion other than banking reform in Mississippi, the Union Bank exacerbated the sorry condition of the local economy.

Within two years of opening its doors, the bank's practices and strapped financial condition became widely known, causing the public to turn against it as an agency inimical to the widely shared vision of a good republic as one in which all producers enjoyed the same opportunity to achieve political and economic independence. Sharing with many southerners a suspicion of paper money, the governor supported reform legislation mandating that banks hold in reserve specie enough to back the paper they issued. Initially, the legislature was reluctant to endorse laws plainly designed to kill specie-poor banks, but in 1840 both houses placed specie reserves under state supervision and required that institutions pay hard currency on demand or surrender their charters. Within a year, nine banks closed; eight more shut in 1841. (By 1860 only two, neither of which existed in 1840, operated in Mississippi.) Dissatisfied with the reform measures and doubtful that recipients of special privileges would consent to meaningful regulation, McNutt in 1841 broached the idea of repudiating debts incurred on behalf of the Union Bank. Were the bank debts paid, the governor argued, citizens would have to raise millions in taxes, and he doubted that "the freemen of Mississippi" were so "degenerate as to submit to heavy taxation to pay a claim not contracted in accordance with their supreme law." Adopting an argument that Democrats frequently employed, he asserted that the supplemental act he signed in 1838 sufficiently altered the charter to require the approval of successive legislatures.[8]

Payment of the bonds then became illegal, "a demand founded neither in justice nor equity," but repudiation promised to reward the virtuous and punish the wicked. "The relief of one portion of our fellow citizens should not be attempted, when detrimental to a more numerous class, who have been less reckless in their operations, and have higher claims on our sympathies," McNutt asserted. Lest anyone doubt the veracity of his portrait of banks as institutions of monopoly and privilege, the governor pointed out that merely 3 percent of the public owned stock in the Union Bank. Extending his attack to all state-chartered banks, he promised that "those who produce nothing, who have long lived on the labor of others, will suffer. The honest planter, the enterprising merchant, and the laborious mechanic will be benefitted" by revocation of bank charters. In 1842 the legislature took the first step toward fulfilling the governor's wishes, resolving not to appropriate funds for the payment of debts incurred under "repugnant

8. Quoting *Mississippi Senate Journal,* 1841, p. 21. On McNutt, see Schweikart, *Banking in the American South,* 23.

laws." The state paid neither the principle nor interest on the bonds after an 1843 act declared them void.[9]

When he founded his appeal for repudiation on the dignity of productive men, McNutt established that the evils associated with unique privileges and heavy taxation stood for the reverse of the Democratic faithful's concepts of liberty and virtue. Submission to taxation, especially when the monies would bestow special privileges upon a select group, suggested that plain folk lacked a lust for liberty. Paying such taxes meant that they consigned the rewards of their material success to foppish bankers. Payment of the debt, McNutt passionately argued, required that the state levy taxes on "the fire that warms us, the bread we eat, the clothes we wear, all articles of produce and every necessary of life." Confronted with heavy taxes, hard working citizens would be forced to acknowledge the inferiority of their inalienable rights and the superior standing of speculators and men of commerce. To such an admission, the Lexington *Union* knew Mississippians would never "submit with pusillanimous tameness," as doing so would coddle "a community strictly mercantile in its character."[10] Other Democrats also embraced the egalitarian sentiments of McNutt's address. Party members in Choctaw County invoked the name of Thomas Jefferson when they derided banks as harmful to the material and moral interests of independent farmers, and McNutt's successor, Tilghman Tucker, agreed that honoring illegally incurred debts rewarded unvirtuous men for precipitating financial disaster through their "reckless extravagance and prodigality."[11]

Whigs used similar terms to chastise Democrats who they said appealed to "the reckless and the turbulent" with their dishonorable talk of repudiation. In their campaign to block repudiation, Mississippi Whigs offered a view of liberty and virtue at odds with that of their Democratic rivals. Moved by a traditional fear of the folk, they doubted that their fellow citizens possessed civic virtue enough to subordinate their self-interest to

9. Quoting *Mississippi Senate Journal,* 1841, p. 21, but see 15–16; *Mississippi Senate Journal,* 1840, pp. 28, 54, but see 18, 49; and *Laws of the State of Mississippi,* 1842, p. 260. See, too, Millsaps, "History of Banking," 41, and the reaction to McNutt's proposals and the legislature's action, Jackson *Mississippian,* October 2, 1840, April 30, 1841; Lexington *Union,* June 13, 1840, October 30, June 5, 1841.

10. Quoting *Mississippi Senate Journal,* 1841, p. 21; Lexington *Union,* March 6, January 30, 1841. See also Millsaps, "History of Banking," 38–41.

11. Tucker quoted in *Mississippi Senate Journal,* 1843, p. 13, but see, too, 30–41; Lexington *Union,* January 30, February 6, 1841. See also, Woodville *Republican,* March 11, June 10, 1843; John A. Quitman to the Editor of the Natchez *Free Trader,* October 27, 1841, in Quitman Family Papers.

the interest of the broader community; even raising the question of repudiation evinced the susceptibility of supposedly virtuous citizens to being led astray. Merely by talking about repudiation, Mississippians announced to their fellow Americans that they wished to be treated like "scoundrels and puppys [*sic*]" ready for a kicking. Frequent electoral defeats explained Whigs' pessimism. Outnumbered, at times overwhelmed, at the polls, they believed that when given a choice voters preferred to sacrifice their individual and collective virtue on the altar of expediency.[12] Little that occurred on the old southwestern frontier during the Jacksonian period encouraged Whigs to expect otherwise. A sense of rowdiness, egalitarianism, and individualism permeated Mississippi. In an atmosphere of energetic self-service, the Whiggish vision of a well-ordered, hierarchical society in which each citizen remained bound to the whole by an overwhelming commonality of interests seemed out of place. "God Save the State and curse the demagogue," Duncan McKenzie wailed when considering the prospect of repudiation. The Franklin County Whig John P. Stewart perhaps best summed up his party's outlook: attacking the idea of repudiation, he proclaimed that "the same policy that would suit a poor man would suit nineteen twentieths of the people of all classes."[13] According to Whigs, all white Mississippians shared an interest in defining liberty-loving and virtuous citizens as those willing to sacrifice personal interests for the good of social order and harmony. Only self-serving demagogues who appealed to the narrow interest of weak-minded residents advocated repudiation.

Unlike Democrats, who saw a natural gulf separating bankers and farmers, Whigs drew upon their ideas of transcendent interests binding the entire community to argue in favor of debt payment. By deemphasizing egalitarian sentiments, they sought consciously to deny the "ultimate supremacy" of the people in directing the course of government. Concern for a society of law and moral behavior informed their support of the Union Bank. In the days leading up to the heated gubernatorial campaign of 1841, in which the only issue discussed was repudiation, Whigs openly assailed the proponents of repudiation as immoral, self-serving, and unvirtuous. Predict-

12. Quoting Vicksburg *Daily Whig*, March 27, 1841, February 8, 1840. Young, "The Mississippi Whigs," 93–100. On the general Whiggish concern for moral development and other core ideas, see Daniel Walker Howe, *The Political Culture of the American Whigs* (Chicago, 1979), 11–42. On Whigs' fear that Mississippians were predisposed to act spontaneously and without regard for the long-term best interest, see Vicksburg *Tri-Weekly Whig*, August 19, 1841.

13. Quoting Duncan McKenzie to Duncan McLaurin, September [?], 1843; John Stewart to McLaurin, July 30, 1840, all in McLaurin Papers.

ing Democratic contender Tilghman Tucker's victory, John Stewart promised to leave the state if the anti-bond-paying Democrat assumed power. A blight on the state was a blight on every white resident: "I certainly will not live among a people who would hold the doctrine that they will not pay their just debts if able. We rank low already in the scale of morals and debt paying." In the election Tucker defeated David O. Shattuck, capturing 54 percent of the vote and all counties except twelve west of the Pearl River.[14]

Democratic arguments that differentiated between moral and legal obligations failed to impress Whigs. Liberty-loving men responded to the duty, both moral and legal, that demanded repayment. From the beginning of the controversy, Whigs (and a small number of bond-paying Democrats) held that the supplemental act of the Union Bank charter did not substantively alter the state's pledge of its faith. The acts passed in 1837 and 1838 allowed the state to make a loan to the bank; in the supplemental act the state staked the bank a smaller amount of start-up capital through its purchase of stock. Even if they granted that the relationship between the bank and the state changed, the meaning of the relationship, Whigs argued, did not. Besides, the election of pro-bank legislators in 1837 indicated citizens' readiness to create a union bank with state aid. In the early 1850s, when Hezron Johnson sued Mississippi for failing to pay either the interest or principle on bank bonds that he held, his attorneys successfully made the same argument. The decision favorable to Whig arguments, however, went for naught as the Democrat-controlled legislature refused to appropriate money to pay Johnson.[15]

Throughout the banking crisis, Democrats offered themselves as defenders of an egalitarian world, a world they believed imperiled by the influence of self-serving aristocrats. They wanted to provide all white Mississippians an equal chance at securing their economic and political liberty. Repudiation promised to do that. On the other hand, Whigs portrayed themselves as facilitators of a harmonious society in which prevailing concerns about honor and the hierarchical arrangement of society bound all

14. Quoting Vicksburg *Daily Whig,* February 11, 1840; John Stewart to Duncan McLaurin, July 30, 1840, in McLaurin Papers. See, too, Young, "The Mississippi Whigs," 11, 134; Miles, *Jacksonian Democracy in Mississippi,* 150–52; William L. Coker, *Repudiation and Reaction: Tilghman M. Tucker and the Mississippi Bond Question* (Floral Park, Fla., 1969), 23–25. Results of the election can be found in the Records of the Secretary of State, Election Returns, 1841, in Record Group 28, MDAH.

15. On bond-paying Democrats, see Natchez *Mississippi Free Trader,* August 30, 1843. Vicksburg *Tri-Weekly Whig,* August 19, 28, 1841; Vicksburg *Daily Whig,* February 27, 1841; *State* v. *Johnson, Mississippi Reports: Reports of Cases Argued and Determined in the High Court of Errors and Appeals of the State of Mississippi,* XXV (Boston, 1854), 625.

citizens, rich and poor. According to both parties, liberty and virtue could only be achieved if citizens resisted the efforts of others (be they bankers or demagogues) to institute the supremacy of one interest. Born in the midst of the repudiation crisis, the second political party system employed class-conscious rhetoric that pitted self-professed protectors of the folk against champions of order. But despite the importance of the debt-payment controversy in initially clarifying the ideologies of political parties, the issue, as well as the class conflict it generated, was transitory. The question of submission that it raised, however, was not. For beyond the confines of the debate over repudiation, the parties shared an aversion to submissive behavior. Exertions undertaken before and after the repudiation crisis to identify and control residents unwilling or unable to prove that liberty and virtue inhered in them testified to Mississippians' essential and all-encompassing unity about what constituted submission.

Throughout most of the antebellum period, anxieties about isolating the underclass subsumed class conflict and bound white Mississippians in a political culture that regarded black enslavement as necessary to secure white liberty, the antithesis of submission.[16] Since all white males had access to the market and the ballot box, and thus could rightly claim to be free and virtuous, Mississippians reasoned that those cut off from the benefits of citizenship constituted an overt threat to the social ethic. Through this kind of reasoning, all who lacked the dignity to avoid submitting to others' will (as evinced by their working for others and their inability to voice their political sentiments), chiefly African Americans, but to a degree also propertyless whites and those without ties to agriculture, fell under the rubric of the underclass. As such, they deserved special scrutiny to ensure the long life of the social ethic and white cultural homogeneity.

Racial chauvinism inherited from preceding generations encouraged white Mississippians to characterize blacks as unvirtuous, and the presence of African Americans in the institution of slavery verified their degeneracy and dependence. Supposedly incapable of asserting their autonomy, and at any rate uninvited to try, blacks saw their activities rigorously circumscribed by state law. Aside from well-known features of the southern

16. On the relationship between white liberty and black enslavement, see Edmund S. Morgan, *American Slavery, American Freedom: The Ordeal of Colonial Virginia* (New York, 1975), 269–70; Shalhope, "Thomas Jefferson's Republicanism," 556; Charles Barinetti, *A Voyage to Mexico and Havana: Including Some General Observations on the United States* (New York, 1841), 126–29; Nehemiah Adams, *A South-Side View of Slavery: Or Three Months at the South, in 1854* (Boston, 1854), 47–49.

states' slave codes that restricted mobility and educational opportunities, Mississippi prohibited slaves from participating in the market. They could neither sell truck-garden vegetables without the consent of their masters, nor own livestock, nor cultivate cotton to sell as their own. Since the law prohibited all but deathbed manumissions for heroic service, lawmakers intended to obstruct slaves' access to local markets in order to preclude black-white social contact and to block them from appropriating one of the signposts of independent behavior, not to prevent them from gaining the means to purchase their freedom. Free blacks enjoyed slightly more liberty. Those who escaped the 1831 exile imposed by the legislature could participate in the market, but they had to register with county courts when they moved. They could not own guns or knives without permits; the state militia could execute any dogs they owned; and assemblies of five or more free blacks and meetings with slaves were forbidden.[17]

Well-defined laws narrowed the contact that whites had with all blacks. Of course, high-minded racial chauvinists had little desire to socialize with African Americans: Mrs. Jared Cook once declared "civilized people" better for the experience if they never spoke to blacks; she fretted that young children "will be ruined" by interaction with them. Yet authors of the state law thought not of Cook and her ilk when they drafted restrictive laws. They intended to keep slaves from socializing with workers in nonagricultural jobs, especially mechanics, barkeepers, and printers, as the public regarded workers at these jobs as outsiders (northerners and foreigners, it was believed) and parasites on the community of market producers. Workers not closely linked to the market, it was feared, would welcome any opportunity to lead a slave revolt. By law, tavern keepers could not sell liquor to blacks. Advocates of abolitionism were barred from working in print shops, serving on juries that heard cases involving slaves, and keeping houses of entertainment.[18] A desire to control blacks' access to liquor and abolitionist literature underlay the laws, though the conviction that free tillers of the earth alone possessed liberty also informed the decision to regulate contact between African Americans and whites who did not farm.

The latter class of residents included white indigents. Even though the Constitution of 1832, as a means of affixing white homogeneity upon the population, opened the suffrage to white males regardless of property holding, citizens continued to distrust their fellows who so lacked virtue as to become penurious.[19] The boom-time economy of the mid-1830s, which

17. On laws dealing with slaves and free blacks, see *Code,* 1840, pp. 155–70, 391.

18. Quoting Cook Diary, January [?], 1857. *Code,* 1828, pp. 328–29, 351.

19. On the suffrage clause of the Constitution of 1832, see May, *John A. Quitman,* 52–57;

cleared the way for farmers of common origin to establish themselves as materially successful, encouraged citizens to look upon poverty and indebtedness as signposts of unvirtuous behavior, specifically indolence or speculation. As Edward Golladay observed from under his mountain of debt, that it was "terrible to be poor & vastly distressing to owe money & not have ability of paying," an acknowledgment that financial bankruptcy signaled moral turpitude and an infantile dependence on others for one's sustenance. According to Mississippi law, if a white resident exhibited such a diminished interest in preserving personal liberty, the state could assume dominion over that person. In reality, however, the state, outside the charity hospital in Natchez, extended no assistance to the poor, though it mandated that counties care for the indigent within their borders and allowed local entities to pass along the cost of housing and feeding the poor to their families. The work of the state and private benevolent societies inadequately met the needs of indigents. But alleviating the suffering of the downtrodden was hardly the goal of the law. Overseeing a potentially dangerous class of people cut off from the market prompted Mississippians to view the poor as the moral equivalent of slaves. Indigents lacked regard for their reputations, for their personal autonomy, and state law restricted their mobility just as it restricted the movement of African Americans. If found outside their native neighborhoods, indigents could be jailed and put to work on public works projects until their home county retrieved them. For those too poor to care for themselves but too proud to confess it, county courts could intervene and place them in a poorhouse, a shame that attached not only to the condemned but to their families as well.[20]

With far less subtlety than state law, James M. Wesson, president of the Mississippi Manufacturing Company, likewise defined the underclass as poor folk without ties to the market economy. Like Matthew Estes, the Columbus pamphleteer who argued that the institution of slavery allowed

---

R. H. Thompson, "Suffrage in Mississippi," Mississippi Historical Society *Publications*, I (1898), 36.

20. Quoting Edward Golladay to "My Dear Brother," January 12, 1861, in George S. Golladay Papers, MDAH. *Code*, 1840, pp. 143–48. On the poor as lazy and venal, see George H. Young to James McDowell, September 25, 1842, in McDowell Papers; Vicksburg *Daily Whig*, March 21, 1840. On families helping their relatives avoid poverty, see H. J. Curtis to Phillip J. Weaver, April 10, 1850, in Phillip J. Weaver Papers, WRP; G. R. Neilson to "Dear Father," April 23, 1853, in Wright Family Papers, MDAH. On benevolent societies, see "Minutes of the Leaders of the Benevolent Society of the Methodist Church, South, at Aberdeen, July 4, 1854," in Columbua Sykes Papers, MDAH. On the shame attached to a family with a loved one consigned to county care, see Darden Diaries, May 26, 1860 (in Darden Papers).

virtuous whites to escape the drudgery of farm labor, Wesson, assuming that yeomen loathed the market, equated nonslaveholding whites with the enslaved. According to him, nonslaveholders deserved the opprobrium of their slaveholding peers because they breached what he perceived as the division of labor based on skin color by working the land and avoiding the market. Contrary to most southerners, who looked upon factory labor as worse than slavery, Wesson thought that once the region possessed a manufacturing system "a large and prosperous class of population will have been created out of the very dregs of society, and it may be in some instanses [*sic*] worse than dregs." Freed from their identity with the labor of African Americans, yeoman farmers-turned-factory-workers would obtain the full potential of their liberty. By operating high-speed machinery, they distinguished themselves from African Americans, and factory workers producing crude shoes and coarse cloth for plantation slaves gained a firm interest in the perpetuation of slavery. White industrial laborers thus affirmed their superiority to dependent blacks and thereby no longer constituted a threat to the social ethic.[21]

Wesson subscribed to a definition of good citizenship more restrictive than other Mississippians, but his broader effort to connect virtue to successful participation in the market fell within the mainstream of contemporary notions of the social ethic. Suspicion of anyone not at least lightly entangled in the web of the market ran high. Occasionally newspapers reported atrocities (some likely real but others based on rumor) that occurred when whites without direct ties to the agricultural market associated with blacks. In 1841 a white mechanic in the area of Bayou Sara supposedly took part in a slave uprising, and in 1846 a riot broke out on Jackson's Pearl Street when "low groceries" sold alcohol to blacks. Similar incidents bolstered distrust of whites without ties to the land, a distrust clearly expressed in the 1835 Madison County slave uprising scare.[22] Occurring on the heels of Nat Turner's revolt in Virginia, the Madison County affair transmitted a clear message to white members of the underclass: despite recent suffrage reform, wholesale changes in concepts of liberty would not be forthcoming. African Americans were reminded, too, that their condition as enslaved people made them suspect of opposing prevailing concepts of liberty and qualified them to receive a full measure of violence.[23] While much

21. J. M. Wesson to J. F. H. Claiborne, August 11, 1858, in James Francis Hamtrack Claiborne Papers, Microfilm, MDAH. Matthew Estes, *A Defense of Negro Slavery,* 43, 143–57.

22. For the reference to "low groceries," see Jackson *Mississippian* September 23, 1846. On the slave revolt at Bayou Sara, see Vicksburg *Tri-Weekly Whig,* July 27, 1841.

23. *Code,* 1828, pp. 328–29. On summary attacks against blacks, see Robert Everest,

about the outbreak of vigilante violence in Madison County has the ring of legend, the extreme response to a rebellion that never came off reveals the importance assigned to controlling the underclass.

The trouble in Madison County began when Virgil Stewart, an adventurer who claimed to have penetrated the secrets of the Murrell Gang, issued a pamphlet about its leader, John A. Murrell, a small-time criminal from Tennessee who, according to Stewart, planned to launch a regional slave insurrection. Central Mississippi planters were familiar with tales of uprisings, but one purportedly organized by a hardened criminal frightened them more than most. By early July, 1835, Madison County planters believed slaves in their community followed Murrell; accusations flew, slaves were interrogated, and a vigilance committee at Livingston questioned several whites about their role in planning the uprising. To ensure peace, Governor Hiram G. Runnels proposed to arm citizens against conspirators, an offer that sanctioned the excesses of night riders, who killed an estimated fifty blacks. The uprising, the investigating committee decided, stemmed from five white men (northerners and Thomasonian steam doctors to boot), all of whom were hanged. Before his death, one of the condemned reportedly explained that the conspirators had wished not to destroy slavery. Even though they had "held out the idea to the negroes that they should be free," they "intended they [the slaves] should work for *us*," a distinction that fell on unsympathetic ears. Mississippians understood the significance of the murderous events in Madison County. On July 4, 1835, an appropriate day for white southerners to rise up in defense of their peculiar brand of liberty and two days after the first of the Livingston executions, a militia company at Vicksburg, also the scene of an uprising scare, violently quieted a group of hecklers at a political rally. By July 6 a spirit of vigilance gripped the city. Citizens, aided by the militia, rounded up peddlers and gamblers on the assumption that they carried the slave revolt germ. Five were executed for holding abolitionist views, and four were stripped, whipped, and set adrift on rafts in the Mississippi River. Similar efforts to control foreigners, gamblers, and n'er-do-wells at Natchez and Grand Gulf ensued; even Columbus, on the eastern boundary of the state, sent its shady characters packing.[24]

A Journey Through the United States and Part of Canada (London, 1855), 96; and an account of two blacks accused of murder being burned to death in Lightsey Diary, February 27, 1851.

24. Quoting Shackleford, *Proceedings of the Citizens of Madison County*, 35. On Murrell, see James Lal Penick, Jr., *The Great Western Land Pirate: John A. Murrell in Legend and History* (Columbia, Mo., 1981), 9–31, 109–33, 146–54; and H. R. Howard, comp., *The His-*

Insightful contemporaries predicted that the reign of Judge Lynch at Livingston and elsewhere "probably quieted the spirit [of resistance] for years," an observation proven by the fact that other rumors of rebellion failed to produce a reaction comparable to that sparked by the Madison County scare.[25] So well were the lessons of the 1835 affair learned that afterwards even questions about slavery's central place in society were rarely heard. Those so bold as to consider rebellion understood that they would be dealt with harshly; consequently, opponents of slavery remained silent. As for whites denied liberty and virtue due to their poverty or their neglect of market production, they too fell under suspicion. By the late 1830s Mississippians believed that only white men who participated in the market without becoming enslaved to it possessed liberty and virtue; notions of proper economic behavior informed concepts of political liberty. In order to foster personal independence, citizens wished to avoid submitting to others' will, or for that matter appearing to do so. Notwithstanding the brief sway enjoyed by the politics of class, defense of African-American enslavement in the antebellum period remained the principle duty of liberty-loving citizens.[26] Anyone who declined to distinguish himself from black slaves or who advocated an end to slavery represented a challenge to the social ethic and its peculiar version of liberty.

During the last fifteen years of the antebellum period, white southerners discerned the formation of a sustained challenge to their ethic, though the challenge developed from outside the region, not from within. First in

---

tory of Virgil A. Stewart and His Adventure in Capturing and Exposing the Great 'Western Land Pirate' and His Gang in Connexion with the Evidence (New York, 1836), 61. On the events at Livingston, see also Edwin A. Miles, "The Mississippi State Insurrection Scare of 1835," *Journal of Negro History,* XLII (1957), 49, 59; Davidson Burns McKibben, "Negro Slave Insurrections in Mississippi, 1800–1865," *Journal of Negro History,* XXXIV (1949), 80–81.

25. Quoting Davidson Burns McKibben, ed., "Extract of a Letter from a Gentleman in Clinton, Mississippi, to a Gentleman in Lynchburg, Virginia, Dated the 5th of July, 1835," *Journal of Negro History,* XXXIV (1949), 91–92. On the aftermath and interpretations of the planned insurrection, see Agnew Diary, December 8, 1856; Lightsey Diary, April 11, 1852.

26. On the central place of slavery in southern politics and the unimportance of class issues, see William J. Cooper, Jr., *The South and the Politics of Slavery, 1828–1856* (Baton Rouge, 1979). Charges and countercharges of abolitionism were common in Mississippi politics during national campaigns; see Lexington *Whig Republican,* October 29, 1840; Jackson *Mississippian,* July 24, October 2, 1840; Vicksburg *Daily Whig,* April 14, 1841; Vicksburg *Tri-Weekly Whig,* August 16, 1845; Liberty *Advocate,* August 5, 1845. On race and class in southern politics, see Robert E. Shalhope, "Race, Class, Slavery, and the American Southern Mind," *Journal of Southern History,* XXXVII (1971), 573.

the uproar created by the Wilmot Proviso and later by the Compromise of 1850, Mississippians perceived the federal government as their enemy, an enemy that purposefully unleashed the determined forces of abolitionism to undermine the social ethic. In response whites rallied around the ethic, forcing the two-party system to undergo significant changes. No single event more starkly signaled those changes than the advent of the rhetoric of resistance, which celebrated citizens' reluctance to submit to encroachment on their liberty. Through that rhetoric Mississippians fomented a united response to opponents of their political culture, which led to the elimination of dissent and eventually to secession.

Changes in the conduct of Fourth of July celebrations illustrate the transformation of Mississippi's political culture. Before the late 1840s Whigs and Democrats welcomed the occasion as an excuse to exalt the Founding Fathers for their creation of the federal Union. During an 1844 celebration Democrats at Patrick's Mill (Scott County) toasted Washington, Jackson, and soldiers of the Revolution for their heroic defense of liberty and virtue. Mention of constitutional liberty (to the Scott County folk the equivalent of egalitarian democracy) also prompted a round of cheers. But as the sectional crisis of the 1850s heated up, southerners turned to the Founding Fathers to justify the legality and propriety of fragmenting the Union. In Attala County, states' rights advocates at an 1851 Fourth of July celebration argued that secession to protect southerners' right to own slaves was a patriotic act. If resistance to tyranny constituted treason, southerners should be "just such traitors . . . as George Washington and his compeers were, when they resisted the tyranny of George the Third." Calls for the South to follow the course of traitors like Washington multiplied in the 1850s, and justifications of resistance to federal authority came evermore to turn upon the Kentucky and Virginia Resolutions as defenders of the social ethic viewed every opponent of the westward extension of slavery a foe of individual liberty and states' rights. According to Mary Davies, July 4, 1854, passed quietly in the eastern counties. The old men who once celebrated the nation's founding had died; the young men who replaced them in the halls of power despised the Union. By the mid-1850s, the uses to which southerners put their national heritage had been reversed. Those who had once castigated every opponent of Jackson as "a dm'd nullifier" (and thus a foe of the Union) pushed the great hero into the basement of their pantheon of saints and waited for the North to commit a significant enough depredation against southern conceptions of liberty to justify revolution.[27]

27. Quoting Jason Niles Diary, November 11, 1851 (SHC); Davies Diary, July 4, 1854

The first inkling that the North might satisfy the wishes of southern firebrands came in 1846, when an unheralded representative from Pennsylvania, David Wilmot, introduced before Congress his famous proviso. Southern reactions to his proposal to prohibit slavery in territory acquired from Mexico quickly followed. Neither political party in Mississippi welcomed the measure, as leaders of each believed it demanded that southerners submit to gross encroachments upon their moral and legal rights to command property.[28] Take away their right to move property west and southerners would become the unvirtuous and enslaved children of the North, poor and despised for submitting to laws repugnant to their individual and collective liberty. Reacting to the Wilmot Proviso, Mississippi Democrats, who wanted to distance themselves from the pernicious measure proposed by one of their fellows, sought to elicit a united southern response, but overcoming the divisiveness inherent in the recently formed party system took more than a decade.

Early in the proviso's career, Whigs, in fact, stated a willingness to compromise on the measure. Indicative of his party's stand, a Whig writer in the Vicksburg newspaper first denounced the proviso then cautioned southerners against "forever prating about the South." The more southerners complained about depredations against their constitutional liberties, the less seriously the rest of the nation took the charges, he warned. Persistently characterizing legislation as "sectional," however harmful to southern concepts of a good republic it might be, suggested to the nation that the South promoted a hidden agenda. In assaulting the proviso's foes the writer proclaimed that southern prating about liberty and virtue epitomized a frenetic defense of slavery, one that led to the creation of a single political party bound to the idea of secession.[29] He, like other Mississippi Whigs, remained as yet unprepared to consign the region's fate to southern hotheads.

However perceptive about Democratic designs the Whig writer proved to be, erasing old party loyalties took time, though the first tentative steps toward doing so occurred in 1849. Following the path blazed by south-

---

(in Davies Papers); Duncan McKenzie to John McLaurin, November 13, 1836, in McLaurin Papers. The Patrick Mills celebration is recounted in the Jackson *Mississippian,* July 5, July 19, 1844. On the patriotism of resistance, see Alexander H. Handy, *A Parallel Between the Great Revolution in England in 1688 and the American Revolution of 1860–1861* (Meridian, Miss., 1864), 4, 20, 40. On the supposition that northerners intended to abolish slavery, see Vicksburg *Tri-Weekly Whig,* August 4, 1849.

28. For examples of reaction to the proviso, see Jackson *Mississippian,* April 20, September 21, 1849.

29. Vicksburg *Tri-Weekly Whig,* September 10, 1846.

ern congressmen, who signed a bipartisan statement criticizing the proviso in January, Mississippi Whigs and Democrats gathered in May to map out a plan for united action against the forces of abolitionism. Leading Whigs, including George Shall Yerger, William Sharkey, and C. K. Marshall, joined the convention, but Democrats controlled it. Jefferson Davis, a Democratic senator at the time, delivered the most celebrated speech of the convention when he argued that seventeen years of issuing ultimatums and then backing away had brought about the current exigency. Like the previously cited Whig writer, Davis believed that the North wished to reshape the southern social ethic, but instead of submitting through a compromise, he proposed that the region secede to prove that it was not crying wolf. Other Democrats endorsed Davis' rhetoric of resistance. In a letter written after the convention, George Calhoun complained that the North lacked respect for peculiar southern liberties guaranteed in the constitution. Its depredations had become so egregious that he called upon southerners to cast their wayward northern brethren from the Union. Whigs attending the convention attempted to douse with old party rhetoric the spirit of disunion. Although they had initially welcomed the bipartisan convention, Whigs, fearful that Davis' speech might set in motion the wheels of secession, began denouncing it, even before adjournment, as an extra legal body without authority, the very sort of body they expected degenerate Democrats to assemble.[30]

John A. Quitman's Democratic gubernatorial campaign, launched soon after the convention, overwhelmed Whig discontent over formation of a fusion party and drew Whigs to Quitman's side, if only briefly. An advocate of southern resistance since the nullification crisis, Quitman attracted Whig followers because he was a Mexican War hero and because he denounced repudiation. To rally support for Quitman, another bipartisan convention was scheduled to convene in October, 1849. As the date for the meeting drew near, T. N. Waul, along with other Democrats, pleaded with Whigs to face down "the perils that are at our door" by supporting the old nullifier. Bipartisan county-level meetings to elect delegates to the October convention echoed the urgency of Waul's statement. The meetings typically issued reports like the one coming from the Pontotoc convocation: Quitman's election would set before the world Mississippi's intention to protect "our property, our feelings, and our honor." As a gauge of fusionist sentiment, the Whigs in their own county conventions, though they

30. Quoting George Calhoun to the Editors of the Jackson *Mississippian*, September 10, 1849. For accounts of events leading up to the convention and the convention itself, see Jackson *Mississippian*, February 23, 1849 and Vicksburg *Weekly Whig*, May 16, 1849.

nominated Thomas Polk of Marshall County for governor, passed resolutions praising Quitman and sounded the death knell of their party.[31]

The interjection of the debt-paying issue into the 1849 election ensured that Quitman, the best-known gubernatorial candidate, would win the contest. His stance on the bond question allowed him to poll a significant Whig vote, while his calls for resistance appealed to Democrats. But the debt-paying issue also revived dormant intraparty contention within the Democratic camp. Reuben Davis, himself an independent gubernatorial candidate, warned that the party abandoned its principles by supporting "mendicants and professional quacks" of Whiggish persuasion when it nominated Quitman. Ex-Governor McNutt, too, blanched at the thought of his party sacrificing its economic platform in order to run a states' rights candidate. He attempted, apparently without much success, to label Quitman a pseudo–states' righter committed more to the cause of bond payment than to resistance of northern aggression. Most Democrats, however, rushed to Quitman's side. Henry Stuart Foote, a previously little-known Jackson attorney, obtained his political reputation (and with it a seat in the U.S. Senate) by debating McNutt and defending Quitman as an heir to "the true Jeffersonian and Calhoun school."[32] With the Whig party running a half-hearted campaign for the governor's office, Mississippians focused on the October 1, 1849, fusion convention through which a statement was made supporting the treatment of slavery as "a domestic institution" fully protected by the Constitution. Delegates also declared that constitutional liberties would be protected only if Congress allowed slavery to be introduced into all territories. While no prominent state's rights Democrats attended the convention, they found comfort in the results of the affair. Besides calling for the South to meet at Nashville in 1850, delegates to the convention cast the state's choice of responses to the proviso in terms clearly favoring resistance. Mississippi faced two choices: it could submit to the "insulting discrimination" of the proposed congressional legislation or resist.[33]

The idea that the South would never, in the words of J. H. Harman-

31. Jackson *Mississippian,* June 20, 22, 1849; Natchez *Mississippi Free Trader and Natchez Gazette,* June 27, 1849.

32. Quoting Reuben Davis, *Recollections of Mississippi and Mississippians* (Boston, 1891), 302–307; Henry Stuart Foote to John A. Quitman, August 9, 1849, in Claiborne, ed., *Life and Correspondence of John A. Quitman,* I, 220. See, too, Jackson *Mississippian,* August 17, 1849. Even though the Whigs endorsed Quitman, they did not concede local races; see Vicksburg *Tri-Weekly Whig,* February 3, 1849.

33. Vicksburg *Tri-Weekly Whig,* October 4, 9, 1849, February 15, 1850.

son, "quietly submit to the insulting arrogance of the Yankee" gained prominence after the convention. Even though the convention avoided specifics about the course that resistance should take, all understood the meaning of the term. Linking abolitionism, the proviso, and death of the social ethic, Sharkey, a Whig and chief justice of Mississippi's High Court of Errors and Appeals, entertained thoughts of secession if the federal government restricted the expansion of slavery. "The Union," he said, "must be dissolved, and the blessings which we enjoy under our Government must become a sacrifice on the altar of fantacism [*sic*]. We must become a degraded people, or abandon our country to the African race. We would say [to northerners] Beware!" for they rush to their "own destruction."[34]

The October convention and Quitman's election catapulted the rhetoric of resistance to prominence and respectability, but another rift in the state Democratic party momentarily scattered the forces that joined in 1849. Because of that division, competitive politics in the state were revived and the life of the Union was perhaps extended. The split had its origins in the debate stemming from the passage of the Compromise of 1850. The hope so recently entertained for the creation of a southern fusion party dissipated as the compromise assumed prominence in political discourse, and as the Mississippi Democratic party divided behind the leadership of its senators, Jefferson Davis and Henry Stuart Foote.

The compromise, originally proposed in January, 1850, by Henry Clay, included seven separate bills delineating congressional action on territorial and slavery issues. Provisions of the bill as passed by Congress included the admission of California to the Union as a state; a new fugitive slave law; and prohibitions against congressional legislation on the slavery question in the lands of the Mexican cession and on the slave trade in Washington, D.C., or Maryland without a popular referendum. The South extracted from Congress a vague promise to protect the free flow of commerce. On the broadest level Davis and Foote agreed that the South conceded too much if it endorsed congressional involvement in slavery legislation in the District of Columbia or permitted California to join the Union as a nonslaveholding state. But where Foote was willing to bend on the California question, proposing at one time the extension of the Missouri Compromise line to the Pacific, Davis was largely inflexible, taking the Calhoun line of ar-

34. Quoting J. H. Harmanson to J. F. H. Claiborne, December 24, 1848, in Claiborne Papers, MDAH. Sharkey quoted in the *Congressional Globe*, 31st Cong., 2nd Sess., 533. Sentiments similar to Sharkey's may be found in Albert Garrel Seal, ed., "Letters from the South: A Mississipian's Defense of Slavery," *Journal of Mississippi History*, II (1940), 216–17, 220.

gument by declaring any line that separated free and slave territory an infringement on southern rights. An examination of key roll-call votes on amendments to the various compromise measures reveals that throughout much of 1850 Foote and Davis maintained their positions on the legislation, but when Congress temporarily voted down California's admission, Davis joined Foote on several occasions to vote for the extension of the 1820 compromise line to the Pacific.[35] His willingness to accept the Missouri Compromise line after Congress dispensed with California's admission suggests also that a paramount commitment to defeating the spirit of the Wilmot Proviso motivated him. Rejection of the proviso's intent was the yardstick by which states' righters like Davis measured loyalty to the southern social ethic. Conversely, Foote, who in 1850 began to emerge as the leader of a Unionist faction in the Mississippi Democratic party, construed commitment to peace within the federal Union as the measure of regional loyalty. The differences between Davis and Foote that came to a head during the compromise debate shaped Mississippi politics until 1854.

Foote, who according to one historian was "the one Mississippian most responsible for his state's acceptance of the compromise and rejection of secession in 1851," lobbied hard to pass the measures. Arrogant and eloquent, Foote was, if not a political opportunist, then at least a political chameleon with strong Whiggish tendencies. Even though he had campaigned for Quitman in 1849 as a bond-paying, states' rights Democrat, Foote by 1851 turned against the governor and adopted Unionism as the best means for protecting the southern social ethic.[36] By his own account of the compromise measure, Foote claimed responsibility for breathing life into the Committee of Thirteen, which eventually wrote the compromise, and for formulating the omnibus format of the legislation—distinctions that Davis happily granted him. Joining with northern Democrats in sup-

35. On the compromise, see David M. Potter, *The Impending Crisis, 1848–1861* (New York, 1976), 90–120; Cleo Heron, "Mississippi and the Compromise of 1850," Mississippi Historical Society *Publications,* XIV (1914), 111, 121, 134–35; *Congressional Globe,* 31st Cong., 1st Sess., 246–47. On the comments and votes of Mississippi's senators, see *Congressional Globe,* 31st Cong., 2nd Sess., 517–20, 531; *Congressional Globe,* 31st Cong., 1st Sess., Appex., 867, 1416–17, 1420, 1455–56, 1479, 1483, 1504.

36. Quoting John Edmond Gonzales, "Henry Stuart Foote: A Forgotten Unionist of the Forties," *Southern Quarterly,* I (1963), 129. See, too, Henry Stuart Foote to John A. Quitman, August 9, 1849, in Claiborne, ed., *Life and Correspondence of John A. Quitman,* I, 220. On Foote's role in the compromise, see Hamilton Holman, "Democratic Senate Leadership and the Compromise of 1850," *Mississippi Valley Historical Review,* XLI (1854), 413–17; John McCardell, "John A. Quitman and the Compromise of 1850," *Journal of Mississippi History,* XXXVII (1975), 239–66; *Congressional Globe,* 31st Cong., 1st Sess., 1830.

port of the compromise, Foote proclaimed it the final resolution of sectional animosity, a position that carried much weight with Union Democrats. At a meeting of Lowndes County Unionists in July, 1850, led by Joseph B. Cobb and William Barksdale, Unionists agreed that however onerous Congress' failure to extend the Missouri Compromise line, they accepted the new settlement until the North committed further aggression against southern notions of a good republic. Until then, they promised, the region would take "such modes and measures of redress as we may deem necessary for protection of the South." Despite the tiresome abolitionism of "our insatiate adversaries" in the North, Foote and other Unionists, unlike Davis, refused to endorse unequivocally the rhetoric of southern resistance and grew impatient with the "treasonable faction" of southerners who opposed the compromise. He did not share with most of his fellow southern congressmen their fear that submission to the compromise measures would result in the death of their social ethic and he denounced the rhetoric of resistance as "the language of sedition." Perhaps because he had played a vital role in pushing the compromise measures through Congress, Foote found himself ever more at odds with traditional defenses of the southern social ethic. "Thank God," he said, "I am no secessionist, no disunionist, and thank God I am in one sense a submissionist. I am, and shall be, I trust willing to submit to any constitutional enactment adopted by Congress, that does not amount to gross oppression."[37] Foote embraced the compromise as a permanent measure for ensuring sectional peace. He was eager as well to collect the political bounty that Mississippians, whom he believed shared his opinions, would offer when he returned home.

Davis, a moderate among states' righters, occupied a precarious position. In order to maintain his standing in the Mississippi party, he articulated the rhetoric of resistance; as a senator speaking to a national audience, he treated the idea of resistance with restraint. When addressing Mississippians, he unleashed a wellspring of demagogic vitriol against the compromise and its backers, outlining before Lowndes County Democrats two possible responses to the measure: southerners could resist implementation of the measure or accept it, and he believed they supported resistance. In Congress Davis tempered his attacks, arguing that the com-

37. *Congressional Globe,* 31st Cong., 1st Sess., Appex., 1491–1500; *Congressional Globe,* 31st Cong., 1st Sess., 585, 587, 594, 1480–81; *Congressional Globe,* 32nd Cong., 2nd Sess., 48; Vicksburg *Weekly Whig,* August 17, 1850. In denouncing the compromise's opponents, Foote argued that only secessionists would oppose a bill promoted by their own party. On Foote and the public reaction to his arguments, see Raymond *Hinds County Gazette,* October 30, 1851; Vicksburg *Weekly Whig,* February 12, October 22, 1851.

promise threatened to undermine property holders' right to move their possessions without regard to territorial boundaries. His own efforts to downplay the rhetoric of resistance clashed with the angry words of fire-eaters like Mississippi Congressman Albert G. Brown, who swore to relinquish all except "principle and honor" to prevent passage of the compromise, and made Davis' attempts to water down threats of secession and war futile. Nevertheless, he implored the Senate to consider the pounding of southern war drums a phantom born of politicians' lust after office and a sound to which no military man in the South marched.[38]

Davis and Foote, then, hedged on the meaning of southern resistance. The former viewed acceptance of the compromise as submission to the northern social ethic, while the latter portrayed rejection of the compromise as submission to southern firebrands and demagogues. In the battle for the hearts and minds of Mississippi voters that followed congressional approval of the compromise, the meaning of the term submission remained a point of contention as long as political rivalries existed.

When the compromise passed Congress, Union Democrats (including the remnants of the Whig party, which had been in hibernation since the fall of 1849) and old-line Democrats began holding separate organizational meetings to coordinate the regional response to the measure. Each rallied behind its chosen acolyte in the U.S. Senate. Talk of fusion ceased. Believing that resisters still carried the day, Governor Quitman called a special session of the legislature to determine a united reply to the compromise. At the same time the sitting legislature, which had been elected prior to passage of the compromise, chastised Foote for his support of the compromise and praised the rest of the state's congressional delegation for its work against the measure. Referring to the actions of "a dominant majority" in the North that subverted "the sovereign power" of the South, legislators barely disguised allusions to secession when they called for counties to send delegates to a statewide convention in November, 1851.[39]

Almost a year passed before the convention met, and in the intervening time Unionists and resisters battled over the region's fate. Congressman

38. *Congressional Globe,* 32nd Cong., 2nd Sess., Appex., 120–21, 1471; *Congressional Globe,* 32nd Cong., 1st Sess., 1003–1006. See Jefferson Davis to Lowndes County Citizens, November 22, 1850, in Lynda Lasswell Crist, ed., *The Papers of Jefferson Davis, 1849–1852* (Baton Rouge, 1983), IV, 139–40.

39. *Laws of the State of Mississippi,* Called Session, 1850, p. 25. See also, the speech of J. A. Wilcox on the development of the Southern Rights faction in the Democratic party, *Congressional Globe,* 32nd Cong., 2nd Sess., Appex., 282–85. On Quitman's motives, see Natchez *Mississippi Free Trader,* June 25, 1851.

Brown fired the opening salvo in this war of words at Ellwood Springs in November, 1850. In one breath Brown, defying logic, argued that he preferred to see his home state remain in the Union but hated to see it buckle with "tame submission to outrageous wrong." Continuing, he proclaimed, "If it has really come to this, that the Southern States dare not assert and maintain their equal position in the Union, for fear of dissolving the Union, then I am free to say that the Union ought to be dissolved." A host of lesser figures picked up Brown's bravado, but generally cast secessionist rhetoric in the more discreet terms of protecting liberty and the social ethic. Signing himself "Jefferson," a writer in the Natchez *Mississippi Free Trader* explained that Mississippians could either protect "the inherent rights of freemen" or submit to northern despotism and black liberty. Similar invocations of Jefferson's name occurred prior to the convention: states' rights legislators addressing the Mississippi House cited the Kentucky and Virginia resolutions when they postulated that southerners possessed "a natural independence against all external pressure." Professing a love for the union, legislators announced nonetheless their intention to fight for the social ethic until death. "There can be no equality of the races," they declared, "They [blacks] cannot live amongst us except as our slaves or as our masters. . . . We must either maintain our superiority or surrender the land of our fathers."[40]

While old-line Democrats bludgeoned Mississippians with calls for resistance, Union Democrats adopted an even-tempered tone. A loose coterie of Whigs and dissident Democrats, they, out of affection for Foote's defense of the compromise, cautiously turned over leadership of their faction to the facile senator. Echoing the sentiments of the Nashville convention, Union Democrats declared that no one loved the compromise, but resistance in the face of sectional give-and-take appeared obdurate. The social ethic could best be protected within the framework of the compromise, the final word on the slavery question, they said. According to the Union Democrat Samuel S. Boyd, Jefferson Davis and his antisubmission allies disingenuously couched their calls for secession in the word "resistance." Their equating of the Kentucky and Virginia resolutions with actual secession was "a perversion of their whole import and language" that consciously obscured the fact that Madison had renounced his resolution as an "extra-

40. Quoting M. W. Cluskey, ed., *Speeches, Messages, and Other Writings of the Honorable Albert G. Brown, a Senator in Congress from the State of Mississippi* (Philadelphia, 1859), 256; Natchez *Mississippi Free Trader and Natchez Gazette,* July 3, 1850, January 8, 1851. On Brown's response to the compromise, see James Byrne Ranck, *Albert Gallatin Brown: Radical Southern Nationalist* (New York, 1937), 51–100.

and ultra-constitutional remedy." Union Democrats also broadcast William Sharkey's warning that Mississippians consider the horrors of a race war that awaited if secession occurred and denounced the States' Rights Association, in Joseph B. Cobb's phrase, as "an unconstitutional and a seditious assemblage."[41]

In 1851 Union Democratic labors to build a consensus of support for the compromise by denouncing old-line Democrats as intractable prevailed. They were aided by the fact the compromise went into effect without destroying the social ethic. Soon after that realization dawned on Mississippians a changed attitude reflecting the Union Democratic view of the compromise descended over the citizenry. Felix Houston discovered when he delivered an address at a Vicksburg political rally that state politicians' dislike of the compromise exceeded that of their constituents. While he believed the Democratic party had to "Quitman" the question of secession, he perceived that the crowd disagreed, and he altered his speech extemporaneously so as to couch pleas for resistance in less forceful terms than he wished to use. Judging from the results of the canvass for delegates to the November, 1851, convention, Houston's audience more thoroughly demonstrated statewide opinion than did Houston himself. For when the convention gathered at Jackson, Unionists occupied more seats than old-line Democrats. Only eighteen counties (all of them in the traditional Democratic strongholds of the Piney Woods and Hill Country, except Sunflower) sent states' rights delegations. Not surprisingly, the document eventually approved by the convention bore the stamp of Union Democratic arguments. Echoing the sentiment of the famous Georgia platform, the Mississippi convention promised to support the Compromise of 1850 if Congress did not attempt to interfere with slavery in the states, outlaw the interstate slave trade, restrict the operation of the peculiar institution in the District of Columbia, refuse admission of any state into the Union because it permitted slavery, or prohibit slavery in any territory. Should

41. Quoting Samuel S. Boyd, *Speech of the Honorable Samuel S. Boyd Delivered at the Great Union Festival Held at Jackson, Mississippi the 16th Day of October, 1851* (Natchez, 1851), 418; Joseph B. Cobb [A Southron], "The True Issue Between Parties in the South, Union or Disunion," *The American Whig*, n.s., XXXVI (1851), 593. On the convention see, too, Raymond *Hinds County Gazette*, October 31, 1850; W. L. Sharkey to the editor of the *Southron* quoted in Vicksburg *Weekly Whig*, October 23, 1850; Sharkey to Luke Lea, December 24, 1850, quoted in Jackson *Mississippian and State Gazette*, January 12, 1851; Jackson *Mississippian*, November 8, 1850; Vicksburg *Weekly Whig*, May 21, 1851. On the 1851 convention and Foote's contention that it was unnecessary, see Foote to John A. Quitman, October 16, 1850, quoted in Jackson *Mississippian*, November 1, 1850.

Congress neglect southern sentiment on these issues, the state would resist with all its might.[42]

Like their old-line Democratic rivals, Union Democrats on the resolution-writing committee never defined the term resistance, but unlike their political foes, they denied explicitly that they intended it to mean secession. In a nonbinding straw poll, seventy-two delegates voted that no right to secession existed; only seventeen voted that it did. (Among those who voted to recognize secession as a legal recourse were the authors of the convention's minority report, William R. Cannon, Wiley P. Harris, and Samuel N. Gilleland, who were joined also by Lowndes County Unionist William Barksdale.) A majority of delegates also favored Joseph B. Cobb's resolution proclaiming the convention an unnecessary contrivance of secessionist demagogues. Secession itself, Cobb added, waged "war with the spirit of republican institutions, and [was] an encroachment on the sovereign power of the people." Liberty might best be protected, the convention concluded, by maintaining the status quo, however troubling it was. So fervently did Union Democrats wish to chastise their rivals, they also overrode old-line Democrats' objections and published in the convention proceedings the U.S. Constitution and President George Washington's Farewell Address, in which he censured factional politicians.[43]

Emboldened by their convention success, Union Democrats, once foes of the creation of a fusion party, believed themselves masters of the state's destiny: the old issues were by and large dead, the question of resistance settled, and the time for creating one Southern political party ripe. By encouraging Mississippians to gather in a fusion party, they opened the way for a crucial political realignment that by 1855 left Mississippi with but one effective political party. As things turned out that party was not the Union Democratic one, but the party of resistance.

Contrary to Union Democratic wishes, talk of resistance persisted after

42. See Felix Houston to J. F. H. Claiborne, September 19, 1850, in Claiborne Papers, MDAH. On the efforts of old-line Democrats to convince voters that the debate over the compromise was not about secession, see K. McKenzie to Duncan McLaurin, November 24, 1851, in McLaurin Papers; Wade Diaries, March 7, 1851; Natchez *Mississippi Free Trader and Natchez Gazette*, January 8, May 17, 1851; Jackson *Mississippian and State Gazette*, September 26, 1851. On the canvass for delegates and the convention, see Jackson *Mississippian and State Gazette*, November 21, May 16, 1851; Vicksburg *Weekly Whig*, November 19, November 26, December 3, 1851; *Journal of the Convention of the State of Mississippi and the Act Calling the Same With the Constitution of the United States and Washington's Farewell Address* (Jackson, 1851).

43. Quoting *Journal of the Convention of the State of Mississippi*, 19–22, but see, too, 16, 18, 47.

the November convention. The gubernatorial election, which occurred soon afterwards and pitted against one another the state's leading resister, Quitman, and its leading Unionist, Foote, kept the issue before the people. Their campaigns began the previous summer when the one-time allies met in public debate seeking votes for their favorite delegates to the 1851 convention. After Quitman withdrew from the race, in part because of legal trouble caused by his involvement in a Latin American filibuster, Jefferson Davis became the states' rights candidate.[44] By 1851 few in Mississippi doubted that when Davis spoke of "resistance" he meant secession, and if the vote for governor is any indication, the state was evenly divided between Unionists and secessionists. Davis, having missed several weeks of the campaign due to illness, lost by 999 votes in an election that polled over 55,000. Even though the majority of Mississippi voters refused to support the gubernatorial candidate who represented resistance, Democratic party leadership derived some satisfaction from the fact that voters hardily declined to submit to other gross encroachments on their individual liberty. In addition to the gubernatorial election, voters were asked to decide whether they wished "to submit" to the payment of state-issued Planters' Bank bonds that had been issued in the 1830s. Nonpayment passed by a wide margin. Only fourteen counties, every one a traditional Whig stronghold, voted for paying the debt. Davis, it should be noted, carried four bond-paying counties, but generally did poorly in Whig strongholds.[45]

Although the Union Democratic party successfully carried the gubernatorial election and elected a majority of state and federal legislators, they enjoyed little success during their brief tenure in office. For a time U.S. representatives J. A. Wilcox, J. D. Freeman, and B. D. Nabors quieted Con-

44. On Quitman's troubles, see the letter signed "Jackson" in the Vicksburg *Weekly Whig,* February 12, 1851; John A. Quitman to R. B. Rhett, January 24, 1851, in Claiborne Papers, MDAH. See, too, an assessment of the effects of Quitman's withdrawal as negligible in James F. Shannon to Absalom F. Dantzler, June 26, 1852, in Dantzler Papers. Controversy over repudiation of the Planters' Bank bond had flashed hot since the early 1840s.

45. On the gubernatorial campaign, see the Vicksburg *Weekly Whig,* February 12, May 7, 21, October 22, 1851; Natchez *Mississippi Free Trader,* June 25, October 8, 1851; Lightsey Diary, August 27, 30, October 3, 1851. For a recounting of the campaign, see Jefferson Davis to Barksdale and Jones, February 2, 1852, in Dunbar Rowland, ed., *Jefferson Davis, Constitutionalist: His Letters, Papers, and Speeches* (2 vols.; Jackson, 1923), II, 126–27. Hudson Strode's *Jefferson Davis, American Patriot, 1808–1861* (2 vols.; New York, 1955), I, 232–35, also includes an account of Davis during the campaign. For the vote count in the gubernatorial election, see *Mississippi House Journal,* 1852, p. 256; for the tally on repudiation, see Records of the Secretary of State, Election Returns 1852, Record Group 28, MDAH. Hearon, "Mississippi and the Compromise of 1850," facing 208, includes the returns, as does Ranck, *Albert Gallatin Brown,* facing 100.

gressman Brown and forced old-line Democrats to follow him in backing away from the rhetoric of resistance. Yet Union Democrats could not capitalize on their electoral victory by consolidating in one party proponents of the compromise and opponents of the regular Democratic leadership. The collapse of the national Whig party hindered their cause, as did Foote, by all accounts an ineffective governor skilled chiefly at alienating people. After his defeat in the 1853 election, Foote, in fact, resigned before his term expired and emigrated to California.[46]

Because of the self-destructive nature of the Union Democratic party, the greatest problem facing its rival during Foote's term involved providing longtime Democrats in the northern part of the state a piece of the political pie.[47] Tensions between the new northern counties and the river counties had always run high, but in 1853 estranged Democrats bolted from the party in the Chickasaw Rebellion. The rebellion began at the Democratic convention of May, 1853. Stirred to action by Foote, who hoped to draw to his side Unionists not previously aligned with him, B. N. Kinyon tried to ramrod through the convention a resolution critical of President Franklin Pierce, a warm friend of old-line Democrats. When Kinyon attempted to pass another resolution calling for the state ticket to be split between Unionist and states' rights candidates, delegates booed and jeered. The measure went down to defeat by an eighty-seven to four vote. Realizing the futility of turning the Democratic party into an extension of Foote's command, Kinyon and his colleague John Horne resigned from the convention in disgust, leaving state's righters to battle over candidates. Personal ambition, brokered deals, and at least one "secret" caucus dominated the nominating process, depriving some aspirants, including the Pontotoc County judge Reuben Davis, of the nominations they desired. Prior to the meeting Davis had attracted some support for his congressional aspirations and tried to build a convention majority by adjudicating a deal between Brown and John J. McRae, each of whom wanted a place in the U.S. Senate. When the convention learned of his behind-the-scenes maneuvering, however, it nominated William Barksdale for the congressional seat that Davis desired. Davis, who had run as an independent in 1849 and entertained Unionist

46. On Foote, see Gonzales, "Henry Stuart Foote," 135; Vicksburg *Tri-Weekly Whig*, September 21, 1852; Vicksburg *Weekly Whig*, May 18, June 29, July 20, 1853. On the Union Democrats and Brown in Congress, see *Congressional Globe*, 32nd Cong., 1st Sess., Appex., 282–86, 356–57; Albert G. Brown to J. F. H. Claiborne, May 6, 1853, in Claiborne Papers, MDAH.

47. See Albert G. Brown to J. F. H. Claiborne, November 14, 1853, in Claiborne Papers, MDAH.

sentiments, deflected support; Barksdale, despite being known for his Unionist sentiments, received the nomination as a reward for his vote favoring the right of secession at the 1851 convention. Talking loudly about a corrupt bargain, Davis cultivated a following in northeastern Mississippi and entered the November election as an independent candidate, but as he had done in 1849, he pulled out of the race before the election.[48]

Just as did the Chickasaw Rebellion, the Know-Nothing party bore witness to the immediate strain placed on the political culture by the collapse of the Whig and Union Democratic parties. Composed mostly of former Whigs, long familiar with a touch of nativism in their party, as well as some out-of-office Democrats, the Know-Nothings denounced their opponents as immoral and shortsighted demagogues. Oddly, however, the party chose as its 1855 gubernatorial candidate a staunch states' righter and anti-bond-payer from Pontotoc, Charles D. Fontaine. Party hacks intended to take advantage of Democratic dissension in the northern counties by nominating Fontaine, who had no idea his name was even being considered for the position. Stranger still, Fontaine apparently accepted the nomination because he believed the Democratic party too gracious toward Unionists, including William Barksdale. While Whigs hoped to use Fontaine to defeat the Democratic party, Fontaine regarded his campaign as a plebiscite to decide who among states' righters (the hard core like himself or weak-minded Democratic party lackeys) should rule at home.[49] A more unusual marriage

48. On the "Chickasaw Rebellion," see the Jackson *Mississippian and State Gazette,* May 6, 13, 27, July 8, 1853. For an assessment of the convention and the Democratic party's strength, see C. S. Tarpley to Jefferson Davis, May 6, 1853, in Rowland, ed., *Jefferson Davis, Constitutionalist,* 213. For a creative account of the "rebellion" and the 1853 campaign, see Davis, *Recollections of Mississippi,* 331–33. But see, too, James W. McKee, Jr., "William Barksdale and the Congressional Election of 1853 in Mississippi," *Journal of Mississippi History,* XXXIV (1972), 129–58, who attributes Davis' withdrawal to the publicity he received after stabbing his opponent.

49. On nativism in Mississippi, see the Jackson *Mississippian,* September 6, 1844; Vicksburg *Weekly Whig,* November 26, 1844, January 3, 1845. On Know-Nothings in Mississippi, see Jackson *Mississippian and State Gazette,* October 24, 1855; Vicksburg *Weekly Whig,* July 18, September 8, 1855; Vicksburg *Tri-Weekly Whig,* July 21, August 4, 1855. On Democratic fears that Know-Nothings were merely Whigs by another name, or perhaps abolitionists, see J. J. McRae to J. F. H. Claiborne, November 18, 1854; Madison McAfee to Claiborne, August 31, 1855; Wiley P. Harris to Claiborne, December 8, 1854, all in Claiborne Papers, MDAH. On Whig disdain for Know-Nothings see Duncan McKenzie to Duncan McLaurin, December 8, 1854, in McLaurin Papers. A prodigious amount of correspondence addresses Fontaine's motivation for accepting the nomination; see, for example, George Foote to Fontaine, April 6, 1855; James Taylor to Fontaine, April 25, 1855; A. T. McWilliams to Fontaine, May 4, 1855; A. C. Owen to Fontaine, May [?], 1855, all in Fontaine Papers.

than the one uniting Fontaine and the Know-Nothings would be difficult to imagine, and the union brought about a premature death for the Know-Nothing party in Mississippi.

Whigs, Union Democrats, Democratic bolters, and Know-Nothings each in turn fell victim to the powerful Democratic machine and their own weaknesses. None of the opposition factions could capitalize on Democratic party diversity, and all except the Union Democrats offered only token opposition. As a measure of Democratic party success, the Vicksburg *Daily Whig*, the leading opposition newspaper, candidly confessed soon after the 1855 elections that overthrowing the Democratic party was impossible and unnecessary: "We maintain that every Whig can carry out his conservative principles now, far more effectively without a separate political organization, than with it." Potential challengers to Democratic hegemony learned through the examples of Foote and Reuben Davis that those who opposed the party for personal reasons or who supported national legislation construed by Democrats as inimical to the social ethic would be castigated as "God d——d abolitionists."[50] Support for the legality of secession and disregard for fusionist tickets resulted in political rewards, as William Barksdale discovered. Isolated from external assistance and lacking a forceful, alternative vision of a good republic, opponents of resistance could only temporize until a sufficiently egregious challenge to the social ethic made further delay impossible.

By 1855 the absence of a well-organized opposition party circumscribed political discourse. Pockets of opposition remained, but by and large Mississippians had come to agree on the nature of the threat to their social ethic. They agreed as well on the nature of resistance. During the last five years of the antebellum period, southern reaction to purported northern aggression (personal liberty laws, the Kansas-Nebraska controversy, and John Brown's raid) became virulent, a predictable reaction considering the poverty of Mississippi's political discourse.[51] Yet secession was not inevitable. Regardless of the diminution of political rhetoric, regardless of the cultural and political homogeneity fostered by devotion to the social ethic, viable

50. Quoting the Vicksburg *Daily Whig*, November 21, 1851; Niles Diary, August 17, 1850.

51. On the collapse of the second party system as a precursor to secession, see Michael F. Holt, *The Political Crisis of the 1850s* (New York, 1978), 222–38, 258–59. On reaction to the Kansas-Nebraska controversy, see John McRae to Simeon R. Adams, February 3, 1858, in Adams Papers. On reaction to John Brown's raid, see Darden Diaries, November 3, 1859 (in Darden Papers).

options to secession existed. Talk of drawing railroad companies to the state and the actual development of lines spurred the growth of secessionist sentiment, however, by bolstering the illusion of political and economic liberty.

Recent historians of the secession crisis have argued that upcountry farmers in South Carolina and Alabama reluctantly answered the call for resistance. Plain folk ignored fire-eaters' rhetoric, but their distaste for encroaching modernization and the taxation necessary to bring internal improvements to the Hill Country propelled them endorse secession as a method of maintaining independence at home.[52] In Mississippi the situation was different. Although Hill Country resentment of planter domination of the Mississippi Democratic party fueled the Chickasaw Rebellion and Fontaine's bid for governor, most residents appreciated Democratic party rule; taxes remained low, and after the disastrous experience with banking in the 1830s, state politicians denied responsibility for sponsoring internal improvements. After 1855, though, yeoman farmers demanded that the web of the market economy be extended through railroad construction. Unlike their contemporaries in Alabama and South Carolina, they believed (in the contradictory language of the social ethic) that railroads signaled economic independence since they provided access to markets. However falsely, they viewed railroads as another sign of their autonomy, and the more independence Mississippians believed themselves to possess, the more willing they were to sever their ties with the Union.[53]

Between 1850 and 1857 the variety of independence promised by railroads seemed imminent as the state chartered no less than seventeen railroads, many of them trunk lines. With railroad fever spreading more rapidly than the secessionist impulse, Mississippi, in the decade of the 1850s and into the early 1860s, placed hundreds of miles of track into operation. The Mobile and Ohio; the New Orleans, Jackson, and Great Northern; the Mississippi Central; the Mississippi and Tennessee; and the Vicksburg and Montgomery railroads completed their construction before 1861, but none

52. Ford, *Origins of Southern Radicalism,* 337; J. Mills Thornton III, *Politics and Power in a Slave Society: Alabama, 1800–1860* (Baton Rouge, 1978), 426–42.

53. On the need for greater economic independence, see A Mississippi Planter, "Production and Manufacture of Cotton," *De Bow's Review,* VIII (1850), 99; J. M. Wesson to J. F. H. Claiborne, August 11, 1858, in Claiborne Papers, MDAH. On the necessity of railroad development before secession, see the Vicksburg *Weekly Whig,* October 16, 1850; Vicksburg *Daily Whig,* July 3, 1858; Jackson *Mississippian and State Gazette,* December 12, 1851, June 11, 1852, June 30, 1857; Jackson *Mississippian,* May 26, June 9, 15, July 21, 1858, July 13, October 12, 19, 1859.

received financial aid from the state. Responsibility for funding railroad construction passed to individuals and the companies themselves, for state law prohibited governmental entities from investing in private enterprises.[54] Such restrictions failed to dissuade Mississippians from anticipating railroads connecting them to distant markets or from wishing for broader power to attract lines to their communities. The editor of the Brandon *Herald* believed the people of south Mississippi willing to pay higher taxes to construct the Gulf and Ship Island line, and in 1852 residents at a mass meeting in Tishomingo County expressed discontent with the state's reluctance to grant the Memphis and Charleston Railroad right-of-way through their county. The refusal, they said, was an affront to "equality in the State and the rights of her citizens under the compact of government." Denying them a railroad threatened their economic liberty, and they beseeched the state for the right to tax themselves, promising that if the legislature neglected their wishes they would withhold contributions to state coffers.[55]

Even as the urgent sectional crisis of 1860 began to take shape, news of railroad development challenged political news for prominence in Mississippi newspapers, but the juxtaposing of railroad and secession news should not surprise. The southern social ethic, after all, required that free men submit to neither political nor economic slavery, and railroads represented access to markets and thus to liberty. Southerners understood the connection between railroad construction and regional economic independence. They also believed that railroads, by extending the market economy into places previously isolated from it, instilled in white residents a deeper affection for the social ethic and the white cultural homogeneity it bred. As one contributor to a states' rights newspaper argued, investment in railroads served to "concentrate wealth at home" and to "diffuse among the masses a higher degree of comfort, intelligence and independence."[56] States' righters were

54. Records of the railroad charters may be found in various volumes of legislative session laws published annually. Only the Gulf and Ship Island, which was not completed until the 1890s, received money from the state's 3 percent fund; see *Laws of the State of Mississippi,* 1857, p. 38. On interest in railroading, see Charles Ripley Johnson, "Railroad Legislation and Building in Mississippi, 1830–1840," *Journal of Mississippi History,* IV (1942), 195–206.

55. Quoting Jackson *Mississippian and State Gazette,* March 26, 1852; the Brandon *Herald* quoted in Jackson *Mississippian and State Gazette,* October 19, 1859, but see also January 9, 1852, and Vicksburg *Weekly Whig,* October 22, 1851. Not everyone was so ebullient about the advent of railroading in Mississippi. Daniel Kelly complained that railroads drained specie from his community; see Daniel Kelly to James Kelly, September 20, 1856, in Kelly Papers.

56. Quoting Jackson *Mississippian and State Gazette,* March 11, 1853. *Journal of the*

not alone in embracing such rhetoric. Even the Unionist-dominated 1851 convention passed a resolution favorable to economic diversification and the establishment of railroads in preparation for secession. Railroads, so the argument went, strengthened the South's economic independence by opening direct lines of trade with southeastern port cities. Mississippi cotton could be shipped to Liverpool via rail connections with New Orleans, Mobile, and Charleston, and producers could shun northern markets altogether. In a letter to Andrew Johnson, B. B. Trousdale, a Corinth Unionist, noted that his neighbors associated the protection of their political liberty with the safeguarding of their economic liberty. They thought that once the South asserted its political freedom from abolitionism, economic prosperity through increased cotton production and direct links to markets would occur.[57]

Because of such associations the appearance of railroads in Mississippi quickened the drift toward secession by fostering confidence in regional and individual independence. Such false expectations infused southerners' faith in cotton and the market economy as key to their economic independence. By the mid-1850s, with railroads traversing the state, Mississippians believed a new day of economic independence had dawned for them. Yet as more and more farmers fell into the web of the market economy, the variety of economic and political independence that they longed to obtain became increasingly elusive. Becoming participants in a modernizing economy voided all claims to the independence that supposedly belonged to farmers who produced for home consumption and the market.

As sectional tension worsened, every imagined depredation against the social ethic provoked a fresh round of secessionist rhetoric. Insightful residents feared for the diminution of liberty. Daniel Kelly, after witnessing citizens in Mobile and Clarke County exile so-called "abolitionists" from their communities, doubted that southern concepts of liberty could survive the tensions of the secession crisis: "I am afraid the time is close at

---

Convention of the State of Mississippi, 18. See, too, Percy Lee Rainwater, *Mississippi: Storm Center of Secession, 1856–1861* (Baton Rouge, 1938), 84, 85, 90.

57. Despite Trousdale's distaste for secession, he embraced the social ethic: "This government was made by white men, and for white men[.] [T]he negro had no part or lot in making it, and the Constitution left the Negro where GOD placed him in a subordinate condition." See B. B. Trousdale to Andrew Johnson, December 17, 1860, in Leroy P. Graf and Ralph W. Haskins, eds., *The Papers of Andrew Johnson, 1858–1860* (Knoxville, 1972), III, 690.

hand, when *Sweet Liberty* will be *bruised* & *mangled,* if not *murdered* & *buried.*" Likewise, Matthew Lyon feared that "a galling and iron despotism was riveted upon the necks of the people" during the secession crisis, as they lost the capacity to so much as utter their distaste for the final act.[58] By 1861, lacking a vibrant political discourse, Mississippians had but one response to forces that threatened to rend the fabric of their social ethic. In order to protect their peculiar versions of economic and political liberty, versions which celebrated dependence on the market economy and black enslavement, Mississippians in January, 1861, severed their relationship with the free states.

With the unchallenged rhetoric of resistance ingrained in southern political culture, secession was inevitable by late 1860. Politicians with Whiggish tendencies continued to mount a feeble opposition to resistance, but after Lincoln's election, the secessionist impulse proved invincible. Even conservatives like A. M. West, a railroad entrepreneur and Unionist, thought the election of a Republican president provocation enough to justify seeking "separate protection and safety." In a similar statement Lucius Quintus Cincinnatus Lamar surmised that Lincoln's election was the first signal that a black and "red republicanism" emanating from the Republican party threatened to subsume the South in the "moral revolution" of abolition. As both sections came to identify protection of their unique social ethics with the success of sectional political parties, the fate of the Union hinged on the outcome of the presidential election. The success that the Democratic party had (in the words of a Pontotoc convention) in making the Republican party "co-eval with the existence of this government" made Mississippians willing to vote for the secession candidate for president, John Breckinridge, in large numbers. The party's success in making its Republican rival the source of all venality made resistance to secession impossible when results of the election became known.[59]

58. Quoting Daniel Kelly to James C. Kelly, September 20, 1856, in Kelly Papers; James A. Lyon Journal, MS in MDAH, 100. John McRae to Simeon R. Adams, February 3, 1858, in Adams Papers, confirmed that adherence to the Democratic party line on all issues of sectional importance was tantamount to the protection of peculiar southern rights.

59. Quoting the Vicksburg *Weekly Whig,* April 11, 1860; *Letter of Lucius Q. C. Lamar in Reply to Honorable P. F. Liddell of Carollton, Mississippi* (N.p., n.d.), 6; Jackson *Weekly Mississippian,* June 13, 1860. Vote totals are available in W. Dean Burnham's *Presidential Ballots, 1836–1892* (Baltimore, 1955), 552–70. For a map of the returns, see Ranck, *Albert Gallatin Brown,* following 200. On opposition to Breckinridge, see R. G. W. Jewell to Stephen Douglas, December 10, 1860; Citizens of Marshall County to Douglas, September 4, 1860; Citizens of Eureka to Douglas, March 10, 1860; Citizens of Central Academy to Douglas, March 10, 1860, all in Stephen A. Douglas Papers, Special Collections, Uni-

Historians have posited a variety of reasons for secession: fear, abolitionism, economic concerns, firebrand politicians. But the Democratic party's resourceful depiction of itself as the sole protector of the southern social ethic perhaps most influenced the decision.[60] For a season, sentiments like those enunciated by C. D. Fontaine held sway. Concerned that no states' righter would step forward to lead the region out of the Union, Fontaine grew distracted: "I greatly fear that the spirit of resistance will be forever quenched, and the flame of Liberty smoulder out in the ashes of base submission." In fact, by the time Fontaine stated his fears, most southerners, deprived of an alternative method of defending the social ethic, could only submit to the despotism of the Democratic party. Dumbfounded by their own paralysis, sensitive southerners knew not what to do. In despair Daniel Kelly wrote: "I hardly know what to say. Civil war is one of the last resorts; the very thought of it is awful & revolting. To submit & become vassals to negrodom is equally so." Yet Kelly was unable to envision another course of action. He could only pray "may God save us from ourselves."[61]

---

versity of Chicago. On the response to Lincoln's election and the erection of "anti-submission poles," see Darden Diaries, December 7, 1860 (in Darden Papers). Gonzales, "Henry Stuart Foote," 137; Jackson *Weekly Mississippian,* December 12, 1860. On the Mississippi Secession Convention, see *Journal of the State Convention, and Ordinances and Resolutions Adopted January 1861, with an Appendix* (Jackson, 1861), 14–15.

60. For an interpretation of secession in Mississippi that emphasizes the role of class conflict and internal pressures, see William L. Barney, *The Secessionist Impulse: Alabama and Mississippi in 1860* (Princeton, 1974), 267–316.

61. Quoting C. D. Fontaine to John J. Pettus, November 12, 1860, in RG 27, MDAH; Daniel Kelly to Ann Kelly, December 3, 1860; Kelly to John N. Kelly, January 1, 1861, all in Kelly Papers. See, too, John Aughey's account of a Unionist's life in Mississippi and the willingness with which his fellows submitted to Democratic party rhetoric: *The Iron Furnace: Or, Slavery and Secession* (Philadelphia, 1863), 5–6, 50.

Part II

The Agencies of Change

There are men who by their sentiments belong to the past and by their ideas to the future. They have a difficult time discovering their place in the present.

—Louis de Bonald

Early in the summer of 1860 Flavellus Nicholson, a bachelor farmer in Noxubee County, watched helplessly but dispassionately as drought withered his crops in the field. Freshets in August arrived too late to nourish his cotton and corn but coincided with the presidential election campaign, interfering with his participation. The floods also hindered his courtship of a young lady. When the rains ceased, Nicholson resumed his activities. He attended a Breckinridge rally and afterwards a "storm party." "Politics is all the go," he enthusiastically commented.[1] The politics of resistance and winning the attention of his female friend occupied more of his time than did anxiety over his crops. Concern that secession might precipitate destruction of the social ethic evaded him as well.

Flush with anticipation of a call to arms, Nicholson believed that on November 6, 1860, he cast his first and final ballot in a U.S. presidential election. A states' rights partisan, he voted for Breckinridge. His choices, after all, were limited: neither Douglas and his "Squatter Sovereignty men" nor John Bell and his "Union Shriekers" nor Lincoln, "the detestable candidate of the foul mouthed Republicans," appealed to him. After the election Nicholson knew his duty. As a lieutenant in the Quitman Light Infantry, he prepared to defend the southern social ethic against the repugnant forces of abolitionism. Patriotic southerners like himself had "determined never to be the slaves of Northern despots, though the assertion & maintenance of their rights should cost them rivers of blood." To Nicholson the war would be a crusade for rights: "Our all depends upon the issues of this great struggle."[2]

1. Flavellus G. Nicholson Diary-Journal, June 13, August 25, 28, 31, 1860, MDAH.
2. *Ibid.*, November 6, December 10, 1860, n.d., 1861.

Four years later, his fever for crusades cooled by the rigors of war, Nicholson nevertheless proved reluctant to concede defeat and attempted to reestablish the antebellum social ethic on his farm. He found freed people uncooperative though. Slowly, the meaning of emancipation sank in: the South had gambled its all in 1861 and lost. Such knowledge offered scant comfort, for in addition to having lost command of his supposed inferiors Nicholson had lost as well his financial wherewithal. No longer able to play the role of a dashing young blood in attendance at a grand soiree, he counted among his "worldly possessions . . . a wife and three children, a little household furniture, and a few mules & horses. Miserum me!" Throughout 1865 and 1866 Nicholson grew ever more embittered, especially toward freed people and farming. He concluded that working his land with free labor would be "neither pleasant nor profitable" and that farming in general was "a most awful bore without any profit." In a more pensive moment he wondered what had been gained by "this terrible war." [3]

For Nicholson and other white southerners, emancipation forever altered their vision of a good republic. Where once the dream of asserting their independence through ownership of a cotton plantation and one hundred slaves fostered a broad-based sense of white cultural homogeneity, the mere presence of free blacks disturbed their understanding of the social order. Some, like Nicholson, bid farewell to Mississippi and farming. Disgusted with his prospects and unwilling to hire "uppity" freed people on their own terms, Nicholson removed to Mobile where he opened a garden supply business in 1868. Two years later he returned to Noxubee County, where he worked as a store clerk before starting his own general store in 1871. His fortune began to change with the death of his father-in-law, T. W. C. Wingate, a substantial planter, who left his estate to Nicholson's wife. Suddenly he felt "better able to cope with the stern realities of life" and used his wife's inheritance to expand his mercantile business. He also began renting land to tenants. His journey from a man of standing in the antebellum order to a man of standing in the New South was complete. More importantly, his attitude underwent a transformation. In 1889, boasting that his children held important positions as railroad agents and store clerks, Nicholson bestowed upon them the highest praise known to citizens of the New South: "My sons are all doing finely—making money." [4] However important the defense of the southern social ethic had been in motivating Mississippi to secede, sustaining antebellum concepts of a good re-

3. *Ibid.*, July 16, 24, 1865, August 10, 23, December 3, 1866.

4. *Ibid.*, December 16, 1875, and August 9, 1889, but see, too, December 3, 1866, January 24, July 3, 1868, June 26, 1870, November 24, 1871.

public, as Nicholson discovered, proved difficult in the years after 1861. The exigencies of war and Reconstruction, as well as the advent of a New South, altered the social order and consequently society's assumptions about the nature of good citizenship and a good republic.

The transformation of society began during the war when the Confederacy and the state of Mississippi imposed policies that citizens had formerly regarded as contrary to the promotion of their liberty. Conscription, impressment, and the granting of special privileges to a few citizens aroused among folk a sense of class-consciousness that the broad commitment to slavery and political and economic liberty had largely submerged. Emancipation contributed further to the demise of white cultural homogeneity by bestowing upon African Americans the title "citizen." Even though white Mississippians retained their unbridled hatred for blacks and fervently wished to return to the days when slavery formed the backbone of the social ethic, the best they could hope for was an uneasy peace with the new order introduced by free labor.

Toward the establishment of that peace, white Mississippians nominally accepted the dictates of the federal government, while employing at the same time legal and extralegal initiatives (political violence, sharecropping arrangements, and the crop-lien law) to ensure that ex-slaves would not, in fact, obtain the virtue necessary to mark liberty as their possession. Economic and political oppression denied ex-slaves the full benefits of citizenship, and they struggled throughout the postwar period to secure their autonomy. Their efforts met with defeat, however, as adversaries installed a version of the antebellum social ethic that relegated them to underclass status. With the social ethic imperiled by war and Reconstruction, leading men moved the postbellum South toward accepting new concepts of a good republic and into the commercial order of the late-nineteenth-century United States. Like Nicholson, they discarded old values and defined liberty and virtue in a manner contrary to prewar southerners: the pursuit of material success through industry, railroading, and store ownership supplanted in importance self-sufficient farming. Yet like their antebellum predecessors, the makers of the New South refused to admit blacks as autonomous players in the new order, causing both familiar and recently embraced values to commingle in the postbellum period. In the process southerners created a political culture that was founded in the commercial order and the racial underpinnings of the antebellum ethic; they fostered the development of a South that was neither thoroughly of the New South nor of the Old.

CHAPTER 4

"THE DISTRESSING INFLUENCE OF WAR"

After the fall of Vicksburg, the hope and ebullience that had led Mississippians to embark upon a war to defend the social ethic devolved into despondency. The war, particularly the Vicksburg siege and its aftermath, caused more profound suffering than most white Mississippians were willing to withstand. Provisions were scarce and prices high; the Confederacy made extraordinary demands on citizens' time and their purses; cavalry units from both sides pillaged at will. Economically and spiritually broken, Mississippians suffered under what H. M. Call labeled "the distressing influence of war."[1] By July, 1863, defeat seemed imminent, and white residents ceased wishing for victory and prayed instead for a speedy return to normalcy. The achievement of normalcy, however, at least when defined as the reinstatement of the social ethic unchanged, was not possible, another of the distressing influences of war.

Throughout both halves of the war to defend white liberty—the labor of war and the post-emancipation war against free labor—the southern social ethic confronted trials destined to alter it. Pristine notions of the social ethic, which had played a prominent role in catapulting the state toward secession, passed into obscurity as the tide of the war turned against the South. When the Confederate states adopted policies of conscription and impressment and created institutions previously deemed inimical to concepts of liberty and virtue, visions of a homogeneous social order seemed sadly irrelevant; notions of the good republic as the protector of political

1. Quoting H. M. Call to "Sister," July 5, 1863, in J. R. Rust Papers, SHC. On the Vicksburg siege and the impression it made on Mississippians, see Willis Herbert Claiborne Diary, April 3, 17, July 14, 1863 (MS in Claiborne Papers), SHC; O. S. Holland to Mahalia Roach, June 8, 1863; Holland to Roach, June 23, 1863, all in Roach and Eggleston Family Papers. Only the fall of New Orleans affected Mississippians more than Vicksburg. See Annie Laurie Broidrick, "A Recollection of Thirty Years Ago," Typescript in SHC, 12.

and economic liberty appeared far removed from reality. Contrary to Mississippians' wishes, the close of hostilities failed to restore normalcy. Wartime conditions (violence, inflation, anxiety) persisted even after 1865, and emancipation further eroded whites' concepts of a good republic. They nevertheless doggedly pursued the restoration of their social ethic during Reconstruction. The introduction of sharecropping arrangements, labor contracts, and the crop-lien law represented efforts to reestablish white liberty and virtue based on the political, social, and economic isolation of African Americans. The necessity of installing these devices of subjugation testified to the newness of the social order fomented by war and Reconstruction.

If white Mississippians had known that their social ethic would encounter the tests that it faced between 1861 and 1877, they might have temporized and reconsidered the wisdom of secession. While farseeing southerners understood that secession likely meant war, few believed that war might mean defeat. Had they wished, however, they might have foretold disaster by observing the devastating results of the drought that struck the eastern half of the state in 1860. Yet extensive crop failures augured disaster to few Mississippians, who believed that they could preserve their social ethic. Such thinking proved to be wishful at best. For the lean season promised by the drought preceded, in William Faulkner's phrase, "the four years fallow." A near decade-long period of adjustment to free labor followed the war. Only a handful of residents, among them William S. Yerger, who designated the ordinance of secession "An Ordinance for the Abolition of Slavery and the Desolation of the South," had premonitions of failure. Judging from commentary contained in their diaries and correspondence, most white Mississippians allowed the days leading up to the firing on Fort Sumter to pass without significant notice. James F. Maury, a student at the state university at Oxford, found his studies and day-to-day concerns more engaging than the prospect of a war. Just weeks before echoes of cannon fire rolled up the Ashley and Cooper rivers, Maury had other things on his mind: "Employed myself killing rats and reading Hume."[2]

Not all Mississippians remained as unconcerned as Maury about the events of 1860 and 1861. Some raised serious questions about the state's ability to keep anarchy at bay once it stepped outside the Union. Other pensive souls conveyed uncertainty about the meaning of secession: the Union-

2. Quoting Faulkner, *Absalom, Absalom!* 161. Yerger quoted in J. T. Trowbridge, *A Picture of the Desolated States: And the Work of Restoration, 1865–1868* (Hartford, 1868), 373. James F. Maury Diary, March 29, 1861, SHC.

ist B. L. C. Wailes believed the election of Jefferson Davis as president of the Confederacy assured an amicable separation from the Union; as late as February, 1861, Susan Sillers Darden, the wife of a staunch secessionist, thought of Lincoln as the president of an undivided nation. But as hope for peace dissipated in the spring of 1861, apprehension grew. According to William Need, a former Mississippian living in the Arizona Territory, secession ensured war and an end to southern commerce and slavery, an ironic circumstance considering that the South precipitated the war to preserve the social ethic. "The people of the Cotton States are insane; great prosperity has made them mad!" he contended.[3]

Most Mississippians sanguinely accepted the consequences of secession. Some, once war seemed inevitable, faced the conflict with alacrity. Onetime Know-Nothing candidate for governor Charles D. Fontaine looked forward to the coming conflict and longed to welcome invading armies with "bloody hands & hospitable graves." Under the influence of a similar enthusiasm, the bishop of the Episcopal Diocese of Mississippi, William Green, decreed that "Confederate States of America" be substituted for "United States" in his parishioners' prayers, and he added to his church's litany a prayer of his own creation seeking a blessing for the southern cause. Zeal for the war ran higher than foreboding or disinterest. Mississippians, young and old, male and female, rushed to defend their liberty and the social ethic: males joined the state militia, home guard units, and vigilance committees; and females formed clubs to darn socks and sew colorful uniforms for their hometown warriors.[4]

As ardor for war mounted, volunteers inundated the ranks of the recently reformed state militia. Prior to 1858 the state had compelled all white males to serve in the militia, but in the wake of the Mexican War, reformers, including Governor Albert G. Brown, heralded the creation of a voluntary militia as a triumph of efficiency, liberty, and patriotism. The much-discussed reformation proceeded slowly. Only in 1860 did the legislature firmly implement voluntary service, authorizing in May the formation of two brigades. Recruitment lagged until Lincoln's election, after which, according to Adjutant General Walter L. Sykes, seven or eight companies

3. Quoting William Need to John J. McRae, February 8, 1861, in John J. McRae Papers, MDAH; Wailes Diaries, February 11, 1861; Darden Diaries, July 10, 1861 (in Darden Papers).

4. Quoting C. D. Fontaine to Sally Ann Fontaine, January 13, 1861, in Fontaine Papers, MDAH; unattached MS, April 24, 1861, in William M. Green Papers, MDAH. See, too, Darden Diaries, July 10, 1861 (in Darden Papers); Cordelia Scales to Loulie Irby, May 18, 1862, in Cordelia Lewis Scales Letters, Typescript in SHC.

enrolled per week. All together eighty-one companies formed before 1861. Wisely, Governor John Pettus refused to accept into state service most of the newly formed companies, citing as his reason a lack of ordnance and provisions. The financial burden of supporting the troops promised to overwhelm the state treasury, as well as the communities called upon to feed them. Pettus' apprehensions about asking a barely self-sufficient and inefficiently armed state to feed and outfit its militia were well founded, as the South's industrial capabilities, especially the products of its munitions manufactures, were minuscule.[5] Supplying the Confederate army proved to be one of the most troublesome tasks of the war, a task unaffected by unbridled enthusiasm.

Despite Pettus' reluctance to accept into the militia all troops that applied, scores of aspiring soldiers formed companies in early 1861 but found no outlet for their martial designs. Before either side had fired a shot, Mississippi troops, many armed only with flintlocks and supported by their officers and private subscription, languished in camps awaiting orders or waiting to be enrolled by the militia. By the spring of 1861 a paltry fifteen hundred Mississippians had been sent to the East. Discontent with camp life spread through the ranks. Eager to enter the fray, bored with inactivity in camp, and suddenly concerned that a drawn-out conflict would keep them from tending their crops, soldiers complained that Governor Pettus accepted into the militia only units led by his political favorites. Soldiers already enrolled in the militia petitioned Pettus to release them from state service or assign them to fighting units. But the governor remained unmoved by all appeals until hostilities began in April, 1861. He then ordered the militia to enroll all companies offering their services. Within one month two hundred companies signed on, forcing Pettus again to stop receiving volunteers, an act which in turn provoked disgruntled citizens into joining the Confederate army instead.[6]

The patriotic fervor of 1861 would be impossible to sustain as the dis-

5. Dunbar Rowland, *Military History of Mississippi, 1803–1898* (1908; rpr. Spartanburg, 1978), 34–35. Bettersworth, *Confederate Mississippi*, 26–28. On the absence of arms in Mississippi and Pettus' refusal to purchase any from a northern firm, see Wailes Diaries, March 29, 1860. On the organization of troops and democratic election of officers, see J. Hardeman Stuart to Annie Elizabeth Stuart, June 6, 1861, in Dimitry Papers. On Pettus, see Robert W. Dubay, *John Jones Pettus, Mississippi Fire-Eater: His Life and Times, 1813–1867* (Jackson, 1975), 95–99.

6. For complaints against Pettus and appeals to be accepted into the state service, see W. C. Falkner to John Pettus, December 28, 1860; J. W. M. Harris to Pettus, May 1, 1861; R. M. F. Lowry to Pettus, May 3, 1861, all in RG 27, MDAH. Bettersworth, *Confederate Mississippi*, 27–28; Rowland, *Military History of Mississippi*, 39.

tressing influences of war diminished the enthusiasm that had led men to enlist in large numbers. Where once the state had been slow to satisfy patriots eager to fight, it eventually proved unable to locate and retain soldiers, much less to rally the support of the civilian population. The brutality of the war and the advancement of governmental policies previously regarded as antagonistic to southern concepts of liberty and virtue prompted the withdrawal of support. In a war to secure liberty, it was ironic that such measures were necessary. Through the inequitable application of conscription and impressment laws and the granting of military exemptions and other special privileges to the planter class, the Confederate and Mississippi governments withdrew their support for egalitarian notions of service and economic opportunity, prompting many citizens to complain that governments asked them to fight a war for the pecuniary benefit of the few.

The appearance of a wartime class consciousness owed to the perception of inequitable sacrifice and to long-standing tensions inherent in the social ethic that surfaced under the strains of war. Reconciling their concepts of liberty with authority had never come easily to southerners, since liberty traditionally belonged to white men if they repelled governmental intrusion into their lives and their communities. Furthermore, the social ethic required that liberty-lovers subscribe to the judgment of the brotherhood of southern white men. Deviations from acceptable behavior were punished. During the war, competing notions of a good republic developed when ordinary citizens accused rebel governments of catering to wealthy men. Even though the war had begun to preserve liberty, it soon became apparent that the war promised to alter antebellum notions of liberty and virtue.

The first indication that the war might harm the cause of liberty appeared on the local level. Vigilance committees, adjuncts of slave night patrols, enforced upon civilians a rigorous code of conduct and conformity. One Winston County committee arrested a local resident for being an "abolitionist." The committee based its judgment on the fact that the farmer had returned a slave to his mother-in-law because he believed the African American imperiled his daughter's moral development. A Lowndes County committee arrested Reverend John Aughey for his opposition to the war and jailed him with a group of deserters, spies, and native guides for the Union calvary. Aughey's son, who attempted to run for the legislature on a platform of peace and reconstruction (but found no one willing to print ballots), landed beside his father in jail. James Lyon, another Lowndes County minister, likewise felt pressured to embrace the southern cause, though he avoided imprisonment. According to Lyon, wicked people in the late 1850s and early 1860s snatched away "the liberties of the people." Moral poverty, or "a fear to speak their opinions[,] their actually giving utterance to opinions & feelings, the exact contrary of what they entertain and feel," resulted. When Lyon treated his congregation to a sermon laced with such sentiments, several members angrily stomped from the church.[7] In the early years of the war citizens condoned the activities of vigilance committees as necessary for the war effort, but when the Confederacy and Mississippi adopted policies to keep order at home and armies in the field, they decried the action as noxious to individual liberties. Although previously willing to make dissenters victims of an iron despotism, the majority of Mississippians turned against policies designed to enforce allegiance to the cause when those policies emanated from outside the community. Opponents of conscription, impressment, and the exemption from military service of large slaveholders bristled at the thought of ordinary citizens sacrificing proportionately more than those rich enough to receive exemptions or to pay someone to serve in their place.

While people like Samuel Agnew believed conscription imperative to raise an adequate army, few in the state vigorously championed the policy. Most regarded it as did Major James C. Rogers. Conscription was, he said, "a fatal blow at our independence," the antipode of the social ethic being defended. Complaints against the policy poured into the governor's office soon after the Confederacy passed it in April, 1862, but in light of the threat of retribution against dissenters, many correspondents refused to sign their names to letters sent to Jackson. One such anonymous letter writer labeled the policy an unconstitutional usurpation of individual liberty. The governor, he said, could "form no earthly idea how much distress & suffering our citizens are subjected to by it." According to him the people would in their own due time agree to serve, "but we do not want [to be compelled] & expect our Governor to arrest the inaugural of Military despotism, tyranny, & oppression." Citizens also complained that local medical boards, charged with classifying conscripts, exempted favorites. In 1864 H. W. Walter reported that 72 percent of conscripts at Brookhaven, generally men with political influence, received medical exemptions. Additionally, he said, 302 of the 537 actually approved for service in the last five months of 1864 deserted before leaving the state. Confusion over who could be drafted led to violent confrontations between Confederate representatives and civilians. In order to prevent healthy males from escaping their duty and vet-

7. Quoting James A. Lyon Journal, February 28, 1862, undated, p. 100; Aughey, *The Iron Furnace*, 50–60, 80.

erans from being conscripted, one of the governor's correspondents proposed that males be branded on the forehead as eligible for service or not. Doubts about the Confederacy's ability to maintain egalitarian concepts of service surged when it amended the conscription law to exempt from military duty planters and overseers with twenty slaves or more under their charge.[8]

Conscription, though moderately successful in raising an army, fostered resentment, and impressment heightened the feeling shared by many white Mississippians that the Confederacy looked exclusively upon ordinary farmers as a source of supplies and manpower. Planters too complained about impressment of slaves and farm implements, but the loudest voice of resistance belonged to small producers who excoriated the government for legalizing the army's plundering ways. Passage of the law accelerated the rate at which Confederate forces appropriated supplies, livestock, and foodstuffs from folk in the countryside. Some sweeps by cavalry units left entire neighborhoods with bare cupboards and stock lots. In the northern part of the state, impressment officers and Union raiders competed for horses and mules, and formerly loyal protectors of the social ethic found it difficult to distinguish between those who destroyed and who protected their liberty.[9] With impressment and draft exemptions in place, small landholders with little means and without labor to spare thought of themselves as bearing most of the burden of war. To their minds the war to secure liberty came to be one to limit personal independence for the sake of preserving the wealth and status of the planter class.

Planters disagreed with the idea that they benefited from the war, for since Lincoln's election they had suffered the consequences of the sectional crisis as surely as had others. By the end of 1860 New Orleans commission houses, anticipating bloodshed and a blockade of southern ports, cut off planters' credit and refused to receive cotton, an action that drove great

8. Quoting Major James C. Rogers to Charles Clark, March 23, 1863; "A Citizen" to John Clark, October 5, 1863, all in RG 27, MDAH. On conscription in Mississippi, see Bettersworth, *Confederate Mississippi,* 64–75, 197–98, 229. See also James Garner to Charles Clark, March 12, 1863, in RG 27, MDAH. U.S. War Department, *The War of the Rebellion: A Compilation of the Official Records of the Union and Confederate Armies* (130 vols.; Washington, D.C., 1880–1901), Ser. I, Vol. III, p. 976, hereinafter cited as *OR.* Unless otherwise indicated, all citations are to Series I. See also, H. L. McKenzie to Duncan McLaurin, September 2, 1863, in McLaurin Papers.

9. Petition of "Planters of Richland, Holmes County" to Charles Clark, March 23, 1863, in RG 27, MDAH; Agnew Diary, February 8, 1864. See, too, Cordelia Scales to Loulie Irby, October 29, 1862, in Scales Letters. On criticism of impressment, see Bettersworth, *Confederate Mississippi,* 81–83.

cotton producers to the point of distraction. An Adams County planter worth no less than $150,000 believed himself "ruined and poor" by the close of the market. His behavior became so erratic that family members carted him off to a lunatic asylum. The diminution of business in the western counties of the state quickly spread east. As early as January, 1861, reports abounded that currency (specie and paper money) ceased to circulate in substantial amounts. Merchants closed their shops, befuddled planters held their cotton, and ordinary business transactions came to a sudden stop. Before closing his dry goods store, Thomas Webber of Bahalia fired a parting shot at the Confederacy illustrative of the general response to the economic decline: "I am confounded. I am ruined. My Country is ruined. Would to God I had never been born."[10]

In order to address the economic collapse brought about by secession, the state assumed powers and granted privileges that antebellum Democrats had rejected as antagonistic to individual liberty. Hoping to invent a medium of exchange and to take advantage of the South's dominant position in the international cotton market, the legislature approved a number of financial bills. None achieved lasting results, but their passage testified to citizens' willingness to forsake momentarily their former prejudices if they believed doing so might preserve the social ethic.

The first of the financial acts passed authorized the state to make loans to cotton planters. The legislature intended that the twenty-year 8-percent bonds paid planters for their cotton would circulate as currency. They never did. Believing that they could weather the financial storm by living off their accumulated assets, planters hoarded the bonds or, as the war progressed, sold them to speculators. Addressing its previous failure to create a circulating medium in the cash-poor state, the legislature passed a second measure, the Cotton Loan Act, in December, 1861, which pledged Mississippi's faith behind $5 million of treasury notes. Issued in denominations from $1 to $100, the legislature effectively gave cotton cultivators advances on their 1860–1861 crop. As envisioned by the state, agents would assess a farmer's baled crop and award the notes based on a maximum price of five cents per pound. The state thus became the owner

10. Quoting Thomas E. Webber Diary, February 28, 1861, WRP. On the negligible influence of the financial collapse upon war enthusiasm, see W. C. Smedes to Stephen A. Douglas, December 10, 1860, in Douglas Papers. See, too, William Leon Coker, "Cotton and Faith: A Social and Political View of Mississippi Wartime Finance, 1861–1865" (Ph.D. dissertation, University of Oklahoma, 1973), 109; Tryphena Fox to "Dear Mother," December 16, 1860, in Tryphena Holder Fox Collection, MDAH; December 16, 1860, in Tryphena Holder Fox Collection, MDAH; Samuel Coleman to William T. Walthall, December 31, 1860, in William T. Walthall Papers, MDAH.

of the cotton, and the producer possessed a currency with which to conduct business. Furthermore, the law required that farmers withhold their cotton from the market until the state called for it. Like the previous attempt to provide a currency, the notes never circulated at par value: one contemporary claimed that the established exchange rate for specie exceeded 2:1. Circulating among a host of currencies issued by other states, the Confederate government, and municipalities, state notes seemed hardly appealing, especially since Mississippi's previous retraction of its financial backing cast an air of suspicion over the wartime pledge.[11]

In still another way the state reclaimed prerogatives it had earlier rejected. Despite the overwhelming antibank sentiment that prevailed in the late antebellum period, Mississippi in 1861 granted a number of banks, railroad companies, and insurance firms the privilege of issuing notes. Stock in the corporations could be purchased with bales of cotton, which the state valued at $125 each, roughly three cents per pound. Curiously, their incorporation by a legislature previously committed to the elimination of special privileges raised few eyebrows. But neither did the new institutions add significant amounts of paper currency to the economy.[12] As surely as recovery from the depression of the 1840s required more than the elimination of financial institutions and state debts, so too did the economic crisis triggered by the Civil War. The key to recovery during both economic calamities hinged on the cotton market, and the wartime market would not recover until after 1865.

Nevertheless, cotton continued to function in the southern economy as a linchpin, albeit a linchpin without strength. As long as Mississippians remained ebullient about victory, cotton planters subscribed to the state a portion of their crops. When battlefield losses multiplied, however, volunteerism among the civilian population vanished. By 1863 most had been reduced to poverty; few residents possessed currency, and those who did held it. To conduct the war the state needed to raise revenue, but legislative efforts to tax a population cut off from the cotton market and without currency garnered the wrath of independent-minded citizens. Unlike currency legislation the collection of taxes became a point of contention in Mississippi. During the January, 1861, Secession Convention, James Z. George and Samuel J. Gholson proposed a progressive tax structure that levied particularly high taxes on the state's most valuable property, slaves. The convention, afraid that planters would reexamine their support for secession,

11. Coker, "Cotton and Faith," 71, 87–88, 94, 138–46; Bettersworth, *Confederate Mississippi,* 93, 98, 102–103; Wailes Diaries, July 4, 1862.

12. Bettersworth, *Confederate Mississippi,* 111.

instead increased taxes across the board, including the tax on slaves, by 50 percent. Nervous about nonslaveholders interpreting the tax structure as regressive, the convention levied an additional tax of twenty cents per one hundred dollars in slave property and instituted a tax of .3 percent on all money controlled, deposited, and loaned, safely submerging class tensions at the start of the war.[13] Within two years the desire to foster white homogeneity, which had led the convention to pursue a golden mean in its taxation policies, fell victim to the war and an entropic tax base.

Until 1863 the state taxed citizens lightly and issued a variety of stay laws prohibiting the collection of private debts until twelve months after the end of the war. Despite the state's attempts to offset higher taxes with policies intended to suggest collateral and egalitarian sacrifice, Union penetration of Confederate lines exacerbated revenue collecting operations and forced Mississippi to discard the fiction that all suffered under the same economic burden. A new law in 1863 levied a direct tax of 8 percent on all property, a graduated license tax, a capital gains tax, and a tax in kind on agricultural produce. For most farmers the latter measure seemed a cruel denial of wartime reality.[14] Exposed to an invading army and southern outlaws, surrendering a portion of their produce left little for home consumption. Citizens greeted the tax in kind as a confession that the state regarded dimly its duty of preserving antebellum concepts of liberty.

With the cotton economy in declension and secondary markets retrenched, the tax in kind aggravated farmers' financial difficulties. Currency, despite the creation of a circulating medium, remained scarce, and the blockade of southern ports kept most cotton from finding a market. In an economy only marginally self-sufficient at best, the combination of inflation, food shortages, and war sank the state into a barter economy. Already reeling from shortages attributable to the drought, residents in eastern and southern Mississippi first felt the pains of war in their stomachs and their pocketbooks. Lacking the necessaries of life, a group of residents from Rankin, Simpson, and Smith counties wrote Governor Pettus that even those who would normally aid the destitute could not. Duncan McKenzie lamented the omnipresence of the poor in his community and cried out, "Great God,

13. Darden Diaries, July 26, 1861 (in Darden Papers); Bettersworth, *Confederate Mississippi*, 93–95; Coker, "Cotton and Faith," 67–71; Charles Hillman Brough, "History of Taxation in Mississippi," Mississippi Historical Society *Publications*, II (1899), 118–20.

14. Coker, "Cotton and Faith," 156; Agnew Diary, February 2, 1865. Although the state taxed citizens lightly, local governments levied steep new taxes. Sunflower County, for instance, charged a local property tax that was twice the state rate. See the report of the Sunflower County Board of Police, October Term, 1861, in Lafayette P. Yerger Papers, MDAH. On the tax-in-kind, see Bettersworth, *Confederate Mississippi*, 124–25.

Uncle, what an age we live in." His Piney Woods neighbors, who planted row crops and sent timber and livestock to New Orleans and Mobile, suffered from a want of bread and cash. Prices cited in diaries and correspondence, however impressionistic, bear out the severity of the hard times experienced during the war. Barrels of pork ranged in price from $25 to $30 cash, and the credit price easily topped $35. Wheat in the first year of the war reportedly doubled to $5 per bushel, and flour went to $55 in some quarters. Corn sold at upwards of $3 a bushel, more than twice its prewar price; a bushel of weevil-eaten ears, according to one report, cost $1. By 1862 the price paid for salt, the chief ingredient used to preserve meats, hovered around $24 a bushel.[15]

Soldiers at the front knew firsthand what food shortages meant to them, and from correspondence, they knew that their children at home often went without. In the antebellum period the measure of independent citizens had been their ability to subsist and to produce for the market. But between 1861 and 1865, state tax policies, the destruction of local markets, and the removal of white males from farms precluded maintenance of ideal notions of economic liberty and virtue. Faced with depleted larders and empty pocketbooks, citizens believed that they had surrendered their liberty and virtue, if only temporarily, for the greater good of society. In return they expected the state to care for them. As construed during the war, liberty and virtue not only inhered in those who worked under the antebellum paradigm, but also in those who sacrificed their livelihoods and future prospects in order to secure the social ethic. In June, 1863, citizens at Benton expressed the idea that, as crusaders for the cause of liberty and virtue, they deserved to receive a supply of food. If the state, they told Governor Pettus, failed to fulfill its patriotic duty to feed citizens, victory would be impossible. "It is very hard for a soldier to remain at his post or to do his full duty, when he knows his wife and children at home are starving," they reminded him.[16]

Others too put aside their misgivings about an intrusive state government and forwarded to Pettus creative plans to distribute food to hungry citizens. One writer from Lauderdale County, noting that the 1860 drought

15. Reports of wartime prices may be found in the following collections: Darden Diaries, July 4, 1861 (in Darden Papers); Sally Ann Fontaine to C. D. Fontaine, September 16, 1862, in Fontaine Papers; Duncan McKenzie to Duncan McLaurin, July 5, 1862, in McLaurin Papers. On salt, see Agnew Diary, November 12, 1862; Wailes Diaries, August 29, October 1, 1862; E. H. Anderson to Eugene Hilgard, August 4, 1862, in Eugene W. Hilgard Papers, MDAH; Ella Lonn, *Salt as a Factor in the Confederacy* (University, Ala., 1965), 54–89; Bettersworth, *Confederate Mississippi,* 153–56.

16. Petition of the Destitute in Rankin, Simpson, Smith Counties, August 18, 1862, but see also Phil H. Gully to John Pettus, March 11, 1863, all in RG 27, MDAH.

had thinned herds of beef cattle so badly that farmers completely ignored their nearly starved stock, argued that the state should confiscate and redistribute cattle among civilians outside the stricken region. According to his plan, the state could pay to feed the cattle, distribute healthy stock to soldiers, and sell beef on the hoof to civilians. His contention that the state had to assume responsibility for feeding citizens represented a new concept of liberty that permitted governmental intrusion into citizens' lives, as long as the state acted at citizens' request and declined to force upon them a particular policy. The shortcomings of his plan became painfully obvious when the state actually attempted to redistribute agricultural produce through the tax in kind. Opponents of forced redistribution knew what Pettus' correspondent failed to concede: the antebellum emphasis on market production complicated the provisioning of a society under the distressing influence of war.[17] Much to the regret of ordinary folk at home, the state, even though it did not bolt at granting privileges to banks and cotton planters, failed to care adequately for the keepers of the social ethic at the front and at home.

Like foodstuffs, finished goods (clothes and shoes primarily) also were coveted before war's end. According to historian John Bettersworth, Mississippi "entered the Civil War a greatly undernourished infant," dependent upon others for manufactured goods, and it inefficiently supplied citizens during the war. Only four major textile factories, including the state penitentiary mill, operated before 1861. While manufacturing establishments turned out $6.5 million in products in 1859, the production of lumber, meal, and flour constituted almost 50 percent of the value of manufactured goods; the lumber industry alone employed almost 25 percent of persons working in manufacturing facilities and accounted for one-quarter of the value of finished goods manufactured. At the start of the war industrial production diminished to a trickle as manpower previously employed in factories joined the military. Production plummeted as well because facilities became targets for Union cavalry and because workers, many of whom went unpaid and hungry, refused to labor long under wartime conditions. Workers at the Mississippi Manufacturing Company at Bankston struck and rioted for wages in 1864. After they threatened to burn down the factory, plant managers invited a cavalry unit attached to General Nathan B. Forrest's command to sweep through Choctaw County arresting rebel-

17. The plan for redistributing cattle can be found in "A Planter" to John Pettus, September 29, 1862, in RG 27, MDAH. For other plans to redistribute wealth, see W. W. McLendon to Pettus, March 12, 1863; James Rives to Pettus, March 26, 1863; William Delay to Charles Clark, November 28, 1863, all in RG 27, MDAH.

lious workers as army deserters. Forrest's action ended the riots for a time, but he embittered the labor force. Several months later, when Union cavalry rode through the area, workers stood aside while troops burned the factory. Manufacturing facilities at Woodville, Jackson, and Columbus (including a large munitions factory that had been removed from Memphis at the latter) likewise fell to Union raiders.[18] Besides destroying cotton and manufacturing facilities, Union troops paid special attention to the destruction of Mississippi's railroad lines. A northern soldier assigned to destroy portions of the Mobile and Ohio and the Mississippi Central railroads boasted that the Union army made "a moral impression on the Citizens of Mississippi." Reflecting on his unit's success, he correctly surmised that residents would "never forget our visit for several generations to come." As if the destruction of railroads by Union soldiers was not enough, Confederate troops laid railroads to waste to block Union armies, and civilians, dissatisfied with Confederate policies and shortages, took part in the destruction, too.[19]

The destruction of Mississippi's scant productive capacity made an impression on contemporaries and led some to begin their own small manufacturing operations. Samuel Agnew, a Presbyterian minister, recognized the need for medical supplies in the army and set out sixteen hundred poppy plants from which to make opium; his father began tinkering in a blacksmith shop and invented an unidentified "new implement of warfare." Besides medical and military materials, ordinary items, like wooden water buckets and cloth, became scarce. Agnew complained that without a bucket school children under his command had to drink stream water filled with "wiggletails." Cotton cloth, even the plain white sheeting manufactured in southern textile mills, was rare, and, according to one report, the cost of a yard exceeded five dollars in early 1862, a price that would eventually be considered low. Because of exorbitant cloth prices, homespun fashions came in vogue. Yet the wartime price of cotton cards (hand-held implements used to strip cotton into fibers) rose from thirty to sixty-five dollars a pair, making the effort to dress one's family a costly one. Farm families in northeast Mississippi wove cloth in their homes and bartered the finished product for foodstuffs. Unlike the penitentiary mill at Jackson, which implemented a

18. Bettersworth, *Confederate Mississippi,* 67–68. On labor unrest at Mississippi Mills and other locations, see J. M. Wesson to Charles Clark, March 26, 1864; Alex Vintress to Clark, February 6, 1864, all in RG 27, MDAH; Agnew Diary, February 25, March 6, 1862.

19. Quoting [?] to "Dear Professor," March 7, 1864, in U.S. Army, Officers and Soldiers Miscellany, MDAH. For accounts of actions by disgruntled civilians, see Agnew Diary, June 23, 28, 1862, March 31, 1863.

system of out work during the war, the farm families contracted directly with cotton producers and sold their wares on the open market. Other entrepreneurs attempted to meet wartime demand for shoes. Seeking to cash in on the high prices commanded by homemade footwear (reportedly eight dollars a pair), Duncan McKenzie purchased from a local herdsman raw sides of leather and engaged an expert to tan the hides.[20] Although most Mississippians realized by 1860 that the southern economy needed industries, they undertook few efforts to establish factories. The demands of the cotton economy and the long antebellum depression retarded development of a diversified, industrial economy, as did notions of the government's role in facilitating improvements. Wartime manufacturing ventures reflected desperate attempts to rescue the southern economy, not a deep-seated commitment to industrialization. Cotton, despite the harsh realities of war, remained the deity to which Mississippians paid homage.

For planters like James L. Alcorn, a dramatic game of hide and seek commenced with the war. At first he hid cotton from zealous Confederates intent on burning it in support of the voluntary program to remove cotton from the market, and later he hid it from Union cavalry. By 1863, as Union forces appeared regularly in the countryside, the state officially adopted a policy of burning cotton, angering the one group of citizens it had previously kept more or less content: planters. Typical of the planter response to enforced withdrawal of cotton, B. L. C. Wailes thought the policy "an act of supreme folly and wantonness, and totally inexcusable." Faced with torch-bearing armies North and South, cotton cultivators nevertheless tried to market their crops. After Memphis fell to the Union army in 1862, north Mississippians especially, despite threats from their patriotic neighbors, traded there. Some, like Simon Spight, exchanged cotton for perishable and rare items, which they sold to their neighbors at exorbitant prices. Spight, for example, sold baking soda for three dollars a box, plugs of tobacco for one dollar, and brandy for five dollars per quart. Although those who traded with Union-held cities had to swear never again to aid the Confederacy in word or deed, few seemed bothered by renouncing their former allegiance. Matthew Dunn, a Confederate soldier, however, anguished over the decision to sell cotton against government orders. "I don't know whether it is

20. Agnew Diary, March 13, 22, 1862, May 12, June 1, October 30, 1863. Duncan McKenzie to Duncan McLaurin, January 28, 1863, in McLaurin Papers. On a scheme to produce salt for the government, see Grafton Baker to Charles Clark, June 21, 1863, in RG 27, MDAH. On the penitentiary factory during the war, see Ledger of Accounts, Mississippi Mills Collection, MDAH. On a leatherworks in southwestern Mississippi, see William A. Stone Diary, January 7, 12, February 2, 24, 1863 (MS in William A. Stone Papers), MDAH.

right or not" to trade with the enemy, he told his wife.[21] For others, feeding their families with the goods that cotton brought concerned them more than allegiance to a dying cause. Whatever rewards line-runners believed awaited them, crossing between Union and Confederate territory for the purpose of trading was a dangerous occupation. Legally, as Martha Cragan learned when she attempted to exchange cotton for salt and cotton cards, trading with the North was prohibited: Confederate troops confiscated her cotton and her team of horses. Seeking recourse through Governor Clark, she received instead a rebuke for breaking the law, though he promised to locate her team.[22]

Despite the general ban on the cotton trade, large planters and brigands had more luck getting their surplus to market than Cragan. In 1863 Governor Clark even signed a contract permitting John M. Syler to transport his cotton, at state expense, across Confederate lines so that he might purchase two thousand pairs of cotton and wool cards at twenty dollars each. The number of such contracts multiplied when the western counties of Mississippi fell under Union control, placing planters in closer proximity to the market. At the same time, unauthorized trade with the enemy increased: at Woodville, an English-born merchant, Mrs. Betty Beaumont, functioned as a factor for contraband goods, a business at which both Union and Confederate troops winked; on the coast, which fell quickly to Union forces, lumbermen shipped tar, pitch, planks, and charcoal unmolested to Union-held New Orleans; organized bands of cattle rustlers, despite the summary executions carried out by vigilance committees, also took advantage of the contraband trade with New Orleans, driving entire herds through Confederate lines.[23] Like the state's efforts to curtail trade with the enemy, local efforts to stymie illegal trade met with uneven success.

21. Quoting Wailes Diaries, June 14, 1862; Matthew A. Dunn to Virginia Dunn, September 5, 1863, in Matthew A. Dunn Family Papers, MDAH. On prices, see James L. Alcorn to Amelia, December 18, 1862, in James Lusk Alcorn and Family Papers, SHC; Agnew Diary, June 7, December 11, 27, 1862, January 1, May 3, 1863. On a soldier's struggle to provide for his family from afar, see Sidney Champion to Matilda Champion, September 13, 1864, in Sidney Champion Papers, WRP.

22. Martha Cragan to Charles Clark, November 28, 1863; Clark to Cragan, December 6, 1863, all in RG 27, MDAH.

23. See unattached contract between Syler and Clark in Box 56, RG 27, MDAH. On a similar arrangement, see J. T. Smylie to Charles Clark, December 21, 1863; F. R. Tinly to Clark, February 1, 1864, all in RG 27, MDAH. Mrs. B[etty]. Beaumont, *Twelve Years of My Life: An Autobiography* (Philadelphia, 1887), 213, 218, 242–53. On wartime cattle rustling in the Piney Woods, see Baxter, "Cattle Raising," 17–19. On trade through the lines, see Bettersworth, *Confederate Mississippi,* 174–87.

Forced to sacrifice to the southern cause their liberty in exchange for suffering, Mississippians' distaste for the war grew as Confederate policies and Union armies exacted their toll. According to a Union officer, Confederate policies had made many citizens in northern Mississippi "unwilling supporters of the rebellion." Besides common thievery, which became the habit of many who faced starvation, resisting Confederate officials became as popular an activity as fighting invading armies had been. The most celebrated case of resistance to the southern war effort occurred in Jones County, where Newton Knight, a former Confederate orderly, assembled a force of disgruntled neighbors to defend themselves against conscription and impressment. Confronting empty smokehouses and frequent cavalry raids, Knight's army of deserters and draft dodgers robbed stores and individuals in Jones County. They fought pitched battles with elements of the Louisiana cavalry in Jasper and Covington counties, too. Similar vagabond armies in the North-Central Hills, particularly in Leake County, protected their young men from conscription officers and opened trade routes. Outbreaks of lawlessness and massive resistance to Confederate policies broke out in the swamps and canebrakes around Natchez as well as those near Utica, where numerous brigands and resisters resided.[24]

The historian John Bettersworth has contended that resistance to the Confederacy in the Piney Woods represented an expression of backcountry onerousness, and in part, he is correct. But, in fact, as former Governor John J. McRae learned when trying to raise a company in south Mississippi, many Piney Woodsmen expressed dismay when asked to leave their homes undefended. Isolated small farmers around the state knew little of the world outside their immediate vicinity and saw no need in fighting a far-away enemy if doing so meant leaving their homes unprotected.[25] Their reluctance to fight on distant battlefields notwithstanding, they perceived Lincoln's election as a threat to their cherished liberty, but once the war be-

24. Quoting John J. Mudd to Lt. Col. John A. Rawlins, in *OR*, Vol. 17, Pt. 1, p. 514. See, too, W. H. Handy to Charles Clark, February 8, 1864; R. S. Hudson to Clark, June 13, 1864, all in RG 27, MDAH. On the Knights of Jones County, see Thomas Knight, "Intimate Sketch of Activities of Newton Knight and the 'Free State of Jones County'" (Typescript in Thomas Knight Papers), LSU, 2–4, and Thomas Knight, "Thomas J. Knight's Story of His Father, Newton Knight" (in Knight Papers), LSU, 2–3, 6–7, 12, 33, 62. On similar bands of deserters and looters, see H. Hunt to Virginia Dunn, April 3, 1865, in Dunn Family Papers; G. W. Mims to Charles Clark, June 8, 1863, in RG 27, MDAH; James Worthington, "Antebellum Slaveholding Aristocracy of Washington County," in *Memoirs of Henry Tillinghast Ireys*, eds. McCain and Capers, 350–65.

25. Bettersworth, *Confederate Mississippi*, 213–45; John J. McRae to Earl Van Dorn, June 28, 1862; McRae to W. P. Chellar, May 21, 1861, all in McRae Papers.

came a destroyer of liberty, they set out to kill the monster. Privileged exemptions from military service granted planters and the perceived unfair burden of support carried by moderate and small landholders turned the very advocates of revolution against the war. The former unity of the white South unraveled as small farmers felt pressed to fight a war they suddenly believed they had been duped into supporting, a war that crushed egalitarian access to markets and political power.

Matthew Dunn, a soldier who served in east central Mississippi, understood the resentment that moved his fellow citizens to resist the war. As part of his soldiering duties, Dunn arrested draft dodgers, one of whom "gritted his teeth at me & asked if I dared to treat him so." As Dunn ascertained, the tide of support that had earlier flowed in favor of the South began to turn in direct proportion to the sacrifices governments demanded citizens and soldiers to make and to the rise in casualty figures. Whispered talk of desertion and even Reconstruction passed through army encampments. Desertions became widespread, and neither rough treatment accorded deserters nor executions stemmed the exodus; such treatment, in fact, turned more citizens against the war. After noting the execution of three deserters, Dunn confessed that "this war is calculated to harden the softest heart." [26] Realizing that victory eluded them and that the price of continuing the fight would be heavy, many Mississippians chose not to allow their hearts to be hardened further. In the last months of the war, some soldiers switched sides and enlisted in the victorious army.

The Civil War exposed the incongruence between antebellum ideals and reality. When faced with a choice of adopting policies to protect the economic liberty of small farmers or that of large planters, the state chose the latter by granting special access to markets and exemptions from military service. As the slaveholders' war became a poor man's fight, there erupted a war within the war led by yeoman farmers and nonslaveholders who accused their wealthy neighbors of callously disregarding their rights within the established political culture. But despite dissatisfaction with the conduct of the war, Mississippians remained averse to surrendering their social ethic, especially their allegiance to notions of the black underclass as a precursor for white liberty. To heal the social divisions occasioned by the war and to return pristine concepts of liberty and virtue to prominence, white Mississippians' primary occupation in the immediate postwar period became the assertion of control over black labor.

* * *

26. Quoting Matthew A. Dunn to Virginia Dunn, April 19, 1864, September 5, 1863, but see, too, Dunn to Dunn, October 12, November 7, October 13, 1863, all in Dunn Family Papers.

In 1865 the state lay in ashes. Solitary chimneys were all that remained in parts of Jackson; pockmarked streets and buildings at Vicksburg testified that a battle had taken place there; forests around Corinth had been leveled. Even small towns like Okolona fell victim to the torch. In the interior of the state, weeds flourished where cotton had once grown; fences and farmhouses sagged after four years without maintenance. Surveying the damage done to her son's plantation, Susan Darden lamented, "Oh, this cruel, cruel war—what ruin it has brought upon us!" More significant even than the physical destruction of the state were the deaths of thousands of residents. No adequate statistics establish the number of Mississippians who died during the war, but the toll on human life certainly exceeded the most gloomy prewar prediction. Wounded participants offered telling evidence of the brutality of the war: according to historian Alfred Garner, Mississippi appropriated 25 percent of its 1866 budget to purchase artificial limbs for veterans. Civilian casualties of the war, black and white, as well as soldiers, filled makeshift cemeteries throughout the countryside. Outside of Vicksburg, Isaac Shoemaker, a northern plantation owner, observed that mass graves, dug shallow and with haste, emitted "an exceeding offensive smell—and I saw crows sitting on them attracted by the effluvia."[27]

While white Mississippians faced an awesome task in rebuilding the state and their lives, accepting the reality of emancipation proved to be the greatest obstacle confronting them. For emancipation created a new class of citizens, one that whites regarded as poorly prepared, even unable, to undertake the independent action that characterized possessors of liberty and virtue. White southerners continued to believe that their identity as free men depended upon the existence of African Americans as something less than citizens. Although Congress, through the Fourteenth and Fifteenth amendments, nominally opened the political arena, it demurred at opening the southern economy to freed people. Indeed, the nation as a whole continued to believe that blacks could best serve the commonweal as laborers. For their part, freed people attempted to make a place for them-

27. Quoting Darden Diaries, January 28, 1866 (in Darden Papers); Isaac Shoemaker Diary, February 11, 1864, WRP. See, too, Robert Somers, *The Southern States Since the War, 1870–1871* (1871; rpr. University, Ala., 1965), 142–44; James Wilford Garner, *Reconstruction in Mississippi* (New York, 1901), 122–23. On Natchez after the war as "a sadly desolated district," see J. Floyd King to Lin, January 9, 1866, in Thomas Butler King Papers, SHC. On financial distress caused by the war, see Alden Spooner Forbes Diary, April 27, 1865, Typescript in MDAH.

selves in the social order as heirs of Jacksonian concepts of liberty, virtue, and equality of opportunism.[28]

Historians of the past three decades have pointed out that enslaved African Americans possessed visions of liberty; day-to-day resistance, folktales, and rebellions testified to their desire for freedom. The visitation of war upon the South intensified slaves' longing, and as the war dragged on, the frequency and intensity of resistance increased. A planned rebellion in the southwestern counties in May, 1861, cost the lives of several slaves, and another slave plot, reportedly hatched by German immigrants, was discovered in the summer of 1862. The presence of an invading army in a countryside depopulated by conscription greatly aided and inspired runaways. Throughout the war, but particularly after the fall of Vicksburg, slaves swarmed Union camps, seeking not only liberty but also food and clothing. The entire populations of some plantations left en masse: a Yazoo County resident awoke one morning to find that only her cook remained. Other planters, like John A. Downey of Corinth, fled Mississippi with their slaves to keep them from escaping. Downey started for Texas with fifty-nine slaves but arrived with forty-four, the remainder having stolen away during the journey. Once in Texas he sold fourteen more to profit from them before they too ran off. Reflecting on the wisdom of his immigration and divestment, Downey wished that he had "kept them and whip'd them till they had forgotten they ever heard of a Yankee."[29]

With the long dreamed of liberty as near as the Union army, slaves, according to Samuel Agnew, began to "carry a high head." Attempting to avoid further chastisement, a runaway from Agnew's neighborhood, shot while trying to escape, feigned lunacy. When she professed to be Jesus Christ on the way to Jerusalem, Agnew recognized her condition as a plea for le-

28. On challenges to white notions of liberty presented by emancipation, see James L. Alcorn to Amelia Alcorn, October 17, 1869, in Alcorn Collection, MDAH. On wartime and postbellum social decline, see J. Floyd King to Lin, January 9, 1866, in King Papers. On American attitudes toward free labor, see Gerald David Jaynes, *Branches Without Roots: Genesis of the Black Working Class in the American South, 1862–1882* (New York, 1986), Chapts. 1–3. For a different view of ex-slaves' goals, see John Scott Strickland, "Traditional Culture and Moral Economy: Social and Economic Change in the South Carolina Low Country, 1865–1910," in *The Countryside in the Age of Capitalist Transformation;* eds. Hahn and Prude, 163–68.

29. Darden Diaries, July 3, 1865, May 8, 10, 12, 17, 19, 1861 (in Darden Papers); Wailes Diaries, July 2, 5, 1862; [?] to Annie F. Stuart, August 15, 1863, in Dimitry Papers. John A. Downey to L. D. Burwell, n.d., in Downey Papers. On the rebellion planned for 1861, see Winthrop D. Jordan, *Tumult and Silence at Second Creek: An Inquiry into a Civil War Slave Conspiracy* (Baton Rouge, 1993).

niency, failing to understand the metaphorical meaning of her playacting. With the collapse of the Confederacy, the opportunity to enter that metaphoric Jerusalem seemed to slaves close at hand. Sympathetic northerners, who witnessed the movement of blacks away from their former masters, thought the scene resembled nothing less than a journey of biblical proportions. Isaac Shoemaker, while searching for a Delta plantation, witnessed five thousand freed people (road-weary, ragged, and somewhat despondent) prepare to embark for Davis Bend and an experimental agricultural village established on the peninsula. The caravan reminded him of "the departure of the Isarlites [*sic*] out of Egypt." [30]

Few former slaves benefited from the direct federal assistance offered those freed people bound for Davis Bend, but an estimated one-third left their familiar slave quarters and masters with little more than a few personal items and hope for the future. A missionary who worked with the American Missionary Association commented on the ex-slaves' optimism: "If they were not the most hopeful race in the world, they certainly would sit down in despair or become desperate." Freed people did not sit down. In fact, of the liberties opened to them by emancipation, mobility was the first they chose to experience. Although most mobile freed people who moved off "old massa's" place simply went to a neighboring farm, several Mississippi towns and cities, as well as the Delta in general, attracted ex-slaves. In the years immediately following the war, Vicksburg, Jackson, Natchez, and Columbus experienced substantial increases in their black populations; between 1860 and 1870 the number of blacks living in Vicksburg grew by almost five times, while the black population in the remaining cities nearly doubled. Of the five largest antebellum towns in Mississippi, only Holly Springs near Memphis saw its black population decrease between 1860 and 1870. The promise of fertile land also drew freed people to the Delta. Hill Country freed people, as well as thousands from outside the state, moved into the river counties and the Black Belt, a trend that continued for more than a decade. In 1881 the state commissioner of Immigration and Agriculture estimated that ten to eleven thousand ex-slaves immigrated into the state during the previous four years.[31]

30. Quoting Agnew Diary, October 30, November 1, 2, 1862, but see, too, June 5, 1863; Shoemaker Diary, March 3, 1864. James L. Roark, *Masters Without Slaves: Southern Planters in the Civil War and Reconstruction* (New York, 1977) provides insight into the institution of slavery during the war.

31. Quoting J. D. Bardwell to Reverend Samuel Hunt, November 2, 1867, American Missionary Association Papers, Amistad Research Center, New Orleans, Microfilm. For a discussion of the Davis Bend experiment, see James Tyson Currie, "Vicksburg, 1863–1876: The

Some freed people, enticed by state and private agents, poured into Mississippi, but others, dissatisfied with their lot, left. Samuel Thomas, assistant commissioner of the Bureau of Refugees, Freedmen, and Abandoned Lands calculated that 100,000 blacks fled the state between 1860 and 1865. Because of the well-known flaws in the 1870 census, accurate estimates of black mobility are impossible to obtain, but scattered literary evidence indicates that labor shortages remained an annual feature of plantation life for several years after the war. Perhaps the most celebrated mass exodus from Mississippi occurred in 1879. Following the depression of the 1870s, a yellow fever epidemic, and the political violence of the decade, scores of African Americans moved to Kansas hoping residents in a state that had never seen slavery established within its borders would accept them as equals. Kansas, like other states at the time, appealed to such sentiments by sending agents south and mailing literature to prospective immigrants. In 1879 alone, between 5,000 and 6,000 ex-slaves from Mississippi accepted the invitation to move to Kansas.[32] Even though a promise of free land drew them there under false pretenses, those who left rightly believed the emergent sharecropping and credit arrangements, as well as violence, restricted their liberty as surely as had slavery.

Even as freed people in the late 1860s began to explore their freedom of movement, white Mississippians reacted badly to the introduction of black liberty. In their minds black mobility, the first signal that freed people would actively claim their place as citizens, foretold the eradication of the social ethic. If elevated to the status of yeoman, freed people would subvert white southerners' perception of the importance of having an underclass primarily identified by race and relegated to field labor. Free labor, after all, would not be disposed to work in others' cotton fields. As evinced by the persistence of the language of slavery, native southerners resisted black freedom. Seven years after the end of the war, the politician-planter Jehu Amaziah Orr continued to speak of his labor force as if enslaved: "Mary broke [the] Singletree & ran away." Susan Darden longed for the days of slavery, so

---

Promise and the Reality of Reconstruction on the Mississippi" (Ph.D. dissertation, University of Virginia, 1976), 103–59. Wharton, *The Negro in Mississippi,* 106–17, discusses mobility among freedmen.

32. Samuel Thomas to O. O. Howard, June 27, 1865, in Records of the Assistant Commissioner for the State of Mississippi, Bureau of Refugees, Freedmen, and Abandoned Lands, Reports of the Sub-Commissioners, National Archives, Microfilm reel 1, hereinafter cited as BRFAL (1). Wharton, *The Negro in Mississippi,* 116–17. Eliza R. McNabb to [?], January 28, 1868, in Eliza R. McNabb Letters, Typescript in MDAH; William Storrow Lovell Plantation Journals, March 4, 7, May 24, 1879, SHC; Agnew Diary, January 3, 1880.

that she could "whip" her domestic servants for their slow movement. Such sentiments received sanction from the government in Washington, particularly President Andrew Johnson (who, according to Samuel Agnew, defined liberty as "freedom to work"), by neglecting the cause of free labor. When Johnson vetoed a bill to extend the Freedmen's Bureau, the bugbear of the southern white imagination, he fortified whites' loathing of free labor.[33] For the first two years after the war, a confrontation occurred between landlords, who intended to produce cotton with cheap and beholden labor, and blacks, who refused to submit meekly to slavery under a different name.

Encouraged by the Johnson administration's timidity, and at any rate resistant to approving wholesale changes in the social ethic, a series of reactions to free labor, ranging from violence to legal restrictions on black liberty, took place. Taking a page from George Fitzhugh, paternalists like Agnew justified appeals for limited liberty on their concern for blacks' welfare. Incapable of caring for themselves because of their savagery, devoid of self-interest, and no longer the beneficiaries of white masters' kindly tutelage, Agnew predicted that the condition of freed people would soon resemble that of the northern "hireling," despondent and inefficient. The mutual respect between master and slave that slavery established, as well as laborers' ability to negotiate, would disappear, too. Less paternalistic justifications of restrictions on black independence were heard in postwar Mississippi. Bearing out the importance of the underclass to their concepts of a good republic, yeoman farmers in the days immediately following the war constituted a far more serious threat to freed people's liberty than even the most unrepentant paternalist. For the exigencies of war brought them to a level of poverty that blurred the line between themselves and African Americans, and as Samuel Thomas observed, enmity for blacks increased in direct relationship to whites' own economic status: "The nearer a white man is to the level of negro equality, and intelligence, and social and political standing, the more he hates him." Neither large planters, who needed labor, nor small farmers, who feared that their liberty in society diminished in proportion to the rise of black liberty, intended to make labor entirely free.[34]

33. Quoting Jehu Amaziah Orr Journal, July 11, 1872 (in Orr Papers), SHC; Agnew Diary, May 8, 1865, but, see, too, May 24, 29, 1865. On whites' interpretation of free labor during Johnson's administration, see R. S. Donaldson to Lt. Stuart Eldridge, October 4, 1865, BRFAL (9).

34. George Fitzhugh, *Sociology for the South: Or the Failure of Free Society* (Richmond, 1854), 9–14; Agnew Diary, May 27, 29, 1865; Samuel Thomas to O. O. Howard, August 5, 1865, in BRFAL (1); Thomas to J. W. Webber, June 26, 1865, BRFAL (1); James L. Alcorn to Amelia Alcorn, March 22, 1864, in Alcorn Family Papers.

Maintaining control over an underclass deemed inferior by virtue of its skin color and previous condition of servitude demanded that every aspect of laborers' lives be regulated. The state, as well as individual whites, employed various methods to curtail freed people's liberty and to regulate the behavior of whites considered friendly to black liberty. Through several incidents reminiscent of the response to the antebellum Madison County slave uprising scare, native southerners proclaimed that they would, despite emancipation and blacks' legal acquisition of rights, continue to distrust apparent supporters of African-American economic autonomy. Merchants who sold groceries to freed laborers without the consent of landlords, and thus interfered with traditional landlord-labor relations, discovered firsthand the persistence of the impulse that had exiled gamblers and peddlers in 1835; Federal troopers learned that their blue uniforms served as a reminder of their status as outsiders; and former slaves realized that emancipation and their newfound liberty meant nothing to native whites, who when given the chance would try to reestablish customary relations.[35]

In the most celebrated instance of whites reconstituting slavery under a new name, the legislature, in November, 1865, passed the infamous Black Code. Designed to reaffirm the social ethic and to maintain traditional planter-labor relations, the code dealt chiefly with matters of vagrancy and apprenticeships. Although many of the clauses resembled northern laws of the time, the code applied only to African Americans. Black orphans could be bound out to planters for fixed terms of service, as could children neglected by their parents, and former masters obtained the privilege of first securing the services of their once-owned property. Freedom of assembly was restricted: gatherings of African Americans or African Americans and whites might be broken up, and the law defined participants in mixed-race meetings as vagrants, subject to arrest and imprisonment.[36] Although institution of the Black Code owed mainly to white southerners' refusal to embrace black liberty and great cotton planters' corresponding desire to command labor, the laws resembled northern ones that defined the relationship between capital and labor. While the efforts of the federal government to establish equality of the races was admirable and nec-

35. Niles Diary, June 5, 11, 12, 18, 1865; Silas May to Lt. Stuart Eldridge, May 3, 1866, BRFAL (15). On attacks against Union troops and other agencies of the federal government, see Thomas Wood to O. O. Howard, June 15, 1865 [?], BRFAL (2).

36. Wharton, *The Negro in Mississippi,* 82–93. For an example of freedmen's children being seized by former owners, see S. S. Leonard's Assistant Commissioner's Report to Bureau of Refugees, Freedmen, and Abandoned Lands, September 21, 1867, and A. W. Preston to Messrs. Kinson and Bowman, December 22, 1866, all in BRFAL (21).

essary, northern failure to offer viable alternatives to the southern vision of a good republic forestalled revolutionary change in the region.[37]

As an agency of change the Freedmen's Bureau, the most prevalent federal authority in the South, confronted a formidable task. Charged with the disposition of abandoned lands and the care of refugees and freed people, the Bureau was hard pressed to impose free labor on a population half of which despised the notion. Northerners, Republicans and Democrats alike, hamstrung the Bureau by refusing to sponsor a thoroughgoing revolution. When called upon to nullify the Black Code, to eliminate the pass system in Mississippi towns, and to protect freed people from the most egregious depredations they suffered on plantations, the Bureau went about its business admirably. Yet its Mississippi agents, reflecting opinion in Washington, lacked the fortitude to distribute abandoned lands to ex-slaves. Samuel Thomas concluded that dispersing among freed people lands confiscated during the war would require "a hero," and making available land to rent would necessitate a "military force to protect the freedmen during the term of their leases." Disturbing the established social and economic order by placing the bottom rail on top fell outside the realm of federal authority, at least according to the government's frontline agents. Throughout the Bureau's life, the protection of freed people's political liberty occupied its time more than did opening doors of economic opportunity. Perhaps indicative of the Bureau's interpretation of its role in Mississippi, Thomas believed that if permitted to achieve equality under the law freed people would contentedly remain mere laborers. The emphasis on political equality suggested by Thomas confirmed that the Bureau, even if unintentionally, assisted white southerners in their war against free labor.[38]

Convinced that the social order could not sustain free black labor, white southerners attempted in two ways to nullify the meaning of emancipation. First, they schemed to remove freed people from the state, or at least to replace their labor with other ethnic groups. Then, when those efforts failed, they initiated steps to control black labor, primarily through the crop-lien law. Without slavery to testify to blacks' place in society, some whites wished to exile them. One of the most curious plans for doing so circulated among a small group of planters hoping to recover part of their capital invested in slaves by selling freed people to Cuban planters. Justifications for abandoning black labor were numerous, but fears of genetic and social amal-

37. Jaynes, *Branches Without Roots*, 57–74; Wharton, *The Negro in Mississippi*, 82.

38. Samuel Thomas to O. O. Howard, n.d., BRFAL (1). Prices for land during the immediate postbellum period were low. Agnew Diary, June 26, 1867, records prices between $3.35 and $5.50 an acre, about 60 percent less than antebellum prices.

gamation, as well as wholesale race war, made the idea attractive to whites. The belief that ex-slaves preferred not to work in cotton fields influenced their decision to turn against black labor. As John Kemp, Jr., speaking for other planters, plainly put it: "Free niggers wont work in the South."[39]

Most whites, however, realized that the region could not rid itself of African Americans. That knowledge did not keep them from looking to Europe and China for suitable replacements. Imported white labor, some planters believed, would reconstruct the buffer (a "white guard" in J. Floyd King's phrase) between landlords and the black underclass previously provided by the institution of slavery. In 1866 King, the innovative manager of a plantation near Natchez, transported one hundred laborers from Germany, Denmark, and the Low Countries. In exchange for free passage to the United States, each laborer contracted to work for one year. As part of the experiment King planned to use experienced black laborers to pace the Europeans in cotton fields. Within weeks of introducing white labor to his plantation, the experiment floundered. Thirty-five of the immigrants left. Those who stayed proved to be more expensive to maintain than ex-slaves: they ate two-thirds more than black field hands and worked only if driven. Failure of the effort notwithstanding, King refused to admit total defeat. As semiskilled laborers and craftsmen, he believed white laborers more desirable as neighbors than freed people, though still susceptible by virtue of their relationship to property and market production to qualify as an underclass upon whom notions of white liberty might again be erected.[40]

Large landholders also looked, with similar results, to the North and the Far East for labor. Nevertheless, isolated incidences of mass immigration to the state bestowed upon southerners hope for a future of the region without African Americans. D. Wyatt Aiken, a South Carolina planter and publisher, estimated that in 1870 alone fourteen hundred northern labor-

39. Quoting John Kemp, Jr. to William J. Pattison, September 12, 1865, in William J. Pattison Papers, SHC. Some whites wished to see freed people removed from the state out of fear of race war; see John Matthews to Robert Matthews, November 19, 1865; Samuel Matthews to John Matthews, September 19, 1867, in James and Samuel Matthews Letters, MDAH. Other whites apparently tolerated the presence of freedmen only because they doubted that suitable replacements for black labor could be found. See J. P. Bardwell to George Whipple, May 30, 1866, American Missionary Association Papers.

40. Quoting J. Floyd King to "My Beloved Sisters," January 8, 1866, but see, too, King to Mallery, January 18, 1866; King to Lin, January 1, February 9, 1866, all in King Papers. On the greater reliability of African-American labor, see Grenada *Sentinel,* November 29, 1890; Natchez *Daily Courier,* January 5, 1866; Macon *New South,* May 28, September 24, 1881.

ers went to Mississippi via the Mobile and Ohio Railroad; another two thousand went by other means. Like King, Aiken imagined that white labor would replace freed people in cotton fields, though he doubted that northerners, who expressed more interest in owning farms and shops than chopping cotton, would fill the South's need for labor. Ventures designed to bring Chinese laborers from the West Coast and the Far East met with no lasting success either, but Mississippi planters throughout the 1870s sent agents to recruit Chinese workers. Encouraged by rumors that they worked for as little as four dollars a month, planters discovered that, in fact, they demanded higher wages and shorter days than even ex-slaves. Defeated in their plans to import labor, landlords slowly agreed to an uneasy truce with black laborers.[41]

In no small measure the truce stemmed from the entrenchment of sharecropping and the development of the crop-lien law. For through these arrangements landlords received what they had looked for in immigrant and white labor: a responsive and attentive peasantry. Writing in 1870 Alfred Huger, another South Carolina planter, saw promise in the newly established landlord-labor relations. Better even than they had during the antebellum period, African Americans and landlords shared an interest in cotton production. Labor relations had evolved in such a fashion as to create "the best 'peasantry' the South could possibly hope for."[42]

Immediately after emancipation, planters had not been so certain that they could preserve the established relationship with labor so thoroughly. Representatives of the federal government, after all, insisted that they negotiate with laborers for their compensation, which was to include at a minimum food and clothing. According to various reports, freed people, however, preferred to rent, own, or lease land, but few whites intended to grant former slaves that much economic independence. Those who signed such agreements with blacks confronted the scorn of their communities and became subject to prosecution under a state law that prohibited blacks from owning or renting land. In lieu of the independence afforded by ownership and rental agreements, freed people entered into straight wage contracts, which typically stipulated that laborers furnish their own food

41. D. Wyatt Aiken, "Agriculture in Mississippi," *Rural Carolinian,* I (1870), 475–76; Aiken, "Immigration and Labor," *Rural Carolinian,* IV (1873), 292–93. On efforts to attract white northern labor, see John Kirby to H. H. Southworth and W. H. Morgan, March 2, 1870, in Yerger Papers. On Chinese immigration to Mississippi, see Wharton, *The Negro in Mississippi,* 97–105; James W. Loewen, *The Mississippi Chinese: Between Black and White* (Cambridge, Mass., 1971), 21–26, 32–37; Robert Seto Quan and Julian B. Roebuck, *Lotus Among the Magnolias: The Mississippi Chinese* (Jackson, 1982), 4–9.

42. Quoted in an editorial in the *Rural Carolinian,* II (1870), 46.

and clothes; monthly salaries ranged between eight and twenty-six dollars, depending on gender and qualifications. Complaints about the wage system emerged as soon as it appeared. Freed people often complained of low wages. A recently discharged black soldier who sought work at J. Floyd King's plantation refused to sign a contract because he could not hope to live on the salary offered (fifteen dollars a month), particularly if he had to find his own rations. Opportunities to draw substantive salaries were limited and remained so even when demand for labor exceeded supply. Once King outlined to the reluctant freedman his options, starvation or subsistence, he signed a contract. Freed people also complained that landlords cheated them. Not infrequently payment for a year's labor fell due at the close of the cotton-selling season, and the freed person, who had eaten from the landlord's smokehouse for a year, found that he had been charged an exorbitant price for the privilege. For their part, landlords, especially those outside the western counties, disliked the wage system because they lacked cash to pay black labor. They complained as well that when guaranteed a wage laborers lacked incentive to work and believed payment resulted whether they produced one bale or three.[43]

Ex-slaves, notwithstanding their complaints, preferred to receive compensation for their labor in cash, though other aspects of the wage system repulsed them; landlords, facing a dearth of cash preferred another system. With the approval of the Freedmen's Bureau, former masters and ex-slaves negotiated to implement the sharecropping system.[44] Through sharecropping, landlords believed risks were dispersed, and tenants liked sharecropping as an intermediate step toward landownership, since it permitted them a measure of autonomy and broke the back of gang labor that persisted under the wage system. Landlords who contracted with labor on a shares basis stipulated production levels to ensure that compensation re-

43. On whites selling land to freed people, see Samuel T. Nicholson to "My Dear Brother," November 18, 1871, in S. T. Nicholson Papers. On resistance to the idea of selling land to ex-slaves, see Roger L. Ransom and Richard Sutch, "The Ex-Slave in the Post-Bellum South: A Study of the Economic Impact of Racism in a Market Environment," *Journal of Economic History,* XXXIII (1973), 135–37. Agnew Diary, July 31, August 1 and 2, 1865; Mrs. Dixon to Harry St. John Dixon, June 2, 1867, in Dixon Papers, SCH; J. Floyd King to Lin, May 17, 1866, in King Papers; Darden Diaries, August 22, 1865 (in Darden Papers); R. S. Donaldson to Lt. Stuart Eldridge, July 22, 1865, in BRFAL (1).

44. On the emergence of the sharecropping system, see Samuel Thomas to O. O. Howard, June 27, 1865; Thomas to Colonel Mayries, June 22, 1865; Thomas to O. O. Howard, September 14, 1865, all in BRFAL (1). Freedmen, according to Annie E. Harper, untitled MS, 1876, MDAH, 63, preferred sharecropping arrangements because they could raise livestock and feed their families while producing cotton for the market economy.

flected the tenant's work effort, but otherwise share contracts took a variety of forms. Most included clauses requiring kind and humane treatment, demanding tenant loyalty, and setting hours of labor. Some contracts, like the one Ned Littlepage signed with his landlord, W. R. Barth, provided ex-slaves no medical care or provisions. Others, like the one P. C. Harrington signed with thirty-two freed people, offered free medical care, food, clothes, and housing. Harrington, however, contracted to receive 90 percent of his hands' crops, while Barth and Littlepage entered into a more complex arrangement. According to their contract, Barth would receive one-half of the cotton and potatoes that Littlepage harvested and one-third of the corn, fodder, and peas. Littlepage purchased some of his seed and furnished one of the three mules he needed. The contract that James Archer signed with freed people contained elements common to both of the above-mentioned ones. Archer received one-half of the cotton picked and deducted from his tenants' percentage of the crop the cost of their food, clothing, and medicine. Besides dictating what freed people could cultivate, landlords exercised a measure of control over ex-slaves' leisure time, too, stipulating that tenants keep "respectable and orderly houses" and that they "use all energy and industry to make a good crop." To enforce such measures, landlords reserved the right to examine croppers' homes. Curtailing freed people's contact with other laborers and isolating them from political activities motivated C. B. Moody to include in one contract a warning that his tenant's home should not become "a place of common resort for Coloured people."[45]

Aspects of labor control derived from slavery times appeared in sharecropping arrangements, but the system was flexible enough to admit a measure of black liberty. Freed people embraced sharecropping because it offered protection from landlords who reneged on wage payments and allowed

45. All quotes derive from the following contracts: W. R. Barth and Ned Littlepage, BRFAL (49); C. B. Moody and Solomon Monroe, BRFAL (48); Eliza Walker and Freedmen, BRFAL (43); Contract with Freedmen, July 18, 1865, in P. C. Harrington Papers, SHC; "Agreement with Freedmen, 1865," in Archer-Finlay-Moore Collection, MDAH. On sharecropping in general, see Joseph D. Reid, Jr., "Sharecropping in History and Theory," *Agricultural History,* XLIX (1975), 426, 429, 437; Lee J. Alston and Robert Higgs, "Contractual Mix in Southern Agriculture Since the Civil War: Facts, Hypothesis, and Tests," *Journal of Economic History,* XLII (1982), 331, 353; John David Smith, "More than Slaves Less than Freedmen: The 'Share Wages' Labor System During Reconstruction," *Civil War History,* XXVI (1980), 256–66. On sharecropping as a means of labor control, see Ransom and Sutch, "The Ex-Slave in the Post-Bellum South," 131–32; Roger Ransom and Richard Sutch, "The Impact of the Civil War and of Emancipation on Southern Agriculture," *Explorations in Economic History,* XII (1975), 1–10.

them the liberty to set their own work rhythm. Except for ex-slaves who signed contracts with large plantation owners soon after the war, tenants negotiated their contracts individually and could extract from landlords favorable rents. A Washington County planter required that his tenants harvest one bale of cotton per five acres rented, an incredibly small yield per acre that permitted freed people to live under conditions similar to those extolled in the antebellum period. They could produce for the market and home consumption.[46] Under the shares system any cotton raised over the required rental fee belonged to the tenant, who sold it to his or her landlord. These arrangements provided freed people a degree of autonomy unknown under slavery or the wage system, but their lack of capital, which fostered a dependence on landlords or merchants for supplies, made ex-slaves susceptible to accumulating debt, particularly after 1868, when the price of cotton and demand for labor stabilized.

The give-and-take that informed sharecropping arrangements failed to relieve tensions between landlords and labor. D. Wyatt Aiken took offense that after having purportedly free labor imposed upon him he still had to furnish clothing and food just as he had when he owned slaves; the social distance that had separated capital and labor withered under the system, and labor expected to negotiate with him face to face. W. B. Jones, a Panola County planter, believed that sharecropping arrangements encouraged tenants to produce as little cotton as they wished, thus robbing him of the material success that he desired. Jones, who tended to rail against free labor more than most planters, accused freed people of using the sharecropping arrangement to drag whites into poverty. Blacks complained about profiteering on the part of landlords, who paid tenants far less than market price for cotton and other farm produce and charged usurious interest rates for supplies. Immediately after the war, whites and blacks also criticized the operation of plantation stores, especially those owned by northerners, for practicing creative bookkeeping. When leveled by whites, those charges reflected more a hate of northerners than a distaste for unsavory business practices, for as soon as they acquired sufficient cash to open their own plantation supply stores, native southerners began fleecing tenants.[47]

46. Mrs. Dixon to Harry St. John Dixon, January 29, 1870, in Dixon Papers. On variety in contracts and the dispersion of risks, see Joseph D. Reid, Jr., "Sharecropping as an Understandable Market Response: The Post-Bellum South," *Journal of Economic History,* XXXIII (1973), 120–21, 129–30.

47. D. Wyatt Aiken, "Labor Contracts," *Rural Carolinian,* III (1871), 114; W. B. Jones Diary, December 31, 1873 (MS in Jones-Smith Plantation Journal), MDAH; J. Floyd King to Mallery, January 18, 1866, in King Papers; J. D. Bardwell to Reverend Samuel Hunt, No-

Even though the high price paid for cotton between 1865 and 1868 protected most renters from accruing great debts, the collapse of the cotton market afterwards made it nearly impossible for sharecroppers to avoid losing money and with it their liberty. In response to ex-slaves' losses the Freedmen's Bureau did little to help tenants survive the changing cotton market. Boards of arbitration formed by the Bureau initially protected tenants from landlords' most perfidious practices, but eventually the boards came to be dominated by men sympathetic to landlords. Their rulings in cases of contract disputes sanctioned what would later become common practice as they ensured that freed people amassed substantial debts, forcing indebted tenants to contract with the same landlord for the following year in order to retire the debt.[48] While the sharecropping system represented a compromise between labor and landlords, freed people's dependence on others for supplies transformed the arrangement into something approaching debt peonage, especially after the collapse of the cotton market and the passage of the crop-lien law.

In 1867 the state provided a means for entrapping free labor in a dependent relationship: the crop-lien law. Officially known as "An Act for the Encouragement of Agriculture," the necessity for the lien law stemmed from confusion over competing claims to property when tenants defaulted on debts. After the war, when landlords lacked cash to purchase plantation supplies for their renters, they had turned to merchants for credit. In some instances the landlord accepted goods in his own name and charged tenants for the supplies used, as well as a substantial interest rate; in other cases, the landlord directed tenants to particular merchants. Competing claims on a tenant's assets resulted when tenants owed money for supplies and rent to different individuals, and the law was intended to clarify the hierarchy of claims that could be held against a tenant and to define assets that could be held in judgment of debts.[49] Initially lenders and landlords were satisfied with the law, for it granted creditors a primary lien on all of a debtor's crops and movable property, including draft animals, while

vember 2, 1866, American Missionary Association Papers. On the common ideas about labor shared by native southerners and northern immigrants, see Lawrence N. Powell, *New Masters: Northern Planters During the Civil War and Reconstruction* (New Haven, 1980), 133–34.

48. On the use of sharecropping agreements and debt to tie ex-slaves to the land, see B. G. Humphreys to O. O. Howard, October 10, 1867; J. A. Shelby to Allen Almay, December 30, 1867, all in BRFAL (3).

49. Prior to the passage of the law, planters took great pains to protect their rental property from seizure. See the unattached Deed of Conveyance, Robert Wilson Papers, WRP.

exempting real property from seizure. Proceedings for attaching property were simple: six months after a delinquent debt fell due the creditor filed suit in Chancery Court, and the county sheriff then confiscated enough property to cancel the debt.[50]

Under the lien law the compromise between planters and laborers as established by the sharecropping system disappeared as tenants lost the ability to produce crops other than cotton. More than the sharecropping arrangement alone, the crop-lien law placed freed people under the control of moneylenders who demanded that they plant mostly cotton, the only widely marketable, nonperishable crop raised in Mississippi. As a labor control device, the crop-lien law carried significant meaning, and it was not coincidental that the law passed just as Mississippi fell under the directives of Radical Reconstruction. Whites, who had long associated ex-slaves' political activities with decreased productivity, recognized no distinction between African Americans' economic and political liberty and sought to crush the one to offset gains made in the other under the watchful eye of the federal government. The cycle of debt resulting from slavish devotion to cotton became inescapable; it also promised to keep labor behind the plow and out of politics.

The Dixon family of Washington County understood the way in which control over ex-slaves' economic and political liberty guaranteed that blacks remained members of the underclass. In 1869 sharecroppers on the Dixon plantation communicated satisfaction with their labor arrangements. Hands who furnished all their provisions received three-fourths of the crop, and those who furnished one-half received 50 percent. High prices for cotton made the Dixon's tenants prosperous and content. But happiness eluded one resident of the plantation. Mr. Dixon was as dissatisfied with the shares system as he had been paying wages. What Dixon considered the wealth and leisure of the sharecropper's life had transformed a once-industrious labor force into a lazy one more interested in politics than in tending crops. In September, 1869, the tenants from the Dixon plantation (self-professed Loyal Leaguers) paraded in front of Dixon's home on horseback, waving the Union flag and playing "Yankee Doodle." Disgusted by such brazen acts, Dixon entertained thoughts of selling the plantation and moving to California. By the close of the next year, however, Dixon changed his mind. Cotton prices had fallen, and the tenants had lost their enthusiasm for politics. They worked in the fields more diligently than ever.

50. *Laws of the State of Mississippi,* 1867, pp. 567–72. On sharecropping and the operation of the lien law, see Lacy K. Ford, "Rednecks and Merchants: Economic Development and Social Tensions in the South Carolina Upcountry, 1865–1900," *Journal of American History,* LXXI (1984), 309–11.

The sharecroppers, Mrs. Dixon noted, had "passed through the Jews hands & have all come out largely in debt: no cash to buy fine horses & mules as they did last year." The tenants, to the pleasure of the Dixons, had learned that with the crop-lien law in place they were not, as another Mississippian observed, "much benefitted by emancipation."[51]

Sharecroppers confirmed that the lien law acted as an agent for their oppression. Wiley Brewer recalled the pains of saving money under the crop-lien law: "I saved my money and bought me a mule, in about 32 years I bought me a farm." Any dreams of receiving from the government forty acres and a mule dissipated by the close of 1865; any hope of living as free men and women died when African Americans realized that whites intended to keep them in a position of service through measures like the crop-lien law. All that they demanded, as one told a representative of the American Missionary Association, was the same price for their corn and cotton and an opportunity to achieve economic autonomy. Yet he also knew that blacks had no chance of doing so as long as the white South forced them to submit to its definition of free labor as bound to the land and fixed permanently as the mudsill of political culture: "We've no chance—the white people's arms are longer than ours. What we want to do is to lengthen the colored people's arms till they can reach as far as their old masters and stand an equal chance."[52] Bound to the land by contracts and the crop-lien law, freed people could only watch as whites diminished their liberties, economic and political. Nevertheless, a change in the social ethic had been admitted. Freed people, though still an underclass relegated to field work, made a place for themselves in the southern economic order. As players in the economy, they drew the hostility of whites trapped by the crop-lien law and unable to distinguish themselves from freed people.[53]

Through the two halves of the Civil War—the labor of war and the war against free labor—the antebellum social ethic survived, though it was diluted. First, it was diluted during the war itself. The urgency of conducting a war to secure liberty and virtue prompted southerners, particularly state and Confederate governments, to embrace policies that trampled the very ideals for which the war was fought. Conscription, impressment, and the

51. Quoting Mrs. Dixon to Harry St. John Dixon, January 29, 1870, but see, too, Dixon to Dixon, November 5, 1869, January 25, 1870, all in Dixon Papers. Also quoting B. W. Herring to Bettie Herring Wright, October 28, 1868, in Wright and Herring Family Papers, SHC.

52. Quoting Rawick, ed., *The American Slave,* Ser. I, Vol. VI, p. 205. [?] to Reverend G. L. Pike, April 7, 1871, American Missionary Association Papers.

53. For a discussion of white farmers' reaction to the crop-lien law, see Chapter 8.

granting of special privileges to large planters and institutions previously deemed antithetical to southern free men boded ill for the preservation of white homogeneity. During the second half of the war for white liberty, emancipation precipitated a further diminution of the antebellum social ethic. The conversion of formerly enslaved labor into free labor threatened to extinguish the race-conscious underpinnings of the social ethic forever. Surmounting the antagonisms and tensions that the Civil War had unleashed, white southerners united in support of sharecropping arrangements and the crop-lien law to reestablish that African Americans remained primarily an underclass of laborers, a class upon whose inferior status property-owning whites could continue to base their concepts of liberty.

Chapter 5

The Political Culture of Racism

In 1865 Carl Schurz, Republican senator from Missouri, foretold with the accuracy of a Jeremiah white southerners' bad reaction to African-American freedom. Former slave masters and their allies, he predicted, would attempt to narrow, if not to retract forcibly, blacks' gains in the areas of economic and political liberty. Like the southern heirs of Andrew Jackson, whose devotion to liberty he doubted, the senator understood the symbiotic relationship between political and economic liberty. As early as 1865 Schurz recommended that the Senate broaden suffrage in the former Confederate states and then permit the moral suasion of freed people's conscientious political behavior to convert southern whites into friends of black liberty. Reconstruction of the southern mind would proceed slowly, but ex-slaves and the Republican party united in their commitment to equality posed a formidable obstacle to any "oppressive class-legislation and individual persecution" that the southern states might undertake.[1] At once expectant and cynical about whites' ability to reverse their habits of thought, and doubtful, too, of the federal government's jurisdiction over the mind of the white South, Schurz cautioned against pursuing measures to secure African-American liberty halfheartedly: "Nothing renders society more restless than a social revolution half accomplished. It naturally tends to develop logical consequences, but it is limited by adverse agencies which work in another direction; nor can it return to the point from which it started."[2]

True to Schurz's augury, white southerners exhibited no ardor for enlarging their version of a good republic so as to include freed people. Landlords and merchants, and even the Freedmen's Bureau, which sanctioned sharecropping arrangements with their pernicious features, restricted the

1. *Senate Executive Documents*, 39th Cong., 1st Sess., No. 2, pp. 38–39, 42–43.
2. *Ibid.*, 37.

scope of free labor. By 1870 the machinery necessary to stymie one-half of the revolution Schurz advocated had been set in motion as African Americans became virtually shackled to the land. The second part of the revolution called for by northern Republicans, the granting of political equality to freedmen, likewise met with "adverse agencies." For roughly ten years whites endeavored to curtail black political rights in order to ensure cultural homogeneity. In the immediate postwar period, "adverse agencies," as well as "oppressive class legislation and individual persecution," blocked the South's Reconstruction. Through legal and extralegal means, whites refused to brook the elevation of African Americans to citizenship. Their success in suppressing the political voice of blacks and other dissenters inaugurated a long period in which designs to identify and bully an underclass played a prominent role in Mississippi politics. By 1877 freedmen passed from slavery to enfranchisement to de facto disfranchisement, and the South fell under the steel-fisted control of the Democratic party, equally determined in 1882 as it had been in 1860 to rule the South or ruin it. Although race, at least in the abstract, had always informed the conduct of southern politics, exertions to undercut black liberty transformed the political culture of liberty and virtue into the political culture of racism, a political culture that cherished white supremacy and homogeneity more than liberty.

Before the Civil War concluded, white Mississippians understood the meaning of Reconstruction and bristled at the thought of a social, economic, and political revolution. Willis Herbert Claiborne, writing in his diary, voiced the sentiments of southerners for generations to come: "'Reconstruction!' Great God, the very word is pregnant with blasted hopes, blighted prospects, and liberty lost forever; degradation, utter misery, and slavery of the most horrible measure." Implicit in the word "reconstruction" lay a rebuke of the ideals that had urged southerners to leave the Union in 1861. Reconstruction meant to whites defeat on the field of battle and erosion of the social ethic's underpinnings. At Clinton, survivors of a slain rebel, repulsed by the thought of Reconstruction, echoed Claiborne's misgivings when they erected a lasting monument to the lost cause and their foreboding: "CAPT ADDISON HARVEY BORN JUNE 1837 KILLED APRIL 19 1865 Just as the Country's Flag was Furled forever Death saved him the pain of defeat." The pain of defeat (emancipation, occupation, political equality) promised an unwelcome revolution, a revolution that would desecrate, to use Robert Somers' phrase, "life and property, virtue, and honour" in what whites considered the hog wallow of black equality.[3]

3. Claiborne Diary, n.d., 1863 [?] (in Claiborne Papers), SHC; V. S. Naipaul, *A Turn in*

James L. Alcorn, the Unionist turned Confederate general, blinked when he caught a glimpse of the new order that freed people envisioned. At an Episcopal church in Helena, Arkansas, he joined a peaceful congregation of black soldiers, white army officers, and townspeople. More disturbing to him than the racially mixed assemblage, however, were "the black wenches who would flaunt down the aisle with their Balmorals well exposed and turn into any pew where a vacant seat remained regardless of the color that had preceded them." Other native southerners responded in similar ways to displays of black disdain for established social conventions. When the Dixons of Washington County confronted their tenants parading Loyal League colors, they excused the action as the product of African-American insensitivity, but they forgave it not: "I don't think they really meant anything more than to imitate *whitefolks*, but it looked to me very much like 'equality' & was of course very distasteful," Mrs. Dixon commented.[4] Not only did the social ethic demand segregation of the races, concepts of virtue and respectability dictated that blacks, as propertyless laborers, behave as members of the underclass.

Whites sensitive to the changed circumstances of the postbellum era typically justified their obdurate insistence that blacks occupy the bottom rung of society as did a South Carolina planter when speaking to J. T. Trowbridge: "They've always been our owned servants, and we've been used to having them mind us without a word of objection, and we can't bear anything else from them now." But others spoke a plainer language of animosity. In 1873 W. B. Jones, a Mississippi planter, posited that the experiment with African-American freedom had rendered no positive changes in the minds and morals of the intended beneficiaries. Without the forceful hand of white masters to guide them, freed people had devolved into a primitive condition, "the condition of the utmost negro simplicity viz a Buckshot a hungry belly & a stink."[5] Echoing Jones's refrain, Samuel and John Matthews, as well as J. Floyd King, argued that "nature's law" propelled the Teutonic race onward and upward while dictating that blacks languish at "the brute level." Attempts by the federal government to in-

---

the South (New York, 1989), 179; Somers, *The Southern States,* 153. On hatred of the Union and Reconstruction, see southerners' response to Fourth of July celebrations: James McClain [?] to Mary Whitehurst, July 4, 1881, in Whitehurst Papers, MDAH; Ball Diary, July 4, 1887.

4. Quoting James L. Alcorn to Amelia Alcorn, March 22, 1864, in Alcorn Papers; Mrs. Dixon to Harry St. John Dixon, November 5, 1870, in Dixon Papers.

5. Quoting J. T. Trowbridge, *A Picture of the Desolated States,* 291; Jones Diary, January 11, 1872, December 31, 1873 (MS in Jones-Smith Plantation Journal).

stitute equality offended their sense of civilization and propriety, for such efforts precluded the white male ("the real man," in Oscar J. E. Stuart's phrase) from exercising the power that nature bestowed upon him. Struck by the state of postwar affairs, Duncan McKenzie bemoaned his misfortune in having to stand by while "a class of beasts in human shape . . . nurtured and raised in such a way that the lash has become a part of their constitution" grasped political and social rights under government protection. Few white southerners attempted to constrain their feelings about black equality. According to an officer in the Freedmen's Bureau, former slaveowners pointedly told him they preferred hogs to eat ex-slaves "rather than they should lose them" as pliable members of the underclass.[6]

Behind statements of revulsion at African-American liberty lay a longstanding fear: if blacks, purportedly incapable of assuming a place in the social order, gained equal access to markets and to civil and political liberty, the social order itself was doomed. The distinctions that established white cultural homogeneity would wither, dragging yeoman whites into the filth and degradation of the underclass; labor, an honorable pursuit (when conducted by liberty-loving and virtuous men), would become sullied if citizenship were extended to the underclass. But white Mississippians feared too a revolution against the social order sponsored by those engaged in drudgery, including yeoman whites made suddenly indistinguishable from ex-slaves by their poverty. African-American political independence, an illogical and dangerous fallacy under the assumptions of white southerners, not only promised to destroy the social ethic but threatened the laws of nature. In the postbellum period whites' concepts of liberty and virtue still depended upon the presence of an underclass without full access to the market or the electoral process.

Responses to black liberty varied narrowly. Planters, recognizing that they needed freed people's labor to cultivate cotton, rarely reacted violently. Socially acceptable, though equally oppressive, avenues were open to them: armed with the crop-lien law, singly and in league with merchants, they wielded power sufficient to manipulate labor and to deny egalitarian-minded tenants places of employment. Plain whites, however, felt obliged to defend with force their status in the social order. Common knowledge among con-

6. Quoting Samuel Matthews to Robert Matthews, November 19, 1865; John Matthews to Robert Matthews, July 26, 1866, in Matthews Letters; J. Floyd King to Lin, September 8, 1866, in King Papers; Oscar J. E. Stuart to Albert G. Brown, November 4, 1875, in Oscar J. E. Stuart and Family Papers, MDAH; Duncan McKenzie to Duncan McLaurin, February 25, 1867, in McLaurin Papers; James H. Matthews to Major George D. Reynolds, November 27, 1865, in *House Reports,* 39th Cong., 1st Sess., No. 30, Pt. 3, p. 185.

temporaries held that the closer a white man stood to African Americans in matters of economics, the more jealously he defended his tenuous status as a free man. In their uncritical acceptance of that notion, and by refusing to relinquish the racial imperatives of the social ethic, leading Mississippians facilitated and sanctioned the violent behavior of others. During the postbellum period, whites of all classes testified to their anxiety about protecting the social order by engaging in public attacks on "sassy" or "impudent" blacks.[7]

The easy brutality bred in a slave society and exacerbated by wartime deprivations became endemic after 1865. "Sacrifice, suffering, and defeat," the historian George Rable observed, "had rubbed emotions raw" during the war. So too did the prospect of former slaves achieving political liberty agitate whites. Much of the violence that occurred in the immediate postwar period germinated in the fecund soil of war-inspired animosities and shortages. The theft of cotton, corn, and horses continued in postbellum Mississippi as residents, who had come to see the war as a sacrificial slaughter conducted for the salvation of slaveholders, sought to avenge their losses by raiding their neighbors' larders. Persistent lawlessness prompted prominent citizens to call for a revival of night patrols. Ostensibly intended to check brigands of both races, the night patrols, a holdover from slavery, functioned also as a reminder that former masters preferred to circumscribe freed people's liberty rather than to risk a revolution of the underclass. Night patrols also warned white desperadoes that honorable citizens regarded depredations against property as affronts to the social ethic.[8] Just as in the 1830s when Madison County residents employed vigilante justice to inform recently enfranchised yeomen that free men were expected to support the peculiar institution, postwar night patrols thundered through the country with a similar message: crimes against property were the hallmark of unvirtuous men who by their behavior or by birth belonged to the underclass. Treating freedmen like autonomous citizens, whites liked to crow, naturally led to bloody insurrection under the leadership of unscrupulous whites and strong-willed African Americans. Therefore, defenders of the social ethic demanded suppression of lawlessness, whether committed by whites or blacks.[9]

7. For the rough treatment accorded "sassy" freedmen, see Agnew Diary, July 5, 14, 1865, April 16, 1867.

8. George Rable, *But There Was No Peace: The Role of Violence in the Politics of Reconstruction* (Athens, 1984), 3. On calls for night patrols, see R. S. Donaldson to Samuel Thomas, August 22, 1865, BRFAL (1).

9. On Mississippians' fears of a race war, see H. C. Shaw to B. B. Butler, December 27,

Fours years of war failed to diminish white zeal for an underclass that lay at the heart of the social ethic; neither did attempts by African Americans and the federal government to guarantee equality lessen the affection that native whites expressed for it. Between 1865 and 1868 resistance to Reconstruction occurred largely in the legislative arena. During the Constitutional Convention of 1865, the first opportunity that Mississippi had to protect black liberties, defense of the antebellum social order more than directives from Washington determined the state's response to emancipation, black suffrage, and the principle of secession. In the ensuing years white citizens so vigorously checked the scope of Reconstruction and black liberty that their defiance moved the federal government to assume direct responsibility for remaking Mississippi.

Composed largely of old Whigs, the Constitutional Convention of 1865 strove to preserve antebellum ideals without alarming the directors of Reconstruction residing in Washington. Pleasing even one resident of the capital city, however, proved to be burdensome. President Johnson, an undemanding advocate of southern Reconstruction, directed his handpicked provisional governor William Sharkey and the convention to institute only a nominal change in southern values. By granting the suffrage to those who could read the U.S. Constitution, who could write their names, and who owned and paid taxes on real estate valued at $250, he hoped to mollify native southerners and to keep his congressional opponents at bay. Endorsing his suffrage proposal, Johnson believed, would assure Radical Republicans of white acquiescence to a view of the good republic remotely similar to theirs and quell the revolutionary intentions of northern congressmen, but the convention refused to adopt his plan, much less more egalitarian ones, and expressly limited the franchise to white males.[10]

In other matters as well, delegates to the August convention refused to renounce beliefs they had fought to preserve. Although old Whigs dominated the convention, a sufficient number of secessionist Democrats won seats in the body to cause a ruckus over rescinding the secession ordinance, another of the elements required by Johnson to ensure readmission to the Union. James F. Trotter, a secession Democrat on the Committee on Or-

---

1867, in Mrs. Roy Rollins Papers, MDAH: "I fear their [*sic*] will be a war between the negroes and white people in the course of another year, if there is I will fight against them to the last, won't you?"

10. The best account of state politics after the war remains Harris, *Presidential Reconstruction,* especially Chapt. 3. See, too, Andrew Johnson to William Sharkey, August 16, 1865, in RG 27, MDAH. *Laws of the State of Mississippi,* 1866, pp. 21, 26.

dinances and Laws, condemned the wording of a proposed statement forswearing secession. Declaring the ordinance of secession "null and void," he cautioned, invited the prosecution of disunionists as traitors. He preferred that the ordinance be "repealed and abrogated," a distinction that enabled participants in the conflict to avoid criminal indictment. Amos Johnston, a Hinds County Whig and author of the committee's majority report, pressed to declare the ordinance null and void to indicate that the ordinance had never, and did not in 1865, carry the weight of law. After considerable wrangling, the actual resolution decreed the ordinance "null and of no binding force," a slight concession to Trotter.[11]

Similarly, the abolition of slavery, which President Johnson required for readmission to the Union, created dissension. The convention debate owed to delegates' self-deluding hope that Congress would compensate slaveowners for their property losses; the intensity of the debate stemmed from efforts by three old Whigs from Hinds County to aggrandize their personal political power. During the campaign to elect convention delegates, the Hinds politicos, all vying for seats in the convention, quarreled over the nature of abolition. George L. Potter advocated the conditional abolition of slavery, as he expected the Johnson administration to offer some form of compensation if slaveholders asked for it. His leading opponents, Amos Johnston and William Yerger, assumed a commonsense stand on the question of abolition, arguing that abolition would position southerners to proclaim themselves reconstructed without undergoing the evils of a thoroughgoing revolution. Since convention delegates won their seats on an at-large basis, all three men attended the convention, infecting the assembly with their campaign squabbling. In the end Yerger carried the day with an impassioned speech calling for abolition if only to appease Radical Republicans in the North, but Potter altered the wording of the abolition amendment to suggest that slavery had been destroyed by force, not voluntarily. Albert T. Morgan, a Yazoo County carpetbagger, denounced the convention's carefully worded addendum, saying the delegates neglected to surrender their claim to reimbursement and "did not mean to estop their successors from resolving that, after all, slavery had not been destroyed."[12]

11. *Journal of the Proceedings and Debates in the Constitutional Convention of the State of Mississippi, August, 1865* (Jackson, 1865), 33–34, 174–76, hereinafter cited as *Journal of the Proceedings, 1865*. Winbourne M. Drake, "The Mississippi Reconstruction Convention of 1865," *Journal of Mississippi History*, XXI (1959), 244. Harris, *Presidential Reconstruction*, 55–56.

12. Quoting Albert T. Morgan, *Yazoo: Or on the Picket Line of Freedom in the South: A Personal Narrative* (1884; rpr. New York, 1968), 204–205; Harris, *Presidential Recon-*

They intended instead to leave the question of abolition and black freedom in doubt.

Freed people understood the convention's intentions. A group of ex-slaves, meeting at Vicksburg to protest the rewritten constitution, predicted that a Mississippi legislature would soon attempt to enslave blacks again, or at least to remove them from the state.[13] While under the watchful eye of federal authorities, the legislature could not undertake the nefarious action predicted by the Vicksburg freed people, but by November, 1865, barely three months after the adjournment of the constitutional convention, Mississippi's first Reconstruction-era legislature began purposefully to fetter the social and political activities of African Americans. Through their deeds legislatures garnered the wrath of Radicals and assured the start of congressional oversight of Reconstruction.

Before adjourning the Constitutional Convention of 1865 appointed a delegation to instruct the legislature in methods of perpetuating the race-conscious assumptions of the antebellum social ethic. Led by Judge Robert S. Hudson of Yazoo County, the delegation filed a report with the legislature calling upon the state to withhold from freed people "some unbridled privileges for the present." Fear of insurrection, the report said, did not enter into the committee's decision; instead, the moral and intellectual inferiority of ex-slaves motivated the call for restrictions on their liberty. Before blacks could achieve full citizenship, they had to be instructed in the "ultimate good" that accrued to those who were industrious and behaved in a seemly fashion: "The wayward and vicious, idle and dishonest, the lawless and reckless, the wicked and improvident, the vagabond and meddler must be smarted, governed, reformed and guided by higher instincts, minds and morals higher and holier than theirs." In language that evoked the militancy of the early 1860s, the Hudson committee invited legislators who disagreed with the outlined policies to resign their positions and to leave the state. But the delegation found numerous adherents to its declaration of racial hatred, among them the newly elected governor, Benjamin G. Humphreys, who inspired the legislature in his annual message to follow the Hudson Committee's instruction: "The purity and progress of both races require that caste must be maintained."[14] In the initial period

struction, 48–50; Donald H. Breese, "Politics in the Lower South During Presidential Reconstruction, April to November, 1865" (Ph.D. dissertation, University of California, Los Angeles, 1963), 395–96; *Journal of the Proceedings, 1865,* 29–30.

13. Harris, *Presidential Reconstruction,* 50.

14. The Hudson Committee report can be found in the *Mississippi House Journal,* Oc-

of Reconstruction, white Mississippians could not reconcile their ideal notions of society with the prospect of African Americans freely involved in the market economy and politics.

Through the passage of the most significant law to emerge from the 1865 legislative session—the Black Code—white Mississippians demonstrated their stalwart refusal to immerse the sickly southern political culture in the curative waters of Reconstruction. The cornerstone of the postbellum laws known as the Black Code appeared under the innocuous title, "An Act to Confer Civil Rights on Freedmen, and for Other Purposes." As passed in the legislature, the law prohibited ex-slaves from owning or renting property in the countryside, required that black town residents receive certificates from local officials entitling them to live within the corporate limits, and prohibited interracial marriages. Despite omnipresent murmurings in favor of the wholesale exile of blacks from Mississippi, a panacea for desperate men, the Black Code also forbade laborers to void their contracts and stipulated punishment for outsiders who enticed labor from the state. Those provisions encountered no animosity from whites, but granting to freedmen the right to sue and to be sued, as well as the right to testify in court cases, elicited a response from the self-professed unreconstructable.[15] The latter provision, more than any other feature of the code, became a sticking point in the debates over the law and slowed its passage.

Diehard foes of any extension of rights to blacks delayed passage of the Black Code for nearly a month by dominating floor discussions of the measure. Samuel J. Gholson, a leading adversary of the measure, labeled as appeasement legislation designed to put freedmen in the witness chair. He asserted that black testimony heralded the inauguration of true African-American equality. Other members of the legislature, including Senator M. D. L. Stephens, took up the debate, enlarging upon Gholson's rhetoric. Tired of the lengthy fracas and eager to pass some form of the bill, Governor Humphreys persuaded both houses to appease northern firebrands by ignoring offensive sections of the law. At the same time, he inserted provisions intended to placate Mississippi firebrands: freed people had to work or be jailed; they were taxed to support indigents of their own race, and the state militia was reorganized in anticipation of a race war "or

tober Term, 1866, pp. 13–17. Humphreys' annual address is reprinted in *Mississippi Senate Journal*, October Term, 1866, pp. 14–17.

15. Harris, *Presidential Reconstruction*, 128–29; *Laws of the State of Mississippi*, 1865, pp. 82–86.

any possible combination of vicious white men and negroes."[16] For moderate southerners like Humphreys, the abolition of chattel slavery sufficiently established all the liberty that blacks should enjoy. Allowing ex-slaves to bear witness in court was merely a concession to the temper of the age, for it did not fundamentally alter blacks' place in the political culture. They remained confined in the underclass, and thus observed, remained peaceful.

African Americans and their friends correctly interpreted the Black Code as evidence that the region, without guidance, refused to reconstruct itself. The Black Code, according to Samuel Thomas, the chief officer of the Freedmen's Bureau in Mississippi, instituted another form of slavery. It returned freedmen to their old masters "to live and work according to their peculiarly southern ideas." Thomas doubted that freed people would meekly assent if whites continued to view them as less than full citizens. Thomas' subordinate at Magnolia, J. H. Matthews, expressed dismay at passage of the Black Code. Although he had hoped the legislature would permit freedmen "the right to live and to own and accumulate property, . . . the ugly fact stares us in the face, that there is a wide gulf between our anticipations and realizations."[17] The legislative debate over permitting blacks to testify in court, as Thomas argued, proved that southerners still considered former slaves to be brutes ready for exploitation.

Even though some whites so abhorred the thought of blacks in the witness chair that they protested the Code, most rallied in its support. Proponents recognized restrictions on vagrants, apprentices, and miscegenists as means of preserving their political culture. The editor of a Natchez newspaper captured the sentiments of many whites when he proclaimed the legislature "remarkably liberal" in conveying rights to ex-slaves without passing laws repugnant to "the good sense of the community."[18] Like demonstrations of unabashed delight with the Black Code verified the prevalence of belief that the social ethic had been resurrected inviolate. White southerners' reluctance to reconstruct their political culture more thoroughly, however, brought the full weight of the nation to bear against the state as passage of

16. Memphis *Appeal,* November 28, 1865, quoted in *Laws of the State of Mississippi,* 1865, pp. 133–34. *Mississippi House Journal,* October Term, 1865, pp. 210–13, 217, 284; *Mississippi Senate Journal,* October Term, 1865, pp. 222–26, 232.

17. Quoting J. H. Matthews to Stuart Eldridge, December 12, 1866, BRFAL (1). Samuel Thomas to [?], n.d., 1865; Thomas to O. O. Howard, December 14, 1865, all in BRFAL (1). See also the report of Eldridge, subcommissioner at Vicksburg, filed in Thomas Wood to O. O. Howard, June 15, 1865, BRFAL (2), in which he recounts the departure of blacks from local plantations trying to avoid the brutality sanctioned by the code.

18. Natchez *Daily Courier,* September 13, 1866.

Black Codes across the region ignited a confrontation between the president and Congress. Primarily in reaction to the Codes, Congress voided the 1865 constitution and placed Reconstruction under the supervision of federal authorities.

Slightly more than a year after passage of the Black Code, military governor General E. O. C. Ord arrived to oversee Reconstruction. Remarkably unfit to implement congressional demands by virtue of his temperament and his sympathy for upper-class southerners, Ord symbolized the birth of a new breed of politician in Mississippi. More committed to the economic reconstruction of the South and the establishment of "normalcy" in social and political relations, Centrists like Ord occupied leading positions in both political parties. Their ascendancy, which lasted until 1873, represented another way in which native whites impeded the revolution in values that Radical Republicans and freed people desired. Notwithstanding Ord's proclivity toward slow movement in matters of Reconstruction, Congress charged him with making certain that Mississippi, in another constitutional convention, recognized the rights and liberties of freed people. His and his successor's failure to convince whites to make additional modifications to the social ethic triggered bloody violence. Their inadequacy also heightened federal interest in the reconstruction of Mississippi and precipitated a split in the Republican party that gave local Radicals the support necessary to gain control of state government.

According to the terms of congressional Reconstruction sent down from Washington, General Ord had to supervise the registration of all eligible males, black and white, in preparation for a new constitutional convention. Once registered, they would vote for or against calling a convention and would elect delegates; to validate the results of the referendum, one-half of registered voters had to cast ballots. Despite resistance from whites, who viewed the command to write another constitution as a usurpation of states' rights, 137,561 citizens registered. Fifty-four percent of the registrants were freedmen—approximately 80 percent of the eligible black population—placing blacks in a position to control the results if they voted as a bloc.[19] The first biracial election in Mississippi history possessed all the features that characterized future Reconstruction-era campaigns: a Republican party committed to equality; cooperative and unreconstructed elements of the Democratic party; and a dedicated, extraparty faction of reactionary whites.

19. William C. Harris, *Day of the Carpetbagger*, 79–82.

Although moderates in Washington lost control of the Reconstruction process with the start of congressional Reconstruction, their allies in Mississippi refused to give up without a fight. Convinced by the results of registration that blacks would participate in the voting process and carry the day in favor of Radical Reconstruction, some old secessionist Democrats tried to garner the support of the newly enfranchised. Former governors Albert G. Brown and John J. McRae, the newspaper editor Ethelbert Barksdale, and the president of the 1861 Secession Convention William S. Barry hastily formed a Cooperationist movement. Their faction became a sanctuary for antebellum politicians who wished to retain their political might by making slight concessions to the emergent new order. With the assistance of black voters, Cooperationists believed they could control the convention and grant restricted liberties to African Americans without sacrificing the old order totally. Theirs was the strategy that had been tried in the Constitutional Convention of 1865 and succeeding legislatures. As it had previously, so too did it falter in 1867 and 1868, though the reasons for its collapse differed. The plan broke down first because the inchoate Republican party in Mississippi exposed Cooperationists' timid and self-serving approach to Reconstruction; Republicans further linked the Ku Klux Klan to all endeavors to hinder the establishment of equality. Second, an alternative strategy developed behind the banner of George Potter and his Constitutional Unionist faction of the Democratic party cut into the appeal of Cooperationists.[20]

In some ways the Potter strategy offered a middle ground between violent resistance to black equality as advocated by the Klan and cooperation with moderate Republicans as advocated by the state's former Democratic leaders. But it carried great risks. Through a strategy of "masterly inactivity" (a boycott) Potter hoped to invalidate the election by encouraging more than one-half of the electorate to refrain from voting. Without a new constitution, Constitutional Unionists believed military rule would continue and soon would provoke sufficient outrage among whites in the North and South to overthrow the Republican party in both sections. Once the foes of military rule united in their opposition to it, the South could reconstruct itself as it saw fit. Unlike the Cooperationists who hoped to woo black voters with promises of friendship, Constitutional Unionists yearned to institute the old order without compromise. The method designed to achieve their goals promised to antagonize Radicals and perhaps to strengthen federal military might in Mississippi, but the end they sought justified any

20. *Ibid.*, 86–90.

temporary setbacks. The strategy of masterly inactivity almost worked. Of the nearly fifty-eight thousand whites registered to vote, it has been estimated that only 20 percent went to the polls.[21]

Had it not been for the Republican party's mobilization of black voters, the Potterites would have carried the day. Approximately four-fifths of the registered black electorate cast ballots in favor of a new constitutional convention, a turnout that surprised even the most optimistic Republican party organizers. Aided by agents of the Freedmen's Bureau and the Loyal League, the party oversaw the politicization of an electorate dedicated to securing its liberty. In their mobilization campaign, organizers were aided by the Ku Klux Klan, an easy foil. The coming convention, Republicans said, pitted loyal men against disloyal men, deserving blacks against obstreperous whites. The Republican party so successfully conveyed the idea that white southerners, if placed in control of the convention, would not recognize black liberty that denouncing Centrists, including General Ord, as soft on former rebels turned Klansmen became the hobby of the party in 1867 and 1868. Not only did the Republican party's encouragement of the black electorate ensure that the constitutional convention would meet, the party elected a majority of delegates from its own ranks, though fewer than twenty of the ninety-seven convention delegates were African Americans.[22]

With the Radical branch of the Republican party holding sway over Congress and with Republicans in command of the convention, citizens expected Reconstruction to proceed through the disqualification of former rebels, and their expectations came to fruition. Freed people and elements of the Republican party believed this step necessary to ensure ex-slaves a place in the political culture. The first suffrage proposal placed before the convention made unquestioned loyalty to the Union during the war necessary for anyone wishing to vote, hold office, serve on juries, and even to teach in public schools. As proposed by Edward J. Castello, it required as well that potential voters take an oath denouncing efforts to deprive anyone of their right to vote and accepting the extension of civil and political liberties to all men. After a stay in the Committee on the Franchise, Castello's bill emerged on the floor with the disqualifying clause applied only to Confederates who had served as federal officeholders in the antebellum period.

21. *Ibid.*, 107–109.

22. *Ibid.*, 57–58, 106–107. For its work mobilizing and educating African Americans, the Freedmen's Bureau was roundly condemned, and not infrequently attacked; see Thomas Wood to O. O. Howard, June 15, 1865, BRFAL (2). On the division of the postbellum South into traitors and loyal men, see the Petition of Wall Street Baptist Church to the Freedmen's Bureau, n.d., BRFAL (8).

Dissatisfied by the alteration, the Yazoo County carpetbagger Albert T. Morgan inserted an amendment disfranchising all rebel soldiers and officials.[23]

Conservatives in the convention, both Democrats and old Whigs, bolted at the proposed suffrage measures. R. B. Mayes, a probate judge in Yazoo County, predicted that the elevation of ex-slaves to full citizenship promised to keep him from winning another election. Former governor Benjamin Humphreys expected to be disfranchised for his participation in the war: "A white man's government is at an end, and perhaps it is well. White folks have certainly shown great incapacity for self government. Perhaps negroes will do better." Yet he distrusted black voters and anticipated retaliation. "At any rate," Humphreys wrote Oscar J. E. Stuart, "the experiment will be tried. You and I will have to take back seats, or be elevated, at the end of a rope—such is the civilization of the age." His despair was not in evidence at the convention, for conservatives proposed numerous amendments to protect white suffrage, including one originating with several old Whigs that instituted property qualifications for the vote. Other amendments directed at preserving Confederates' suffrage were tried: one removed disabilities for all soldiers below the rank of brigadier general; another granted ex-Confederates the suffrage if they had voted in favor of the constitutional convention; and another called for disabilities to be attached only to rebels disqualified by the Fourteenth Amendment and the Reconstruction Acts of 1867. Largely because the boycott strategy had left the convention without a significant number of white conservative delegates, none of the amendments passed, but delegates killed the Morgan amendment. When the suffrage measure, as written by the Committee on the Franchise, came to a vote before the full convention, it carried by a fourty-four to twenty-five margin, sending the convention into an uproar. Opponents of the disqualifying clause turned the floor into a scene of pandemonium. Charles Townsend, a leading conservative, chastised the president of the convention, Beroth B. Eggleston, for packing the franchise committee with friends of disqualification. For his bilious remarks Townsend was voted out of the body, and within twenty-four hours of the amendment's passage, more than a dozen dissatisfied delegates voluntarily followed him.[24]

23. Harris, *Day of the Carpetbagger,* 139–93; *Journal of the Proceedings in the Constitutional Convention of the State of Mississippi, 1868* (Jackson, 1871), 63–68, hereinafter cited as *Journal of the Proceedings, 1868.*

24. Quoting Benjamin Humphreys to Oscar J. E. Stuart, August 8, 1867, in Dimitry Papers. R. B. Mayes to Oscar J. E. Stuart, July 4, 1867, in Stuart Papers; Harris, *Day of the Carpetbagger,* 145; *Journal of the Proceedings, 1868, passim.* See, too, the roll call analysis of convention Radicals in the Subject File Collection, "Reconstruction," MDAH.

As finally amended, the franchise measure attached temporary voting disabilities to about twenty-five hundred antebellum politicians who had joined the Confederacy as soldiers or officials. The law stipulated that county registrars might lift the disabilities without legislative approval in the near future. Even though those whose participation in the war had cost them their political liberties declared themselves outraged by the convention's action, most Mississippians, as military commander General Alvan Gillem (Ord's replacement) observed, cared little about the suffrage restriction. They balked, however, at the portion of the Castello law requiring all voters to swear support for political and civil equality. Gillem noted that most voters in the state loathed the thought of ex-slaves receiving equitable treatment before the law and considered African-American liberty a challenge to their own status as virtuous citizens. Incredibly, he imagined they would do nothing about the perceived change of their position in the social order because upper-class citizens—and Gillem included himself among that group—asked them to remain peaceful.[25] While Gillem may have been correct about the sentiments of well-heeled residents, he miscalculated the broader distaste for blacks active in politics, especially when juxtaposed with the disqualification of white voters.

With the constitution written, Mississippi citizens voted against its ratification in June, 1868. Political factions participating in the ratification election employed the same tactics that they had in 1867. In Mississippi's second biracial election, however, the Republican party sought not only the support of freed people but made direct appeals to white voters, hoping to expand its base; the attempt to solicit native whites' votes met with disaster, though, as few of the targeted audience supported the constitution and as some African Americans, suspecting that Republicans intended to neglect black liberty, refused to vote in the election. Previously, freedmen had been attracted to the party with promises to divide the South into loyal and disloyal men with the latter playing a minor role, if any at all, in politics, but the sudden emphasis on wooing whites into Republican ranks caused loyal freedmen to doubt the intentions of party leadership, including General Gillem. At a Grenada meeting of Republicans, evidence of the rupture between black and white Republicans appeared. With approximately one thousand freed people gathered to hear a group of Republican speakers, local Democratic luminaries intruded on the meeting. Republicans on the podium cheered for the crowd to mob the Democrats, but rank-and-file members called for an open debate. For their part the Democrats ac-

25. Alvan Gillem to Joseph S. Fowler, March 17, 1867, in Joseph S. Fowler Papers, SHC.

tively exploited Republican points of contention. Leaders of the party encouraged black voters to restore voting rights to all whites as repayment for their allowing blacks to participate in the 1867 election.[26] Their Machiavellian appeals duped few freed people, undoubtedly because violence, the case of Grenada notwithstanding, generally accompanied such pleas. The fractious division of the Republican party contributed to the defeat of the constitution as differences over strategy prohibited the solidification of the black voting bloc. By vigorously engaging in voter intimidation and capitalizing on Republican divisions (benefiting mostly from the former) Democratic opponents of the constitution negated the seventeen thousand majority enjoyed by registered blacks.

Beginning in 1868 political violence crept into the Democrats' bag of tricks, especially in the campaign to defeat the constitution and to oust Republicans in national elections. As it had during the sectional crisis of the 1850s the party's rhetoric turned frenzied and hyperbolic with Democrats admonishing their fellows to vote the straight ticket, beginning with voting "Against the Constitution." Vigilance groups organized to ensure that wavering voters cast their ballots properly, and a volume of congressional testimony recounts Democratic success in their 1868 campaign of intimidation. Robert W. Flournoy, a leading scalawag from Georgia known for his firm commitment to equality, told the congressional committee investigating election outrages that Democrats in northeast Mississippi brandished guns and knives at polling places and broke the leg of one Republican candidate for superintendent of education. Other witnesses who appeared before the committee told of more subtle forms of intimidation and fraud. A. Morley Patterson reported that white men in disguises warned blacks that their names would be written down if they voted and that they would be punished after the election. Patterson took threats against him so seriously that he refused to return home for three months after the election. In Copiah County, according to various witnesses, night riders told blacks that merchants would cut off their farm supplies if they attended the election. Blacks who tried to vote encountered drunken crowds armed with ropes and brick bats; some reported that they could not find tickets; others said election supervisors refused to accept their ballots.[27]

26. Harris, *Day of the Carpetbagger,* 166–88, 193–95. For an account of the Grenada Republican meeting, see the letter signed "M" published in the Democratic newspaper, Jackson *Daily Clarion,* June 8, 1868. On Gillem's opinion of the 1868 election, see *House Miscellaneous Documents,* 40th Cong., 3rd Sess., No. 53, p. 64.

27. On the violence used to carry the 1868 ratification election, see *House Miscellaneous Documents,* 40th Cong., 3rd Sess., No. 53, pp. 23–24, 148–49, 172–73.

Perhaps the most brazen instance of intimidation occurred after the election. During the constitutional convention, delegates appointed a Committee of Five, headed by Republican William Gibbs, to rule on the validity of the election, and the committee began collecting complaints about election fraud soon after the polls closed. Reports of heinous depredations in seven counties nearly convinced committee members to throw out the entire vote tallied there. While gathered to consider their options, a party of twenty-five prominent men, including William Sharkey, George Potter, and John J. McRae burst into the meeting room and ordered members to count all ballots cast. Several of the intruders allowed the Committee of Five to see pistols they carried in their belts. According to the original count, the Democrats carried the election to defeat the constitution by a 7,600 majority, but stirred by reports of intimidation and outraged by its own experience with the gentlemen's mob, the committee discarded ballots cast in the counties whose vote counts it questioned. The previous Democratic majority became a Republican majority of 3,380. For a brief moment it seemed to stalwart Republicans that right had emerged victorious over might. Yet General Gillem, who believed "a *fairer* expression of opinions" was not possible under existing circumstances, refused to approve the committee's action. Publicly, he argued that the committee lacked authority to decide the matter.[28] Aided by Gillem the Democratic party leapt its first hurdle on the way toward defeating what it perceived as anarchy, corruption, and misrule. The discounting of votes, they hoped, would provoke a virulent native reaction to congressional Reconstruction and lead to its overthrow.

The strenuous exertions of the Democratic party to defeat the constitution failed to produce the desired results, however, as the nation sent a Republican majority to Congress and Ulysses S. Grant to the White House. Among Democrats, Grant evoked fear and suspicion, but as events developed those anxieties seemed unwarranted. Lacking a constitution, Mississippi's fate remained in doubt until early 1869, when Grant, at the request of conservative state politicians, pressured Congress to permit a vote on the constitution with a separate referendum to be taken on the measures

28. Quoting Alvan C. Gillem to Joseph S. Fowler, July 27, 1868, in Fowler Papers. Gillem's phrase, "a *fairer* expression of opinions," testified to his private belief that white Mississippians would not and could not be expected to endorse black suffrage (emphasis mine). See also *House Miscellaneous Documents,* 40th Cong., 3rd Sess., No. 53, pp. 2–3, 8. On Gillem's reflections on the constitution itself, see Brooks D. Simpson, *Let Us Have Peace: Ulysses S. Grant and the Politics of War and Reconstruction, 1861–1868* (Chapel Hill, 1991), 250. On whites' reaction to the defeat of the constitution, see Natchez *Weekly Democrat,* July 6, 1868.

excluding certain whites from voting. The election, slated for November, 1869, also featured a race for governor between Louis Dent, Grant's brother-in-law, who favored ratification of the disqualifying measures, and James L. Alcorn, a recent convert to the Republican party, who preferred the constitution without its proscriptive features. Although rabid conservatives tried to mount another campaign of "masterly inactivity" to defeat the constitution, they made little headway among a people who believed the Centrist policy of bending without breaking could best preserve their social ethic. Without a strong opposition party to agitate against ratification of the constitution, voters not only approved it and placed Alcorn in the governor's office, but they ratified the Fourteenth and Fifteenth amendments.[29]

According to historian Michael Perman, the much-delayed passage of the constitution and Alcorn's victory represented the pinnacle of Centrist achievement in Mississippi politics. Centrists had always played a prominent role in state Reconstruction, but ratification of the constitution, without its fainthearted proscriptive amendments, propelled Centrist thought to greater prominence. Some converts to Centrism likely acted out of a spirit of opportunism. Alcorn and Horatio Simrall, the chair of the committee that had written the Black Code, calculated that agitation over political equality would soon end, and they longed to position themselves to assume command of the state's economic reconstruction. Accordingly, they, like other Centrists, accepted the extension of lesser liberties to freed people in order to avoid wholesale social and political revolution. Alcorn, a Delta planter who before the war directed efforts to construct a levee system, explained his move into the Centrist wing of the Republican party as a defensive one. Acting as a moderate, he believed he could lead the state's economic revitalization while quieting pleas for social egalitarianism. In his phrase, he wanted "to pluck our common liberty and common prosperity out of the jaws of inevitable ruin" that would follow if the notion of free labor and free men reigned unchecked. Most of all Alcorn feared the yeoman white response to Radical calls for social justice. If because of emancipation and the extension of civil rights yeomen recognized that nothing separated them from the condition of African Americans, Alcorn predicted class warfare, and he preferred that the social ethic remain anchored in the political culture of racism, not class.[30]

29. Harris, *Day of the Carpetbagger,* 199–264.

30. Quoting James L. Alcorn, *Views of the Honorable James L. Alcorn on the Political Situation of Mississippi* (Friar's Point, Miss., 1867), 4. Michael Perman, *The Road to Redemption: Southern Politics, 1869–1879* (Chapel Hill, 1984), 45–48. On the opprobrium at-

Between 1865 and 1868 black Mississippians passed from slavery to citizenship. While the extension of citizenship encouraged defenders of black liberty, the election of a Centrist-dominated state government foretold that bloodshed would accompany the perpetuation of political egalitarianism. From the time of Alcorn's election until the overthrow of his Radical successor, Adelbert Ames, Centrists in the Republican and Democratic parties spoke of protecting black liberty, though in fact those belonging to the former party turned a deaf ear to remonstrations for protection under the law, and those in the latter party slyly sanctioned acts of racial violence. In downplaying governmental protection of black liberty, they revealed their aversion to equality and their interest in drawing the state into the national economic order. Moderate Republicans in the North came eventually to agree tacitly that too much emphasis had been placed on black liberty and not enough on spanning the economic chasm that separated the sections.

The elevation of Centrism also boded ill for unanimity within the Republican party. Because of Alcorn's circumspect advocacy of black liberty, his ascendancy to the governor's mansion widened the division that had earlier appeared in the Republican party. From its birth in Mississippi, the party had been torn between supporting black liberty or advocating halfhearted support for the reform of southern society. As long as the question of disfranchising former rebels occupied party politics in Mississippi, Republicans avoided internecine struggles over black equality. Yet approval of the constitution and the election of Grant, who appeared ready to abandon congressional Radicals, brought to the fore questions of freedmen's role in the party. The sudden conversion to Centrist dogma by prominent secessionists Ethelbert Barksdale and Albert G. Brown caused the Radical wing of the party further dismay. It had been, after all, largely at the insistence of just such Centrists that Grant pushed through Congress the plan for separate votes on the disqualifying measures of the constitution and abandoned his kinsman, Dent, in the gubernatorial election.[31] To Radical Republicans the union of significant whites with a faction of their party

tached to Democrats who joined the Republican party, see Darden Diaries, October 10, 1868 (in Darden Papers). On the connection between Centrist ascendancy and economic development, see Mark W. Summers, *Railroads, Reconstruction, and the Gospel of Prosperity: Aid Under the Radical Republicans, 1865–1877* (Princeton, 1984), Chapts. 1–2.

31. Harris, *Day of the Carpetbagger,* 203, 207–208, 214–17, 223; Perman, *Road to Redemption,* Chapts. 2–3. See, too, Columbus *Southern Sentinel,* March 23, 26, 1867. On the self-serving nature of Democrats' sudden conversion to Centrism, see E. P. Jacobson to

brought to mind images of the lion and lamb together at rest. Shortly before Alcorn's election, Robert W. Flournoy had estimated that there was "not a foot square in this state where a meeting of white and black persons would be permitted to organize a republican party. Mobs and murder would certainly be the result." So in 1869, when county-level Democratic meetings lavished praise on their adversaries for supposedly rejecting disfranchisement of some whites, Radicals were wary of the peace overture; the combination of moderates behind the slogan "fair treatment" for freed people promised to divert Mississippi politics from equality and toward economic reconstruction. At the same time that African Americans and their Radical allies sensed a retreat from revolutionary social reformation, the Loyal League, freed people's warmest political ally, also began to wither.[32] Abandoned by Centrists and without effective local organizations to offer support, blacks (and their white allies) during Alcorn's administration faced severe challenges to their only recently obtained liberty.

Their fears proved justified between the years 1868 and 1875. While leading Democratic politicians followed members of the opposition party into the middle ground of Centrism, most white Mississippians remained less willing than their leaders to utter rhetoric, even for the sake of appearances, endorsing black equality. A correspondent of the Forest *Weekly Register,* "Friend of the Right," equated the extension of political and civil liberties to freedmen with the empowerment of mules and asses. Others agreed that "Plows and Politics" did not mix. Despite the ascendancy of Centrists in Mississippi and the removal of most federal troops with Alcorn's election, many whites believed the social order doomed under moderate rule. Defense of traditional visions of a good republic through attacks on black equality and federal authority, the twin demons of the unreconstructed, continued unabated.[33]

During the late 1860s and early 1870s the Ku Klux Klan became the primary vehicle through which the unreconstructed carried out their defense

---

J. F. H. Claiborne, November 8, 1872, in Claiborne Papers, MDAH. On Republican anger over Alcorn's cooperation with Democrats, see A. W. Ross to James L. Alcorn, March 21, 1871, in RG 27, MDAH. See, too, Pereyra, *James Lusk Alcorn,* 99–103, 104–47.

32. Robert W. Flournoy to Benjamin F. Butler, May 23, 1867, quoted in Michael Fitzgerald, *The Union League Movement in the Deep South* (Baton Rouge, 1989), 52, but see 48, 98, for accounts of League activities in 1868 and 1869.

33. Forest *Weekly Register,* January 9, 1869; Columbus *Southern Sentinel,* April 23, 1866. See, too, Forest *Weekly Register,* February 19, 1870; J. Floyd King to Lin, June 22, 1867, King Papers. On conservative whites' loathing of federal authority, see L. Q. C. Lamar to Jimmy, August 11, 1869, in Lucius Quintus Cincinnatus Lamar Papers, Typescript in SHC.

of the social ethic's undiluted racial assumptions. Most studies of the Klan link the group to lower-class whites, but an examination of ninety-one north Mississippians indicted for violating federal civil rights laws indicates that middling folk outnumbered yeomen in the Klan. Three-quarters of them were farmers, and the remainder held a variety of occupations ranging from common laborer to salesman. On average the indicted Klansmen held $1,660 of real property and $1,614 of personal property. The occupations of the accused, as well as the group's moderate wealth holdings, suggest that the Klan appealed to a cross section of rural southerners, and it certainly received the support of Lucius Q. C. Lamar and Edward C. Walthall. Even though Lamar and Walthall publicly denounced Klan depredations as excessive and detrimental to their goal of allaying federal apprehension about the success of Reconstruction, they abetted violence by constantly decrying "black rule" and by defending accused members in court.[34]

Unable to block Klan violence, the Centrist peace with black liberty that Alcorn encouraged lasted little more than two years. Its collapse left Republican politicians who clung to the faith without a constituency and irreparably rent their party. In contrast, Democratic Centrists discovered during the overthrow of Republican Centrists an alternative path through Reconstruction that bypassed black liberty. They learned from the Klan's example that they need not endorse black liberty in order to have the opportunity to restore the social ethic. Attacks against the perceived enemies of the social ethic multiplied in the wake of Alcorn's 1869 election and the tenure in office of his Centrist successor Ridgely C. Powers. Besides "uppity" freedmen and an occasional federal officer, the Klan, along with the unorganized foes of black liberty, attacked the signposts of the new order: Republicans, schools, and northern merchants. Alcorn opposed bloodshed as an impediment to economic revitalization and attempted to quash the Klan by passing laws that prohibited the wearing of disguises,

34. On Klan violence, see Allen Trelease, *White Terror: The Ku Klux Klan Conspiracy and Southern Reconstruction* (Westport, Conn., 1971), 88, 274, 296. On prominent Mississippians in the Klan, see Fred M. Witty, "Reconstruction in Carroll and Montgomery Counties," Mississippi Historical Society *Publications*, X (1909), 131; James B. Murphy, *L. Q. C. Lamar: Pragmatic Patriot* (Baton Rouge, 1973), 100, 101. The data base of persons indicted under violations of the Enforcement Acts was derived from an unattached report in the Source-Chronological File, Northern and Southern Districts of Mississippi, January 1871 to December 1875, General Records of the Department of Justice, RG 60, National Archives, Microcopy rolls 1–4, hereinafter cited as DJ (reel number). It should be noted that the mean value of real estate holdings for those reporting was $988 and the mean value of personal property was $600. Both figures are substantially lower than the averages, suggesting great disparities in the wealth of Klansmen.

established a state criminal investigative unit, and placed the militia under his command. None of the measures dealt the Klan a death blow. Alcorn's refusal to heed the suggestion of his Republican rival Adelbert Ames that he call for federal troops in violent times provided Radicals reason to portray the governor, in the words of Henry Niles, as "a tired Demagogue." Niles further posited that "many of his [Alcorn's] superiors in honor are in the Penitentiary; and many of his superiors in morals and piety are in Hell." Black voters, too, wearied of the governor's "reasonable, sensible management" of the party and state.[35] To them, Centrists appeared immune to the suffering caused by outrages like the whipping of carpetbagger Allen P. Huggins and the Meridian race riot of 1871. While the governor was apparently unmoved, or least limited by his view of Reconstruction, to respond to the deeds of unreconstructed southerners, the federal government responded to Huggins' bloody shirt and the riot by passing the Ku Klux Klan and Enforcement acts.[36]

Four years of Centrist leadership in the Republican party precipitated a fierce intraparty gubernatorial campaign in 1873. Moderate Republicans, again led by Alcorn, vied with Radicals behind Ames for the office. Not since the days of the 1868 ratification vote had the choice between ballots been depicted in such racially charged terms. The election would determine whether the state remained on its course of Centrist rule or whether it would take a new path leading to equality behind Ames. The editors of the race-baiting Forest *Weekly Register* recorded the typical white response to Ames in a prayer it suggested readers adopt: "Lord send meningitis, small

35. Quoting Henry Niles Diary, May 6, 1870 (Microfilm copy in Jason Niles Diary). Alcorn to R. H. Walker in the Jackson *Mississippi Pilot,* September 25, 1873, clipping in Alcorn Family Papers. See, too, Harris, *Day of the Carpetbaggers,* 380–402. For accounts of Klan violence and the response to it, see Lieutenant Governor Ridgely C. Powers to E. P. Jacobson, June 14, 1871, in DJ (2); *House Reports,* 42nd Cong., 2nd Sess., No. 22, Vol. XI, pp. 484, 487, 496, 590; Witty, "Reconstruction in Carroll and Montgomery Counties," 129–30; W. H. Braden, "Reconstruction in Lee County," Mississippi Historical Society *Publications,* X (1909), 144; E. C. Coleman, Jr., "Reconstruction in Attala County," Mississippi Historical Society *Publications* X (1911), 159.

36. Accounts of the two outrages can be found in George Leftwich, "Reconstruction in Monroe County," Mississippi Historical Society *Publications,* IX (1906), 57; E. F. Puckett, "Reconstruction in Monroe County," Mississippi Historical Society *Publications,* XI (1910), 127; Jennie Shaw to "My Beloved Sister," March 30, 1871, in Rollins Papers; Fitzgerald, *The Union League Movement,* 197–99. See, too, Allen P. Huggins to A. T. Ackerman, January 14, June 28, 1871; John H. Pierce to Ackerman, January 24, 1871; G. Wiley Wells to Ackerman, August 21, 1871, all in DJ (1). On the Enforcement Acts and the work of the Justice Department in Mississippi, see Stephen E. Cresswell, "Resistance and Enforcement: The United States Department of Justice, 1870–1893" (Ph.D. dissertation, University of Virginia, 1986), 20–32.

pox, cholera, measles, whooping cough, if we have incurred your divine displeasure. Heap upon us all the imprecations of the 109th Psalm; but we implore thee, that our state be not cursed with such small Ames." Centrist Democrats considered the threat of his election serious enough to disband their party and focus their voting strength on Alcorn. "Old issues," Democrat Hiram Cassedy, Sr. observed, "have become extinct, and party names have lost their prestige, the Democratic name serves no other purpose now than to arouse fears, North and South, by which alone the Republican party are enabled to keep up their organization."[37] Even if it meant the dissolution of the party of their fathers, Democrats determined to defeat resurgent Radicalism. Yet, for all their efforts, the Centrist Alcorn lost.

Soon after Ames's victory Democratic-Conservatives, stung by the advent of Radical rule, abandoned cooperation for the color line, a strategy based on protracted conflict against black liberty, a strategy they had learned from the Klan. Dissatisfaction with the prospects of Radical ascendancy developed even before Ames took the oath of office. Less than a month after the election, in fact, prominent whites in east Mississippi fired the first signal flares of the coming Redemption when they began reorganizing the Democratic-Conservative party. Most historians separate the practitioners of the color line from more cooperative tacticians in the Democratic camp, but by 1874 the distinction between them blurred. Embracing Centrist doctrines, Democratic-Conservatives in the reorganized party came to suspect, had cost them the 1873 election. To recoup their losses they needed to separate themselves from Republicans of every stripe, and they extended to all Republicans the description "negrophilist" that they had reserved previously only for Ames and his allies. Burr H. Polk noted the sudden vitriol his Democratic-Conservative acquaintances reserved for him: "Those people can hardly be fair or just in any way to a Republican." Ames's victory, according to the emerging proponents of the color line, certified that black voters lacked virtue to make wise decisions at the polls. But moderate Republicans vilified Ames as well for sacrificing members of his own party when they refused to align with him. "Sorehead" Republicans and Democrats were all the same to Ames, making it difficult for some Republican Centrists to support their party.[38]

37. Quoting Forest *Weekly Register,* April 9, 1873; Hiram Cassedy, Sr. to the Editor, Jackson *Weekly Clarion,* September 4, 1873. See, too, Perman, *Road to Redemption,* 155.

38. Quoting Burr H. Polk to Captain A. C. Fisk, n.d., in DJ (4). On Mississippians' view of the Klan and its role in ending Reconstruction, see Robert Phillip Howell, "Memoirs," MS in SHC, 24–25. See, too, Jackson *Weekly Clarion,* December 3, 1874; Harris, *Day*

Aided indirectly by Grant, who, after the election of 1872, wearied of the constant flurry of affairs in the South and began vigorously courting Democratic-Conservatives, native whites searched for a strategy to unseat Ames. The "very salutary effect" of federal prosecutions under the Enforcement Act (which resulted in a 39 percent conviction rate) convinced whites that excessive and open denouncements of Republican rule when coupled with plainly racist rhetoric could not overthrow the Radicals. More subtle tactics were needed. In late 1874 the new focus of Democratic politics was discovered: taxes. "If you would know how poor a man is," or so said a New Yorker who owned land in the state, "just ascertain the number of acres he owns and pays taxes on in Mississippi." Opponents of Reconstruction had long complained that taxes exceeded the ability of farmers to pay. But the taxpayers' movement that sprang from the reorganized Democratic-Conservative party wanted more than retrenchment and reform. It also sought to overthrow Radical, or as they liked to say, "black" rule. According to Michael Perman, the bipartisan nature of the early taxpayers' associations offered a method for accomplishing both goals without alerting Radical sensitivity to race-baiting. The subtlety of the tactic did not escape supporters of Ames. C. P. Lincoln, county clerk at Grenada, argued that the "same rebellious spirit that prompted them in 1861" moved white Mississippians to join the taxpayers' movement; an editor of the Jackson *Weekly Pilot* suspected in the new strategy a revival of "Ku Klux Democracy."[39]

A statewide taxpayers' convention met at Jackson on January 4, 1875. Even though a number of Alcorn Republicans attended the meeting, Democrats (many of them members of the agricultural reform society, the Patrons of Husbandry) dominated the proceedings. The convention's address to Mississippi taxpayers focused on farmers' economic distress, chiefly low cotton prices, high taxes, and the forced sale of their land. "By reason of the general poverty of the people, and the greatly depressed values of all property, and especially of our great staple," the address read, "the present rate of taxation is an intolerable burden and much beyond their ability to

---

of the Carpetbagger, 422–23, 619. On the popularity of Ames among Radical Republicans, see John Adolphus to Adelbert Ames, April 10, 1874, in RG 27, MDAH. On whites' fears of Ames as a plotter of race war, see Agnew Diary, July 3, 1873.

39. Quoting C. P. Lincoln to J. E. Carpenter, n.d., in DJ (1); Jackson *Weekly Pilot,* February 13, 1875, quoted in Harris, *Day of the Carpetbagger,* 631. See, too, Perman, *Road to Redemption,* 163, 165–68, and "H" to the Editor, Water Valley *Courier,* quoted in the Jackson *Daily Clarion,* January 30, 1875.

pay." In 1869, according to the convention, taxes on land valued at one hundred dollars amounted to ten cents, but since the inauguration of Republican rule the rate had gone up to forty cents, depriving the keepers of the social ethic of their land. Republicans' spending habits equally outraged the convention. Government salaries, common schools, and the cost of public printing all fell under the taxpayers' carefully phrased indictment of Radicalism.[40]

Every clause of the convention address heralded conservatives' efforts to preserve the antebellum social ethic. High taxes and debt (the bane of free men), the breakup of plantations (the master class's loss of direct authority over labor), and extravagant expenditures for schools and other public institutions (the specter of social equality) represented attacks on the ethic. In veiled language, language that careful observers nonetheless deciphered, the convention suggested that rectifying the extravagant and wasteful practices of Reconstruction meant retracting the liberty extended to blacks. Ames understood the intention of the taxpayers' convention: "The true sentiment of the assembly was the 'color line,'" he said, "though the platform said nothing about it."[41]

As the taxpayers' movement took wings, white-liners (the most virulent advocates of the color line), began organizing in force. Led by William H. McCardle of the Vicksburg *Herald,* they used the off-year elections of 1874 to register their disdain for Radical rule. In Columbus, according to Henry B. Whitfield, "a lot of rowdies" distributed handbills reading "Bread or No Bread" to intimidate blacks into voting the Democratic ticket or not voting at all. Through the influence of intimidation, elections ceased to resemble the democratic events that Whitfield's forefathers had enjoyed and rated not the name election; "outrage" better described the 1874 canvass of voters. Henry Bickerstaff preferred the term "mobocracy." In Iuka, Bickerstaff told Attorney General George H. Williams, "all the efforts possible are being made to re-enslave the Negro." White-liners and taxpayers had driven from Tishomingo County all except a handful of black and four

40. Quoting Jackson *Daily Clarion,* January 6, 1875. For a sympathetic treatment of the taxpayers' complaints, see Ross Moore, "Social and Economic Conditions in Mississippi During Reconstruction" (Ph.D. dissertation, Duke University, 1938), 71; Brough, "History of Taxation in Mississippi," 121–23. On taxes, see Batt Moore, Jr. to John Fewell, February 12, 1876; L. B. Brown to Fewell, January 14, 1867, all in John W. Fewell Papers, MDAH; A. Q. Withers to George H. Williams, October 25, 1874, DJ (1).

41. Quoting Adelbert Ames to E. Benjamin Andrews, ary 24, 1895, in Adelbert Ames Papers, MDAH. Wharton, *The Negro in Mississippi,* 177–79, convincingly argues that Republican fiscal policy was just and necessary to repair damage to the state's infrastructure caused by the war and to inaugurate services needed by the state.

white Republicans.[42] Informed, at least theoretically, by diverse sentiments, the white-line and taxpayers' movements differed mainly on tactics. Republicans' tendency to lump the movements together grew out of the events that occurred at Vicksburg in December, 1874.

The circumstances that led to racial warfare at Vicksburg originated with the 1873 election of freedman Peter Crosby to the post of sheriff. Soon after his election, citizens opposed to him and Ames organized a taxpayers' union and a white league. The clubs dedicated themselves to identifying mismanagement and fraud in local government and intended to unseat black officials. Without much effort the taxpayers' union discovered that one of Crosby's surety guarantors had died without posting the bond necessary for Crosby to hold his office, and they set about removing him. Whites gloated at the possibility of expelling a "corrupt" black official, especially Crosby, who as sheriff had the power to seat juries. But their interests extended beyond the sheriff's office. To carry the November, 1874, elections, white-liners, using threats of violence, forced the registrar of voters, a Radical Republican, to take flight; then, capitalizing on the information gathered against Crosby by the taxpayers' union, they forced Crosby to resign. A mob appointed a new sheriff. Despite the growing air of violence in Vicksburg, a sufficient number of strong-willed Republicans remained in office to block the complete success of the white-liners. On December 7 a band of armed whites stormed into town to arrest Crosby, who continued to organize resistance to the emerging mob rule. With Crosby out of the way, they chased freed people out of the city where another company of brigands awaited to fire upon them as they crossed an open field. Simultaneous attacks in other quarters of the city ensued, and for several days vigilantes rode through the countryside killing blacks at every turn. As news of the riot spread, whites from as far away as Trinity, Texas, wired messages indicative of white southerners' villainous intentions: "Do you want any men? Can raise good crowd within twenty four hours to kill out your negroes."[43]

The murder spree ended only after Ames convinced President Grant to send federal troops, an action that bolstered white resolve to end Radical rule. Politically astute whites knew that preventing federal intervention in

42. Quoting Henry B. Whitfield to G. Wiley Wells, December 9, 1874; Henry Bickerstaff to George H. Williams, September 1874; but see, too, R. A. Hill to Williams, September 18, 1874, all in DJ (1).

43. Quoting *House Reports,* 43rd Cong., 2nd Sess., No. 265, p. ix, but see, too, ii–xvii. Darden Diaries, December 7, 1874 (in Darden Papers) records the efforts of Jefferson County residents to help the white population at Vicksburg. Harris, *Day of the Carpetbagger,* 647–49.

Mississippi dictated the use of legitimate means once the opposition had been suppressed. Toward that end Lucius Q. C. Lamar dispatched several friends to speak to the congressional committee that investigated the Vicksburg outrage. Lamar informed E. D. Clark that he should emphasize Crosby's corruption as the driving force behind the riot, and he should try to keep the extremist McCardle away from the committee. Clark, along with Thomas Catchings and other Democrats, complied with Lamar's wishes and argued before the assembled congressmen that blacks had precipitated the mob action by electing corrupt officials and marching through town in support of Crosby.[44]

Despite the widespread sentiment among Republicans that, in C. P. Lincoln's phrase, only "a 'color line' of blue" would dislodge anti-Radical forces, Grant turned a blind eye to Ames's plight. With the opening provided by a disinterested president, white politicians used the familiar fear of insurrection to mobilize the electorate. While their rhetoric might seem to twentieth-century readers mere fear-mongering, Democratic party leaders apparently suspected Ames would do anything to remain in office. Responding to the governor's control over the state militia, Lamar told his wife that the governor intended to sacrifice "his negro regiments" in order to persuade Grant to "take possession for him." Distemper among leading Democratic-Conservatives grew daily as the election of 1875 approached, and they exploited apprehensions of a race war that infected the general population. Democratic-Conservatives, who revived their party in August, 1875, put forward a statewide ticket for the first time since the Centrist victory of 1868 and swore to preserve white liberty against all challengers. The party platform adopted in the convention included statements of allegiance to political and civil liberties for all and support for public education, as well as calls for reduced state expenditures, farm relief, and levee construction. The party even took tentative steps to woo freedmen, "and thus," according to the Jackson *Weekly Clarion,* "give permanence and success to our party and its principles."[45]

Although white-liners in the Democratic-Conservative convention bolted at the idea of appealing to black voters, party leadership quieted their dis-

44. L. Q. C. Lamar to Edward Donaldson Clark, December 24, 1874, in Lucius Quintus Cincinnatus Lamar Collection, UM; Lamar to Clark, December 24, 1874, in Kate Freeman Clark Collection, Microfilm in MDAH.

45. Quoting C. P. Lincoln to J. E. Carpenter, n.d., DJ (1); L. Q. C. Lamar to "Wife," February 15, 1875, in Edward Mayes, ed., *L. Q. C. Lamar: His Life, Times and Speeches, 1825–1893* (Nashville, 1896), 211; Jackson *Daily Clarion,* March 4, 1875, but see, too, January 27, 1875.

sent by suggesting that the appeals were for northern consumption only. No one took seriously the idea of converting large numbers of faithful Republican voters. The planter W. B. Jones, for instance, complained that his tenants viewed the election as another opportunity to further remind whites that the bottom rail was on top, and he intended to submit no longer. Their enthusiasm for the election notwithstanding, Jones blocked them from voting: "These niggers did not attend," he reported. Others also realized that Democratic-Conservative appeals to justice meant little in Mississippi. Ames predicted that white-liners would carry the day in November, even if they did not in the August convention; bloodthirsty whites would punish those who had ever voted the Republican ticket. The convergence of the white line and taxpayers' policies in the reorganized Democratic-Conservative party foretold white Mississippians' willingness to carry the election by any means necessary.[46]

In some areas the tactic led Democratic-Conservatives to stage two-party meetings, hoping to convert black voters to their cause. At those affairs Democratic speakers like Edward C. Walthall promised that "colored men shall be protected in the free exercise of their right to vote if it takes white men's blood to do it." But his hyperbole served less as a commitment to black voting rights than as a warning that bloodshed was anticipated. A Republican newspaper, the Jackson *Pilot,* saw through the rhetoric: "While the platform is peace, the canvass will be war." Fully aware of the party's strategy after the Vicksburg riot, Susan S. Darden, the wife of a prominent Franklin County planter and Democrat, worried about a Republican in-law's safety: "What could have induced him to act so? Oh, Lord have mercy upon him & stop him in his mad career." Although they offered freedmen the proverbial carrot, Democrats more often used a literal stick to control black votes; they disrupted Republican meetings and wantonly attacked blacks at work in the fields. W. F. Simonton reported that a group of young whites threatened to hold five blacks in a sweltering boxcar until they promised to vote the Democratic-Conservative ticket.[47]

46. Quoting Jackson *Weekly Clarion,* August 4, 1875; W. B. Jones Diary, November 1–3, 1875 (in Jones-Smith Plantation Journal). See Adelbert Ames to Blanche Ames, August 4, 1875, in Blanche Ames, comp., *Chronicles from the Nineteenth Century: Family Letters of Blanche Butler and Adelbert Ames* (2 vols; Clinton, Mass., 1957), I, 124.

47. Quoting Darden Diaries, August 28, 1875 (in Darden Papers); Walthall quoted in the Jackson *Weekly Clarion,* September 13, 1875; Jackson *Weekly Pilot,* August 14, 1875, quoted in Perman, *Road to Redemption,* 168. See, too, W. F. Simonton to Adelbert Ames, September 13, 1875; E. C. Walker to Adelbert Ames, August 26, 1875; J. B. Algood to Ames, September 12, 1875; J. A. Orr to Ames, April 16, 1875, all in RG 27, MDAH. On the election, see Keith Ian Polakoff, *The Election of 1876 and the End of Reconstruction* (Baton Rouge, 1973), 179–80.

In Monroe County, Democrats' intimidation so often converged with their proselytizing that blacks had difficulty distinguishing between the various tactics. Reuben Reynolds attempted to convince African Americans of the excesses of Reconstruction, but the effort met with mixed results. In 1875 he told an audience that his party had ex-slaves' best interest in mind when it advocated an end to Radical rule; he was greeted with jeers and guffaws. Even after summarily firing a tenant on his wife's plantation for badgering him, the taunting continued. Chiding his listeners for their recalcitrance, Reynolds reminded them that they owned no property and possessed no means for securing a livelihood: "The only way you can rid yourselves of the white people is to catch yourselves by the seats of your pants and lift yourselves 200 yards above the tops of the trees, d——n you!"[48] Another Monroe County Democrat, Reuben Davis, achieved equally dismal results when he spoke before black audiences. Unlike Reynolds, who first treated his hearers as children before turning violent in his rhetoric, Davis dwelled little on niceties and patronizing words. At one point he sarcastically asked if his audience believed whites so foolish as "to feed and clothe you and then let you vote for the d——n carpet bagger?" A lone voice in the back of the room cried, "Yes." As Davis reached for his pistol to punish the impertinent commentator, friends of the freedman pointed out that he suffered a hearing impairment and perhaps misunderstood the question, so Davis resumed his speech. When Davis proclaimed himself ready "for war and bloody war to the knife, and the knife to the hilt," the black man, who had obviously feigned his deafness, answered, "Me, too," and the crowd raced out the windows to escape the coming fracas. However much Reynolds and Davis wished to dictate and control freed people's political opinions, the new citizens fought back when possible. But in 1875, confronted with what Allen M. Green called the "Ku Klux Democracy and the Weak Knead [*sic*] Republican President of the North," halting men like Reynolds, Davis, and their minions was inconceivable.[49]

The riot at Clinton just two months before the election bore witness to the influence of violence and the uses to which white-liners put such affairs. At Clinton, a small hamlet west of Jackson, the full force of white-line strategy was displayed, and Grant was forced to show his hand. On September 4, 1875, shots rang out at a biracial political meeting, and within twenty-four hours trainloads of Vicksburg residents, the state's best practiced ri-

48. Leftwich, "Reconstruction in Monroe County," 75–77.

49. Quoting *ibid.;* Allen M. Green to Edward Pierepont, September 23, 1875, DJ (3). On black resistance to violence, see H. L. Lott to A. B. Hunt, October 29, 1876; D. H. Sessions to John M. Stone, n.d., all in RG 27, MDAH.

oters, arrived to add to the mayhem. Rumors spread among Clinton's white population that African Americans prepared for them a wholesale slaughter; freedwomen would dispatch white females and children while black men killed adult males. Tension in the community spread when Ames, after failing to convince Grant to send troops, ordered the state militia into town. To whites' eyes, black troops marching through Clinton suggested a revolution, social and political. Although no one knew who had started the riot, Democrats blamed Ames, who, they claimed, intended through the riot to provoke national outrage. The incident left scores of people dead and permitted Democratic-Conservatives to turn the dead whites into martyrs of their counterrevolution to secure the liberty and virtue of whites based on black subjugation. Transparent images of those slain, backlighted by flaming pine knots, became the focus of a pre-election parade in Jackson. Sarah Chilton, whose son died in the riot, proudly informed a friend that the incident had "roused the people like the trump of Gabriel, and after that left nothing undone to secure our rights, and to crush anarchy." To Republicans the Clinton affair and John Marshall Stone's November victory signaled the nation's readiness to allow "a portion of her citizens to be killed and slaughtered up at the will and pleasure of another portion just because they differ in Color and political Sentiment."[50]

By November, 1875, the Democratic policy of rule or ruin had successfully proven itself. So staggering had the violence been that even though a federal grand jury investigating election outrages in north Mississippi believed it could indict thousands of election law violators, it chose not to, fearing additional violence. Democratic policy and national Republican acquiescence prompted the grand jury foreman, William D. Frazee, to bid "farewell to liberty, farewell to the freedom of the ballot box."[51] Not even the federal courts could stem the wave of intimidation and violence that passed over Mississippi politics after 1874; the liberty that freed people once believed possible to achieve seemed suddenly distant. In the new era of Democratic rule, former distinctions between Centrists and the unreconstructed disappeared as violence and the color line dominated Mississippi politics. Bloody and fraudulent as the 1875 election was, it differed only in matters of detail from the abuses of the 1876 presidential election and those elections that followed.

50. Quoting Sarah Chilton to Mrs. L. N. Brown, November 13, 1875, but see Chilton to Brown, September 17, 25, 1875, October 1, 17, 24, 28, 1875, in Norton-Chilton-Dameron Family Papers, SHC. Harris, *Day of the Carpetbagger,* 660–61.

51. Quoting Grand Jury Report, July 8, 1876, DJ (3). On violence committed during the election of 1875, see *Senate Reports,* 44th Cong., 1st Sess., No. 527, *passim.*

The political culture of racism owed its coronation in part to the complicity of the national Republican party, which ignored outrages committed against black voters. The party in Mississippi, though never completely wiped out in the post-Redemption era, foundered for direction, and splintered after 1875. A candidate for the U.S. House in 1876 felt so alone in his effort to fight the Democrats that he sought assurances from the attorney general that northern Republicans actually wanted him to win. Democratic exertions in 1875 and 1876 so completely overwhelmed the Radical party that another Republican suggested that "each Republican . . . ought just to choose his Democratic master and go scripture fashion, and have his ear nailed to the Doorpost of the misery in which he is to remain a slave forever!" As for African Americans, Mississippi's white Republicans believed, the national party abandoned them altogether except when it needed a southern outrage to carry the vote in the North.[52]

For the mass of black voters, developments within Mississippi and the national Republican party between 1875 and 1876 meant the loss of their civil and political liberties. Yet the black leadership of the state Republican party continued to curry the favor of national leaders and to control patronage, and through a complicated arrangement with state Democratic bosses, the black wing of the Republican party received local offices, too, allowing the Democratic party to accomplish two goals in the process: it could portray all its enemies as friends of black Republicanism, since only the black wing of the party enjoyed power; and it could more easily win national offices, as white foes lived in isolation from Republican patronage and the support of party leadership.[53] But the arrangement effectively ended black participation in elections. Despite the arguments of leading Democrats, Lamar among them, that disfranchisement was not "a political possibility," the reality of black voting in the Redeemer period proved that de facto disfranchisement was achieved. From a high of 80 percent in 1868, black voter participation fell to 16.8 percent in the 1882 congressional elections. Without similar statistics to back their claims of intimidation, opponents of the political culture of racism found it impossible to prove that subtle forms of oppression supplanted the highly publicized

52. The quote can be found in a bundle of unsigned letters from Mississippians submitted to the Department of Justice by Ira Tarbell, August 25, 1876, DJ (3). See, too, Judge T. Walton to Alphonso Taft, September 3, 1876, DJ (2); J. H. Pierce to Taft, September 3, August 21, 1876; T. J. Reed to Taft, September 3, 1876; John R. Cavett to Taft, August 23, 1876; H. R. Ware to Taft, November 11, 1876, all in DJ (3).

53. On black denunciations of violence, see "A Negro" to John M. Stone, September 26, 1878, in John Marshall Stone Papers, MDAH.

variety of 1875 and 1876. But Republicans like William Baskin understood the significance of blacks' retreat from the polls. He noted that by the early 1880s their opinions ceased to carry significant weight with either party.[54]

Subtle forms of oppression were not the only ones that Mississippi Democrats employed, but their increasing dependence on vote fraud and intimidation allowed them to deny that election bullies hindered blacks in exercising the suffrage. Lamar, in an article published in the *North American Review,* made much the same argument, and his words shortly became standard Democratic doctrine: those who declared that blacks could be bullied into voting the Democratic ticket admitted that freedmen lacked the independence of mind necessary for citizenship.[55] The argument was entirely specious, of course, but pronouncements purporting to recognize African-American political autonomy kept critics of the South off balance.

The overwhelming success that Democrats enjoyed in eliminating black influence at the polls embedded in Mississippi politics a faith in violence when used against African Americans so bold as to claim liberty and virtue. That culture, which originally stood for violence against blacks, however, devolved into one that suppressed white dissent as well. Anyone with the temerity to test the Democratic party, the self-proclaimed keeper of the social ethic by virtue of its victory over Radicalism, received the opprobrious label "Black Republican." After 1876 the political culture of racism, then, assured that freed people would not return to the polls in large numbers and that intraparty and third-party challenges to the Democractic party would be regarded as threats to white domination of politics and society. Where once the social ethic had fostered cultural homogeneity under the rubric of white liberty and black enslavement, the political culture that emerged from Reconstruction made no promises of securing political liberty to whites. It promised only to maintain the racial division of society and to persecute anyone, white or black, who questioned Democratic rule.

54. Quoting L. Q. C. Lamar *et al.* "Ought the Negro to be Disfranchised?" *North American Review,* LXXVIII (1879), 231–38. William Baskin to "Dear Sister," August 26, 1876, William Baskin to Mary Middleton, August 19, 1876, in Middleton Family Papers, MDAH.

55. Quoting Lamar, "Ought the Negro to be Disfranchised?" 231–38. On the rise of bulldozing, see D. L. Smythe to John M. Stone, April 27, 1876; T. C. Catchings to Stone, April 22, 1876; J. B. Chrisman to Stone, April 2, 1879; J. M. Patrick to James Hill, May 23, 1877, in RG 27, MDAH.

Chapter 6

Of Merchants and Railroads

Despite the reification of the social ethic's racial underpinnings, the ethic itself emerged from the period of Reconstruction changed; the presence of even nominally free blacks cracked the foundation upon which liberty had been traditionally erected. Even though white citizens had not wished it, the South stood poised to become a New South. Some reacted quickly to the promise of a different order. Less than a year after Robert E. Lee surrendered his command at Appomattox Courthouse, Elizabeth R. McNabb discerned a change among the young men living in her neighborhood: "Simon Catchings is coming back to Summitt[.] [H]e and J. B. Quinn are going to have a store. Everybody wants to be merchants, doctors, or lawyers. Lucius Quinn is reading medecine [*sic*] so is Will Lamkin[,] John Quinn, Dick Bridges, Frank Martin[,] and a host of others." [1] These men, longtime Pike County residents all, understood that the Confederacy's demise and black liberty heralded a new age. Like their kinsmen, the purposeful settlers of the old southwestern cotton kingdom, they invented the South anew, making a place for themselves on the postbellum frontier.

Sensing that the war had devalued once sacrosanct ideals, those Pike County men eschewed the habits of their fathers and assumed new ones. Unlike historians who have occasionally bludgeoned each other over questions about continuity and change in the South, contemporaries understood that they lived in a new world. Four years of war and the promise of Reconstruction did not bode well for the full resurrection of the Old South's myths and realities. Most obviously, military defeat and emancipation made the dream of owning a cotton plantation and one hundred slaves impos-

1. Elizabeth R. McNabb to "My Dearest Friend," March 29, 1866, in McNabb Letters (Typescript in MDAH). On the rapidity with which citizens embraced commerce, see the clipping titled "Mississippi's Industrial Advance" in McCool Family Papers, MDAH.

sible.[2] Without the mastery over labor afforded by slavery, operating a plantation after 1865 became an odious task for many surviving whites with dreams of material success. Furthermore, events in the mid- to late 1860s suggested that the federal government intended to close the material and moral gap separating the South from the rest of the nation. White Mississippians, while accepting material progress for themselves, rejected ex-slaves' claims to the economic and political fruits of free labor. They clung to tenets of the social ethic that bolstered their economic standing, but forsook other aspects of the ethic in order to seek success in fields not planted in cotton, proclaiming through their actions that liberty and virtue in the postbellum era inhered in those who accumulated great riches, regardless of their relationship to the land.

Emancipation, with its explicit profanation of the antebellum social ethic, explained in part the eagerness with which some Mississippians pursued material success away from the farm, but as Harold Woodman has pointed out, ascertaining why the transformation from Old South to New South took place consumes less energy than determining how it came about.[3] For if the late-nineteenth-century South deserves to be called "New," historians must explicate the course of the transformation. Changes in public policy opened the way for creation of a new social and economic order. Commercial and industrial entrepreneurs benefited from state-proffered tax exemptions, the Subsidy Act, and the Abatement Act; in a similar fashion, rural merchants used the crop-lien law to appropriate the function of antebellum cotton factors and to re-create themselves as a new class of prestigious men in the countryside. But the most significant change took place outside legislative halls. Insightful men had learned during the war and Reconstruction that if the state was to rise Phoenix-like from the ashes of defeat, they would have to embrace the signposts of the new age: industry and commerce that closely linked the South to the national economy. Drawing themselves and the South into the vortex of the national commercial order required that they alter their assumptions about a good republic and good citizenship. Their willingness to do so suggests that the real change that swept over the postwar South occurred in the realm of ideas.

* * *

2. For a review of the literature dealing with the themes of consensus and change, see Harold Woodman, "Economic Reconstruction and the Rise of the New South, 1865–1900," in *Interpreting Southern History: Historiographical Essays in Honor of Sanford W. Higginbotham,* eds. John B. Boles and Evelyn Thomas Nolen (Baton Rouge, 1987), 254–307. See, too, Michael Wayne, *The Reshaping of Plantation Society,* 203. The reference to owning a plantation and one hundred slaves derives from Kellar, ed., "A Journey Through the South," 356.

3. Woodman, "Economic Reconstruction" in *Interpreting Southern History,* 282–83.

Few of the ideas that propelled McNabb's friends and others like them to seek success in uniquely New South ways originated with their generation. The seed of the New South Creed, defined by historian Paul Gaston as a body of ideas about material progress with commerce at the center, had been planted by farsighted railroad promoters and levee builders during the antebellum period.[4] Neither were the ideas embodied in the creed new: economic diversity, railroad development, and an emphasis on wealth as the measure of good citizenship had animated generations of Mississippians. The popularity of the ideas and the fervor with which residents embraced them, however, were peculiar to the New South. Whereas antebellum prophecies of a diversified economy well-integrated into the national one fell from the lips of exceptional men, the number and zeal of the progress-minded increased exponentially after 1865.

While New South prophets envisioned a southern landscape dotted with mills and laced with rail lines, they continued to believe cotton the region's trump card. The difference between their view of cotton's significance and that of antebellum promoters lay in the fact that they did not intend themselves to cultivate it. Other work awaited them. New South prophets foresaw a day when the state was home to factories that refined and marketed cotton as finished goods. Increased cotton production, according to a postbellum Noxubee County newspaper editor, would not only revitalize southern agriculture but would spark an explosion in manufacturing and industrial development of all types. The fortunes that wise investors amassed in the southern commercial order, or so another editor claimed, assured that northern fathers would amend Horace Greeley's famous command for young men to move West and instead tell their children to "go South."[5] Notwithstanding the persisting belief that Mississippi's age of economic splendor depended on cotton, New South prophets, by stressing the industrial-commercial component of their vision, depicted a world in which they wished to live. The new Mississippi would be a land of cotton fields *and* textile mills, truck gardens *and* country stores. (Occasionally an adventurous soul even added mining to the list of activities that would push the state into the mainstream of national economic development.) Ensuring the triumphant ascension of a New South, however, required its advocates to disavow some of the region's self-conscious peculiarities. In their

4. Paul Gaston, *The New South Creed: A Study in Southern Mythmaking* (New York, 1970), 15–42. For an impassioned statement on the overweening importance of commercial development, see the clipping of an article appearing in the New Orleans *Picayune*, McCool Family Papers.

5. Quoting Macon *Mississippi Sun*, February 24, 1884, but see, too, Grenada *Sentinel*, November 17, 1883, June 3, 1882; Vicksburg *Evening Banner*, May 4, 1887.

language the sectional conflict and Civil War became anomalies, times when barbarism reigned among a peaceful and progressive people. Penitent for their transgressions, they proclaimed the region's grasp for independence foolhardy; olden times and ways were forever forgotten. In the view of a Natchez editor, Mississippians stood ready to "take up with the new habits, the new methods, the new tastes, which the new condition of affairs renders necessary." As "a new people," they prepared to enter "the battle of life" with their contemporaries in the rest of the nation.[6] To compete with the industrializing North and the expansive West, New South prophets, without forswearing cotton, recognized the need for a diverse economy.

Industrial facilities and railroads, however, were merely outward manifestations of the South's newness and testimony to New South prophets' commitment to commerce. The transforming experience of the postwar period, the experience that permitted the expansion of the commercial order into the state, occurred far removed from public view and moved with such stealth that individuals often failed to recognize its onset. Where antebellum ideals had espoused the virtues of debt-free living and self-sufficient production within the market economy to assure personal political independence, New South ideals heralded the virtues of a Yankee-like lust for money and interdependent economic relationships. Few late-nineteenth-century southerners would have announced that they had forsaken self-sufficiency, but creating a South of plantations, factories, and railroads required a degree of interconnectedness with the market economy that antebellum citizens, despite their desire for the rewards of the market, had not known. If antebellum Mississippians simply dabbled in the web of the market economy, their descendants submitted to the entangling grasp of a far more intricate web. By surrendering to the pull of the postwar market, erecting a rail system, and encouraging industrial growth, cash-oriented businessmen supplanted mythological self-sufficient farmers as God's-chosen people.

The desire to obtain great riches had always led men to the Deep South frontier, but after the war, with the wealth-creating opportunity of slavery closed, cash took on added significance. To some postbellum Mississippians, accumulating money took precedence over the antebellum moral

6. Quoting Natchez *Daily Democrat,* November 20, 1875. On the development of industries not directly dependent on cotton, see Natchez *Daily Democrat and Courier,* February 3, 19, March 17, May 2, 1887; Macon *Mississippi Sun,* March 19, 1888. On mining, see Lucius Q. C. Lamar to S. A. Jonas, June 15, 1884, in S. A. Jonas Papers, MDAH; James Hubbard to Eugene Hilgard, February 8, 1872, in Hilgard Papers. On the Civil War as a time of barbarism, see Natchez *Daily Democrat and Courier,* January 5, 1877.

imperative that exalted achievement of economic independence. The Leake County representative of the credit-ranking firm R. G. Dun and Company paid Hector H. Howard, Jr. a singularly New South compliment suggestive of the changed values. Howard, a druggist and general store owner, appeared "to understand his bus[iness]. very well and will make money (Yankee like)." Some residents lost their perspective on life when their pecuniary success seemed impossible. Philip M. Catchings, a planter and merchant in Simpson County, while contemplating the impending death of his infant child and his looming financial failure, had difficulty distinguishing which more deeply affected him. "Our Baby has been expected to die for a week. I think will die this morning in a few hours[.] I am about ruined. I don't think that I will Ever recover my losses from this overflow[.] The Baby died at 8 oclock [*sic*] at night." In a new age that appreciated wealth more than independence, others faced temptations to engage in illegal activities. It is not known how J. E. Reynolds responded to an offer to pass counterfeit money in Mississippi, but the promise of being placed "upon the highway to fortune and affluance [*sic*]" would surely have appealed to many New South citizens.[7]

Other southerners sought temporal rewards in distinctly New South fashion. J. F. Herndon knew of nothing that would hinder his journey toward fortune and affluence. With a resolution unrivaled even by William Faulkner's fictional Flem Snopes, Herndon set out to make a place for himself in the economic order of the postbellum world. Reversing the course that his predecessors had taken, Herndon, a store clerk, decided to move east in search of the riches that eluded him in Texas: "I intend to have money if I am sent to the Dry Tortugas or to Hell for it." Such determination, literally Herndon's selling his soul to the devil, knew no bounds. After purchasing "a Spring stock of goods" in New York, he hoped to return South, "look out for breakers," and make a handsome profit on his two thousand dollar investment. In February, 1871, Herndon opened a store at the crossroads town of Brooksville in Noxubee County, but his dreams of achieving the easy wealth of a merchant soon encountered the realities of the rural trade. Six months after his arrival the local representative employed by R. G. Dun and Company characterized his prospects as hopeless and warned

7. Quoting Dun and Company, Noxubee County, 14H; Catchings Diary, December 8, 1880 (in Catchings Collection); B. B. Walker to "Dear Sir," January 1871, in J. E. Reynolds Papers, MDAH. For a contrary view of cash, see R. A. Evans' condemnation of his brother for teaching his children to love money: "I think you are courting a great error in teaching them to love it so & their clothes don't amount to much in the eyes of the lord. So you can tell them to go to church." See R. A. Evans to "Dear Brother," June 6, 1872, in Evans Papers.

potential creditors that Herndon spoke of moving on. With an unsalable stock valued at between five and eight hundred dollars, Herndon lived in a hell on earth bound by poverty and creditors' demands for payment. By June, 1872, he had sold his business, but not before leaving a lasting impression on the Dun representative, who described him as given to "trickery & sharp." [8] Although Herndon might have been more willing than most to engage in questionable practices, he shared with innumerable postbellum Mississippians a yearning to become a new man in the New South.

Herndon's selling of his soul to the devil in exchange for a country store is suggestive. For the country store, as much as cotton and railroads, served as a symbol of the New South. Many acquisitive souls, newcomers and longtime residents alike, looked upon the retail trade as a promising way to achieve success in postemancipation Mississippi. The store itself, quite often a ramshackle building with a bowed roof and sagging floor, served as a polling place, gossip mill, and center of rural social life. More importantly, as merchants evolved into plantation suppliers and venture capitalists, the country store connected the cotton kingdom of the New South to the commercial order of the late nineteenth century and thus served as an intermediate stage of integration into the national economy.

In the immediate postwar period, rural merchants took over the lending duties previously performed by commission houses, most of which had shut down during the Civil War. Like their predecessors in the world of rural finance, the cotton market dictated their fate. Since furnishing merchants served an exclusively rural clientele as cotton brokers and suppliers of farming materials, they survived or failed according to the fluctuations of the cotton market. Scattered references in the credit ledgers of R. G. Dun and Company suggest the tightness with which the fate of merchants and farmers were intertwined. Of one merchandising concern Dun observed, "their success depends upon the cotton crop;" of another, "their future success depends almost entirely on the crop this year therefore a fair precaution should be used;" and of another, "he advances the planters & is entirely dependent on them." [9] Unlike antebellum cotton factors, postbellum country store operators also served small-scale cotton cultivators. With the

8. Dun and Company, Noxubee County, 38.

9. Quoting Dun and Company, Leake County, 10; Warren County, 82; Marshall County, 106. On the postbellum country store, see in Thomas D. Clark, *Pills, Petticoats, and Plows: The Southern Country Store* (Indianapolis, 1944); Ransom and Sutch, *One Kind of Freedom*, 120–25; Woodman, *King Cotton and His Retainers*, 295–313. During the great flood of 1882, the close relationship between country store owners and petty cotton producers became evi-

crop-lien law protecting against financial loss, they furnished the new yeoman class that emerged in response to emancipation and whose ranks grew during the depression of the 1870s.

Even though postbellum merchants replaced cotton factors as the primary financiers and suppliers in the rural economy, some merchants continued to act as little more than agents for surviving commission houses. Jacob Halberg, a Noxubee County planter and merchant, dealt exclusively with the Mobile firm of Foster and Gardner. Other merchants, in a practice rarer still, continued the antebellum tradition of country store owners becoming commission merchants. At Greenville, Samuel Worthington, Davis M. Buckner, and William Mason, along with their wives, formed a dry goods and banking house in 1871. Capitalized with $125,000, which Worthington had won in a law suit, their company specialized in "buy[ing] and sell[ing] exchange [sic] and shave[ing] notes." The company, like similar furnishing agencies, suffered greatly during the Panic of 1873, and in the mid-1870s the Bank of Greenville bought them out, transforming what had been a sophisticated furnishing business into a modern banking institution.[10]

In the late 1860s and early 1870s most merchants lacked the capital to engage in complicated furnishing and currency speculation operations. To obtain credit for a stock of goods, they turned instead to wholesale houses based in St. Louis, Cincinnati, New York, and Boston. Wholesalers, confusingly referred to at times as commission merchants, were happy to oblige them and to offer liberal terms; they looked upon the South as a new market recently made accessible by nascent transportation and communication revolutions. Typically, wholesalers tendered a supply of goods on commission and carried the full cost of the shipment on their accounts until the first of the year, when merchants' customers sold their cotton. Under the arrangement, risks were dispersed and wholesalers expanded their markets without laying out a prodigious amount of capital. Merchants, some of whom viewed the retail trade as simply a route to success more lucrative and less wearisome than farming, became the cornerstone of modern American business in the South. Their close working relationship with vertically integrated wholesalers allowed them to play in late-nineteenth-century America a role similar to that enjoyed by railroads: they

dent as flood waters made it impossible to plant a crop. See E. F. Walker to Robert Lowry, June 1, 1882; Thomas Mount to Lowry, March 23, 1882, all in RG 27, MDAH.

10. Dun and Company, Noxubee County, 38; Washington County, 37, 53, 86–87.

symbolically and actually linked the South to the commercial United States. Whereas in the antebellum period country merchants often acted merely as adjuncts to southern cotton factors, after the war they provided a firm connection between isolated consumers/producers and large markets. As such, their suppliers expected them to follow closely the dictates of modern business, and R. G. Dun's representatives, agents of modernity themselves, reported their acumen and personal habits to potential creditors.[11] Although the first generation of postbellum merchants lacked the expertise possessed by later ones, they were nonetheless makers of an intermediate stage of economic advance.

While the arrangements between merchants and distant wholesalers secured the South's access to the commercial order, merchants exploited the crop-lien law to make a place for themselves in the countryside. Store owners, who began their enterprises with nothing more than a good name, farmland for collateral, and a supply of nonperishable items obtained on consignment, used the law to amass plantations. When they acquired land, they rented it to sharecroppers, who purchased goods from their stores. Planters, who wished to perfect their control of labor, observed the success of merchants, and they too soon opened stores to serve their tenants.

Originally passed in 1867, the lien law permitted lenders first claim on the crops and unfixed assets of defaulting debtors, turning over to lenders in cash-poor Mississippi enormous power over the rural economy. Not only did crop-lien-wielding merchants wrest from planters control over labor, they also expanded their lending operations to include small-scale white producers, who turned to them for plantation supplies and sustenance until crops were harvested. Under the protection of the lien law, merchants furnished even the smallest producer, hedging against losses by charging substantial interest for their services. In the unlikely event that a farmer paid off his debt and interest, the merchant benefited by clearing a name from his books. But if the farmer failed to retire his debt, the merchant could seize assets (generally cotton but in the case of indebted landowners the land itself), and place a lien on other assets, including the next year's crop. (When the merchant seized land, he likely rented it the following year, and perhaps to the same defaulting farmer.) Thus, with the proceeds of one year wiped out and a debt carried over, the farmer faced another year in which he worked in essence for the merchant. As a virtual employee, he had to plant mostly cotton, the only crop that promised a market, in-

11. On merchants' reliance on wholesalers, see Dun and Company, Lowndes County, 24, 112, 162. On the Dun Company and merchants as signposts of a new era, see Ransom and Sutch, *One Kind of Freedom,* 120–22.

creasing his dependence on the merchant for even more of his supplies.[12]

The cycle of receiving supplies, planting cotton, borrowing against the crop for foodstuffs, and falling further into debt at the end of the year spun endlessly. Debts, like stores and plantations, passed from one generation to the next. Robert Somers, traveling through the South during Reconstruction, accurately observed the effect that the furnishing business had upon the rural economy: "A new class of [business] houses are springing up . . . whose conditions of advance are almost necessarily marked by a degree of rigour that was unknown in former times, and that will probably grind and impoverish the mass of poorer cultivators, white and black, for a long time to come." Besides dictating that their debtors plant pretty much all cotton, store owners demanded too a kind of fealty, insisting that clients maintain accounts and sell produce only at their stores, demands that tended to limit the number of clients that patronized a particular merchant. (In 1880, Roger Ransom and Richard Sutch have estimated, the typical country store furnished only seventy tenants.)[13] Requiring indebted customers to trade exclusively with them also limited the capital required to operate a country store. Few customers meant few goods lined the shelves.

Because of the limited nature of the country merchant's business, owning a rural store had obvious appeal to substantial landowners. Using their land as collateral, they could receive from a wholesale house a stock of goods to sell to tenants who worked their land. Labor, after all, needed supplies to plant cotton, as well as foodstuffs to feed their families; by supplying his own tenants, the planter-merchant avoided sticky legal questions that arose over control of the crop. In 1878 W. M. Connor of Fox Trap, who rented land to tenants enough to produce about four hundred bales of cotton, opened a store to supply his hands. He apparently supplied few other rural folk. Other planter-merchants expanded their retail operations to furnish neighboring farmers. B. R. Long and five old planters of Marshall County began a small general store so that they could control their tenants' crops. Not long after opening, however, local farmers called on them for supplies, and they broadened their business to include the purchasing of cotton "on a small scale principally from patrons." Still other

12. On the country merchant and the crop-lien law, see Ransom and Sutch, *One Kind of Freedom,* 120–22, 156–61; Woodman, *King Cotton and His Retainers,* 310–11; Joseph D. Reid, Jr., "White Land, Black Labor, and Agricultural Stagnation: The Causes and Effects of Sharecropping in the Postbellum South," *Explorations in Economic History,* XVI (1979), 31–35; Roger Ransom and Richard Sutch, "Debt Peonage in the Cotton South After the Civil War," *Journal of Economic History,* XXXII (1972), 641–69.

13. Somers quoted in Ransom and Sutch, *One Kind of Freedom,* 156, but see, too, 137.

planters became silent partners in country stores. S. C. English of Panola County kept afloat a rural concern in the lean postbellum years and undoubtedly viewed his investment a lucrative one that enabled him to retain a measure of control over his tenants and their crop.[14] For store owners who established furnishing monopolies, rich rewards awaited.

Since land ownership, cotton cultivation, and furnishing went hand in hand, merchants became large landowners and large landowners became merchants. In 1847 Norfleet R. Sledge migrated to Mississippi and carved a plantation from the loess hills of Panola County. At the same time he opened a dry goods store, which remained in operation for eleven years, and brokered cotton for his neighbors. A progress-minded planter, Sledge used his position as a director of the fledgling Mississippi and Tennessee Railroad Company to ensure that the line ran near his home, offering easy access to Memphis and Jackson, and indirectly to New Orleans. By 1861 he held, according to credit reports, nearly $500,000 in property, 10 percent of which he loaned at interest. Then, the war came. The effects of the war on Sledge's prosperity remain unclear, but like Robert Penn Warren's Gilbert Mastern, he "who had made one fortune with his bare hands, out of the very air, could now, with all his experience and cunning and hardness . . . snatch another one, much greater than the first." Even before the war drew to a close, Sledge set about snatching another fortune. Taking a partner to bolster his depleted capital, Sledge reentered the retail business and remained involved in the store until his death in 1881. During the postbellum period he also groomed his sons to assume control of the country store; as well-taught pupils, they expanded their father's trade. Norfleet, Jr. owned stores in Memphis, Lula, Mastodon, and Como. With his brother, O. D., Norfleet also held two plantations, one of five thousand acres in Panola County and another that produced one thousand bales of cotton each year.[15]

In snatching their fortunes the Sledges undoubtedly benefited from the crop-lien law, their father's experience, and the access to Memphis and beyond provided by the railroad. Railroads not only permitted merchants access to wholesalers, but facilitated their development of furnishing mo-

14. Quoting Dun and Company, Marshall County, 99, but see, too, Noxubee County, 54; Panola County, 78 a/4.

15. Quoting Warren, *All The King's Men,* 162. On the Norfleets, see Dun and Company, Panola County, 63, 78T, 78E; Goodspeed Brothers, *Biographical and Historical Memoirs of Mississippi . . . and a Record of the Lives of Many of the Most Worthy and Illustrious Families and Individuals* (2 vols.; Chicago, 1891), II, 785–86; *Sixth Annual Report of the President and Directors of the Mississippi and Tennessee Railroad. . . .* (Memphis, 1859).

nopolies by opening ready markets for the cotton they purchased. Often times obtaining oligarchic authority over the furnishing business in a neighborhood depended on a railroad connection to cotton markets and wholesale houses, for any merchant who operated on a railroad line stood a better chance of success than one who opened a store far removed from a line. W. H. Scales, a Lowndes County merchant, understood the importance of railroads in postbellum Mississippi and built a furnishing empire along the Mobile and Ohio. Scales's father, N. F. Scales, a doctor, planter, and merchant, had migrated to Lowndes County before 1860. The younger Scales at first seemed uninterested in following in his father's footsteps and conducted a pair of schools in northeast Mississippi. Around 1856, however, W. H. removed to Camden, Arkansas, a converging point for travelers to the West, where he opened a general store. After the war Scales returned to Mississippi and took over his father's enterprises. Like other merchants of the time, Scales struggled to build a successful furnishing trade in the unsettled political and economic atmosphere of the 1870s. With the assistance of a partner's bankroll, he opened stores at West Point, Crawfordsville, Starkville, Brooksville, Macon, and Mobile. By 1890 he held twelve hundred acres of land and brokered cotton transactions down the length of the Mobile and Ohio line.[16] As dominating forces in the local credit and cotton markets, country store owners utilized the residual influence of their antebellum wealth and reputations to carve small monopolies in their neighborhoods that in turn let them consolidate large landholdings; merchants who started their careers as planters simply reversed the process. Regardless of the course they took, furnishing merchants developed a strong grasp on the rural economy.

To an entire generation of postbellum men seeking a respite from the backbreaking and unrewarding labor of farming, the business world beckoned. Yet relatively few plain farmers answered the call, and fewer still, Faulkner's Flem Snopes excepted, likely lasted long in business. Among 106 postbellum business owners identified in the Dun ledgers, only one might be considered of yeoman background. In 1879 J. A. Bowie, a twenty-five-year-old laborer, opened a drug store at Edinburgh in Leake County. Dun's representative noted that Bowie had "very little education" but believed him "likely to succeed & to gain slowly." [17] Businessmen (country store op-

16. On Scales, see Dun and Company, Lowndes County, 13, 100; Noxubee County, 17. Goodspeed Brothers, *Biographical and Historical Memoirs of Mississippi*, II, 722–23.

17. Quoting Dun and Company, Leake County, 25. William Faulkner, *The Hamlet* (1931; rpr. New York, 1964), 3–67. The survey of merchants listed in the Dun files was conducted for the following counties: Copiah, Harrison, Jones, Leake, Lowndes, Marshall, Noxubee,

erators, as well as other merchants) needed cash or credit to open their concerns, and aside from established farmers who held real estate, Mississippians lacked assets to secure the faith of wholesalers. New men of the Snopes variety simply lacked the reputation and skill needed to break into the commercial order. Plain folk eking out an existence had not been movers and shakers in the Old South economy, and their vaulting to prominence remained unlikely in the postbellum period.

Before ascending into the merchant class, entrepreneurs had to possess mortgageable assets, and in the immediate postwar period, only owners of moderate or substantial acreage held adequate land to secure credit. So important was land to securing credit and a customer base, a significant minority of rural merchants continued to farm after opening their businesses. Among the sampled businessmen who, according to the Dun files, started their concerns after 1867, approximately 20 percent listed their occupation in the 1870 census as farmer or planter. A survey of lumber mill owners operating in 1884 further suggests that commercial entrepreneurs continued to farm; of thirteen mill operators sampled, eight listed their occupations in the 1880 census as farmers. Although the small number of observed businessmen-farmers precludes drawing meaningful conclusions about their wealth, census data indicate they were longtime residents and likely well-established members of their communities. Taken together, the samples suggest that in the postbellum period business owners traveled the short distance from established farmer to retail trader.[18]

Even though most of the business owners identified were men who held some land and other assets, many might be considered newcomers to the commercial order for other reasons: they entered the commercial world after the war, and a number of them hailed from foreign lands. Approximately 81 percent opened their operations after the Civil War, and most first ap-

---

Panola, Pontotoc, Warren, Washington, and Wilkinson. Forty-nine of the 106 merchants identified owned grocery or general stores; 15 manufactured finished products such as carriages or furniture. The other businessmen owned saloons, hotels, drugstores, wholesale groceries, seafood shops, or practiced a trade.

18. Business owners were sampled in the Dun and Company Mercantile Agency Credit Ledgers for the counties listed in the above note. They were then located in the Manuscript Census, Schedule I: Free Population, 1860 and 1870, Mississippi. The sample of lumber mill operators was drawn from *Directory and Shipping Guide of Lumber Mills and Lumber Dealers in the United States and Canada* (Chicago, 1884), 239–46. Only operators who listed their addresses in the twelve selected counties used throughout this study were sampled. Additional information about them is found in the Manuscript Census, Schedule I: Population, 1880, various counties, Mississippi.

peared in the Dun ledgers within twenty-four months of 1870. Curiously, a relatively large number (nearly 20 percent) of postbellum business operators had immigrated from European nations, particularly the German states. Most of those identified in the census as immigrants worked in skilled trades, though several peddled goods or operated country stores. The immigrants, especially the Jewish merchants, perhaps maintained an advantage over native southern country store owners: with family relations in the New York or New Orleans supply houses, they obtained slightly advantageous terms for dry goods while offering their clientele exceptional brokerage service.[19] Not every immigrant businessman enjoyed such a relationship with distant suppliers, of course. Morris Weiss, a Jewish immigrant, apparently made his way as a store owner without the help of kinsmen. In 1868, with the assistance of a local partner, he opened a dry goods store. Four years later, just before the onset of the panic and the devastating Greenville fire of 1874, Weiss mortgaged everything he owned in order to buy out his partner's interest. Simultaneous disasters in 1873 and 1874 seemed not to slow Weiss's ascent in the commercial world. In 1875 he built two tall brick stores from which he conducted his business.[20] A new man in the New South, Weiss stood out among his contemporaries largely because of his success.

As intermediate agents of economic modernization, postbellum men of commerce, generally reputable men of status and wealth, led Mississippi into the vortex of the commercial economy. The appearance of a commercial class, composed of old planters or at least property holders, validated an economic and social elite that resembled in manner, attitude, and often in name the antebellum one. The urge to succeed in the post-emancipation South propelled these men to seek riches in occupations other than farming. They communicated this desire for material success through their commercial enterprises, and though not of itself foreign to antebellum notions of good citizenship, the course they chose to take in pursuit of wealth reflected a response to changed conditions. Commerce offered a path to success in a world no longer supportive of the dream of owning a cotton plantation and one hundred slaves. Inspired by new conditions to embrace the commercial order, merchants opened the way for Mississippi to enter

19. Dun and Company, Marshall County, 57, 75; Panola County, 78L, 78H. On Jewish merchants with New Orleans commercial connections, see Elliott Ashkenazi, *The Business of Jews in Louisiana, 1840–1875* (Tuscaloosa, 1988), 64–103, 142–56.

20. On Weiss, see Dun and Company, Washington County, 20, 32, 64, but see, too, Washington County, 10, 63; Goodspeed Brothers, *Biographical and Historical Memoirs of Mississippi*, I, 299.

the national economy of the postbellum period. With an impulse analogous to the one that drove their antebellum predecessors who pursued virtuous citizenship through material success, they continued to depend on land, labor, and cotton.

The transformation of Mississippi, which began soon after the war and which was symbolized by the rise of the merchant class, impressed the Panola County planter Samuel Matthews. Writing to his brother, who had emigrated to Arizona, Matthews tried to lure him back to the state with assurances of a coming racial peace and industrial development: "There is a general feeling among our people to cease to depend on negro labor, to build up manufactures and as soon as possible cease to export raw cotton but work it up at home." [21] Like postbellum southerners in every state, Matthews looked beyond the intermediate level of economic advance embodied in commerce and counted on industry impacting his state with revolutionary force. Even though he omitted reference to railroads, Matthew's vision of a Mississippi rebuilt on a native textile industry required completion of an efficient transportation system. Some Mississippians more clearly placed their faith in railroads, believing steam engines and iron tracks were destined to bring great joy. Fannie E. Eaton commented that the people in her community "all have the railroad fits very bad, some very bad indeed." Others spoke about distinct advantages that derived from railroad development. James F. H. Claiborne, a proponent of economic expansion in the coastal counties, coupled all progress, agricultural and industrial, to the fulfillment of his dream of a railroad penetrating the Piney Woods. "The great want of this country," he said, "is a railroad, with proper feeders to lift this mighty forest and bring it, as it were, to the lap of the ocean." Whether coastal entrepreneurs pursued their position in the New South through forest industries or the cultivation of scuppernongs, rice, tobacco, or cotton, they needed efficient and cost-effective access to markets that railroads provided.[22]

Notwithstanding Mississippians' excitement over railroads, progress in laying tracks proceeded at a snail's pace. The wartime destruction of Mississippi's 862 miles of track, the lingering economic malaise of the Reconstruction period, and the state's reluctance to commit its resources to private enterprise discouraged builders interested in exploiting the state. Lines

21. Samuel Matthews to John Matthews, September 19, 1867, in Matthews Letters.

22. Quoting Fannie E. Eaton to Mary A. Barnes, n.d., in Barnes Family Papers, MDAH; Claiborne quoted in E. G. Wall, *The State of Mississippi: Resources, Condition and Wants. . . .* (Jackson, 1879), 78, 81.

in north and central Mississippi had borne the brunt of the war's destructive impact. The Mississippi Central, which ran between Jackson and the Tennessee border, lost equipment valued at $750,000 between 1861 and 1865. Replacing or repairing wartime damage took years. Traveling on the Mississippi Central, Whitelaw Reid complained of a "dismal night of thumpings over broken rails and contortions of the cars" relieved only by a midnight portage at a burned-out bridge. Cordelia Scales, who lived along the Mississippi Central in Marshall County, nonchalantly informed Loulie Irby that "the train fell through the trussel [*sic*] in our field yesterday," but, anxious to see her friend, she added, "*don't let it detain you*, for you get off *this side* of the breakage."[23] Faced with such conditions but believing that railroads could rapidly restore prosperity, residents first intended to repair war-ravaged track and then to build other lines. They lacked capital, however, to undertake such enterprises. Beginning in the Reconstruction period, a pattern of railroad development emerged that would continue throughout the nineteenth century: unable themselves to reconstruct or extend lines, Mississippians depended on the infusion of capital and the management skills of northern and foreign entrepreneurs, as well as government assistance.

In the postbellum period the infusion of outside capital into the construction and operation of Mississippi railroads became common. After the economic disaster of the Civil War, few Mississippians, despite their desire to rebuild the cotton kingdom and open the state to development, possessed the financial wherewithal to invest in expensive projects. The Mississippi Central Railroad Company, after coming close to bankruptcy during Reconstruction and passing through the hands of Delaware developer Henry McComb, was purchased by the Illinois Central company, which soon became the broker of other railroad enterprises in central and western Mississippi. Immediately after the war, investors like McComb represented the best hope for railroad development since native promoters could not count on state assistance. The disastrous experience with state-funded banks and repudiation in the 1830s and 1840s shaped the Constitution of 1868, which prohibited the state from aiding private enterprises and required local governments interested in subscribing to the stock of an enterprise to pass bond

23. Quoting Whitelaw Reid, *After the War: A Southern Tour, May 11, 1865 to May 1866* (Cincinnati, 1866), 425; Cordelia Scales to Loulie Irby, December 11, 1866, in Scales Letters. See, too, Charles E. Dameron to "Grandma," March 4, 1866, in Norton-Chilton-Dameron Papers. For a report of the condition of the railroad after the war, see *Ninth Annual Report of the President and Directors of the Mississippi and Tennessee Railroad. . . .* (Memphis, 1865), 31–37.

issues by a two-thirds majority of voters who had been specifically registered for the election.[24] During the 1870s and early 1880s, outright hostility toward railroads rarely appeared, but citizens' advocacy of low taxes and government retrenchment boded ill for broad support of local bond issues. Designed to skirt constitutional restrictions without alarming taxpayers, the state passed legislation (including the Subsidy Act and the Abatement Act) to encourage construction, exempted railroad companies from taxation, and made convict labor available to companies.

The first legislation passed to aid in the construction of railroads, the Subsidy Act, was the brainchild of William D'Alton Mann, a former Union army officer and owner of the Mobile *Register*. Having previously convinced the state to grant his Mobile and Northwestern Railroad all state-owned lands within twenty miles of the projected route of the line (approximately 1 million acres) and to sell the company 750,000 acres of swampland for two cents an acre, Mann beseeched the legislature to pass the even more favorable Subsidy Act. The 1871 law appropriated four thousand dollars for each mile of track laid by any railroad company, provided that at least twenty-five miles were completed by September, 1875. Legislative support for the measure originated with representatives through whose districts the proposed route would pass, and since the projected line was to traverse the state from southeast to northwest, a number of legislators warmly backed Mann's project, believing that lumber industries and cotton mills would accompany the railroad. Passage of the measure did not ensure its success, however. From the time that it received Governor Alcorn's signature, the capitol rumor mill hummed with reports of undue influence (some said bribes) that Mann brought to bear against reluctant legislators.[25] In 1872, responding to the whispered charges against Mann, Governor Powers threatened to repeal the law as unconstitutional. Yet Mann prevailed upon him to submit questions about the law's constitutionality to Attorney General Joshua S. Morris. Unbeknownst to the governor, Mann had secretly retained Morris as his counsel and promised him a bonus if he ruled in favor of the Subsidy Act, which he did. With dissent about the constitutionality of the law quelled, Mann's scheme ran its course.

24. On postbellum laws regarding stock subscription, see *Laws of the State of Mississippi* 1877, pp. 28, 31–32; *Laws of the State of Mississippi* 1882, pp. 52–53. On McComb and the Mississippi Central, see John F. Stover, *History of the Illinois Central Railroad* (New York, 1975), 150–51; John F. Stover, *The Railroads of the South, 1865–1900: A Study in Finance and Control* (Chapel Hill, 1955), 162–79.

25. On Mann, see Harris, *Day of the Carpetbagger,* 532–40. For the Subsidy Act, see *Laws of the State of Mississippi,* 1871, pp. 745–48.

In September, 1875, when time for railroads to earn their construction bounty expired, only a north Mississippi railroad qualified to receive any money. The state, however, professing penury, paid but a portion of the promised cash. For all his exertions Mann and the Mobile and Northwestern received not a single cent from the state and little from private sources. For when word of Mann's surreptitious dealings with the legislature spread, construction firms and communities doubted his trustworthiness and retracted their commitments to the railroad.[26]

Even with the $4,000-per-mile bounty promised railroad companies, the Subsidy Act failed to draw entrepreneurs to the state. The political climate in the early 1870s undoubtedly caused many prospective builders to look elsewhere. Then, too, despite the professions of the state's Centrist leadership that Mississippi wished to advance economically, the depression of the early 1870s caused investors to shrink from adventurous moves. Passage of the Abatement Act in 1875 (the second concession, albeit an indirect one, made to railroad builders) opened Mississippi to entrepreneurs. As suggested by its title, the Abatement Act rendered relief to delinquent taxpayers. According to Redeemer Democrats, state and local taxes levied by Republican administrations stymied private efforts to build up the planting and manufacturing interest of Mississippi. Landowners, especially Delta planters, who paid antebellum levee taxes as well as current ones, viewed the taxes as excessive. The situation in the Delta was unique. As much as three-quarters of the acreage owned in the region was unimproved swampland that friendly antebellum tax assessors had undervalued on the tax rolls. Republican administrations in the late 1860s, however, began enforcing the strict assessment provisions of the 1868 constitution, placing unproductive swamp- and woodland on the tax rolls at their full value. Property taxes in the Delta skyrocketed when Reconstruction governments applied assessment laws equitably. Planters in the river counties also annually owed up to five dollars per acre to retire old levee debts and paid additional taxes to reconstruct new levees. Unable to pay their taxes, many planters saw their land revert to the state; in 1871 nearly 1.37 million acres were abandoned for delinquent taxes in seven northern Delta counties; more than 2 million acres reverted to the state in 1878.[27] With the land vacant, railroad companies saw no reason to venture into the region.

Designed to relieve farmers of their tax debts for the years 1865 to 1874, the Abatement Act proved of little assistance until after the depression lifted.

26. On the investigation into Mann's dealings with the state, see *Mississippi House Journal*, 1873, pp. 1532–72.

27. Brandfon, *Cotton Kingdom of the New South*, 42–49.

But in the long run the return to economic stability and the moratorium on outstanding taxes invited speculators to purchase state lands at reduced prices without paying back taxes. Through a series of legal suits, investors who held levee bonds secured the right to purchase forfeited lands with 5 percent cash and the remainder in bonds and scrip issued by the Liquidating Levee Board, the body charged with erasing antebellum debts. Lands that had long been dormant went on the market and fell into the hands of speculators, and as Robert Brandfon has observed, "land speculation was the starting point for progress" in the Delta. All told the Abatement Act and court action restored approximately two million acres of land to the tax rolls by 1881, and increased ownership of land led to the production of larger cotton crops, which in turn swayed railroad builders to place track through the heart of the Delta.[28] Undoubtedly, forces other than the Abatement Act (the end of the depression, the crop-lien law, and the settlement of labor questions to name three) promoted the Delta's recovery. Cotton production and railroad development surely benefited from the state's changed tax policies that opened vacated land at low cost to speculative buyers and allowed companies to purchase forfeited railroad charters without incurring delinquent tax burdens.

Special privileges granted railroads, however indirectly, soon paid off, particularly for developers interested in the Delta. Some speculators sold their holdings to cotton producers and lumbermen, but others held out, selling to railroads suddenly interested in the fertile region. The companies' interest had been piqued by the availability of land and charters held by defunct concerns that had previously tried to construct lines between Vicksburg and the Mississippi Gulf Coast. In 1882 the western railroad builder Collis P. Huntington purchased two unfinished Delta lines, including 750,000 acres of formerly abandoned land owned by them. Within two years, he completed a 450-mile track between New Orleans and Memphis—the Louisville, New Orleans, and Texas Railway—and continued to purchase small lines and land throughout the 1880s.[29] Running parallel to the Illinois Central (ICRR) and about 80 miles to the west, Huntington's railroad competed with the Chicago-based company. J. C. Clarke, president of the

28. *Ibid.*, 49. *Report of the Auditor of the Public Accounts, 1881* (Jackson, 1881), 55–56. For the Abatement Act, see *Laws of the State of Mississippi,* January, 1875, pp. 11–21. On postbellum cotton production, see Watkins, *King Cotton,* 171.

29. On Huntington's activities and early railroads in the Delta see *Yazoo and Mississippi Valley Company: Laws and Documents* (2 vols.; n.p., n.d.), I, 562–63, 829–38. See, too, William McCaughlan to John M. Stone, August 5, 1878, in RG 27, MDAH.

ICRR, watched jealously as Huntington "traverse[d] the Richest and most thickly populated portion of Mississippi." He entertained notions of constructing a rival feeder line from Jackson or Canton to the Mississippi River opposite Arkansas City. The competition between the two lines lasted until 1892, when Huntington's debts forced him to sell some of his assets, including the Louisville, New Orleans, and Texas to the ICRR.[30] Fueled by ready access to markets and the availability of cheap company-owned lands, the Delta boom of the nineteenth century gained speed in earnest once the ICRR obtained Huntington's line, known thereafter as the Yazoo and Mississippi Valley (Y&MVRR).

In spite of the state's liberation of lands through the Abatement Act, the anticipated railroad boom of the late nineteenth century awaited the implementation of even more favorable legislation, including tax exemptions. Writing to the president of the Vidalia and Western Railroad, J. C. Clarke surmised that until "a more enlightened and liberal policy shall manifest itself in reference to railroads" investment in Mississippi would remain minuscule. Clarke neglected to name which policies discouraged railroad entrepreneurs, but the legislature certainly felt pressure from its agrarian members to apply tax laws evenhandedly. Striking a balance between a desire for rail transportation with a perhaps even more widespread demand for low personal taxes propelled the state to charge railroads privilege taxes ranging from $37.50 to $75.00 per mile of track in 1875. Privilege taxes rose to $40.00 per mile for short lines and $80.00 for long ones in 1880. Four years later the largest lines in the state paid $100.00 per mile. In addition to privilege taxes, the state in the early years of the Redeemer period levied taxes on acreage owned by railroad companies but not used for railroad purposes.[31] None of the taxes, of course, amounted to crippling amounts, especially since railroads had yet to own large tracts of land.

On one hand, Mississippi treated railroads as any other entity, but the legislature also passed laws to facilitate railroad construction and profitability. One such law relieved companies of civil and criminal liabilities if they permitted passengers to ride atop freight trains, and another extended the Abatement Act to purchasers of foreclosed railroads. Then, in 1880,

30. J. C. Clarke to James Fentress, July 15, 1881, July 19, 1880, in J. C. Clarke Out-Letters, 1880–83, III, Chicago, St. Louis, and New Orleans Railroad Company Papers, NL; Brandfon, *Cotton Kingdom of the New South,* 70–72, 80.

31. J. C. Clarke to H. M. Gastrell, July 19, 1880, in Clarke Out-Letters, 1880–83, III, Chicago, St. Louis, and New Orleans Railroad Company Papers. *Laws of the State of Mississippi,* January, 1875, pp. 66–67; *Laws of the State of Mississippi,* 1876, pp. 264–65; *Laws of the State of Mississippi,* 1878, p. 87; *Laws of the State of Mississippi,* 1884, pp. 29–31.

the legislature exempted railroads from paying state property taxes, except taxes on vacant land. In the past, short lines had received tax-exempt status, but the 1880 law applied to all companies without discrimination. Unlike the Subsidy and Abatement acts, tax exemption had an immediate impact on railroad building in the state. As the table below suggests, real growth in railroad mileage occurred in the decade of the 1880s. Also, the number of railroad companies chartered increased rapidly. Prior to passage of the tax exemption (in the period from 1878 to 1880), the state chartered nine railroads. But in the 1882 and 1884 legislative sessions, the state granted sixteen charters, in 1888 thirteen, and in 1890 twelve. Passage of the various acts beneficial to railroads, as well as the return to quiet on the political front, furnished a climate conducive to the construction of railroads.[32] By 1880 the old quarrel about lending state aid to private enterprises seemed to have been settled, and the ever-increasing amount of railroad track in the state testified to the wisdom of the policy, at least according to proponents of the New South Creed.

TABLE 7 Railroad Mileage and Percentage Change, 1860–1910

Year	Miles in Operation	Percentage Change
1860	862	—
1870	990	14.80
1880	1127	13.80
1890	2397	112.7
1900	2788	16.30
1910	4342	55.70

Sources: Henry V. Poor, *Manual of the Railroads of the United States, 1890* (New York, 1890); Henry V. Poor, *Manual of the Railroads of the United States, 1900* (New York, 1900); Henry V. Poor, *Manual of the Railroads of the United States, 1910* (New York, 1910).

Besides tax exemptions, railroad companies enjoyed lucrative arrangements with the state that enabled them to use convict labor in laying their track. A part of Redeemers' efforts at retrenchment, the leasing of convicts began in 1876. French and Jobes, the company that acquired the first contract for prisoners, leased convicts for $1.10 each per annum and agreed

32. Before 1880 several lines received tax exemptions. See the charter of the Port Gibson, Utica, and Crystal Springs Railroad Company, *Laws of the State of Mississippi,* 1878, pp. 463–83. On tax exemptions for railroads, see *Code,* 1880, p. 197; *Laws of the State of Mississippi,* 1884, p. 31.

to furnish them food, clothing, and medicine. They sublet gangs of men to planters and railroad companies as common labor. Eventually, James A. Hoskins and Jones S. Hamilton, planters and New South entrepreneurs, obtained the lease and used their charges to cultivate a relationship (at times tempestuous) with the Illinois Central to supply gravel to the railroad. They also employed convicts in an experimental jute bag factory and built "a plug lumber [railroad] line" between Brookhaven and the Pearl River that they hoped to develop into a trunk line connecting with the ICRR. Since the railroad line ran through prime forest lands, ICRR officials subsidized its construction by selling Hamilton and Hoskins old iron rails, plates, bolts, and nuts at a discount in exchange for the privilege of buying hardwood fuel at the bargain rate of $2.25 a cord. In 1881 Hamilton and Hoskins sold the ICRR between two thousand and twenty-five hundred cords. Delays in completing the line through to the Pearl River forced them to forgo their railroading operation and sell off hardware and land to raise capital.[33]

Using convict labor to build their railroad, Hamilton and Hoskins realized only short-term success. The Gulf and Ship Island Railroad (G&SIRR), however, reaped great benefits from its lease. Although not the first coast-bound railroad to secure convict labor (the Ship Island, Ripley, and Kentucky achieved that distinction), the G&SIRR depended on convict labor. Chartered before the Civil War, the original company received a large grant of land from the federal government to facilitate its construction, but the war intervened and hindered completion of a single mile of track. In 1882 the state legislature resurrected the vision of a railroad between the Gulf Coast and Jackson, and construction on the line began in 1886 with the arrival of some seven hundred convict laborers; within months prisoners completed twenty-five miles of railroad running north of present-day Gulfport. Company officials also wielded convicts as leverage to secure construction financing, one of the railroad's most persistent burdens. The prime mover associated with the G&SIRR, William H. Hardy, spent much of 1888 and 1889 trying to convince New York and English bankers to in-

33. Albert Kirwan, *Revolt of the Rednecks,* 167–68. On Hamilton's and Hoskins' association with the Illinois Central, see J. C. Clarke to J. S. Hamilton, August 3, 1880, in Clarke Out-Letters, II, Chicago, St. Louis, and New Orleans Railroad Company Papers. On Hamilton's financial distress and discounted prices offered him, see Clarke to J. A. Deaton, January 14, 1881; Clarke to A. M. West, October 14, 1880, all in Clarke Out-Letters, II, Chicago, St. Louis, and New Orleans Railroad Papers. On a railroad that began as a dummy line, see Sammy O. Cranford, "The Fernwood, Columbia, and Gulf: A Railroad in the Piney Woods of South Mississippi" (Ph.D. dissertation, Mississippi State University, 1983), 1–93.

vest in the company. When he convinced them of the low cost and predictability of convict labor, they agreed to a series of small loans, but the loans, Hardy lamented, were just enough "to keep my convicts fed and clothed & worked," a fact borne out by his eventual loss of control over the company.[34]

By the mid-1880s the Subsidy and Abatement acts as well as railroad companies' access to tax exemptions and convict labor exposed Mississippi to developers, and additional miles of track began rolling across the state. Even though the first generation of visionaries had imagined that rails would open the cotton kingdom to distant markets, postbellum dreamers intended to employ rail lines as conduits for a host of other goods, chiefly the finished products made in Mississippi factories.

W. W. Willis, of Wheeler and Willis, a Corinth manufacturer of flooring, ceiling, and siding, perceived the significance that a railroad would have for his business. Writing to Governor Stone, Willis said that with sufficient financing a railroad between Burrusville and the Tennessee River would link the "Superior Stone Land" of his neighborhood to Mobile. The northeastern section of the state would become a great supplier of glass, porcelain, and clay, Willis believed, and farms would be occupied by new immigrants to the region. Merchants, too, attempted to use railroads to expand their businesses. In 1879 a group of store owners at Kosciusko cajoled officials of the Chicago, St. Louis, and New Orleans into lowering rates for goods bound for and departing their central Mississippi town. With lower rates, they argued, more goods could be bought and sold in their stores, and business over the railroad would increase proportionately. After a one-year experiment with special rates for Kosciusko, J. C. Clarke wrote the merchants that his company had not seen an increase in business and would end the deal.[35] Willis and the Kosciusko merchants understood the importance of railroads in postbellum Mississippi. They were symbols of New South progress and symbiotically linked cotton cultivators, merchants, and neophyte industrialists to the national economy.

34. For memorials in favor of the Gulf and Ship Island, see *Laws of the State of Mississippi,* 1878, p. 225–27, 251–55. Stover, *History of the Illinois Central Railroad,* 293. On Hardy's experiences in London and New York, see William H. Hardy to Hattie Hardy, July 30, 1888, November 4, 15, 1889, all in William H. and Hattie Lott Hardy Papers, Cook Memorial Library, University of Southern Mississippi, Hattiesburg.

35. W. W. Willis to John M. Stone, April 20, 1880, in RG 27, MDAH; J. C. Clarke to A. Hay, October 10, 1880, Clarke Out-Letters, II, Chicago, St. Louis, and New Orleans Railroad Company Papers.

Railroads were more than symbols, however. They were agents of New South economic expansion. Yet even with the promise of great wealth and spectacular growth, Mississippians at times only reluctantly donated land for depots and shops or subscribed to railroad stock. Counterpoised to the reluctant were local boosters, in some instances hired by the companies, who attempted to bring isolated communities into the modern age. James Fentress, chief counsel for the Chicago, St. Louis, and New Orleans, explained to L. P. Yerger his duties as a railroad attorney. He was "to use your influence to conserve the good will of the people towards the Railroad Company and help them to realize that their interests and ours do not conflict." Yerger played a similar role with the Georgia Pacific and extracted from his Leflore County neighbors a pledge to purchase Y&MVRR stock. As a new man of the New South, he did more to re-create the region than promote railroads. Lending agencies in Jackson, New Orleans, Vicksburg, and Memphis employed him to collect on planters' debts and paid him a commission for directing prospective borrowers to their companies; he also worked for the Schlitz Brewery Company, though employer and employee had a rocky relationship.[36] Yerger's ever-increasing association with the symbols and agents of the New South began with his employment as a railroad attorney. His career, in fact, mirrored the state's economic advance. Even though he started as a railroad attorney, filing real estate transactions and conducting other common legal business, Yerger became a booster for more than one railroad, a loan originator to the builders of the new cotton kingdom, and an agent for a large industry interested in moving to Mississippi.

Yerger's postbellum career began with railroads; so too did late-nineteenth-century economic progress. While Yerger's involvement with the agents of the New South might serve as a metaphor for New South development, he barely concerned himself with the one element most crucial to Mississippi's commercial development, the availability of which facilitated the railroad boom: land. To railroad companies, land was an asset. Companies needed land on which to build their tracks, depots, and shops, of course, but they also demanded vacant land surrounding their lines that could be sold to potential rail users. James F. McCool, an Attala

36. Quoting James Fentress to L. P. Yerger, September 29, 1885, in Yerger Papers. On Yerger's other ventures, see J. W. Johnston to Yerger, March 15, 1888; S. R. Benton to Yerger, February 22, 1888; Chaffe and Powell to Yerger, April 28, 1888; P. M. Hardy to Yerger, October 3, 1889; W. D. Lawson to Yerger, October 2, 1889; Graves and Vinton to Yerger, October 9, 1890; F. E. Kalberg to Yerger, August 1, 1890; Eugene Westhoff to Yerger, February 19, 1892, all in Yerger Papers.

County attorney and state legislator, concentrated his law practice on securing land for the Canton, Aberdeen, and Nashville Railroad (CANRR). James Fentress, who also served as chief counsel for the CANRR, charged McCool with obtaining rights of way for the line. McCool, Fentress said, must "go to work and have your people show enterprise and public spirit." Ideally, the CANRR wanted to obtain rights of way through Attala County before a rival line could do so and thus ensure that the company had the best available land on which to build.[37]

McCool, however, had other plans, plans that would transform him into a new man of the New South. Instead of transferring titles to the CANRR, he purchased prime lands so that he could found a town on the railway line. When word of McCool's extracurricular activities reached Fentress, he berated his local attorney: "I would be glad to see you get rich and if I can aid you will do so—and as soon as a line is located & rights of way gotten I hope you will buy lands that will make you rich." His undercutting operation found out, McCool admitted to Fentress that he had purchased some land but fully intended to transfer the rights of way to the company.[38] He did not explain to the solicitor, and likely did not need to, that the best price for land could be obtained before the company laid its track. McCool's efforts to secure land pointed to a central truth about railroad development: companies had to acquire cheap, vacant lands that they could sell to farmers, town builders, and businessmen. If enticing railroads to the state depended on the companies' ability to acquire land cheaply, their success depended on the companies' selling land after completion of their lines.

Two postbellum railroads, the Yazoo and Mississippi Valley and the Gulf and Ship Island, obtained extensive acreage, which they sold to businessmen as well as settlers. With approximately 600,000 acres in the mid-1890s, the Y&MVRR undertook a program to lure immigrants to the Delta. Like the state of Mississippi, which had its own settler recruitment program, J. C. Clarke of the line's parent company, the Illinois Central, hoped to attract "the right kind, [of immigrant] to this country." Mississippi's commissioner of immigration agreed that the state needed most of all "people of kindred races, that we may be homogeneous." But the state and the railroad company wanted more than common laborers and white tenant farmers; they aspired to entice "settlers who will bring along with

37. Quoting James Fentress to C. L. Anderson and James F. McCool, June 15, 1882, but see, too, Fentress to McCool, May 5, June 4, 1880, all in McCool Family Papers.

38. James Fentress to C. L. Anderson and James McCool, May 4, June 6, 1882; Fentress to McCool, April 12, 1882; Fentress to Anderson, May 1, 1882, all in McCool Family Papers.

them means and energy to enter upon business for themselves, to buy our cheap lands, become permanent residents, and help to build up the prosperity of the state." Both sets of boosters devoted extraordinary energy to discrediting what they referred to as myths about Mississippi, especially stories of poverty and persistent disease. "We do not continually eat pork, nor drink whiskey or creek water, and thus we have good health," a New Yorker explained to prospective purchasers. Actual settlers discovered that extracting a living from the alluvial plain was more difficult than advertised. Johnny Parrott, who purchased 80 acres of Delta woodlands in the mid-1880s and began clearing it to plant cotton, disputed railroads' claims about the health of Mississippians. Residents bore signs of hard work and of living in a miasmic climate, he said, "especially the women look like they were half dead." [39]

Cheap and fertile land, of course, was the main lure used by the Y&MVRR to attract settlers. The Delta, a railroad pamphlet boasted, comprised 10 percent of the state's acreage but produced 27 percent of Mississippi's staples and foodstuffs. Cotton flourished in the region, and so too did a variety of other crops. According to company propaganda, a farmer, after deadening timber and clearing land for three years, could expect to produce on forty-five acres of railroad land corn, peas, and hogs worth $4,750. The pamphlet advertised land at $7 per acre, with 20 percent down and the remainder due at 6 percent interest for seven years. During the three years it took to clear the land, settlers could sell timber, as Parrott did, and scrape by with a small garden. In case the prospect of barely making a living frightened farmers, the railroad hedged its bet by boasting of vast virgin woodlands: "LUMBERMEN CAN MAKE FORTUNES." Cypress swamps stood ready for harvest, and best of all, pamphleteers for the railroad said, farmers and lumbermen could find easy access to Memphis, Vicksburg, Baton Rouge, Chicago, and points east on the Y&MVRR.[40]

Before guides could show potential settlers company lands, a few businessmen obtained huge tracts from the Y&MVRR. In the mid-1890s the

39. Quoting J. C. Clarke to E. G. Wall, February 5, 1881, Clarke Out-Letters, II, Chicago, St. Louis, and New Orleans Railroad Company Papers; E. G. Wall, *Handbook of the State of Mississippi* (Jackson, 1882), 30; Johnny Parrott Diary, June 15, 1887. See, too, Illinois Central Railroad Company, *Railroad Lands for Sale Owned by the Yazoo and Mississippi Valley Railroad Company in the Famous Yazoo Valley of Mississippi* (N.p., 1896), 7; S. M. Tracy, *Mississippi As It Is: A Handbook of Facts for Immigrants* (Jackson, 1895), 27–28, 78, 133.

40. Illinois Central Railroad Company, *Railroad Lands for Sale,* 3, 9, 13, 19–21, 31, 37. For other efforts by the ICRR to attract investors to the region, see Illinois Central Railroad Company, *One Hundred Cities and Towns Wanting Industries . . . on the Lines of the Illinois Central Railroad and Yazoo and Mississippi Valley Railroad* (Chicago, n.d.), 96–125.

Delta Pine and Land Company, N. T. Burroughs, the Southern Land Company, the Moffatt Company of Denver, and a consortium of Milwaukee breweries grabbed hundreds of sections of land in Tallahatchie, Leflore, Sharkey, and Quitman counties. The Delta Pine and Land Company, a Chicago-based group of investors headed by Thomas Watson and his two sons, originally acquired about 450,000 acres in the late 1880s. Company policy at the time required that land purchasers buy with cash a minimum of 10,000 acres. Delta Pine and Land Company acreage passed generally into the hands of large lumber cutters until the timber was harvested, and then the land was sold as improved acreage at higher prices to farmers. Land companies representing outside interests were not alone in the Mississippi Delta. The Jackson firm of Swan and Burroughs possessed 300,000 acres of timberland, some of which they sold in 31,000-acre blocks. The great land bonanza opened by the Illinois Central and the Yazoo and Mississippi Valley brought as much attention to the Delta's cypress as to its fertile cotton lands.[41] Concentration of land ownership and interest in Delta timber proceeded naturally out of the spirit of the New South in which service to nonagricultural commerce reigned supreme.

Unlike the Y&MVRR, which possessed its acreage without contention, the Gulf and Ship Island had trouble selling land because it lacked a clear title. In 1856 the federal government committed to the company alternate sections of land on either side of its track provided that the line passed from Mississippi City to Jackson within ten years. Had the railroad been completed, it stood to gain 120 sections of land, or nearly 11,000 acres. The only restriction attached to the land grant prohibited settlers from obtaining title to company lands until the railroad completed its work. Much happened in the ten years allotted the company for construction of the line. The war, first of all, disrupted plans to link the coast and the capital. Then, in the postwar period, the G&SIRR temporarily lost its charter. In the 1880s agrarians began asking Congress to cancel land grants made to unfinished railroads, and Congress complied in 1890, leaving the G&SIRR virtually landless the year before the Illinois Central acquired it. William Hardy, the railroad's booster, had planned to reap a fortune for his years

41. The extent of landholding among the five large owners named may be viewed on the map "Illinois Central Railroad Lands for Sale in the Famous Yazoo-Mississippi Delta" (1897[?]), in the Map Collection of the Illinois Central Railroad Archives, NL. On the Delta Pine and Land Company, see Brandfon, *Cotton Kingdom of the New South,* 61–67. For other large landholders and attempts by outsiders to monopolize the Delta's assets, see F. C. Nelson to L. P. Yerger, Augut 3, 1889; W. W. Marmuke to Yerger, March 28, 1890, in Yerger Papers.

of labor by selling company lands along the line. Completion of the track, he told his wife, would "make us indepent [*sic*] financially in our old age." Loss of the land and company, however, prompted him to look to lands other than those owned by the G&SIRR to make him rich: "My only chance is to make my fortune out of the Gulfport Lands owned by me and Milton."[42]

Even though the Gulf and Ship Island lost most of its land, its purchaser, the Illinois Central, considered the vacant public domain through which it passed ripe for development. In the 1880s Illinois Central officials had viewed shipping lumber as a nuisance, or at best a civic duty that assisted poor farmers who occupied the "dull season" of the year by cutting timber. Shipping lumber by rail, Chicago-based officials argued, required special cars, cars that returned to the South empty. Nevertheless, the ICRR encouraged lumbermen to continue their work "in the hope that it [the land] may then be available for some agricultural production." For decades independent woodcutters had cut over the public domain, but thousands of acres of virgin pine forests still stood in south central Mississippi. Some timber cutters followed the practice of their antebellum predecessors, cutting logs and floating them to Biloxi where millers fashioned them into railroad car sills and other finished products. Others harvested turpentine; A. C. Danner, for instance, leased 750,000 acres from the Mobile and Ohio Railroad and sublet it to small producers. Soon after the government forced the Hardy's G&SIRR to forfeit its land claims, lumbermen who had clear-cut the forests of the Old Northwest immigrated to the state, seeking a share of the longleaf pine forests south of Jackson that contained an estimated 18.2 billion feet of merchantable timber.[43] The anemic condition of forest industries in the Piney Woods changed when the ICRR took command of Hardy's railroad.

42. Quoting William H. Hardy to Hattie Hardy, July 25, 1888, June 28, 1897, in Hardy Papers. David Maldwyn Ellis, "The Forfeiture of Railroad Land Grants, 1867–1894," *Mississippi Valley Historical Review,* XXXIII (1946), 31, 53–54; Stover, *History of the Illinois Central Railroad,* 290.

43. Quoting J. C. Clarke to J. M. Wesson, October, 1882, in Clarke Out-Letters, II, Chicago, St. Louis, and New Orleans Railroad Company; James Fentress to Stuyvesant Fish, October 22, 1887, in Stuyvesant Fish In-Letters, II, Chicago, St. Louis, and New Orleans Railroad Company, NL. Hickman, *Mississippi Harvest,* 46, 55, 58, 65; Cyril Edward Cain, ed., *Four Centuries on the Pascagoula: History and Genealogy of the Pascagoula River Country* (2 vols.; rpr. Spartanburg, 1983), II, 43–45. On the availability of merchantable pine timber, see U.S. Department of the Treasury, *Report on the Internal Commerce of the United States: Part II of Commerce and Navigation: The Commercial, Industrial, Transportation, and Other Industries of the Southern States* (1886), 491.

Technical improvements made in sawmill machinery, the arrival of northwestern investors, and the completion of the G&SIRR and other lines opened the Piney Woods to industrialization. As early as the mid-1880s the Mississippi Gulf Coast began to feel the impact of railroads. Along part of the Louisville and Nashville that stretched between New Orleans and Mobile, timber cutters annually shipped from twenty Mississippi depots millions of tons of lumber and timber; in 1885 the West Pascagoula station alone sent over 3 million tons of lumber and logs. Most of the timber was sent out of the area to be processed. The Louisville and Nashville shipped more than lumber, however. Vegetables and fruits received at coastal harbors traveled by rail to the burgeoning mill towns of the area. In fiscal year 1884–1885, the L & N shipped 146,000 pounds of vegetables, and in the following twelve months, 251,800 pounds. The New Orleans and Northeastern, which operated through the interior of the Piney Woods between the Crescent City and Meridian, shipped 5.8 million pounds of vegetables.[44]

Both the Gulf and Ship Island and the New Orleans and Northeastern reached into the interior counties of the state, providing lumber barons access to the forests of south central Mississippi. The railroads intersected at Hattiesburg, a way station founded by William Hardy. Even though small timber cutters had operated near the settlement for a number of years, the completion of railroads attracted large operators to the area. By 1893 Hattiesburg mills produced 1 million feet of lumber a day and saw an additional 6 million feet pass through the city via the rail lines; in 1911 thirty lumber wholesalers, selling mostly sawn timber, had offices in the city. Besides the virgin forests of the Piney Woods, northern lumbermen were attracted to the area by land prices, reportedly as low as $1.25 an acre. In one transaction Fenwick Peck, a Pennsylvania native, purchased 400,000 acres at that low price; within several years he had cut from the land approximately 200 million feet of timber. John Kamper, who opened his first mill at Laurel, thirty miles north of Hattiesburg on the New Orleans and Northeastern, sold 16,000 acres at $4.00 per acre to an Iowa-based company headed by George and Silas Gardiner and Lauren Eastman. Taking advantage of cheap lands, plentiful timber, and railroads, the Gardiner-Eastman Company dominated the south central Mississippi lumber trade. During a one month period in 1903, for instance, they shipped on average seven hundred train cars of lumber every twenty-four hours.[45]

44. O. B. Collins to A. C. Falconer, February 4, 1877, in RG 27, MDAH; U.S. Department of the Treasury, *Report on the Internal Commerce of the United States,* 476–83, 496, 501.

45. Jo Dent Hodge, "The Lumber Industry in Laurel, Mississippi, at the Turn of the Nine-

With railroads penetrating the state, industrial development followed, most dramatically perhaps in the Piney Woods. Between 1880 and 1890 capital investment in Jones County (Laurel) industries leaped from $3,200 to $358,000, a 11,088 percent change; Perry County (Hattiesburg) saw a 7,346 percent change in the amount of capital invested in industries. At the same time the value of goods manufactured in the counties increased by 4,774 percent and 9,104 percent, respectively. Across the state the money invested in manufacturing and the value of manufactured products grew. Between 1880 and 1900 the value of manufactured products increased by more than 150 percent, and in the same period capital investments in industry rose by nearly 350 percent.[46] The statewide increase in the value of manufactured products might best be explained by the proliferation of manufacturing establishments, most of which were small. In 1870 Mississippi manufacturing establishments employed on average 3.93 hands; by 1890 the average number of laborers increased to only 9.34. The size of industrial establishments notwithstanding, data included in the 1880 and 1900 censuses suggest that the explosion in the number of facilities caused a corresponding increase in production capacity. Lumber (planed and sawn) was valued at $2 million in 1880, but in 1900 mills produced lumber worth $15.7 million; the value of cotton goods manufactured rose from less than $700,000 to $1.5 million; cotton compressing and ginning mills saw the worth of their production increase from $3,250 to $2.2 million; and the value of cottonseed oil and cakes, barely at $500,000 in 1880, hit the $6.7 million mark in 1900.[47]

As the web of the market spun from railroads and industries more and more complicated interlocking strands, the amateur store owner and the

teenth Century," *Journal of Mississippi History*, XXV (1973), 361–63, 371. John Ray Skates, "The Early Years," in *Hattiesburg: A Pictorial History*, ed. Kenneth G. McCarty (Jackson, 1982), 6–11.

46. *Report on the Manufacturing of the United States at the Tenth Census, June 1, 1880, Embracing General Statistics* (1883), 140–41; *Report on Manufacturing Industries in the United States at the Eleventh Census, 1890: Part I, Totals for States and Industries* (1895), 484–87; *Twelfth Census, 1900: Manufactures, Part II: States and Territories* (1902), 462–71. For an overview of economic progress in the Piney Woods, see Arthell Kelly and Robert C. Spillman, "Sequence Occupancy of the Piney Woods in Southeastern Mississippi, 1805–1976," *Mississippi Geographer*, IV (1976), 32–34.

47. In addition to the sources cited above, see, too, *The Statistics of the Wealth and Industry of the United States . . . Compiled from the Original Returns of the Ninth Census* (1872), III, 537–38.

industrialist of the immediate postwar period came to be replaced by specialists. Some of those specialists had recently arrived from the North. Master mechanics and railroad engineers kept the commercial order running smoothly, and many of them, by virtue of their skills and recent immigration to the state, were truly new men of the New South.[48] By 1900 conducting the affairs of even small country stores could be nearly as complicated as operating a train. Men with special skills (typing, accounting, shorthand) found positions with retail merchants. To obtain their skills, retail specialists of the late nineteenth and early twentieth centuries attended training schools, like the Harris Practical Business College at Jackson ("The Only Business University of the South") and Eastman National Business College in Poughkeepsie, New York. A 1908 directory of Eastman alumni listed 158 Mississippi graduates. Some were merchants and planters, but many held positions indicative of the thoroughgoing commercial and ideological revolutions that had taken place in the New South. They worked as clerks, bookkeepers, and traveling salesmen for produce and wholesale supply houses, railroads, cotton buying firms, and banks. Many, like J. H. Tyrone, a shoe salesman at Aberdeen, boasted that the education they received at Eastman prepared them for the illustrious positions they held. Others, like T. R. Trotter, Jr., a Winona bookkeeper, credited Eastman with their "financial birth." All who contributed comments to the directory looked upon their training at Eastman as security against what Philip M. Essig called "the cold business world." [49] Even more than skilled railroad workers, the Mississippians who traveled to Poughkeepsie served as signposts of the new order, for they became Mississippi's first generation of professional commercial men dedicated to perpetuating and extending the order in which they thrived.

In spite of the transformation of postbellum society that the emergence

48. Taking the names of engineers and mechanics listed on the back of an 1884 photograph of Chicago, St. Louis, and New Orleans employees, I positively identified eight as living in Mississippi in 1880. Of the eight, four hailed from northern states and foreign lands. None of those whose years of residence could be ascertained had lived in Mississippi more than seven years. See the roundhouse photo in the Photograph Collection, Illinois Central Railroad Company Archives, NL.

49. Quoting *Directory by States and Counties of More Than Eight Thousand of the Students and Graduates of Eastman, Poughkeepsie, New York: Part Two, Southern and Gulf States* (N.p., 1908), 143, 150, but see, too, 143–55. Reference to the Harris school can be located in *Maloney's 1907 Jackson City Directory* (N.p., n.d.), 88. See also, the advertisement for the Commercial College of Kentucky University that appeared in the Ackerman *Choctaw Plaindealer,* November 16, 1894.

of a commercial class, railroads, and industry evinced, aspects of life in Mississippi remained static as white beneficiaries of the commercial order retained one feature of the social ethic: the founding of liberty and virtue in African Americans' relegation to a peripheral role in society. Noting that "the war has hewn a pathway for Southern energies in a new direction," a newspaper editor at Columbus took up the New South's clarion call when he pleaded for a rapprochement between the races in order to promote industry in the state. Mostly, he said, Mississippi needed "men of labor and skill to settle among us, capital to export our latent resources, and train and elevate the negro to be able to do his part of the great work of Southern economic development." On the surface, such language vowed protection of freed people in their right to free labor. Subsequent editorials in the same newspaper, however, questioned their capacity to function autonomously in the new order and reminded ex-slaves that they should not seek employment away from the plantation. Another editor, writing in the 1880s, likewise intimated that industrial advance promoted racial peace, but suggested too that blacks would be left behind. The prospects of a cottonseed oil mill being built in Grenada threatened to release "a set of forces that will convert this little dull old town into an active commercial centre." Fearful that Grenada would fall under the spell of foreign ideas, the writer warned that industrialization should occur "under the restraing [*sic*] influence of a high moral public sentiment," or, in other words, that industrial development should occur within the boundaries set by traditional notions of blacks' place in society.[50]

Stripping away the boosterism of the New South Creed leaves a formula for economic advancement as old as the cotton kingdom itself: black labor, working in fields of cotton, would produce a crop that southern white men would manufacture into yarn, cloth, and clothes. In this way, white cultural homogeneity might be maintained. Other white men would construct railroads, operate factories, market truck-garden vegetables, and control the retail trade. Blacks, except in the lumber camps of south Mississippi, would remain conspicuously absent from the commercial world.[51] Much of the rhetoric that poured from the region immediately after the war lamented the victory of free-labor ideology, for nothing inherent in the creation of a New South required acceptance of black liberty. Consequently, Mississippi's economic advancement took place without removing large

50. Columbus *Southern Sentinel,* November 26, 1867, but see, too, December 10, 20, 1867; *Sentinel,* June 3, 1882.

51. On African-American labor in the lumber camps, see Hickman, "Black Labor in the Forest Industries," in *Mississippi's Piney Woods,* ed. Polk, 152–74.

numbers of freed people from cotton fields. Considering merchants' central role in creating a New South and their dependence on the crop-lien law, it might be argued that the commercial revolution demanded that freed people remain tied to the land so that the social ethic could survive. Despite the evolution of Mississippi's economy, the variety of economic and political advances that certain theorists associate with the advent of modernity awaited the future when white Mississippians no longer cared whether their clothes, furniture, or canned goods had been processed by black hands.[52]

52. On Mississippians' desire to keep blacks from working in industrial facilities, see Jackson *Weekly Clarion,* August 25, 1886.

Part III

Accepting and Rejecting Change

We cannot escape history.

—Abraham Lincoln

Memory is the thread of personal identity, history of public identity. Men who have achieved any civic existence at all must, to sustain it, have some kind of history, though it may be history that is partly mythological or simply untrue. That the business of history always involves a subtle transaction with civic identity has long been understood, even in America where the sense of time is shallow.

—Richard Hofstadter

In Mississippi, still a relatively young state in 1880, a strong sense of history informed concepts of a good republic and proper economic behavior. Even had they wished, residents could not have put out of mind their collective past. White citizens, because of the events and phenomena that challenged white cultural homogeneity and their antebellum social ethic—Civil War, Reconstruction, commercial development—enveloped themselves in remembrances of another time. They especially found solace in the racial theories underpinning the social ethic, and thus hindered the wholesale transformation of their political culture.

The new state capitol, finished in 1903, symbolized white Mississippians' inability to escape their history and their unwillingness to do so, as its completion represented an effort to construct upon the ruins of the past a bright and prosperous future. According to a twentieth-century commentator, the new capitol was "the product of a new century, a place of power and utility rather than of tradition." In imitation of the national capitol, designers of the state house used Bedford stone in its construction, and they capped the dome with that all-American symbol, an eagle. Further symbolizing the new age in which Mississippians lived, the builders accepted a gift from the Illinois Central Railroad, a short line connecting the construction site to the company's main track. Built atop the ruins of the old penitentiary, much about the new building suggested that white Mississippians derived their civic identity from the postbellum commercial order, but in fact, the laying of the building's capstone on June 3, Jefferson Davis' birthday, served as a vivid reminder that they founded concepts of a good republic on the sentiments his memory evoked.[1]

Despite the social, economic, and ideological changes inaugurated by the commercial order, white Mississippians—cultivators as well as men of commerce and industry—clung to certain moral imperatives that had traditionally defined notions of the social ethic. They continued to place a high value on individual success in the market economy and to award the title "liberty-loving and virtuous citizen" solely to members of their own race. Postbellum Mississippians, like their antebellum ancestors, espoused an interpretation of history reflective of their ideology, but in the postbellum period two significant groups of postbellum residents, reacting to the new age in which they lived, espoused different views of the past and consequently different ideal visions of a good republic. One of the visions originated with the makers and keepers of the new order, the other with plain farmers.

According to the middle-class beneficiaries of the new order, emancipation destroyed the homogeneous South. They doubted that the altered social order could be restored to its original condition but longed to fix upon the region a version of homogeneity similar to the one they imagined in operation during the prewar period. Like antebellum whites who feared that residents undeserving of liberty, especially blacks, threatened achievement of a good republic, the makers of the commercial world considered those left behind by the postbellum advance as anathema to political, social, and cultural uniformity. Controlling the ignorant and vile through prohibition, as well as sanitary, educational, and suffrage reform, became the duty of middle-class reformers who wished to eliminate evidence of heterogeneity in society. Agrarians too viewed postbellum society as splintered and contentious, but unlike their middle-class contemporaries, they rested blame for the demise of homogeneity on the commercial order itself. Suffering the consequences of the crop-lien law, railroads, industry, and merchants, tillers of the earth ceased to be self-sufficient producers within the context of market production and became instead enslaved to the market and thus unvirtuous. Like beneficiaries of the commercial order, agrari-

1. Quoting *Mississippi: A Guide to the Magnolia State: Compiled and Written by the Federal Writers' Project of the Works Progress Administration* (New York, 1938), 217. Mrs. Albert G. Weems, "Work of the United Daughters of the Confederacy," Mississippi Historical Society *Publications,* IV (1901), 73–78.

ans wished to recapture the halcyon days of antebellum Mississippi. Their vision of an homogeneous social order, founded as it was on concepts of Jacksonian egalitarianism, contrasted sharply with the vision of a good republic common to middle-class reformers.

Two diverse groups presented competing visions of good citizenship and a good republic. The first attempted to create an homogeneous society by blocking from political and social authority the undeserving (whose low economic standing, if not whose race alone, proved their depravity); the second attempted to remove distinctions among whites brought about by the advent of the commercial era. Accomplishing the goals of either group was impossible: emancipation and the triumph of a national commercial order ensured the heterogeneity of society. Yet by the turn of the century the two groups of reformers achieved an accord. They agreed that as white citizens they would put aside their differences and concentrate on the single artifact of the past they all revered: the theories of race that had forever secured the foundation of white liberty in black subjugation. That vision of the social ethic found expression in the rise of a new breed of politician—the redneck—who evinced a commitment to maintaining agrarians' class-conscious critique of the commercial order and, oddly, to preserving the commercial order. Only by resuscitating theories of race, which demanded the presence of a black underclass upon whose back all whites might stand, could the rednecks successfully combine (and thereby expurgate the meaning of) agrarian class-consciousness with the class-conscious ideology of the makers and keepers of the commercial order.

Chapter 7

To Create a Homogeneous Society

The makers and keepers of the New South's commercial order, the middle class, seized responsibility for creating a good society—a homogeneous one in which liberty-loving and virtuous citizens exalted order, duty, and respectability. Some historians would prefer to discard the idea of a self-conscious and unique "middle class" on the grounds that it undercuts the centrality of ethno-cultural identities in the late nineteenth century; others contend that the middle class was an ephemeral social group. Consensus historians, however, insightfully maintain that a self-conscious middle class existed. Unfortunately, they argue that it served mainly as a link in the cultural formation of liberalism and deserves no serious consideration in its own right.[1] Yet the Southern middle class of the late nineteenth century was unique. Because of its blending of the New South Creed with traditional defenses of white cultural homogeneity, the middle class construed notions of a good republic based on a class-conscious awareness of its place in the new commercial order. The beneficiaries of that order believed that, the loathsome revolution in social relations notwithstanding, reestablishment of white cultural homogeneity remained possible.

Where once the white population, rich and poor, had been bound by a common allegiance to the social ethic, middle-class reformers traced to emancipation and the advent of commerce the stark disparities of the late nineteenth century. The apparition of blacks posing as virtuous citizens and

1. For an overview of the historiography of the middle class, see Stuart M. Blumin, "The Hypothesis of Middle-Class Formation in Nineteenth Century America: A Critique and Some Proposals," *American Historical Review,* XC (1985), 302–303, 312, 338. As used herein, *middle class* denotes less an economically defined group than one committed to a common set of ideas about good citizenship and a good republic. For a similar definition, see C. Robert Haywood, *Victorian West: Class and Culture in Kansas Cattle Towns* (Lawrence, Kan., 1991), 4.

the age of the machine tore at traditional values of the white South. A homogeneous republic no longer existed, and a sense of great loss overshadowed middle-class pleasure with the economic benefits of the new order. To soften the rough edges of the commercial order without fundamentally altering its reign, they embraced numerous reforms that promoted order and respectability among deserving but alienated whites: they insisted that their cities undertake waterworks projects and frowned on their neighbors' derelict maintenance of sidewalks; they formed building and loan associations so that clerks and skilled laborers might acquire homes and obtain with home ownership a degree of responsibility and belonging that residence in a boardinghouse could not provide; they also indulged in movements of self-reformation. Many believed, in L. B. Garrett's phrase, that as badly as Mississippi needed commerce to ameliorate societal malaise, it needed even more "good, neat respectable houses of worship;" the message preached by traveling ministers like Sam Jones—that contentment might be found in the joining of temporal respectability and heavenly rewards—was an exciting prospect for folk unfamiliar with their changing world.[2] Regardless of their sorrow for the Old South's passing, few late-nineteenth-century Mississippians wanted to return to it. Those who spoke in mournful tones about the end of an era enjoyed an exalted status in society and wished to preserve it. What they wanted was the establishment of a part of the Old South in the New. Their refusal to surrender their racial chauvinism made possible the continuance of the social ethic's core assumption under greatly changed circumstances.

Not unlike Howard Odum, who a generation later mixed romantic remembrances of his boyhood South with a firm commitment to progress, beneficiaries of the commercial order wanted to keep alive the best of both worlds. Never willing to stage a counterrevolution against the commercial order, middle-class reformers wished to ameliorate it by finding a place in the new order for meritorious whites. Once protected from what B. W. Griffith referred to as "the chill of commercialism" and disorder of their age,

2. Quoting Carthage *Carthaginian,* June 2, 1888. On waterworks and beautification projects, see Jackson *Weekly Clarion-Ledger,* December 8, 1886, April 12, 1888, October 12, 1884, May 16, 1889, and Carthage *Carthaginian,* July 8, 1892. On building and loan associations, see Crystal Springs *Meteor,* March 30, 1889; Jackson *Evening News,* February 18, 1898. On traveling ministers, see Ackerman *Choctaw Plaindealer,* August 1, 1890, February 5, 1897; Hazelhurst *Copiah Signal,* June 20, 1889; Agnew Diary, April 3, 1893. For assessments of social declension, see the clipping of the Atlanta *Constitution,* May 9, 1887, in Benjamin F. Ward Family Papers, MDAH; Belle Kearney, "Patrician Days in Madison County" (Typescript copy in MDAH), 16; Letitia D. Miller, "Recollections," 15, MDAH; Broidrick, "A Recollection," unpaginated.

whites—beneficiaries of the new order as well as those left behind—would once again form a homogeneous society.[3] As a result of their ambivalence toward the new order, middle-class citizens concentrated their impulse for reform in two broad tracks, each in its own way moral and political. They sought to eradicate evidence of their contemporaries' shortcomings by alternately uplifting the degenerate and by pressing them to the periphery of society. Teachers and physicians, through the formation of professional organizations, secured their place in the new order and foisted upon society uniform educational and sanitary practices as a means of abolishing evidence of inequities among whites. In reactionary fashion, middle-class proponents of white cultural homogeneity also endeavored to isolate the supposed morally and intellectually inferior, a pool that included ignorant whites (the illiterate and alcoholics) but especially African Americans. The disfranchising clause of the Constitution of 1890 represented the pinnacle of their struggle to redefine the underclass and to reify the besieged social ethic. With the social order affirmed, middle-class reformers believed that moral and economic uplift would proceed conterminously.

Professionals had long attempted to organize themselves into associations, and success for most came in the 1870s and 1880s, though some groups struggled to place their fraternities on a permanent footing even after the turn of the century.[4] Through their associations professionals sought to formulate a set of standards by which all practitioners of their crafts would be judged. Establishing standards for judging potential professionals, they hoped, would force bogus practitioners to resign while anointing admitted members as possessors of unique knowledge, knowledge that benefited the state in its transition from Old South to New. As self-professed

3. Quoting B. W. Griffith, "Address Before the Southern Commercial Congress" (Typescript copy in B. W. Griffith and Rondo A. Westbrook Papers), MDAH, unpaginated; Howard Odum, *An American Epoch: Southern Portraiture in the National Picture* (New York, 1930), 3–16.

4. The focus herein is on teachers and physicians, but others organized, too. Bankers formed a professional society in the 1880s and maintained it; see *Proceedings of the Mississippi Bankers' Association: Twenty-Fifth Annual Convention, West Point, Mississippi, May 20–21, 1913* (Jackson, 1913). A bar association formed in 1885, passed out of existence in the 1890s, and reappeared in 1906. See *Proceedings of the Mississippi Bar Association at its 6th Annual Meeting Held January 6, 1891* (Jackson, 1892); *Report of the Second Annual Meeting of the Mississippi State Bar Association Held at Vicksburg, Mississippi, May 7th, 8th, and 9th, 1907* (N.p., n.d.). Teachers and physicians struggled as well to form associations. See Jackson *Mississippian,* September 12, 1848; Vicksburg *Tri-Weekly Whig,* June 2, 1849.

commanders of such knowledge, professionals argued, they deserved the praise and status their positions demanded. Middle-class beneficiaries of commercial advance viewed associations as bulwarks against the heterogeneity of the late nineteenth century; they were homogenizing agencies in a fractured world. Based on the activities of two professional groups—teachers and physicians—the makers and keepers of the New South undertook a two-pronged attack on heterogeneity. On the one hand, poor whites merited inclusion in the new order, and reformers strove to improve their lot. But blacks did not deserve elevation, so reformers ignored them or consciously sought to relegate them to a lesser place in society. Notwithstanding blacks' elevation to citizenship, middle-class reformers thought them too degenerate to be included in their ideal notions of a homogeneous society.

Teachers ranked among the most influential professionals in the late nineteenth century. Even though the foundation of public schools in the Reconstruction era provoked racist and antitax sentiments among whites, fresh interest in education appeared in the 1880s. Undoubtedly, the introduction of industry and railroads accounted for the changed attitudes, as did settlement of questions about black liberty. Renewed interest in public education vaulted teachers into the role of protectors of the new order. For when the public again conveyed concern about children's education, it charged teachers with improving the social and religious condition of communities (perceived preconditions for commercial development) and with fomenting a sense of respectability among future leaders of the state. In the phrase of one newspaperman, citizens expected teachers to take "the bantling fresh from the nest" and, through "toil and patience and soul weariness," to fashion a respectable citizen. Makers of the new order so believed that better schools would make children better managers and workers in industry and commerce that one correspondent of a Jackson newspaper proposed higher taxes as a remedy for educational deficiencies. Similar calls, backed by the support of public schoolteachers, to "educate girls and get good teachers in every household" led the state to charter the Industrial Institute and College at Columbus (II&C), in 1884, the first female school of its kind in the nation.[5] Its primary function, like that of the Agricultural and

5. Quoting Ackerman *Choctaw Plaindealer,* September 3, 1897; "Old Boots" in the Jackson *Weekly Clarion,* September 2, 1885. For an overview of public school history, see Percy Easom, "Public School Legislation in Mississippi, 1860 to 1930" (Ph.D. dissertation, George Peabody College for Teachers, 1937), 21–26, and David G. Sansing, *Making Haste Slowly: The Troubled History of Higher Education in Mississippi* (Jackson, 1990), 65–68. On perceptions of the duties of schools and teachers, see Jackson *New Mississippian,* November 15, 1887; Jackson *Weekly Clarion,* September 2, 1885.

Mechanical College founded in 1878 and public schools in general, was to provide young people with the acumen necessary for responsible citizenship in the commercial world.

Teachers' efforts to establish for themselves a select position in the New South contributed to the renewed concern for educational reform. In response to the public's calls for better schools, teachers supported the II&C as a training academy for teachers and gathered in a professional association that allowed them to head the reform effort. At the 1884 statewide teachers' convention, one of the first in Mississippi, participants asked the state to create a method for rooting out ill-prepared teachers who gave their profession a bad name. Two years later, with the support of Education Superintendent John Preston, a state-sponsored qualifying examination for teachers was approved. Administered by county school superintendents, the licensing examinations tested teachers' subject knowledge and their competency to teach particular grades: any score over 75 percent entitled a teacher to a certificate, but a low passing score relegated a teacher to the lower grades where lower pay was commonplace. Teachers' successful lobbying for the implementation of a certification program bore fruit immediately. In 1886, according to Leake County superintendent D. E. Sullivan, a large number of test-takers failed even to complete half of the exam, testimony to the intellectual poverty of those who intended to teach in Mississippi schools.[6]

Teachers were not content with the results of the first year's testing and educated themselves to pass. The inauguration of teachers' institutes in 1887 perhaps helped improve scores, though some superintendents complained that few potential instructors attended the early training sessions. Typically, a school principal or district superintendent conducted an institute one month prior to the scheduled exams. Some, however, held Saturday classes once a month throughout the year, and summer institutes were regular features on the academic calendar. Separate days of instruction were set aside for white and black teachers. Tuition for the normal classes ran to $2.25, plus the price of room, board, laundry services, and book rental. Topics covered included purely pedagogical ones such as "Theory and Practice of Teaching," but a newspaper editor at Ackerman reported that Choctaw County teachers addressed in addition to questions of "practical benefit . . . many questions of importance to the fraternity."[7]

6. Easom, "Public School Legislation in Mississippi," 47; Jackson, *New Mississippian,* January 1, 1884; Carthage *Carthaginian,* October 8, 1886. For a report of the business conducted at the Northeast Mississippi Teachers Association meeting, see Dabney Lipscomb to John L. Johnson, July 5, 1886, in Johnson Papers.

7. Carthage *Carthaginian,* April 11, 1889; Ackerman *Choctaw Plaindealer,* August 1,

By taking for themselves the right to govern admission into their profession and by training themselves in sound educational principles, teachers claimed to be respectable New South citizens. As such, they captured the educational reform movement and promised to make over in their own image the youth assigned them.

Annual teachers' association meetings augmented the work done at training institutes. Participants heard essays delivered on subjects ranging from the benefits of agricultural instruction in the schools to the positive and negative aspects of the grading system to the proper use of dictionaries as spelling aids. They also discussed teaching methods, the role of education in society, and passed resolutions aimed at reforming public schools and protecting their status. In a series of resolutions passed in 1889 the association asked Mississippi to raise teachers' pay, to charter a normal school, and to pay the cost of summer institutes.[8] They reminded the state as well of the importance of educating black children (in segregated schools) and posited the benefits of uniform textbooks, if not for the entire state, then within each county. The final request drew fire from critics who objected to paying higher property taxes for the sake of uniform textbooks, but in some counties textbook committees acted immediately upon the association's request. Mississippi tentatively settled the matter in 1890 when it chartered a textbook commission.[9]

In exchange for passage of educational reforms and the prestige accorded keepers of the New South, teachers promised to inculcate students with a sense of good behavior and respectability. Teachers had long professed to be in the business of forming good citizens, but when late-nineteenth-century teachers spoke of shaping children into moral citizens, an urgency

1890. See, too, Carthage *Carthaginian*, April 23, May 28, November 19, 1887, April 21, 1888. Although several private schools professed to train teachers, the state founded a teachers' school only in 1910. See Sansing, *Making Haste Slowly*, 81. On summer institutes for teachers and organization of the State Teachers' Association, see Robert B. Fulton, "Educational Progress in Mississippi," in *Annals of the American Academy of Political and Social Science* (September, 1903), 61–65, rpr. in Alfred Holt Stone Collection, MDAH.

8. Jackson *Weekly Clarion-Ledger*, January 3, 1889. It is not clear whether the state teachers' association was affiliated with any national organization, but advertisements for discounted rail fares to the Nashville meeting of the National Education Association appeared in the Hazelhurst *Copiah Signal*, July 11, 1889.

9. Jackson *Weekly Clarion-Ledger*, January 3, 1889. On the textbook controversy, see the letter signed "What Next," Raymond *Hinds County Gazette*, October 18, 1890; Carthage *Carthaginian*, May 21, August 15, 1890; Easom, "Public School Legislation in Mississippi," 156; speech of Miss Anna Tillman in Raymond *Hinds County Gazette*, March 21, 1891.

not previously heard resounded in their voices. In a world perceived as badly splintered, teachers had an audience eager to hear that society might once again achieve homogeneity. Yet they struggled to define good citizenship and a good republic where they appeared to move with purpose. Defining such weighty matters in the new order provoked controversy. Differing opinions about what constituted virtue appeared at the 1889 Copiah County teachers' institute. A proponent of classical education, for example, argued that schools should not "turn out mere money making machines," while another "professor" suggested that good citizenship and wealth went hand in hand. Good citizens grew wealthy and created jobs for others less suited for leadership roles in the commercial order. The terms of the debate reflected falsely dichotomous views of the good republic that had been the Old South: educators believed they had a choice of re-creating a republic of yeomen farmers or a republic of market producers, failing to realize that their ancestors had not thought of themselves as belonging to one class or the other but to both. Margaret Lackey's address, "Qualifications of Teachers," however, put to rest the debate that opened before the Copiah conventioneers, perhaps by shaming them; she argued that teachers should be more concerned with imparting to students a love of God, man, and the Ten Commandments than teaching them arithmetic or Latin.[10]

Controversy over the moral imperatives to be conveyed in public schools raged only at teachers' conventions. School administrators and the public believed it possible to mold young minds into conformity with the commercial order and the precepts of communitarian thought. In the official curriculum for Hattiesburg public schools, administrators outlined ideal notions of good citizenship that derived from various modes of thought. By the early twentieth century, Hattiesburg was a quintessential New South city, prosperous but rife with the disparities of the era. Wealthy sawmill owners lived in large Victorian homes on the southern fringe of town. Not far beyond the trolley car line, which carried lumber barons to their offices, but not as far as the cutover timber lands to the west of town, prostitutes and mill workers lived in what middle-class citizens considered a moral and social abyss. Providing the children of those trapped between the Bay Street trolley line and the denuded pine barrens sufficient moral fortitude to resist the easy temptations of their world fell upon the shoulders of Hattiesburg's teachers.[11]

The public schools manual directed almost every aspect of teachers' conduct, within the classroom and without. It reminded teachers to set good

10. Hazelhurst *Copiah Signal,* February 14, 1889.

11. Skates, "The Early Years," in *Hattiesburg: A Pictorial History,* 6–11.

examples for their students and to "make every study and every school duty do effective work in moral training." It also suggested that success in the commercial order required more than knowledge obtained from books; virtuous citizens needed to possess control over their bodies as well as their minds. The enlargement of students' minds took place in classes that taught algebra, elocution, agriculture, and history; fourth graders were expected to begin cultivating "an abiding taste for the best literature." To place a child in charge of his or her body and conscience, the manual encouraged teachers to employ a combination of stern and gentle rebukes, as well as the force of their own good example. Lessons in physiology and hygiene (code words for prohibition instruction) appeared in the curriculum, too. But most importantly, students were to learn that "the will" must hold sway over common passions. In its directions to teachers, the district advised a formula guaranteed to produce respectability and success in the New South: knowledge awakens feeling, feeling solicits the will, the will determines conduct. Virtuous citizens who avoided "sin and selfishness" would obtain happiness through an appreciation of beauty and capital accumulation.[12] As promoters of the New South's commercial order, teachers instructed students in the benefits of clean living, hard work, and self-sacrifice so that they exited the schools ready to assume their places as respectable laborers and managers. The old signposts of virtuous citizenship served new purposes.

Teachers were not alone in claiming the privilege of defining virtue in the New South; physicians, too, wished to instill among citizens and their profession a sense of self-control and proper behavior. Dr. Benjamin F. Ward, delivering the commencement address before the Memphis Hospital Medical College graduating class, reminded the young doctors of the qualities demanded by their profession: "Manhood is the vertebral column that gives support and stamina to professional character. . . . No man rises to the full standard of the true physician who is a moral or physical coward."[13] Doctors had not only to meet the challenges of practicing their profession (long hours in service of a dispersed population and mental exhaustion), but they had also to set a moral tone for their communities. As exemplars of good behavior, Ward contended, physicians might legitimately profess to be keepers of the New South. Like teachers, they asserted that their profession

12. Quoting *Manual of the Public Schools of Hattiesburg, Mississippi, 1910–1911* (Hattiesburg, n.d.), 65, 13, 23, 64, but see, too, 14, 34.

13. Clipping of "Address to the Graduating Class of the Memphis Hospital Medical College," 111, in Ward Family Papers.

played a pivotal role in softening some of the commercial order's rough edges. To establish themselves as paladins of the new order, physicians interpreted their role in society as facilitators of good health and prosperity. As early as the first statewide meeting of doctors in 1856, physicians equated Mississippi's physical well-being with its economic health, and after the war, doctors on the state Board of Health broadcast the message that good health fostered prosperity. Across the state, doctors measured their success and failure as healers in terms of dollars and cents. Dr. P. H. Griffin of Meridian counted that city's losses during the 1878 and 1879 yellow fever epidemic not by the number of deaths but by the amount of money lost due to lost wages, drug costs, the quarantine, and the replacement of destroyed bedding and clothing. In 1909 the link between health and wealth received prominent billing at the masthead of the state's first public health bulletin: "Public health is the foundation on which reposes the happiness of the people and the prosperity and power of the country." [14] According to physicians, good citizens were healthy and wealthy, and assuring that virtuous residents achieved those goals galvanized physicians to organize practitioners of their craft.

Like other professionals in the late nineteenth century, medical caregivers formed a professional society, chartering the Mississippi Medical Association in 1868 for the express purpose of elevating the "character and the protection of the proper rights and interests of those engaged in the practice of medicine." The state association pledged to follow the rules governing the American Medical Association, to initiate only graduates of respectable medical colleges, and to disassociate with members guilty of gross misconduct in the profession or society.[15] Membership in the state association grew slowly but steadily. In 1872 about 80 doctors belonged, but in 1904 that number had shot up to approximately 520.[16] One of the

14. Quoting the pamphlet "Tuberculosis: Its Causes, Prevention, and Cures," in *Report of the Board of Health of Mississippi from September 30, 1909 to June 30, 1911* (Nashville, 1911), 105. See, too, Griffin's comments, *Report of the Board of Health for the Years 1878–1879*, 159; and *Biennial Report of the Mississippi State Board of Health, 1880–1881*, 45; *Biennial Report of the Board of Health of the State of Mississippi from September 30, 1905 to September 30, 1907* (Nashville, 1907), 5.

15. "Constitution and By-Laws of the Mississippi Medical Association as Revised and Proposed by the President, Dr. W. G. Kiger," *Mississippi Medical Monthly*, II (1892), 73. *Transactions of the Mississippi State Medical Association at the Fifth Annual Session Held at Holly Springs April 3rd and 4th, 1872, with Constitution and By-Laws and Roll of Members* (Columbus, 1872), 16–19.

16. *Transactions of the Mississippi State Medical Association, 1872*, 20; *Transactions of the Twenty-Seventh Annual Session of the Mississippi State Medical Association Held at Jack-*

chief functions of professional organizations in the late nineteenth and early twentieth centuries was the regulation of those who wished to practice a craft. While teachers were successfully challenging admission of the untrained into the schoolhouse, members of the state medical association battled corrupt pharmacists and quacks. Numerous articles appeared in the association's official journal warning physicians to be wary of shysters in the drug business, who substituted cheap ingredients for those prescribed by doctors. The practices of the nefarious became so deleterious to good physicians' reputations that the editor of the *Mississippi Medical Monthly* called upon the Board of State Medical Examiners to investigate pharmacists. Fear of druggists' deceptive ways led I. J. M. Goss to warn doctors that "the manufacture of drugs is too much like many other things now, it is to make money; and the jobber thinks nothing of imposing his old worthless stock, upon any unsuspecting physician who does not have time to make his own tinctures, or upon such as are too indolent to do so." He encouraged doctors to make their own drugs. Despite physicians' distrust of pharmacists, the medical association categorically refused to approve alliances between doctors and honest pharmacists or to sanction physicians taking out patents for medicines.[17] An exaggerated sense of propriety and concern for professional ethics informed the association's fear of pharmacists and the medical marketplace.

Quacks, even more so than druggists, alarmed physicians, though sometimes the medical association defined illegitimate practitioners in a self-serving manner.[18] Before 1860 those who wished to advertise themselves as

---

son April 4th, 5th, and 6th, 1894, with Rolls of Members (Jackson, 1894), 23. Leon S. Lippincott, "History of the Mississippi State Medical Association" (1931), Typescript, MDAH, unpaginated.

17. Goss quoted in Marice C. Brown, "Early Pharmaceutics in the Deep South," *Mississippi Folklore Register,* VIII (1974), 234. A native of Georgia, Goss published a volume, *New Medicines and Their Special Therapeutics,* describing concoctions based on ingredients such as alcohol, herbs, and cobwebs. For attacks on druggists, see J. W. Carthart, "Substitution of Cheap Pharmaceuticals in the Filling of Prescriptions," *Mississippi Medical Monthly,* I (1891), 149–53; "Incompetent Boards of State Medical Examiners," *Mississippi Medical Monthly,* I (1891), 157–58. See, too, "Constitution and By-Laws of the Mississippi State Medical Association," *Mississippi Medical Monthly,* 73.

18. After Dr. T. T. Beall published a pamphlet, "Arraignment of the Official Conduct of the Mississippi State Medical Association," the association, regarding him as just another crackpot and calling his tract "a tissue of misrepresentation of facts and misconstruction of motives," drummed him out. See *Transactions of the Twenty-Fourth Annual Session of the Mississippi State Medical Association Held at Meridian April 16th and 17th, 1891* (Jackson, 1891), 36.

doctors had only to purchase a license. Except for the cost of the certificate, nothing prohibited self-proclaimed physicians from practicing any brand of healing they wished. Describing the antebellum licensing process, which continued until the early 1880s, Dr. W. R. Blailock, chief health officer for Leake County, acerbically noted that any doctor could be licensed "even if the sum total of his knowledge consists in his having seen at some period of his life, through a powerful telescope, some of the fly-leaves of an antiquated work on midwifery." Beginning in 1875 with the formation of the Board of Health, interest in professionalizing the corps of health-care providers took shape under the auspices of physicians. Citizens, too, demanded that doctors bear a stamp of approval. In the wake of the yellow fever epidemic of 1878 and 1879, the board's warning about sanitary conditions in the state awakened Mississippians even more to the importance of trained physicians. The financial cost, both the immediate price tag of fighting the fever and the long-term damage to the state's business climate, threatened to weaken Mississippi's appeal as an investment. In 1882 new regulatory laws requiring that applicants for medical licenses pass an examination went into effect.[19]

Critics of the regulatory laws judged the means of certification a species of class legislation, but physicians insisted that protecting the reputation of legitimate doctors formed the sole purpose of the tests, a hair-splitting distinction to opponents.[20] As with the teachers examinations, licensing tests proved to be a stumbling block for many prospective physicians. According to Ward, nearly one-half of the medical school graduates taking the test between 1900 and 1904 failed; inadequate writing skills and a lack of scientific knowledge kept most from receiving their license. Judging from the responses elicited from test-takers in 1894, deficiencies in knowledge accounted for the large number of failures. Employing all of his scientific erudition, one test-taker succinctly described the male heart as "larger than the female"; one listed the elements of the body as "animal and vegetable"; one said without a doubt that the umbilical cord should be cut, "when the head is born"; and another ascribed to Divine Providence the inability of the stomach to digest itself. Such examples notwithstanding, of the

19. Blailock quoted in *Biennial Report of the Board of Health, 1880–1881*, 45. On the early work of the Board of Health, see *Report of the Board of Health, 1878–1879*, 1. On the regulation of physicians, see, too, Legan, "Evolution of Public Health Services," 81; *Biennial Report of the Board of Health, 1884–1885*, 9; *Biennial Report of the Board of Health, 1886–1887*, 4–5.

20. See the remarks of E. P. Sale, president of the Board of Health, *Biennial Report of the Board of Health, 1886–1887*, 4.

forty-three young men taking the exam in 1894, thirty-two received their certificates; among the eleven who failed, seven had completed medical school. With an eye toward protecting the public from unlicensed practitioners and discrediting mediocre medical schools, the state Board of Health heaped insult upon injury when it published in local newspapers the names of failures along with the colleges they attended.[21]

Besides using professional associations to protect their standing in the New South, physicians also educated themselves about their work through state- and county-level meetings and publications. In the early 1890s the state association began publishing its own quarterly journal. Since the journal editors, N. L. Clarke and M. J. Lowry, fancied themselves specialists in obstetrics, an inordinate number of the essays dwelt on techniques for delivering children. Other physicians, however, also published their clinical findings and explained unique cures that they had discovered. Techniques and treatments that passed for safe and even progressive medical practice would shock twentieth-century patients, but doctors expressed confidence in their methodology and the logic they used to cure ailments.[22] Even when discussing a subject like mosquito abatement as a method of preventing yellow fever, Mississippi doctors revealed a frightening lack of medical knowledge. In 1904, despite recent findings in Cuba and the long-running contention of the Mississippi Board of Health that stagnant water and by association mosquitoes preceded outbreaks of yellow fever, physicians attending a convention engaged in heated debate about the vectors of the disease. Dr. J. T. B. Berry, a former member of the Havana Commission, could not convince his stodgy peers of mosquitoes' responsibility for carrying yellow fever. In fact, the convention passed a resolution denying the claim and petitioned the federal government to remove to Dry Tortugas the quaran-

21. Quoted in "Meeting of the State Board of Health," *Mississippi Medical Monthly,* III (1894), 261–62. *Biennial Report of the Board of Health, 1903–1905,* 8.

22. On the dissemination of medical knowledge, see N. L. Clarke, "The Faulty Practice of Obstetrics: A Factor in the Production of Invalidism in Women," *Mississippi Medical Monthly,* III (1894), 233–39; M. J. Long, "Induction of Abortion for the Relief of Pernicious Vomiting of Pregnancy and Puerperal Nephritis, with Report of Cases," *Mississippi Medical Monthly,* I (September, 1891), 8–10; W. S. Sims, "Syphilitic Affliction of the Eye, Ear, Throat and Nose," *Mississippi Medical Monthly,* I (October, 1891), 20–27. On noxious medical practices hailed as advances, see the praise bestowed upon the scientific success of Mississippi native Dr. F. E. Daniel, in part for his article, "Castration of Sexual Perverts," in "F. E. Daniel," *Mississippi Medical Monthly,* III (December, 1894), 253–55. On local medical association meetings and papers presented, see *Transactions of the Mississippi State Medical Association at the Fifth Annual Session, 1872,* 58; "Society Proceedings: Choctaw County Medical Society," *Mississippi Medical Monthly,* II (January, 1893), 211–13.

tine station at Ship Island and to thus eliminate the threat of infection to which coastal residents were exposed.[23]

Although the development and dissemination of medical knowledge proceeded slowly, physicians vigorously pursued improvements in public health, particularly those improvements that directly affected poor whites. By the early 1890s the focus of work conducted by the medical association and the Board of Health fell under the heading of sanitation. Hard lessons about hogpens and unkept outhouses had been learned in the yellow fever outbreak of 1878 and 1879, and physicians wished to avoid another epidemic. Putting aside differences over the causes and cures of disease, they united to improve the sanitary conditions of the state as a means of ameliorating some of the disparities of life in the New South. Altering long-established sanitary practices, however, proved nearly insuperable. Many practices, especially those that dealt with water use and the disposal of excrement, had been born on the frontier and passed from generation to generation. Writing in her memoirs, Letitia Miller recalled that before the Civil War members of her family regularly suffered from various stomach ailments. With knowledge acquired during the late nineteenth century, she realized that her family's habit of drinking water obtained from a cow lot well likely caused the dreaded outbreaks of diarrhea with which she had grown up.[24] Spreading such elementary sanitary knowledge among Mississippians, rural and urban residents alike, prompted the state Board of Health to undertake an ambitious educational program.

The Board of Health singled out what it labeled "soil pollution," a euphemism for the practice of contaminating the ground with bodily waste, as the chief enemy of good health. A number of ailments, particularly hookworm disease, could be traced directly to Mississippians' unsanitary methods of waste disposal. The incidence of hookworm disease, an intestinal disease caused by parasites that retarded growth and occasionally caused death, apparently escalated in the late 1800s as a transient population filled Piney Woods lumber mill encampments. Ill-prepared to care adequately for a large population, rural communities found themselves harboring a set of

23. *Transactions of the Mississippi State Medical Association, 1901,* 2–9. On fears that the yellow fever would spread to Mississippi from Ship Island, see Edward Cary Walthall to William T. Walthall, January 26, 1888, in Walthall Papers.

24. In 1894 a group of physicians organized a society to rival the Mississippi Medical Association. But according to "The Medical and Surgical Society of Mississippi," *Mississippi Medical Monthly,* II (December, 1891), 257–59, the competing associations shared a commitment to the "promotion of sanitary science in the state." Miller, "Recollections," unpaginated.

rough and poorly educated men more wild than tame; sanitary facilities, where they existed, became overloaded, and bodily waste escaped into the water supply. Drinking contaminated water, as well as coming into contact with polluted soil, transported the parasites to humans. Mill workers alone are undeserving of blame for the spread of hookworms. In 1911 the Board of Health found that of 20,979 farm households surveyed in forty-three counties 60 percent had no outdoor toilets. Males, the board reported, often used barns and sheds as restrooms; children regarded all of the outdoors as a suitable privy. Not surprisingly, infection rates among children (many of whom spent their summers out of doors and shoeless) ranged as high as 91 percent of those attending school.[25]

Concerned that the presence of hookworms threatened the health and prosperity of worthy citizens, the state Board of Health sponsored a campaign to eradicate the parasites. In a pamphlet designed for general distribution, the board advised Mississippians to install proper privies, to refrain from spitting on floors, and to protect against mosquito and fly infestation of privies. To inspire healthful behavior, the pamphlet attacked unsanitary practices on several fronts: it cited biblical injunctions against soil pollution and juxtaposed dramatic photographs of the unaffected and hookworm sufferers, whose dwarfed and hollowed frames caused them to appear a decade or more older than they were. The pamphlet contained as well working drawings for sanitary privies with automatically closing lids. Additional steps to eliminate hookworm disease began in 1916 with an experimental program conducted in four Pearl River County communities. With the assistance of the Picayune city government, lumber mill operators, and public schools, doctors took stool samples, initiated treatment for the afflicted, constructed sanitary privies, and implemented strict guidelines for maintaining outhouses. Citizens cooperating with the Board of Health had their names listed in the county newspaper and at rural post offices. In other remote communities, enthusiastic physicians enticed residents to participate in eradication programs by allowing them to observe under a microscope hookworms twisting in stool samples.[26]

25. *Report of the Board of Health, 1909–1911*, 121–24. On the survey of farm households, see, *Report of the Board of Health of Mississippi from July 1, 1911 to June 30, 1913* (Nashville, 1913), 73–74.

26. On photographic evidence of the effects of hookworms, see the pamphlet, "Hookworm Disease" in *Report of the Board of Health, 1909–1911*, 121–42. The biblical injunction cited may be found in Deut. 23:12–13. On the Pearl River County eradication program, see *Report of the Board of Health of Mississippi from June 1, 1915 to June 30, 1917* (Memphis, 1917), 49–60. See, too, a report of similar work on a smaller scale at other sites, *Report of the Board of Health, 1913–1915*, 23–24.

Physicians sought to eliminate other diseases that threatened Mississippians, but with less vigor than they had employed in the hookworm campaign. Neither the Board of Health nor doctors in general revealed as much concern for ridding the state of pellagra and tuberculosis, diseases from which African Americans more often died than whites. In 1914, for instance, deaths per 100,000 attributable to pellagra stood at 30.8 among whites and 87.6 among blacks; for tuberculosis, the difference between the death rate for whites and blacks broadened. The absence of proper medical treatment for blacks, a product of physicians' lack of concern for blacks' health, in part accounted for the higher mortality; the white physician Benjamin Ward suggested that because of their innate inferiority, moral and intellectual, blacks could not be lifted from the conditions in which they lived. Even had racist insights like Ward's not existed, physicians would have been hard pressed to mount a campaign against either pellagra or tuberculosis. Both diseases were products of the New South's commercial order: impoverished diets accounted for rampant pellagra among sharecroppers trapped under the crop lien; foul water and cramped living quarters nurtured tuberculosis.[27] Physicians, for all their concern about creating a virtuous and homogeneous society, healthy and wealthy, failed to include among their goals eradication of the economic disparities that blacks suffered or even to extend medical benevolence toward them.

White middle-class reformers believed emancipated African Americans poorly suited to function in the commercial order. By the late 1880s and early 1890s, even as a black middle-class emerged in the Jim Crow world, the makers and keepers of the new order resolutely continued to view blacks as field hands, important to society as mudsills but individually dispensable, the bane of a homogeneous society.[28] As before the war, when white

27. For Dr. Benjamin Ward's comments regarding tuberculosis, see *Biennial Report of the Board of Health, 1903–1905,* 6. On concern over the spread of tuberculosis, see *Report of the Board of Health, 1909–1911,* 44, 61; *Report of the Board of Health, 1913–1915,* 63. Pellagra, an indication of low protein levels and deficient amounts of niacin (a catalyst of metabolism and a coenzyme derived from leafy vegetables), captured the attention of the federal government before Mississippi exhibited concern for its sufferers. See U.S. Department of Agriculture, *Dietary Studies with Reference to Food of the Negro in Alabama, 1895–1896* (1897), 8, 11, 20, 55–64.

28. On the black middle class, see Neil R. McMillen, *Dark Journey: Black Mississippians in the Age of Jim Crow* (Urbana, 1989), 164–86; D. W. Woodward, *Negro Progress in a Mississippi Town: Being a Study of Conditions in Jackson, Mississippi* (Cheyney, Penn., 1908); Charles Banks, *Negro Bankers of Mississippi* (Cheyney, Penn., 1908). Dun and Company, Warren County, 81M, 217. See, too, the argument advanced by black entrepreneurs that blacks

southerners isolated blacks in the underclass, late-nineteenth-century reformers set about defining liberty-loving and virtuous citizenship in such a way as to deny African Americans an influential stake in the predominant political culture or society.

No post-Redemption Mississippian better characterized white attitudes toward blacks than Horace S. Fulkerson, the Vicksburg newspaper editor. In his racist diatribe, *The Negro: As He Was; As He Is; As He Will Be,* Fulkerson bespoke his generation's bewilderment at living in a world populated by emancipated blacks. Like his antebellum predecessors who had penned similar sentiments, he shrank in horror from the consequences of an empowered underclass and assumed that blacks possessed an inherent depravity and intellectual impotence that made them unworthy of citizenship. According to Fulkerson, trouble for African Americans and the South began when Reconstruction governments extended to ex-slaves responsibilities they were incapable of bearing; the high number of black convicts in the penitentiary (87 percent of the prison population) proved their unfitness for freedom. To Fulkerson the whole of American civilization depended on the emergence of "an Ideal American," a type which through the "homogeneity and assimilating qualities of the people" would foster a good republic. Instead of facilitating the ascension of the well-adjusted "Ideal American," emancipation and the federal government forced upon both races "an unequal yoking; a yoking forbidden of reason, forbidden of instinct, forbidden of Heaven!" Through such a yoking the social equilibrium of the antebellum world had been disrupted and an obnoxious but necessary caste system installed to prevent racial amalgamation. In order to right the incongruence of the federal government's nominal devotion to equality and blacks' inability to exhibit even an inkling of moral courage and civic responsibility, Fulkerson proposed that the United States purchase the maritime provinces and certain Caribbean islands as a homeland for ex-slaves.[29] Removing from the South the perceived cause of postbellum injury and insult, Fulkerson and middle-class reformers believed the region again could achieve the social and political homogeneity that had propelled it to greatness in the antebellum era.

---

working in black-owned factories served to convince whites they should not attack blacks as degenerate members of the underclass, Jackson *Evening News,* April 6, 1899.

29. Quoting H. S. Fulkerson, *The Negro; As He Was; As He Is; As He Will Be* (Vicksburg, 1887), 69, but see, too, 14, 34, 47, 99, 110, 118. On white southerners' concepts of African Americans' inherent incapacity for living in a free social order, see John S. Hughes, "Labeling and Treating Black Mental Illness in Alabama, 1861–1910," *Journal of Southern History,* LVIII (1992), 436–39.

Fulkerson's solution to the problem of a heterogeneous and contentious social order found few admirers, but his sentiments broadly reflected the view of reformers who longed to alienate blacks from the social, political, and economic mainstream of southern life. To argue that blacks could not, despite the protection offered by the federal Constitution, achieve liberty and virtue required that middle-class whites associate perceived rampant social and political disintegration with free blacks. One kind of linkage they pursued involved prohibition. Prohibitionists took advantage of whites' horror of an immoral and uncontrollable black population to argue that blacks were the chief consumers of alcohol, and thus the chief destroyers of order; they stigmatized white allies of the whiskey trade as friends of disorder, the postbellum equivalent of branding whites coconspirators in slave insurrections. Advocates of prohibition had difficulty escaping the rhetoric of racial division embodied in the racial underpinnings of the southern social ethic. In a National Temperance Society publication, A. Burwell urged Mississippi residents to adopt a strict law against the sale of alcoholic beverages by pointing out that Mississippi's poverty might be traced to the omnipresence of whiskey drinkers among the working class. Consumers of alcohol were ineffective producers and poor, and all poor people owed their condition to a moral failing, likely whiskey drinking. The proceeds of the cotton crop, Burwell said, "just about pays for the whiskey" consumed in Mississippi, if not exclusively, then mainly, by those who worked the crop. When Charles Betts Galloway, Episcopal bishop of the state, called for Mississippi to forsake liquor, he also connected the whiskey trade with emancipation-related disruptions. In his mind prohibition was "the watchword of moral reform," and no group would more benefit from the abolition of liquor sales than African Americans. But Galloway, like other prohibitionists, wished not to see black reformation for the sake of elevating freed people to respectability; instead, he preferred that reformation ensure they fulfilled their God-ordained role in society as dependable workers.[30]

Since the antebellum period, temperance advocates had regarded their cause as a means of securing social homogeneity, but they had not bothered to equate African Americans with the social evils they wished to address; their firm commitment to black enslavement sufficed to prove the

30. Quoting A. Burwell, *Dramshops, Industry and Taxes: Address to the People of Mississippi* (New York, 1875), 22. Charles B. Galloway, *Handbook of Prohibition: Specially Designed for Circulation in the State of Mississippi* (N.p., 1886), 3, 87. For an outsider's perspective of motivations for prohibition, see James Hancock, "Mississippi's Experience with Prohibition," in *The 1916 Year Book of the United States Brewer's Association,* 105, rpr. in MDAH.

degeneracy of blacks. Before the war, conspicuous consumers of liquor were regarded as men submissive to their brutal passions—the moral, if not actual, equivalent of murderers, liars, and adulterers. Postbellum prohibitionists, however, discerned an indisputable connection between the social ills of the South and emancipation. Closing taverns and banning the sale of liquor, they argued, would restore vigor and efficiency to white laborers made unproductive by their love of strong drink. Citizens of Greenville believed prohibiting alcohol sales would force brothels and gambling dens to shut down as well, since their clientele consisted largely of whiskey drinkers.[31] Eliminating liquor from the state, prohibitionists liked to think, would not only make Mississippians more productive, it would also elevate to the status of virtuous those white citizens who distinguished themselves from African Americans by their teetotaling ways. Consequently, during the early days of black freedom, petitions arrived at the state capitol asking that the sale of alcohol be declared illegal within certain counties or smaller entities. Private laws arising from citizens' petitions, however, proved ineffective because counterpetitions could as easily sway the next legislature to sanction the trade.[32]

The campaign to pass antiliquor laws began in earnest after Frances Willard of the Woman's Christian Temperance Union toured the state and spoke before the legislature in 1882. A state chapter of the WCTU formed soon after Willard's tour, and prohibition speakers, bearing sentimental tracts and pamphlets that portrayed the consequences of enslavement to liquor, followed her. By 1885 the WCTU, led largely by the wives of longtime prohibition leaders, had chapters in 80 percent of Mississippi counties. Initial success in founding a united activist prohibition movement waned as supporters of a local option law and a blanket abolition of liquor sales, the choice of the WCTU, split. In 1886 proponents of local option cajoled the legislature into approving a law that required counties to

31. On the undesirable behavior attributed to the whiskey trade, see Agnew Diary, June 24, 1867, July 29, 1886; Mrs. E. O. Miller to John M. Stone, February 15, 1893, in RG 27, MDAH; Jehu Amaziah Orr Diary, June 28, 1890 (MS in Orr Papers). For a sense of how little prohibitionists' attacks on alcohol changed over time, compare Holcombe Books, January 20, 1855; Duncan McKenzie to Duncan McLaurin, May 5, 1844, McLaurin Papers; L. L. Pickett to E. L. Noel, March 6, 1908, RG 27, MDAH. See also petition to "The Honorable Mayor and City Council of Greenville," N.d., in Leroy Percy Papers, LSU.

32. On the struggles of one community to knock out the liquor trade, see Ackerman *Choctaw Plaindealer,* September 28, 1888, February 5, July 30, 1897. See, too, the petition "A Majority of the Legal Voters of Iuka" to Robert Lowry, February 1, 1882, in RG 27, MDAH; Jackson *Weekly Clarion,* January 14, 1888. *Laws of the State of Mississippi,* 1870, pp. 380–84.

stage a referendum if they desired to go dry. Within four years, thirty-nine counties voted to ban sales. Even though the WCTU had initially looked upon local option as a mere political expedient, it pointed to the salutary effects of such laws. Twelve months after Lincoln County banned liquor sales, the number of criminal cases on court dockets plummeted from 114 to 37, school attendance rose, and the county produced two thousand more bales of cotton. Regardless of such signs of moral renewal, the WCTU continued agitating for a ban on liquor, a campaign that culminated in 1908 with statewide prohibition.[33]

Portrayals of alcohol as a thief of prosperity and a gateway to other immoral behaviors frequently appeared in the prohibitionist press. By linking the consumption of alcohol to other pernicious habits and by labeling whiskey drinkers the moral equivalent of African Americans, self-enslavers, and the otherwise unvirtuous, prohibitionists ensured that their cause would become the central means through which certain members of the middle-class defined good citizenship. Aspects of educational reform, women's suffrage agitation, and the effort to disfranchise African Americans sprang directly from the prohibition movement. Not only did leading proponents of the ban on liquor provide a core of support for other reform movements, the movements shared a common impulse to advance middle-class status in the social order through the elimination of degenerate residents.

According to prohibitionists, the presence of alcohol in society aroused the unvirtuous to engage in a host of immoral activities in which Christian men and the government itself tacitly acquiesced. Particularly upsetting to prohibitionists was the fact that public schools received a portion of their funding from the licensing fees charged tavern keepers. The funding of schools through the whiskey tax, prohibitionists claimed, undermined the attempt to foster homogeneity and self-control by implying to children their preparation for good citizenship owed to whiskey drinking. In 1884

33. General histories of prohibition include: William Graham Davis, "Attacking the 'Matchless Evil': Temperance and Prohibition in Mississippi, 1817–1908" (Ph.D. dissertation, Mississippi State University, 1975), 10–49, 81–110; T. J. Bailey, *Prohibition in Mississippi: or Anti-Liquor Legislation from Territorial Days, with its Results in the Counties* (Jackson, 1917), 127; W. H. Patton, "History of the Prohibition Movement in Mississippi," Mississippi Historical Society *Publications,* X (1909), 181–85, 193. On traveling speakers, see the advertisement for Luther Benson's tour, Jackson *Weekly Clarion,* January 21, 1885. On the split among prohibitionists, see Meridian *Mississippi White Ribbon,* July 15, 1889; Raymond *Hinds County Gazette,* February 9, 1884; Crystal Springs *Meteor,* November 28, 1885. For a list of dry counties, see Meridian *Mississippi White Ribbon,* March 15, 1890. For glowing reports on the effects of local option, see Meridian *Mississippi White Ribbon,* September, 1888; Wesson *Times* quoted in Jackson *Weekly Clarion,* October 14, 1885.

L. S. Foster of Jefferson County labeled the funding device evidence of moral pusillanimity and political cowardice. Such funding was immoral and equipped foes of educational expenditures with an excuse for arguing that since schools received money from licensing fees higher property taxes were unnecessary. According to Foster, little of the whiskey money made its way to students. Roughly two-thirds of the fees collected in his county paid for the detention and trial of criminals who committed their misdeeds under the influence of alcohol, leaving thirty-six cents on the dollar to be spent on each child. Incensed by the parsimonious funding of education sustained by dependence on the liquor trade, Foster calculated that each child was maintained in school six days a year. "At this rate everyone would be as old as Methuselah before he learned to spell ba-ba." [34]

With the spread of local prohibition ordinances the necessity of abolishing the hypocritical funding of one variety of moral reform by its antithesis diminished. But prohibitionist groups, especially the WCTU, undertook other efforts that aimed at the moral reformation of children through the elimination of the whiskey trade. In 1888 and 1890 the WCTU convinced the state legislature to require that school districts teach courses in health and hygiene. Ostensibly designed to take the backwoods edge off of students and make them at least appear as miniature burghers, lessons in the course delivered a strong antiliquor and antinarcotic message. Governor Robert Lowry, a party lackey who held office without enthusiastic support, vetoed the first bill, but when John Stone retook the governor's mansion in 1890, he approved it.[35] Molding virtuous and productive citizens into servants of the commercial order motivated teachers and prohibitionists to counter the pervasive appeal of strong drink. The image of children lurking in pool rooms and saloons or running errands for brothels and gamblers stirred the WCTU to action, and early in the 1890s the temperance union employed a youth chapter organizer, Belle Kearney. Unlike the adult union, the "Y's," as they were known, welcomed all children, regardless of gender, if they swore to wear "the white flower of a blameless life." Besides working among school-age children, the WCTU actively recruited members at the II&C and boasted that the two hundred student members attending the school would become fierce opponents of liquor, cigarettes, and Coca-Cola when they entered their chosen careers in factories, schools, and homes.[36]

34. Jackson *Weekly Clarion,* December 31, 1884.

35. Bailey, *Prohibition in Mississippi,* 127.

36. Quoting Meridian *Mississippi White Ribbon,* September 15, 1890. On youthful alcoholics serving as couriers and lookouts for gamblers and brothels, see petition to "The Hon-

Of all the campaigns to create a homogeneous and moral society undertaken by the WCTU, none, outside of women's rights agitation, distinguished it from other reform groups as much as did the effort to reform the penal system. Dramatic changes in prisons occurred during the 1890s under the impetus of farmers' organizations, but the WCTU focused its penal reform energies on juvenile offenders. In one of the first issues of the WCTU newspaper, editor Harriet B. Kells called for her fellow female prohibitionists to welcome ex-convicts back into society. Even the simplest gesture would do much to wipe away the indignity of a conviction, and the effort might go a long way toward converting a degenerate soul into a virtuous one. Kells suggested that the WCTU clothe convicts when they exited prison. At the same time, she initiated a campaign to build separate facilities for youthful convicts whose numbers had escalated throughout the post-Reconstruction period and whose poor treatment at the hands of jailers became bothersome to respectable folk. Advocacy of more substantive relief of juvenile prisoners followed. In 1896 the legislature passed a bill to establish a juvenile reformatory, but the governor vetoed it. Stymied but not deterred, the WCTU and other reform groups continued to advocate construction of a reformatory. An experimental program at the Rankin County prison farm set up by several reform-minded organizations opened in 1910. Testimony provided by the teacher hired to educate the boys, Emily Butts, pointed to a miraculous transformation of a ragged bunch of gamblers, swearers, and smokers. When the little convicts left the program, they did so as decorous and gainfully employed citizens.[37]

---

orable Mayor and City Council of Greenville," N.d., in Percy Papers. On activities of the youth section of the WCTU, see Meridian *Mississippi White Ribbon,* February 28, May 15, June 30, 1890. On activities of the WCTU at the Industrial Institute and College, see Meridian *Mississippi White Ribbon,* August, 1888. On WCTU attacks on Coca-Cola, see *Mississippi Woman's Christian Temperance Union: Report of the Thirtieth Annual Convention, Held in Tupelo, Mississippi, October 11th to 14th, 1914* (Jackson, 1914), 21, 56; *Mississippi Woman's Christian Temperance Union: Report of the Thirty First Annual Convention, Held in Eupora, Mississippi, October 23rd to 26th, 1915* (N.p., n.d.), 46.

37. Meridian *Mississippi White Ribbon,* November, 1888, January 15, 1890; *Mississippi Boy Convicts* (Jackson, 1911), 2–7. On the treatment of juveniles, see petition to Robert Lowry, May 5, 1883; R. A. Pickett to John M. Stone, November 8, 1890; S. S. Henderson to Stone, November 8, 1890, all in RG 27, MDAH. See especially the account a fourteen-year-old runaway charged with fighting in public: "They are whipping me and treating me badly[.] . . . Pa for god sake come to my relief and you will make a good pious girl out of me." Roberta Johnson to Rubin Johnson, July 18, 1881; W. W. Cook to Stone, December 20, 1881, all in RG 27, MDAH.

As feverish reformers of society, members of the WCTU sought to convert children into teetotalers. Through Sunday schools and YMCAs where they recruited members for the "Y's," in public schools where they warned against the evils of strong drink and drugs, and in prisons where juveniles exchanged their bad habits for good ones, the WCTU attempted to ensure that white children avoided the perils of the commercial order and instead adapted to it.

Out of the prohibition movement also sprang a kindred reform crusade dedicated to securing the position of white women in southern society. Early in the era of postbellum reform, middle-class males turned to their natural allies, white women, for support in ameliorating the disruptions caused by the commercial revolution and in creating a homogeneous social order by relegating African Americans to underclass status. At first, male reformers accepted women into their temperance society but denied them the privilege of speaking at meetings. With the formation of the WCTU in the early 1880s, however, women obtained a voice in the prohibition movement, a voice that soon drowned out their male counterparts. They also used their newfound voice to enlarge their role in society.[38] As a unique organization composed solely of women, the WCTU soon incorporated women's rights into its struggle to obliterate the whiskey trade, a union of two concerns that promised to elevate women to prominence as virtuous keepers of order and morality. Testimony to the wedding of moral reform and agitation to secure women's place in society appeared at the masthead of the *Mississippi White Ribbon*, the official newspaper of the WCTU: "Woman's Protest Against the Destruction of her 'Business'—Home-Keeping." Women might not only protest the political powers that permitted alcohol a free reign, but they took their traditional role as defenders of the domestic sphere seriously, characterizing it in the language of the New South as a "Business." According to the WCTU, men, not all but perhaps most, were the chief enemies of the home. They were "unstable prohibitionists," or "Christian men out of line with the declared policy of their churches," or farmers who worked their wives like slaves during the week and binged on Saturday.[39] Each in his own way challenged the autonomy and virtuous work of moral education that women undertook at home.

38. Davis, "Attacking the 'Matchless Evil,'" 97. Many Mississippi county seat newspapers recognized the influence of the WCTU by permitting local chapters a full column in their editions. For examples, see the Jackson *New Mississippian,* May 11, 1886; Crystal Springs *Meteor,* July 30, 1886.

39. Quoting Meridian *Mississippi White Ribbon,* April 30, 1889, October 15, 1890, but

African-American males in particular suffered the wrath of the temperance union. Even though the WCTU pitched its cause to black ministers, many of whom united with antiwhiskey forces, it regarded black males as the primary obstacle to passage of statewide prohibition. Kells rested blame for the obstruction of local option laws on black males who, she said, voted as a bloc in favor of whiskey. In a phrase worthy of H. S. Fulkerson, she characterized blacks as "the ignorant, vicious, non-tax-paying population," which "legislates for the enlightened Christian property holder." While in kinder moments she encouraged her readers to proselytize in the black community so that African Americans would be rescued from "a bondage more hopeless than their former slavery," Kells associated southern social declension with the presence of freed men, who proved themselves incapable of becoming liberty-loving and virtuous citizens in the social order.[40] Canceling the sway that black males exercised in political culture would take place, Kells said, if virtuous white women (who proved their moral superiority to black and white men through their stand on prohibition) obtained the suffrage.

The emergence of sentiment in favor of female rights within the WCTU ignited debate about women's role in politics. Some women, even some within the ranks of the WCTU, frowned upon the extension of political rights. Dora Dunbar of West Point protested that if women voted, prohibition—the cause that asserted their superiority—would exchange its moral appeal for political force. Their success in disrupting Democratic political domination (and she did not doubt that women could defeat party regulars by uniting with the Prohibition party), Dunbar continued, would result in an effect precisely opposite of the one women desired: blacks would regain the political power they possessed during Reconstruction and use it for terrible purposes. Regardless of the power women obtained at the

---

see, too, July 30, 1889, and New York *Tribune* quoted June 15, 1889. As used here, the term *women's rights* refers to political rights, but the WCTU wished to establish equality in the workplace, too. See a proposal to found a female-owned-and-operated undergarment factory at Crystal Springs, Meridian *Mississippi White Ribbon,* January, 1889. Other women, imbued with a sense of their rights, considered running for office; see Jackson *Weekly Clarion-Ledger,* July 11, 1889. On other women's reform efforts and the holistic scope of their vision, see, too, Nellie Nugent Somerville, "History of the Mississippi Woman's Suffrage Association, 1897–1919" (Microfilm copy in Nellie Nugent Somerville Papers), MDAH, 6, 13.

40. Quoting Meridian *Mississippi White Ribbon,* October, 1888, August, 1888. On appeals to blacks to support prohibition, see Jackson *Weekly Clarion,* October 14, 1885. On fears of a union between wets and blacks, see B. T. Hobbs to Andrew W. Longino, March 8, 1900, in RG 27, MDAH.

voting booth, she believed they could neither match the influence of men nor the moral appeal of prohibition; in the process of becoming mere political operators, women would forsake the moral leadership they assumed in the community and in their homes. Mollie McGee Snell likewise objected to the granting of political rights to women: as keepers of the home they possessed the most important political power they might ever wish; they encouraged their children and husbands to vote in a responsible manner. The suffrage would ostensibly augment women's authority in the public sphere, but it would also diminish their might at home.[41]

Behind the opposition to the extension of suffrage lay misgivings about women breaking the strong hold that the Democratic party had on southern politics. Although some reform-minded women welcomed the idea of female prohibitionists upsetting the unholy alliance of the Democratic party and whiskey brokers, most quaked at the possibility of substituting for the evils of a whiskey government another Reconstruction-like era of "Black Republicanism."[42] In the late 1880s, as the ranks of the WCTU filled with prohibitionists and suffrage advocates, politicians grew alarmed at the possibility of a vibrant Prohibition party uniting with Democratic bolters. Even though leadership of the WCTU remained uncertain about allying with the national third party, their willingness to consider the benefits of a union separated them from their male counterparts. Repeatedly the male-dominated State Prohibition Executive Committee, headed by W. C. Black, declared its enmity toward the third party and portrayed as soreheads the few thousand Mississippians who enrolled in it. The WCTU, on the other hand, agonized over the decision to unite with the Prohibitionists, dragging out familiar arguments in rejection of the third party and inverting them to justify a split with the Democratic party. For example, the WCTU argued that if a sufficient number of southern females joined the party of prohibition and the party won a presidential election, the Prohibitionists would usher in a new day of southern political domination. The dream of an unreconstructed, even a resurgent, South infected females who assumed the moral high ground offered by prohibitionist arguments. At the sixth

41. Jackson *Weekly Clarion,* April 1, 1885; Meridian *Mississippi White Ribbon,* September, 1888. See, too, the letter signed "Embard" in Jackson *Weekly Clarion-Ledger,* August 22, 1889, and the antisuffrage speech of Annie C. Peyton, an early advocate of the II&C, in Jackson *Weekly Clarion,* July 14, 1886. On the moral influence of women, see, too, Crystal Springs *Meteor,* November 28, 1885.

42. The WCTU frequently loosed bitter denunciations of the Democratically controlled state government. See, Meridian *Mississippi White Ribbon,* January 15, 1890. Males' arguments against female suffrage may be found in Jackson *Weekly Clarion-Ledger,* June 7, 1888.

annual WCTU convention in 1889 Kells advocated that the union support the Prohibitionist party in order to sever all dependence on African Americans in the dry crusade. But the misgivings awakened by the prospects of a third party exterminating the color line kept the WCTU from officially embracing it.[43] Maintaining and strengthening the color line, an object collateral to fostering a homogeneous society, was, after all, a kind of moral reform encouraged by the WCTU and made all the more important in an age of immoral politicians.

Since the Redeemer victories of 1874 and 1875, disgruntled office seekers had frequently run independent campaigns against regular party nominees. Some of the bolters united with Republicans and Greenbackers and overtly wooed black voters. Prohibitionist sentiment introduced into the political fracases of the 1880s another active coterie with which the Democratic party had to reckon. The anxiety generated by the threat of prohibitionists entering the political arena made it imperative that official party candidates reach out to them, and events surrounding the 1886 battle for the Democratic congressional nomination in the central district of the state went a long way toward sealing prohibitionists' allegiance to the Democratic party. Within months of the passage of a statewide local option law, C. E. Hooker, a favorite son among Democrats and prohibitionists, faced longtime bolter and occasional party loyalist Ethelbert Barksdale in the primary election. Barksdale, a member of a prominent political family and a former newspaper editor, assembled a cast of supporters regarded by many as politically dangerous and "wet." The presence of two prominent wets among Barksdale's supporters (Jones S. Hamilton, leaseholder of the state penitentiary, and John McGill, the white Republican mayor of Jackson) ensured that "drys" would portray the election as a moratorium on moral rule. Charges and countercharges of corruption permeated county conventions, but Hooker received the nomination.[44]

Even though the 1886 election and passage of the local option law by a Democratically controlled legislature settled the question of party loyalty for most prohibitionists, they remained relentless in their attempt to remove from office the friends of alcohol and immorality. Several of Barksdale's allies during the election emerged as central figures in a far more important political battle over moral reform and Democratic control of political

43. See Jackson *New Mississippian,* October 24, 1885; Meridian *Mississippi White Ribbon,* December, 1888, April 30, 1889; Jackson, *Weekly Clarion,* December 24, 1884.

44. Accounts of the contested primary appeared in many south central Mississippi newspapers, but for the most insightful, see Jackson *New Mississippian,* August 24, 1886.

machinery. In January, 1888, John McGill lost his bid for reelection. On the surface, his defeat appeared to be little more than a classic Redeemer-era battle between Democrats and "Black Republicans." Considering his alliance with the Barksdale faction two years earlier, however, it might be argued that his overthrow was a matter of revenge orchestrated by party regulars. But much more was at stake in the 1888 election than party loyalty or "home rule."

The white Republican McGill counted on finding few friends among Jackson's Democrats, a search made all the more strenuous by his courtship of Barksdale. Despite the opposition McGill faced, most citizens, even rabid Democrats, agreed that the mayor had lowered their tax burden, retired most of the city's debt, and augmented internal improvements. His fiscal accountability, though, did not silence critics of immoral government and "Black rule." For all of his success in managing the city's affairs, McGill's tenure in office had been tempestuous. Over his objections that prohibition would drive the whiskey trade underground and away from his watchful eye, prohibitionists took advantage of the local option law and outlawed the sale of alcohol in quantities less than one gallon. His opposition to the gallon law alienated advocates of moral reform even more. Rumors circulated that McGill secretly favored prohibition but wished, through his public rejection of it, to drive his enemies into the dry entourage. With taverns closed, his critics charged, McGill hoped to gain control of the black market whiskey trade.[45]

Ascribing to the mayor such Machiavellian motives permitted prohibitionists to label him the instigator of all enmity and criminal activities. The whiskey trade tolerated by the dishonorable mayor, prohibitionists said, accounted for the presence of prostitutes on the streets and three murders that occurred between 1886 and 1888. One murder involved the shooting of a town drunk, who became obnoxious at a tavern; the second left Roderick Gambrell dead and Jones S. Hamilton charged with the crime. Gambrell, the editor of a prohibition newspaper, the *Sword and Shield,* had passionately denounced Hamilton during the 1886 election campaign, and Hamilton retaliated with sharp words of his own. The exchanges between Gambrell and Hamilton soon provoked intense feelings on the streets of Jackson as residents chose sides in the debate. When someone ambushed Gambrell as he walked across the Pearl River bridge, the city knew that the

45. *Senate Miscellaneous Document,* 50th Cong., 1st Sess., No. 166, pp. 5, 10–11, 391, 402. See, too, reports of the testimony in New Orleans *Picayune,* quoted in Jackson *Weekly Clarion-Ledger,* April 19, May 17, 1888. On long-standing suppositions that Jackson mayors allied with unscrupulous blacks, see Jackson *New Mississippian,* January 1, 1884.

tensions of the past two years would soon come to a head.[46] On December 24, 1887, as Hamilton sat in the city jail awaiting trial, the city erupted. Traditionally a night of boisterous celebration, Christmas Eve turned bloody on South President Street when McWillie Mitchell, grandson of ex-Governor William McWillie, had his throat slashed. His assailant, an African American named Bob Whitesides, was mortally wounded by Percy Gambrell, one of Mitchell's companions and a relative of Roderick. Investigators generally agreed that Mitchell, Gambrell, and another white youth had spent their evening blowing horns and shooting firecrackers on the streets, though accounts differed as to whether they had been drinking. They also agreed that prior to Mitchell's death, the white youths exchanged words with Whitesides and several of his friends, who were drinking whiskey on a street corner. The exchange provoked Whitesides to rush into a butcher shop and snatch a knife with which he attacked Mitchell. More so than the murder itself, reports that a black police officer, one of the mayor's henchmen, had instigated it by commanding Whitesides to "carve him" excited the passions of the anti-McGill forces.[47]

According to civic reformers, McGill's refusal to break with his black constituents and clean up the city nurtured the evil ways of Jackson's murderous and immoral. McGill's political allegiances and the composition of the police force, approximately one-half of which was black, riled moral reformers, too. Just days after Mitchell's murder, Democrats and Republicans, including representatives of the federal government, organized a Committee of 100 to rid the city of debauched agents. Predictably, race became a focus of the anti-McGillites. Appealing to virtuous citizens to unite, the Committee of 100 and the Young Men of Jackson, a hastily formed vigilance committee, linked straight-out Democratic politics with moral reform. "One of our number [was] coldly, cruelly, and hellishly murdered in the dark by a negro bully set on by a negro policeman of this negro-cursed city." Nothing short of overthrowing "this black and damnable machine miscalled a government" would satisfy them. Legitimate political organizations also took up the cause of political revolution. The Democratic Reform ticket, headed by William Henry, quickly adopted as its motto "Down with negro policemen and jailers." Faced with such opposition and fearful of election day violence, McGill consulted with the Republican faithful, Democratic soreheads, and black community leaders, who agreed that all black candidates should resign from the Republican ticket,

46. *Senate Miscellaneous Document,* 50th Cong., 1st Sess., No. 166, pp. 2–4, 7–8.
47. *Ibid.*, 5.

and he received from the black community a pledge to boycott the election.[48]

Three weeks after the Jackson mayoral election, U.S. Senator James Z. George wrote Governor Robert Lowry a congratulatory note for his handling of the affair. Bloodshed had been avoided, and the election, judging by its results, seemed to the former leader of the Revolution of 1875 a well-managed one. Nevertheless, the events of December and January had been disruptive to the good order normally enjoyed in Mississippi. To avoid future disruptions George recommended that the governor ignore calls for a constitutional convention and veto any measure that the legislature passed convening one.[49] Public sentiment in favor of a convention heightened after the Jackson election in which dramatic reminders of the perils of black citizenship coupled with the drive for moral reform; after all, forces that coalesced to overthrow McGill (middle-class distaste for African-American liberty and class-conscious suspicions that the degenerate held excessive power) flowed together in the disfranchising clause of the Constitution of 1890.

Historians previously have properly credited the calling of the convention to a multitude of forces. The Farmers' Alliance, particularly chapters in the eastern counties of the state, had since the mid-1880s advocated a convention as a means of correcting injustices committed against poor white counties and farmers, but middle-class reformers had remained cool toward the idea of a convention until the late 1880s. Undoubtedly, the affair at Jackson swayed them to embrace the convention, as did the apparent awakening of black voters indicated by the 1889 reorganization of the Republican party and the political stirring among white critics of the Democratic party. Tangible threats to the creation of a homogeneous body politic congealed in affairs like the Jackson mayoral race, and disfranchisement of the ignorant and the vile—black and white—seemed the practical solution.[50]

48. *Ibid.*, 14, 17, 23.

49. James Z. George to Robert Lowry, January 25, 1888, in RG 27, MDAH. Justifications for calling a convention changed through the years. Originally, unbridled hatred for anything reminiscent of Reconstruction motivated the calls, but by 1885, advocates of a new constitution pointed to a host of changes needed—none of which included disfranchisement. Only in the late 1880s did disfranchisement assume importance. See Jackson *Weekly Clarion*, September 16, 1885.

50. For a discussion of farmers' motivations in advocating a convention, see Chapter 8. On views sympathetic to disfranchisement, see Edward C. Walthall to William T. Walthall, May 2, 1890; John B. Gordon to William T. Walthall, January 26, 1894, all in Walthall Pa-

After two failed efforts to call a convention, Governor John Stone and both houses of the legislature approved the measure in 1890. Portrayed by middle-class reformers as a panacea for restoring social harmony, the convention meant to revoke black voting rights. The line of reasoning employed to cover, if barely, the state's sinister motives proclaimed that politicians, Democrats especially, taught their children a sad lesson when they resorted to physical violence and vote fraud to offset African-American votes. In the plain terms of Frederic Speed, Mississippians decided in the convention that it was "cheaper to out count the niggers than to kill them." [51] Through disfranchisement, regular Democrats and white reformers hoped to foster political peace. Ideally, the relegation of African Americans to the periphery of political culture would return them to a voiceless and powerless status in society similar to that known while under slavery. Others among the advocates of disfranchisement had broader dreams. Convention president Solomon S. Calhoon argued that disfranchisement was the first step in fulfilling the vision of Horace S. Fulkerson, a separate nation for African Americans. As things stood in 1890, "conflicting aspirations & apprehensions must lead to continual jars & frequent hostile collisions, which would not occur with homogeneous races" living apart, if not actually then metaphorically.[52]

Aside from the rhetoric that promoted the permanent settling of (as William S. McAllister put it) "our race problem on the safe basis of intelligent supremacy," some Mississippians demurred at calling a convention. As previously noted, Senator George initially headed the ranks of the opponents, and had he been otherwise able to placate his agrarian constituents, he would have declared against it in the end. His colleague in the senate, Edward C. Walthall, acting as a latter-day grandee, refused to support the convention, too. Masterful politicians like himself, he believed, knew how

---

pers. Both J. Morgan Kousser, *The Shaping of Southern Politics: Suffrage Restriction and the Establishment of the One-Party South, 1880–1910* (New Haven, 1974), 139–45, and Kirwan, *Revolt of the Rednecks,* 58–64, emphasize the influence of internal and external political pressures in calling the convention. James P. Coleman, "The Origin of the Constitution of 1890," *Journal of Mississippi History,* XIX (1957), 69–92, and Eric Charles Clark, "The Mississippi Constitutional Convention of 1890: A Political Analysis" (M.A. thesis, University of Mississippi, 1975), concentrate on the role of agrarian discontent. Neither view lacks merit, but the emphasis here is on the constitution as a means of reestablishing the antebellum social ethic.

51. Frederic Speed to A. M. Paxton, September 23, 1894, in A. H. Stone Collection.

52. Quoting Solomon S. Calhoon, untitled speech delivered in Illinois, 1910 (MS in Solomon S. Calhoon Papers), MDAH, 10.

to control black voters, or at least to keep them in their place, and need not run the risk of arousing anew the nation's animosity. Walthall understood as well that the Fifteenth Amendment prevented the outright revocation of black voting rights. For firm supporters of the convention, hatred for the amendment strengthened their resolve to restrict suffrage.[53]

Plans to erase blacks from the political, and thus the social and economic, world came in many guises. In 1890 Mississippians trotted out sincere, quixotic, and even facetious disfranchising measures, but most represented some form of educational or property qualification. J. A. P. Campbell, a former judge, became the fiercest advocate of property qualifications as a means of restricting voting rights. Realizing that the Farmers' Alliance viewed the convention as their opportunity to unseat the staid Redeemer clique, Campbell tried to sell his idea as a surefire method of restoring the political equality ordained in the Constitution of 1832, which first granted to all white males the right to vote. Like his predecessors who pledged that the formation of a broad electorate would spread a sense of shared responsibility and unite all classes, Campbell argued that the obliteration of venal voters, who threatened white cultural homogeneity, presented the best defense against what he imagined to be the encroaching rule of the underclass. Under his plan the privilege of voting (for it was not a natural right) accrued to the worthy. For every eighty acres of land owned, one vote would be granted; additional votes would be allowed for every five hundred to one thousand dollars' worth of real estate owned with a maximum of five to ten votes per male citizen. Black voters, though eligible to vote, would be counted out under his plural voting scheme, but according to his calculations, only 20 percent of whites stood to lose the suffrage. Best of all, in Campbell's mind, plural voting based on property qualifications stimulated whites to abandon tenancy and eradicate the growing class division apparent in the rise of agrarianism.[54] However ebullient he was about the chances of his plan's success, few Mississippians embraced it, and one writer called it "the most dangerous proposition ever offered our people." The

53. Quoting William McAllister in Raymond *Hinds County Gazette,* May 1, 1886. On hatred of the Fifteenth Amendment, see Jackson *Weekly Clarion,* August 29, 1889; Andrew C. McLaughlin, "Mississippi and the Negro Question," *Atlantic Monthly,* LXX (1892), 828–37. On Walthall, see Jackson *Clarion-Ledger,* October 31, 1889; Edward C. Walthall to W. H. McCardle, July 20, 1890, in William H. McCardle Papers, MDAH. On his post-convention defense of the constitution, see Grenada *Sentinel,* November 1, 1890; *Congressional Record,* 51st Cong., 2nd Sess., 1362–63; *Congressional Record,* 51st Cong., 2nd Sess., Appex., 72.

54. Jackson *New Mississippian,* July 31, 1889, April 30, 1890, June 4, 1890; Raymond *Hinds County Gazette,* April 5, 1890.

plural vote scheme based on property was so unpopular, in fact, that Campbell failed to win a seat in the convention. His son, a Washington County delegate, provided the body its lone voice in favor of the plan.[55]

With the idea of property qualifications doomed before the convention met, and knowing that the Fifteenth Amendment prohibited a frontal assault on African-American voting rights, delegates adopted another approach to disfranchisement: literacy qualifications. The WCTU, long the enemy of the irresponsible and immoral, perhaps best represented the spirit of the convention. Although women occupied no seats in the assemblage, defenders of their cause interpreted the meeting as a chance to wage war against "the *ignorant, vicious, negro* vote," the very enemy that the women accused of siding with the whiskey lobby and ringleaders to block prohibition legislation. In order to remedy the "great mistake" committed under the auspices of federal constitutional amendments (the unleashing of a " 'free negro' spirit" and the founding of "equality of two antagonistic races on the same ground and under the same laws") the convention needed to reestablish the cultural homogeneity of the morally and mentally superior by casting aside the deficient.[56]

During the constitutional convention the WCTU denounced voters identified by prohibition leader J. B. Chrisman as "white ignoramuses," not to mention blacks. So committed to disfranchisement of the depraved was Kells that she chastised delegates unwilling to sacrifice through educational qualifications an estimated twelve thousand white voters for the sake of disfranchising ninety thousand blacks. Any delegate who refused, Kells said, was "unworthy of the gift of the office of constable from the people"; he was as unfit for leadership as the degenerate were unfit for citizenship.[57] Her attacks against those left behind by the commercial order of the New South opened the door for women to seek the franchise. For

55. Quoting "Pro Bono" in the Carthage *Carthaginian,* June 27, 1890. On the treatment accorded the Campbell plan in convention, see the correspondence of Irvin Miller, Carthage *Carthaginian,* August 22, 1890. Plans mocking Campbell's included one proposed by Samuel D. Harper that involved plural votes for legitimately born household heads (provided they had fathered no bastard children); another wag advocated "the fat man[']s plan for the restriction of votes" by which males weighing over two hundred pounds received multiple votes and bonus votes if their wives tipped the scales at the same weight. See Raymond *Hinds County Gazette,* April 19, 1890; J. Foote to Charles K. Regan, July 30, 1890, in Charles K. Regan Papers, MDAH.

56. Quoting Meridian *Mississippi White Ribbon,* June 15, 1890, July 15, 1889, November, 1888.

57. Quoting J. B. Chrisman in Carthage *Carthaginian,* September 19, 1890; Kells in Meridian *Mississippi White Ribbon,* July 15, 1889.

by giving women the right to vote, the WCTU argued, the state's moral leaders received justice and "the progressive spirit of the age" was ensured. Such contentions notwithstanding the convention voiced concern about safeguarding the moral influence of "our women" against the tumult of the political fray.[58] In late August, less than ten days after the convention began, J. W. Fewell of Meridian put forward a proposal to grant women who owned, or whose husbands owned, three hundred dollars of unencumbered real estate the right to vote; a similar preconvention plan had been proposed by Judge Warren Cowan. According to Cowan's calculation, the enfranchisement of women would turn a twenty-two thousand black majority into a fifteen thousand white majority without antagonizing northern observers. After much heated debate over Fewell's amendment and consideration of many substitutes, the franchise committee, headed by Senator George, voted it down by one vote. For years the WCTU and later-day women's suffrage advocates looked back wistfully to the preconvention days when they felt certain their political rights would be secured. The poll tax and residence requirements passed by the convention appealed to them, but the "understanding clause," which excused illiterates from educational qualifications, prolonged in their view the rule of "white ignoramuses" at the expense of virtuous women.[59]

58. Quoting Raymond *Hinds County Gazette,* August 30, 1889; Carthage *Carthaginian,* August 29, 1890. The last quote may be found in Irvin Miller's letter from the convention in which he also related a proposition to disfranchise wife-beaters. See, too, an assessment of women's moral superiority and the implied need to protect them from the sullying effects of politics in Solomon S. Calhoon, "Address to the Madison County Fair, 1891" (MS in Calhoon Papers), unpaginated.

59. Clark, "The Mississippi Constitutional Convention," 106–107. On Cowan, see Meridian *Mississippi White Ribbon,* April 15, 1890; *Woman's Journal* quoted in Jackson *New Mississippian,* April 30, 1890. *Mississippi Women's Christian Temperance Union: Report of the Thirtieth Annual Convention, Held in Tupelo, Mississippi, October 11th to 14th, 1914* (Jackson, 1914), 20. On the franchise measures passed in the convention, see *Journal of the Proceedings of the Constitutional Convention of the State of Mississippi Begun at the City of Jackson on August 12, 1890 and Concluded November 1, 1890* (Jackson, 1890), 228–30, 628–33. After defeat of women's suffrage, female activists began arguing that "American institutions can not be preserved without the infusion into the body politic of a new moral force." Disfranchised women could not teach their sons the proper and patriotic use of the ballot. See Somerville's "Address Before the First Annual Woman's Suffrage Convention, March 28, 1898" (MS in Nellie Nugent Somerville Papers), MDAH, unpaginated; Nellie Nugent Somerville, *Moral Leadership: The True Basis of Woman Suffrage* (Greenville, n.d.), *passim*; Somerville, "Address of the State President Before the Woman's Suffrage Club of Clarksdale, Mississippi, U.S.A., November 18, 1898" (MS in Somerville Papers), unpaginated. See, too, Ball Diary, February 11, 1895.

To middle-class reformers, the constitution achieved mixed results: one class of voters considered ignorant and vile retained the right of suffrage, though blacks were effectively disfranchised; amendments prohibiting the sale of alcohol failed, but a permanent ban on lotteries passed. Because of the constitution's shortcomings, reform agitation persisted into the twentieth century, and occasional triumphs were achieved: a state reformatory for juvenile criminals and a sanitarium for tuberculosis patients were founded; eventually, women received the right to vote. But the ambiguous achievements of the constitutional convention suggest that the task of creating a homogeneous society was too daunting. The political tensions, in part set loose by the Constitution of 1890, opened white Mississippians' eyes even more to the heterogeneity of their age. They came to realize that if, as Solomon Calhoon said, "the great object of political economy is to equalize the distinctions of wealth," the goal of creating an homogeneous society was no nearer to achievement than it had been in 1865.[60] It was the nature of the commercial order, after all, to divide society between the famous and the infamous, between those committed to the present, who based their concepts of a good republic on oppressive aspects of the antebellum social ethic and those uneasy in the present, who based their concepts of a good republic on communitarian and egalitarian aspects of the social ethic. The world that middle-class reformers wanted to foster, one in which they continued to reap the rewards of the commercial order while suppressing the venal under the weight of their class- and race-conscious rhetoric, was based on a curious vision of homogeneity that excluded all blacks and many whites as inherently unqualified to be good citizens. To middle-class reformers the presence of degenerate souls at the bottom of the social order verified that they deserved not to be included in their version of homogeneity.

Regardless of the permanent divisions in white society precipitated by the commercial order and emancipation, both halves of the white world—middle-class reformers and agrarians—sought symbolically and actually to remove blacks from the New South, or at least to diminish their influence. As in the 1840s and 1860s, class concerns eventually disappeared under the surge of race-consciousness and tentatively united whites of all classes against their common foe. Turning against racial prejudices would have done much to institute the homogeneous order desired by middle-class reformers and agrarians, but as Adelbert Ames observed, white southern-

60. Quoting Solomon S. Calhoon, "Address to Confederate Veterans" (MS in Calhoon Papers), 14.

ers possessed neither forbearance nor equanimity. Their sense of a good republic depended upon the existence of a black underclass. Until the supposed mudsills of society were elevated, Ames knew that depredations against blacks would continue: "The days are many before Christ's Sermon on the Mount will be our practical religion. Mississippi like other states has a weary task before it." [61]

61. Quoting Adelbert Ames to Dunbar Rowland, March 20, 1929, in Ames Papers.

CHAPTER 8

ANOTHER VERSION OF HOMOGENEITY

Motivated by a desire to create a society that conformed to their idealized remembrances of the Old South, benefactors of the commercial order attacked postbellum social ills. Physicians and teachers, prohibitionists and advocates of disfranchisement, believing that residents obviously left behind by the commercial order retarded the state's economic and moral advance, worked to restore social unity by eliminating ignorance, disease, and immorality. Agrarians (an amorphous group of rural reformers bound by their dedication to prosperity in the countryside) as well remembered fondly a homogeneous social order and wished to reestablish it. They embraced a vision of the past and of the good republic counterpoised to the new order, one that emphasized liberal and egalitarian concepts of liberty derived from their understanding of Jacksonian America. To eradicate from the recently fomented age of commerce agencies detrimental to farmers, agrarians proposed restoration of a just polity and a "humane economy" that rewarded tillers of the soil their rightful inheritance: material success and independence, economic and political.[1]

The agrarian critique of the commercial order grew out of a class-conscious suspicion that farmers lived in a society disdainful of their labor. Railroads and merchants, bondholders and opponents of an inflationary currency supplanted cultivators in the social order and consciously blocked their achievement of material success. Working in league with the Democratic party, agents of the new order denied farmers liberty while securing their own pecuniary interests. Those agents, however, fell short of guaran-

1. See Norman Pollack, *The Humane Economy: Populism, Capitalism, and Democracy* (New Brunswick, N.J., 1990), Chapt. 1. For a definition of agrarians as those so poor that they opposed private property, see "Negro Agrarianism," *De Bow's Review,* After the War Series, V (February, 1868), 134–38.

teeing their own independence, for as Martin W. Phillips observed, of one hundred clerks, merchants, and industrial employees "not more than three" acquire liberty.[2] In a world that rewarded unvirtuous men, farmers became victims of the crop-lien law, an inflexible currency, and the Democratic party's steel-fisted control of state politics, making them a penurious and powerless class of laborers unable to distinguish themselves from African Americans.

To ameliorate their circumstances, angry postbellum farmers proposed various measures to redirect the flow of wealth and power into the countryside.[3] On the economic front, they aimed to lessen the power of merchants by amending the crop-lien law, diversifying agricultural production, and purchasing supplies through farmer-owned cooperatives. They also sought to end the state's leasing of convicts because the practice represented a special privilege beneficial to wealthy planters and railroad companies alone; likewise, they advocated creation of a state railroad commission to chasten their exploiters. Emboldened by their reform program, which if implemented stood to affirm their status as free and virtuous, agrarians extended their challenge to corporate power by taking on the Democratic party, first from within its ranks and later through fusion tickets and Populism. Self-described revolutionaries dedicated to altering the commercial order, agrarians were as well backward-looking defenders of market-oriented values who longed to take part in the economic bonanza of the late nineteenth century without surrendering traditional concepts of liberty that venerated tillers of the earth as God's chosen people. They were a conflicted group, as surely as middle-class reformers, with their aspirations grounded in both the Old South and the New.

By the end of the nineteenth century, designs to restore egalitarian concepts of political and economic liberty met with defeat. Advocates of a restored agrarian capitalism and democracy remained in the position they had occupied in 1877: they were subject to the commercial order and the corporate politics that it fostered. Their subjugation owed to three circumstances. First, as manifested by their inability to discard market-oriented values, the appeal of the commercial order proved too seductive

2. *The Southern Farmer,* IV (February, 1870), 52; *The Southern Farmer,* IV (May, 1871), 197.

3. This interpretation of late-nineteenth-century farm protesters as agrarian capitalists, not revolutionaries intent on halting the progress of modernity, is similar to arguments made by Robert F. Durden, *The Climax of Populism: The Election of 1896* (Lexington, Ky., 1965), 3–6, and Bruce Palmer, *"Man Over Money": The Southern Populist Critique of American Capitalism* (Chapel Hill, 1980), xvii, 20–38.

to subdue. Agrarian reformers undercut their own professed desire to subvert the new order by seeking merely to orient the flow of money and power toward the countryside and by refusing to divorce themselves from commerce. Second, during a key moment of their siege on corporate authority in politics, farmers divided over the subtreasury plan and the wisdom of creating a third political party. But, most importantly, they bungled their opportunity to rearrange the relationship between commerce and the countryside when like their foes, who used the political culture of racism to pommel blacks into submission, agrarians neglected to pursue the political backing of their natural allies. Doing so avouched that, despite their pronouncements about the evils of the commercial order, the essence of their ideal notions of citizenship derived strength from their belief that a good republic allowed white men equal access to markets and political power, while blacks sat on the periphery unable to obtain liberty and virtue.

In the postbellum period, southern farmers thought of themselves as a besieged minority facing twin catastrophes—one economic, the other ideological. Some of farmers' problems, agrarian reformers said, proceeded from cultivators' own failures. Unlike their forefathers who, they imagined, had fed their families and produced for the market, late-nineteenth-century cultivators eschewed foodstuff production for cotton. Then again, agrarians argued, they overproduced cotton under duress. In part the depression of the 1870s, which broke many farmers economically and precipitated an utter dependence on credit, dictated that they make too much of the great staple. For when farmers turned to merchants, they encountered extraordinary interest rates and the crop-lien law, which their creditors wielded to insist that they plant mostly cotton. The intrusion of representatives of the commercial order into the countryside led to farmers' decline. They became a class of enslaved producers that labored not for its own benefit but for others; they lost their farms and were compelled to enter the growing ranks of tenants or to seek employment in rural mills or to leave the state forever.

Farmers in the postbellum South knew that through the operation of multifarious agents, primarily a short supply of specie coupled with the overproduction of cotton, they had become poor. Across the nation their fellows weathered similar circumstances. In the age in which they lived, commodity prices, reflecting an international glut of staples and a dearth of gold and silver, declined steadily; so too did farm incomes. Southern cotton farmers especially suffered the sting of deflation and persistently lobbied the federal government to inflate the currency through greenback issue and silver coinage. They recognized too that the overproduction of

TABLE 8 Ratio of Cotton to Grain Crop Production, 1850–1900

Year	Ratio of Cotton to Grain Crops (1,000 bales*/1,000,000 bushels*
1850	15.26
1860	31.85
1870	26.93
1880	38.24
1890	39.43
1900	32.42

Sources: See footnote 4.

*For the period from 1850 to 1870, bales of cotton, as reported in the census, were assumed to weigh 400 pounds; in 1880, 475 pounds; in 1890, 477 pounds; in 1900, 500 pounds. On bale weights see William J. Cooper, Jr., "The Cotton Crisis in the Antebellum South: Another Look," *Agricultural History,* XLIX (1975), 388. Cotton was converted into 500-pound bale equivalents. Major grains were converted into corn equivalents at the following rates: wheat 1.3:1 bushels of corn; potatoes 4:1; oats 2:1; peas and beans 1.285:1.

cotton and their inability to make grains contributed to rural poverty.[4] Even more than their antebellum predecessors, postbellum farmers planted cotton at the expense of grain crops. Between 1870 and 1880 cotton production more than doubled, and in the following decade it increased by another 25 percent. At the same time, grain crop production fell. In comparative terms, bale production, when expressed as a percentage of grain output, rose by 30 percent between 1860 and 1890. In 1860 farmers had produced 31.85 bales of cotton for every thousand bushels of enumerated foodstuffs; in 1890 the ratio between cotton and corn increased to 39.43.[5]

4. Warren and Pearson, *Prices,* 32, 70, 78–79. Economic historians differ over the reason for farmers' poverty. Those who trace it to overproduction of cotton include, Roger Ransom and Richard Sutch, "The 'Lock-In' Mechanism and Overproduction of Cotton in the Postbellum South," *Agricultural History,* IL (1975), 405–25, and Wright and Kunreuther, "Cotton, Corn and Risk," 526–51. For criticism of this view, see McGuire and Higgs, "Cotton, Corn, and Risk: Another View," 167–95; and Stephen DeCanio, "Cotton 'Overproduction' in Late Nineteenth-Century Southern Agriculture," *Journal of Economic History,* XXXIII (1973), 608–33.

5. *Seventh Census, 1850,* 457–58; *Agriculture of the United States, 1860,* 85; *The Statistics of Wealth and Industry of the United States . . . Ninth Census,* III, 185–86; *Report on the Production of Agriculture as Returned at the Tenth Census* (1883), 194–95, 231; *Report on the Statistics of Agriculture of the United States at the Eleventh Census: 1890* (1895), 372–73, 395, 477; *Twelfth Census, 1900: Agriculture, Part 2: Crops and Irrigation,* 170–71, 377–78, 432, 599–60.

All around them, farmers saw the effects of their overproduction of cotton and the shortage of specie: their crops sold low in the market, and the value of their farms fell sharply after 1865. Between 1860 and 1870 average farm values declined from $5,169 to $1,203 (a 77 percent decrease). The greatest change in values occurred in the Piney Woods, where farms dropped 88 percent of their value, falling from $2,599 to $315; the Delta region, with an 86 percent decrease, and the Black Prairie region, with a 79 percent decrease, typified the change recorded by other regions. The Northern Bluffs, which saw values decrease from $4,586 to $1,173 (74 percent), recorded the least dramatic change of any region. Over the next two decades, notwithstanding increases in the worth of farms in the Piney Woods (a 146 percent change) and North-Central Hills (a 38 percent change)—increases that owed to railroad development and lumber booms—statewide values decreased by another 1.5 percent before 1890. Other regions experienced declines in average farm values of between 3 percent (in the Northern Bluffs) and 32 percent (in the Southern Bluffs). The shrinking size of the average farm in part accounts for the precipitous fall in farm values. From the eve of the Civil War until 1890, farms of less than fifty acres increased from 38 percent of the total to 48 percent, a consequence of emancipation and the division of plantations into smaller tracts for the purpose of renting.[6] Yet in agrarians' minds the rapid proliferation of small and poorly valued farms bore witness to their diminished status in the commercial order.

Other signs as well warned that farmers had become too poor to be regarded as keepers of the good republic. With every advance of the commercial order, they sensed that their position in the political culture dropped, and few developments more alarmed them than the appearance of factories in the countryside. Even though workers employed in industry never exceeded 20 percent of the total work force in the nineteenth century, a substantial increase in the number of such workers employed in several counties startled farmers, who dreaded that they might find themselves working in a mill. Besides Piney Woods counties and others like Carroll, Copiah, and Pike that contained well-known manufacturing operations, the number of workers in manufacturing facilities located in Alcorn and Lee counties, for example, more than doubled. In 1880 industries in Alcorn County employed 139 workers, but in 1900, 598 worked there. Over the same period the number of industrial workers in Lee County went from 62 to 175. Statewide the industrial labor population exploded from 5,805 in

6. *Agriculture of the United States, 1860*, 84; *The Statistics of Wealth and Industry, Ninth Census*, 184; *Report on the Statistics of Agriculture, Eleventh Census*, 215–16.

1880 to 26,418 in 1900, while the count of manufacturing establishments posted a 225 percent increase, topping out at 4,772 at the turn of the century.[7] The appearance of factories in the countryside daily reminded farmers that if they neglected to safeguard their liberty and virtue, the commercial order awaited to remove them from the only labor that could make them free.

Rather than work in a mill, some farmers, tired of their poverty in Mississippi, chose to leave. Fleeing the state promised another opportunity at farming. Like a previous generation that moved to Texas during the depression of the 1840s, a constant stream of residents made their way west in the last decades of the nineteenth century. In the depression years of 1877 and 1893 Reverend Samuel A. Agnew witnessed an exodus of his neighbors, and though he doubted that moving would benefit them, since Texas suffered under economic and political conditions similar to those in Mississippi, he sympathized with their desperation. The decision to emigrate, however, entailed for many nearly insuperable complications. Low values assigned land meant that those desirous of leaving sold their farms at a loss (if they sold them at all) and indebted Mississippians skirted the law if they fled without repaying creditors. Jeff Aldridge of Alcorn County considered leaving Mississippi, but he felt first obliged to retire debts accrued under the crop-lien law. Ridding himself of some livestock in order to build his reserve of corn, which he anticipated selling locally, would be a good initial step, Aldridge believed. Turning over to his creditor the full bale of cotton he hoped to cultivate on seven or eight acres would also help. Whatever the sacrifice, Aldridge assigned emigration a high priority: "I become more discouraged about this country the longer I stay [in] it but how in the thunder am I to get out of it[.] I am owing some and it seems that every year puts me in a little worse but if I am spared to make a crop next year if I can't come out one way I will another." [8]

Understanding that depressed commodity prices and the overproduction of cotton made them poor came easily to farmers. Finding solutions to their problems was a different matter altogether. For, according to agrarians, agents of the commercial order (chiefly merchants armed with crop liens) dictated their economic behavior. Defeating those agents was imperative. For poverty meant not only that an economic catastrophe had be-

7. Department of the Treasury, *Report of the Internal Commerce of the United States: Part II*, 493.

8. Quoting Jeff Aldridge to B. A. Aldridge, October 5, 1881, in Aldridge Family Letters, MDAH; Agnew Diary, November 23, December 18, 1877, August 2, October 23, 1893.

fallen them but that an ideological one had as well.[9] Restoring farmers to their formerly exalted status in the social order required that they alter their cultivation practices to produce for household consumption as well as the market, and that they destroy their enemies.

Thinking of themselves as an oppressed minority, agrarians articulated a class-consciousness that had been dormant in Mississippi since the inauguration of Civil War–era policies. Solomon S. Calhoon, addressing an audience of farmers in 1895, struck upon a favorite theme of agrarians, exploitation by the powerful. It is, he told farmers, "you against the strong, against the schemes of blood-sucking wealth." Even the private secretary to New South booster Lucius Q. C. Lamar, the poet S. A. Jonas, employed a similar dichotomy when describing the inequities of the period. Enslaved to speculators at Liverpool and New York, southern cultivators, he said, should take up the cry: "The time has come / for the farmer to be free." The Clay County farmer W. W. Graham, who has achieved among twentieth-century students of agrarian reform a celebrity that surpassed his contemporary fame, also depicted society as divided between "haves" and "have-nots." In two letters dated 1877, Graham blamed the loss of his farm on the machinations of "men who wear gauntlet gloves [and] make a living and riches off of farmers." The "disinning [*sic*] tricksters" of the courthouse clique had arranged an estate auction to purchase his farm after the original mortgage holder died. Tenancy seemed his fate. But he refused to enter that condition of servitude without a fight. Writing to Governor John Stone, he complained: "We have a class and always have had that is dominating over and plundering the farmers and it has been growing worse. . . . If any farmer in the South was in any condition there would be just such an uprising as there is now in the North." [10] To Graham and other agrarians, the new order drew life from producers and recognized the false claims to liberty and virtue espoused by self-serving men of commerce.

9. On the ideological crisis created by the commercial order, see Ted Ownby, "The Defeated Generation at Work: White Farmers in the Deep South, 1865–1890," *Southern Studies,* XXIII (1984), 341, 345.

10. Quoting Solomon S. Calhoon, "Silver Address, 12 June 1895" (MS in Calhoon Papers), 5; S. A. Jonas, untitled poem, in Jonas Papers; W. W. Graham to John Stone, November 15, 1877, Graham to Stone December 6, 1877, in RG 27, MDAH. Both James Sharborough Ferguson, "Agrarianism in Mississippi, 1871–1900: A Study in Non-Conformity" (Ph.D. dissertation, University of North Carolina, 1952), 265–66, and Michael R. Hyman, *The Anti-Redeemers: Hill County Political Dissenters in the Lower South from Redemption to Populism* (Baton Rouge, 1990), 1–2, quote Graham extensively. The northern unrest that Graham mentioned was the railroad strikes of 1877.

Poor and indebted, entangled in the web of the market economy and dependent on merchants for their sustenance, agrarians fretted that white tillers of the earth stood perilously close to losing their liberty and virtue. Their proximity to a large black population that labored, as did many whites, on land owned by others heightened apprehensions about the corrupting influence of the commercial order and the dangers of becoming members of the underclass. Where once participating in the market economy had been considered an act inconsequential to one's independence and had, in fact, because of its racially exclusive nature, verified the virtue of participants, the transformation of the market economy into a part of the commercial order prompted agrarians to change their opinion. In the postbellum period the market became an enslaver as the makers and keepers of the commercial order used their intimate knowledge and command of it to shackle farmers to cotton production. In the process, they created a world turned upside down, one in which men of commerce obtained great wealth while farmers lost their liberty in the web of the market economy. Reestablishing an egalitarian social order (or more properly white cultural homogeneity) by crushing the dictatorship of corporate capitalism necessitated, agrarians proclaimed, a redistribution of wealth. Channeling wealth away from agents of the commercial order constrained farmers to behave as they imagined their predecessors had in the halcyon days of the antebellum period. Becoming self-sufficient within the context of market production assured that they would disrupt the commercial order.[11]

Imbued with a sense of class-consciousness, agrarians blamed their inability to survive as free men on the presence of a powerful elite that dragged them into the integrated national economy. (Demons disguised as merchants bore the brunt of farmers' animosity for enslaving them to the market through the crop-lien law and their monopolistic control of the rural economy.) Restoring egalitarian qualities to the economy, however, would enable producers to achieve self-sufficiency while producing for the market. In an 1885 statement of their credo, members of the Pike County Farmers and Mechanics Club swore allegiance to the market economy and foodstuff production in order to destroy corporate capitalism. They intended "to devote the larger and best of land to food crops, making cotton a sur-

11. For a different interpretation of agrarians' response to the commercial order, see Hahn, *The Roots of Southern Populism*, 137–203, who argues that farmers participated in the market economy in a significant manner only after the Civil War, and their experiences in the market drove them to plot its destruction. For interpretations of postbellum yeomen as self-sufficient, see Hyman, *The Anti-Redeemers*, Chapt. 1, and Reidy, *From Slavery to Agrarian Capitalism*, 217.

plus and independent crop, thus doing away with so much labor which is required in the present all cotton system." Curtailing staple production would drive prices upward and cause black labor to leave the state, removing forever the underclass and creating a truly egalitarian social ethic. Just as they imagined their antebellum ancestors had, Pike County Farmers Club members planned to secure their economic liberty by simultaneously producing for home consumption and the market. Balanced production led to material success and allowed white farmers to separate their labor from that of African Americans, who would remain subservient to the will of others through the operation of the crop-lien law.[12]

Agrarian advocates of self-sufficiency within the context of market production encouraged independence-minded farmers to specialize in stock raising and dairy farming. To the extent that farmers converted cotton fields into garden spots and pasturage, reformers said, the supply of cotton would decrease, and the price would increase. Furthermore, the great cities of the North and burgeoning southern ones demanded fresh meat and beasts of burden, making stock raising, in the minds of some Mississippians, the best means of curtailing their cotton production without forsaking market production. Stephen D. Lee, the former Confederate general and president of the Agricultural and Mechanical College, discerned additional advantages in stock raising and dairy production. Neither enterprise required a large capital investment, and each demanded practically no labor. Predicting that the Hill Country would soon be without black labor as tenants moved into the Yazoo Basin to work on great plantations, Lee told a gathering of farmers that the exodus of African Americans was inevitable and that they had best prepare for it by taking advantage of the good grass country in which they lived. Particularly farmers in the eastern half of the state where native grasses flourished stood to benefit by becoming professional stock raisers. Apparently, reformers' admonitions influenced some cultivators to diversify their agricultural production. In the late 1880s reports of north Mississippi men, and even some women, quickly making "independent fortunes" by raising "fancy breeds of horses, mules, and cattle" kindled interest in stock raising. But such observations were impressionistic and based on the development of specialized farms, not the widespread abandonment of cotton cultivation. Between 1860 and 1890, as the value of livestock on

12. Carthage *Carthaginian,* January 17, 1885. For another justification of diversified production, see the apocryphal story of a young boy who, through his own success as a corn farmer, convinced his father to become more cost-conscious and self-sufficient in *Proceedings of the Twenty-Sixth Annual Convention: Mississippi Bankers' Association, Vicksburg, May 5–6, 1914* (N.p., n.d.), 40–41.

farms plummeted steadily from $1,135.90 to $234.80, the average number of swine per farm fell from 41.5 to 8, and the population of milk cows on farms decreased from 5.7 to 2.2. Less dramatic declines in the number of horses and mules occurred as well.[13] Mississippi's projected transformation into a stock-raising country must be considered a failure, the loud crowing of agricultural reformers notwithstanding.

In farmers' minds, diversification represented a rational response to postbellum economic exigencies and an initial step in the resurrection of a moral and egalitarian economy. Producing corn, molasses, sugarcane, and poultry, agrarian reformers liked to say, extended to farmers disdainful of enslavement to cotton continued access to the broader market and ensured that they could feed their families. Other advantages also accrued to self-sufficient farmers. According to Samuel Meek, if farmers produced for household consumption and the market, they might again profess to do "a noble work" and rightfully magnify themselves as liberty-loving and virtuous citizens. Harking back to the rhetoric of the Jacksonian period, Meek told the Philotecnic Society at the A and M College that "one such [self-sufficient] man, in his plain garb and unpretending simplicity is worth ten thousand of those butterfly fopplings, who infest every circle of society—who toil not and neither do they spin, but, surpass Solomon, in all of his glory, in the magnificent splendor of their nothingness." Another agricultural reformer given to poetry recommended that farmers take to heart an inspiring jingle to remind them that safe habits of production led to liberty and virtue: "Remember 'tis not what you sell, but what you save, / That makes a farmer free instead of a slave." And the state geologist, Eugene Hilgard, likewise proposed that "it is *home-making*, not money-making, that evokes the willing help of every member of a rural household" and preserves the autonomous farmer "from fortune's freaks."[14]

13. Lee quoted in Jackson *Weekly Clarion*, December 29, 1886; quoting Hazelhurst *Copiah Signal*, March 8, 1888. See too, Carthage *Carthaginian*, January 24, 1885; Editorial in *The Southern Farmer*, IV (February, 1870), 52. *Proceedings of the Twenty-Sixth Annual Convention: Mississippi Bankers' Association, 1914*, 71, 113; B. W. Griffith, "Helping the Southern Farmer" (Typescript in Griffith and Westbrook Papers). *Agriculture of the United States, 1860*, 84; *The Statistics of Wealth and Industry, Ninth Census*, 184; *Report on the Production of Agriculture, Tenth Census*, 159–60; *Report on the Statistics of Agriculture, Eleventh Census*, 215–16, 294–95, 335.

14. Quoting Samuel Meek, "Address to the Philotecnic Society of the A & M College" (MS in Samuel Meek Papers), MDAH; Crystal Springs *Meteor*, March 17, 1883; Eugene Hilgard, "All Cotton and No Comfort," *Rural Carolinian*, IX (1873), 629–30. See too, S. A. Jonas, untitled address (MS in Jonas Papers), and Solomon S. Calhoon, "Address to the Madison County Fair" (MS in Calhoon Papers), unpaginated.

Agrarians, of course, realized that before curtailing staple-crop cultivation and returning to self-sufficient habits of production, they would have to break the back of the commercial order and its local agent, the country merchant. Merchants, after all, demanded that farmers produce mostly cotton in order to secure loans and charged high rates of interest for the privilege of running accounts for them. Farmers never liked the crop-lien law. Soon after its passage they began characterizing merchants as thieves and worried that liberty and virtue were becoming as scarce in the countryside as a farm-raised beef. Among agrarian advocates of self-sufficiency, members of the Grange (the Patrons of Husbandry) first proclaimed that ending farmers' subservience to commercial men would return farmers to their status as deserving claimants of liberty and virtue. Speaking to the Bowling Green Grange in 1886 T. S. Wright voiced the familiar appeal that farmers abandon cotton. "Make your farms self-sustaining and cotton the surplus crop," he encouraged, "and at no distint [*sic*] day we will be able to fix our own price upon the products of our farms, and no longer be under the control of speculators." Members of the Bowling Green Grange frequently discussed the best method for divorcing themselves from cotton production. Some spoke of forsaking cotton, others argued for an equal division of resources between corn and cotton, while others still believed commercial fertilizers promised to lift farmers out of poverty. Regardless of the method employed, Grangers advocated diversification as the best means of upsetting the entrenched power of merchants and speculators. Another speaker at the Bowling Green Grange argued that "if we as farmers & grangers will pay more attention to the raising of every thing at home . . . we would be the most independent people that lives; for to no man living need he bow, the man that walks behind the plow." [15] By diversifying their production and purchasing all necessities with cash, farmers would destroy merchants' monopoly power and recapture the liberty that rightfully belonged to them.

Nothing short of cultivators' liberty and virtue was at stake in the drive to upset corporate capitalism in the countryside. For under the influence of the crop-lien law, especially during the depression of the 1870s, farmers accumulated debts, lost control over their labor, and overproduced cotton. Foreclosure and tenancy, the signposts of poverty and dependence that farmers most feared, followed. The spread of tenancy in postbellum Mississippi is undeniable, and though landless farmers tended more often to be African Americans, whites increasingly joined the ranks of renters. In 1880 tenants operated 44 percent of farms in Mississippi; 27 percent of

15. Quoting Patrons of Husbandry, Mississippi State Grange Papers, April 8, 1886, May 17, 1884, but see, too, February 16, 1884, MDAH.

tenant farms rented for a share of the crop. In 1890 tenants rented 53 percent of all farms, and the percentage rented for a share of the crop rose to 32. By 1900 tenants rented two-thirds of all Mississippi farms.[16] (See Table 9.) Regions with large black populations (the Delta and bluffs regions) had the most tenant farms, but even in the predominantly white Piney Woods and North-Central Hills, tenancy became pervasive by 1900. Tenancy nevertheless concentrated in black majority counties. From 1880 until 1900 the total number of white majority counties with a percentage of tenant farms ranging between 26 and 50 rose from 18 to 21. At the same time, the number of black majority counties with rented farms equal to more than 75 percent of the total increased dramatically from 1 to 22. (See Table 10.) Put another way, tenancy concentrated in black majority counties, while white majority counties had a smaller number of rented farms (and a smaller percentage of tenants within each county). By 1900, 36 percent of all white farmers either rented their land for cash or a share of the crop, but 85 percent of African Americans who farmed rented acreage.[17]

TABLE 9 Tenant Farms as a Percentage of All Farms (Including the Percentage of Farms Rented for a Share of the Crop), 1880–1890

Region	1880	1890	1900
Southern Bluffs	50.9	55.1	64.0
	(28.4)	(32.8)	(23.3)
Northern Bluffs	46.3	52.5	68.7
	(29.0)	(38.5)	(35.9)
Black Prairie	56.4	68.2	24.0
	(28.8)	(28.5)	(12.9)
Delta	56.9	77.9	85.8
	(32.3)	(41.9)	(39.5)
North-Cental Hills	35.0	37.0	45.6
	(25.6)	(26.5)	(33.1)
Piney Woods	19.1	25.2	71.8
	(8.9)	(14.9)	(24.4)
State	44.0	52.8	66.2
	(26.7)	(31.8)	(32.2)

Sources: See footnote 16.

16. *Report on the Production of Agriculture, Tenth Census*, 66–67; *Report on the Statistics of Agriculture, Eleventh Census*, 156–59; *Twelfth Census, 1900: Agriculture, Part 1: Farms, Live Stock, and Animal Products*, 96–97.

17. See note 16. *Statistics of the Population of the United States, Tenth Census*, 397–98; *Compendium of the Eleventh Census, 1890: Part 1, Population*, 618–21; *Twelfth Census, 1900: Population: Part 1*, 589–90.

TABLE 10 Tenancy and Race: Number of Counties with Percentage Tenant Farms in Specified Quartile, 1880–1900

White Majority Counties:

Year	1st Tenancy Quartile	2nd Tenancy Quartile	3rd Tenancy Quartile	4th Tenancy Quartile
1880	14	18	3	0
1890	15	20	0	0
1900	11	21	6	0

Black Majority Counties:

Year	1st Tenancy Quartile	2nd Tenancy Quartile	3rd Tenancy Quartile	4th Tenancy Quartile
1880	2	17	18	1
1890	0	7	21	10
1900	0	1	14	22

Sources: See footnote 17.

As long as the crop-lien law operated to keep African-American labor tied to the land, white farmers found no reason to object to it; maintaining an underclass of landless labor with black skin fostered their own claims to liberty. When more whites passed from landownership to tenancy, however, attitudes changed. In the mid-1880s agrarians petitioned the legislature to reform the crop-lien law to protect farmers from its worst elements and to keep them from the ranks of tenants. Specifically, they wanted to outlaw the practice known as "hypothecation" that permitted lenders to execute liens against future crops; by preventing such liens, the legislature would safeguard farmers against long-term revolving debt and the overproduction of cotton. Governor Robert Lowry and an agrarian legislature, overriding merchant-planter opposition to the new law, approved it in 1886.[18] Rural celebrations of the new lien law were short-lived. For farmers needing credit remained subject to the whims of merchants, and they

18. Jackson *Weekly Clarion,* September 23, 30, 1885, March 3, September 1, December 15, 1886; Carthage *Carthaginian,* October 10, 1885, February 10, March 20, 1886. On hypothecation, see Crystal Springs *Meteor,* May 19, 1883. On planters' support for hypothecation, see Macon *New South,* October 22, 1881; Jackson *New Mississippian,* November 27, 1883; and the letter signed "Amite," in Jackson *Weekly Clarion,* October 7, 1885. See, too, Jackson *Weekly Clarion,* February 3, 1886, for a criticism of the new law as weak. For a positive response to the new law, see Grenada *Sentinel,* February 6, 1886.

still had to plant cotton at the expense of foodstuffs. Regardless of agrarians' self-proclaimed triumph in 1886, their relationship to the commercial order had not been significantly altered. The simultaneous economic and ideological catastrophes of the postbellum period persisted unabated.

Their inability to check merchant authority over the countryside never deterred agrarians from believing that liberty and virtue might still inhere in their class, if they could escape the strangulating commercial order. Reestablishing farmers as keepers of the good republic dictated that they revise their relationship with railroads, merchants, and the Democratic party. Toward that end, agrarians launched two campaigns to create cooperative stores, attempted (if only briefly) to bankrupt trusts, lobbied for a governmental institution to regulate railroads, and otherwise challenged the Democratic party's association with agents of the new order.

Through advocacy of a cooperative culture, agrarians counterpoised their vision of a "democratic economy" to the hegemony of the commercial economy.[19] Their cooperative vision appeared at the same time that laws demanding that communities maintain roads, rivers, and levees fell out of favor and confirmed their affection for communitarian values. The cooperative spirit that agrarians imagined descending over the land found expression in farmer-owned stores through which group buying and selling promoted egalitarian access to the market economy and emboldened farmers to act in union with their neighbors. Cooperation as proposed by the Patrons of Husbandry and its successor—the Farmers' Alliance—described a spirit of brotherhood among farmers and a tool that might smash merchant hegemony. By empowering farmers as active and autonomous players in the commercial order, an ironic role for agrarians to desire since they professed a loathing for the new order, cooperation promised to ease rural distress. It also offered agrarians a refuge from the bitterly competitive new order and promised to preserve traditional values.

Nearly a decade before the Farmers' Alliance most famously verbalized a cooperative ethos, the Grange launched an experiment in cooperative buying. According to Grangers' assessment, farmers' dependence upon merchants for their sustenance might be broken if they joined forces against their oppressors. Merchant-bashing became one of the Grange's chief occupations, and members of the organization publicly castigated opponents

19. Lawrence Goodwyn, *The Populist Moment: A Short History of the Agrarian Revolt in America* (New York, 1978), 54, but see also 55–93, which addresses the concerns that prompted the cooperative movement and the causes of its failure. See, too, Hahn, *The Roots of Southern Populism,* 293.

of agrarian capitalism. Because of their energetic efforts, observers like Reverend Samuel Agnew determined quickly that "the object [of the Grange] is to break down the merchants." Eventually, they confronted their overlords directly, but in the 1870s local Granges took more tentative steps. They bestowed upon particular merchants, generally members of the organization or at least store owners who agreed to offer Grangers discounted prices, a stamp of approval. All members of a local Grange agreed to trade only with the select merchant. But the relationship between the Grange merchants and farmers often lasted for a short time as store owners refused to honor the agreements they had struck.[20] In the 1880s, as the informal arrangements disintegrated, Grangers tried their hand at cooperative stores. Their successful establishment promised to accomplish what previous efforts at uniting farmers had failed to do: they would create a farmer-sanctioned monopoly of the rural trade and thereby drive from business all other merchants.[21]

However grandiose and important Grangers thought their venture into cooperative merchandising, their stores failed to relieve farmers of their economic distress. A breakdown might have been predicted since membership in the organization began to decline as its cooperative vision emerged, and since most members who remained in the dying Patrons of Husbandry thought of it as little more than a fraternal order. Grangers also guaranteed that their stores would fold when they insisted that all business be conducted on a cash-only basis, a ludicrous operating principle considering rural folks' lack of money.[22] Most county Granges organized a cooperative store and asked participating chapters to underwrite store stock. Once the designated capital of a store had been collected, individual farmers placed orders for goods (generally nonperishable farm supplies) through their local chapters, and managers of the cooperative stores pooled the orders, using volume buying as leverage to negotiate the lowest possible price. A popularly elected board of directors that controlled day-to-day opera-

20. Quoting Agnew Diary, October 2, 1886. On the difficulty of finding a permanent Grange merchant, see Darden Diaries, May 9, 1874 (in Darden Papers).

21. Patrons of Husbandry, Mississippi State Grange Papers, March 17, 1883. On the evils committed by merchants and the wealth that accrued to farmers when they bankrupted their enemies, see the letter signed "Suvatco," in Hazelhurst *Copiah Signal,* June 28, 1888.

22. On the decline of the Grange, see Ferguson, "Agrarianism in Mississippi," 75, 83. From a high of thirty-one thousand in 1875, membership in the Grange declined to ten thousand in 1878 and dipped below four thousand in 1885. On the fraternal nature of the Grange, see Alexander Diary and Account Ledger, February 8, 10, 1873; A. B. Grosh to R. B. Mayes, May, 1869, in Dimitry Papers; Sallie Stone Trotter Ledgers, Midway Grange Account Book, No. 199, MSU.

tions at each store set the retail price for goods just over the wholesale cost. Despite their well-laid plans, the Grange experiment in bulk buying floundered. Its failure owed largely to the fact that a single cooperative store was established in each county, making it inconvenient for many farmers to conduct business. The brief history of the Holmes County cooperative verified the struggle of Grange stores. In 1880 Holmes County Grangers opened a store at Lexington but in 1881 moved it to Bowling Green, where the store survived only one year more before permanently closing its doors.[23]

The Farmers' Alliance succeeded no better than the Grange in infusing the commercial order with its cooperative vision. In 1887, the first year that the Alliance appeared in Mississippi, local chapters opened cooperative stores. In some quarters, merchants sought to drive them out of business by boycotting wholesalers who supplied cooperatives, but alliance men responded in kind with counterboycotts of wholesalers who dealt with non-Alliance merchants. Hoping to ward off the fate that befell Grange stores, the Mississippi Alliance drew a lesson from its sister organization in Texas and founded a state Exchange in 1888. The Exchange functioned as a cooperative clearinghouse, pooling the capital raised by sub-Alliances and bulk ordering farm supplies and staples. Unfortunately, like Grange stores, it operated on a strictly cash basis. After receiving from sub-Alliances a large share of its operating capital and taking advantage of tax exemptions tendered by the city of Winona, the Exchange opened in February, 1888. Rumors of a corrupt management and the absence of an efficient distribution system caused the business to close three years later without offering a lasting challenge to the commercial order.[24]

The Farmers' Alliance, born out of agrarians' frustration with the commercial order and the collapse of the Grange, sought not only through cooperative stores to overturn the influence of merchants and supply men, but it also determined to eradicate the bugbear of the age: trusts. When Mississippi Alliance men spoke in their constitution about promoting brotherhood, social harmony, and a government friendly to farmers, they had in mind the creation of an economy based on egalitarian principles. In order to achieve their version of homogeneity, the Alliance, at least in its early

23. Patrons of Husbandry, Mississippi State Grange Papers, January 3, 17, March 6, 1880, April 1, 1881, May 19, 1883, February 16, September 20, 1884, July 11, 1889.

24. Ferguson, "Agrarianism in Mississippi," 144–51; Jackson *Weekly Clarion-Ledger,* August 30, 1888; Hazelhurst *Copiah Signal,* March 8, 1888, February 21, 1889; Grenada *Sentinel,* March 8, 1884. On the necessity of operating the Exchange on a cash basis, see David Russell Hearn Diary, October 9, 1890 (MS in David Russell Hearn and Family Papers), MDAH; Agnew Diary, February 21, 1887.

days, forsook politics and preached that "their own mutual benefit, educationally and financially" demanded unity. They invoked republican sentiments of self-sacrifice for the good of all when they decried "the prostitution of the public service to the advancement of selfish ends." [25] Among the agencies that prostituted public service, none suffered the wrath of the Alliance more than monopolies. G. A. Wilson, an Alliance man and candidate for Congress in 1888, included the Yazoo and Mississippi Valley Railroad on his list of trusts that cheated productive men. Besides possessing great tracts of land tax-free, the railroad had purchased its land for eight cents an acre and sold it to farmers for five to thirteen dollars. "Their charter," Wilson complained, "gives them the right to buy up the earth on a speculation and hold it free from taxation," and they combined with other companies to set shipping prices. Besides the insidious and oppressive business practices of railroad companies, agrarians identified the jute-bagging trust as the incarnation of evil.[26] The trust, a collection of manufacturers who turned out the crude sacks in which bales of cotton were shipped, set prices and eliminated competition.

To recapture the economic liberty that residents of the countryside had once possessed, the Alliance, only months after its birth, began planning to defeat the trust. A circular letter issued by the state executive committee called upon sub-Alliances to fight the jute-baggers: "For the first time since our organization you are called upon to exhibit your valor in doing battle against our avowed enemy—monopoly—to prove your devotion to the principles upon which our organization is founded." The original plan put forward by the committee focused on construction of a farmer-owned bagging plant backed by $500,000 capital. Stock in the company would sell for $5 a share, an amount that most farmers could afford, organizers surmised. Like the Exchange, the bagging factory would depend on farmers pooling their orders for bags through sub-Alliances and conducting all business on a cash basis. Although the plan arrived too late to defeat the jute-baggers in 1888, the Alliance hoped to have its plant in operation by the close of the next summer. In the meantime the committee encouraged farmers to use any bagging other than jute and suggested

25. Quoting Jackson *Weekly Clarion,* December 15, 1886; Carthage *Carthaginian,* July 23, 1887; see too, "Constitution and By-Laws of the Mississippi Farmers' Alliance," 1887, as reprinted in the Jackson *New Mississippian,* n.d., 1890, in the Brad Carter Papers, MSU.

26. Jackson *Weekly Clarion-Ledger,* February 23, 1888; Carthage *Carthaginian,* April 25, 1890. On jute, see U.S. Department of Agriculture, *Report of the Secretary of Agriculture, 1893* (1894), 570.

pine straw and cotton as substitutes; some Alliance men also advocated that farmers use the interim to petition Congress to remove jute from the list of items protected by the tariff.[27]

From 1888 until the Alliance bagging factory opened in 1889, trust-busting rhetoric propelled the growth of the farmers' movement. One observer of the Alliance estimated that by mid-1889 the number of sub-Alliances and Agricultural Wheels in Mississippi exceeded two thousand; chapters for blacks raised the total by eight hundred. In April, 1889, twenty-one county Alliances sent representatives to Jackson to negotiate a lease with the Penitentiary Board of Control for use of the old prison factory. Only $10,000 of the originally projected capital stock had been subscribed, but the Alliance representatives sold another $15,000 worth to the Jackson Board of Trade. Despite the project's undercapitalization the Alliance signed a $225 per month lease with the penitentiary board and received the right to use prisoners in their factory, a privilege agrarians happily accepted even though they criticized the state for leasing prisoners to railroads and planters. The favorable terms of its lease notwithstanding, the bagging factory folded in 1891, as did the Exchange, amid rumors of malfeasance.[28]

Agrarian forays into cooperative buying failed to nurture farmers' idea of a brotherhood of producers; their insistence that cooperative ventures operate on a cash-only basis served mainly the interest of those who had not yet acquired debts under the crop-lien law. The great body of Mississippi farmers, the very individuals that agrarians intended to help, found themselves shut out of the brotherhood, a sad commentary on the limitations of the agrarian vision. Solomon S. Calhoon believed other circumstances contributed to the breakdown of cooperative ventures. Speaking before an audience of farmers at the Madison County Fair in 1891, he attributed their demise to a lack of expertise. Conducting a business, even in a local market, required a dependence on distant suppliers, railroads, and commercial credit, and farmers set themselves up to fail by employing unqualified members of their own ranks as agents. Destruction of the commercial order, he said, necessitated hiring experienced members of the financial community: "Some day, after about three hundred and thirty thousand flat failures, we will learn that brains, experience, long training and

27. Quoting "Circular Letter to Members of the Farmers Alliance of Mississippi," n.d., but see also "Letter from the Executive Committee, September 17, 1888," in Baskin Family Papers, MSU; Macon *Mississippi Sun*, August 17, 1888; Carthage *Carthaginian*, June 21, 1889.

28. Jackson *New Mississippian*, August 28, 1889; Jackson *Weekly Clarion-Ledger*, April 4, 11, 1889; Carthage *Carthaginian*, April 4, May 3, June 21, 1889, August 1, 1890.

careful accurate business honesty are never cheap in any country and that the true economy is to buy them at a high price." Other observers made similar statements. Praising the operation of a Yazoo County cooperative livestock farm, one newspaper editor predicted success for the enterprise because businessmen, trained in the ways of the late-nineteenth-century commercial order, managed it.[29] Suggestions that farmers hire men of the commercial order to run their cooperatives represented a candid confession that agrarians' vision of a brotherhood of producers was incompatible with the New South. Even though agrarians were unwilling to admit it, their desire to participate in the market economy compelled them to suffer its excesses. Their only other option was to withdraw from the market, a step that would imperil their liberty as surely as enslavement to the market.

In like fashion, agrarians, though they longed to redirect political power away from courthouse cliques and to draw power toward producers in the countryside, proved unwilling to forsake the political culture of racism. They remained captives of a political system that they abhorred. Agrarians particularly despised it for breeding a malevolent class of politician: the loyal servant of the Democratic party, invariably the child of the New Departure or commercial-industrial school of thought, who appeared immune to farmers' remonstrances for justice but who eagerly legislated in favor of bondholders, railroads, and merchants. The results of New Departure hegemony were undeniable. Farmers paid high taxes, railroads gouged the land and producers, currency was in short supply, and political candidates silenced dissenters. As the Democratic party fell victim to the maneuvering of those "most trusted ringsters," support for the commercial order more than meritorious service to the party determined winners of political nominations. Not even in political conventions could agrarians exert their influence. For pernicious combinations and the surreptitious swapping of votes disadvantaged them, neutralizing any challenge to corporate politics.[30]

The source of agrarians' political impotence rested on their vision of a good republic. Since the days of Reconstruction, they had accepted for the sake of their own political liberty the maintenance of an underclass of black laborers removed from political power. Long-standing racial prejudices in-

29. Solomon S. Calhoon, "Address to the Madison County Fair" (MS in Calhoon Papers), unpaginated; Hazelhurst *Copiah Signal,* March 14, 1889.

30. "Ringsters" quote from George C. Dillard to B. T. Hobbs, September 17, 1887, in Hobbs Family Papers, MSU.

vigorated their devotion to white political homogeneity, and their involvement in the taxpayers' movement of the 1870s cemented their relationship with the Democratic party. The Grange leader Putnam Darden, by heading a mob during the 1874 Vicksburg riot, set the tone for farmers during Redemption and established farmers' identity with the political culture of racism. So firmly did they believe that white liberty revolved around the suppression of black voting rights, farmers embraced the fiction voiced by Democrats that all who opposed the party of white supremacy were "Black Republicans." In the mid-1870s farmers, in the words of James Z. George, happily "lay aside all prejudices and preferences" and voted with fellow Democrats "for the common good." They learned to equate party loyalty with devotion to a white man's republic. J. H. Doss paid respect to the political culture that farmers endorsed when he wrote the governor's office asking for an appointment as county registrar. He claimed to be not merely a loyal Democrat but "a '*full blooded white man*' " as well.[31] Farmers' Reconstruction-era willingness to accept the Democratic party's heavy-handed tactics and their insistence that loyal white men vote the straight Democratic ticket facilitated the rise of clique men and established a pattern of behavior that agrarians found difficult to break.

Soon after Redemption, in response to the political oppression farmers faced, a long line of dissidents queued up to test Democratic hegemony. Initially, out-of-office Democrats resentful of their party's neglect headed breakaway campaigns without making direct appeals to agrarian concerns. They nevertheless discovered, as did Reuben Davis (the perennial office seeker from Monroe County) when he made an independent grab for the first congressional seat in 1878, that their former Democratic colleagues blanched not at using violence against old friends.[32] Beginning in the 1880s dissidents changed their strategy. Pointing to the machinations of the commercial-industrial wing of the party and its evasion of farmers' concerns, they tentatively sought support from cultivators. Adopting agrarian class-conscious rhetoric to pick up white farmers' votes, the bolters bemoaned the fate of farmers, who had been pressed to the periphery of po-

31. Quoting James Z. George to Colonel L. A. Outlaw, n.d., in Yerger Papers; J. H. Doss to A. C. Falconer, March 2, 1877, in RG 27, MDAH.

32. Davis was representative of the bolters who made oblique appeals to agrarians, but unlike other white dissidents, he made direct appeals to blacks for support, a disingenuous action considering his Reconstruction-era attacks on black voting rights. On his campaign and the response to it, see Clarke Leonard Miller, "'Let Us Die to Make Men Free': Political Terrorism in Post-Reconstruction Mississippi, 1877–1896" (Ph.D. dissertation, University of Minnesota, 1983), 24–38.

litical culture and otherwise treated like unvirtuous blacks. Their overt appeals to dislodge the New Departure wing of the party invited violent suppression, but also suggested to those weary of Democratic-commercial hegemony that together farmers posed a serious threat to carefree politicians.

In 1880 intraparty challengers of Redeemer rule and advocates of the free coinage of silver combined to hand the Democratic party a minor defeat in the senatorial nomination. The canvass for the nomination intimated that agrarians viewed the Democratic party as an enemy of economic liberty and that, as one agrarian put it, foes of the commercial order refused to be carried by "the democratic party in its breeches pocket." Trouble between industrial-commercial Democrats (led by Lucius Q. C. Lamar) and dissidents had been in the making since Redemption. Ethelbert Barksdale, chair of the party executive committee from 1877 to 1879, acted as informal leader of the anti-Lamar faction. Barksdale, who first opposed Lamar because he believed the senator kept him out of elective office, turned Lamar's refusal to vote for remonetization of silver in 1878 against him. He thus captured agrarian support, as farmers believed the senator's opposition to the measure connoted an identification with the interests of the commercial order.[33] His well-known coolness toward the payment of government bonds in greenbacks also stimulated agrarians to portray him as an enemy of an egalitarian and just economy. With intraparty tensions on the rise, Blanche K. Bruce announced his resignation from the Senate, opening an office for which Barksdale might contend, but fearful that Barksdale's presence in the Senate would precipitate his own demise in Mississippi political circles, Lamar initiated a whispering campaign to arouse support for his former law partner and ex-Confederate general Edward C. Walthall. Yet Walthall was reluctant to campaign for the nomination as he thought his candidacy would needlessly turn the nomination into a referendum on financial questions and disrupt party unity.[34]

Upsetting the Democratic party's hold on the dispensation of patronage and policy decisions was precisely what Barksdale had in mind when he

33. Quoting "Demockratia" to A. J. Frantz, April 21, 1879, in Henry Papers, MDAH. Most Mississippians apparently supported the Bland Silver Bill for its inflationary impact, as more money in circulation augured the increased value of property and crops. H. L. Muldrow perhaps spoke for other residents when he said that inflationary policies might result in better prices for land, which meant to him the restoration of wealth in the agricultural sector of the economy. See H. L. Muldrow to Lafayette Reynolds, March 3, 1878, in Reynolds Papers.

34. L. Q. C. Lamar to Edward Donaldson Clark, February 18, 1879; Edward C. Walthall to Clark, December 5, 1879, all in Clark Collection. See, too, Bradley G. Bond, "Edward C. Walthall and the 1880 Senatorial Nomination: Politics of Balance in the Redeemer Era," *Journal of Mississippi History,* L (1988), 1–20.

made Lamar's stand on the financial issues of the day fodder for the canvass. Otho R. Singleton, an unequivocal advocate of the free coinage of silver and greenback issuance, also vigorously campaigned for the office and, in fact, received the endorsement of the state Grange newspaper, the *Patron of Husbandry.* Among farmers hard hit by the depression and the Crime of 1873, Singleton's advocacy of dual inflationary policies rang true. Barksdale, on the other hand, something of a moderate among agrarians (or more accurately a disgruntled office seeker seeking agrarian support) opposed the Greenback measure of a fiat monetary system, though he endorsed another of agrarians' favorite inflationary policies: free and unlimited coinage of silver and gold. So as not to distance himself from agrarians or from Lamar, Walthall held to the Democratic party line, supporting free silver and greenback issue but refusing to criticize Lamar's vote against the Bland Bill. Most of all, he wished to see the nation establish a stable currency without pursuing what he considered extremely inflationary policies; he wanted as well the state Democratic party to march in lockstep behind his friend's leadership. Because of his refusal to denounce Lamar, attacks on him as a "Bond holder and Bond Holding loving autocrat" circulated, ensuring that he would gain few agrarian supporters.[35]

When the Democratic legislative caucus met to choose a candidate for the Senate in January, 1880, public debate about the senatorial nominees had not produced an outright favorite, but since Lamar controlled the administration of the meeting, Walthall's nomination seemed certain. After exhausting his political capital to fend off an attempt by Barksdale's forces to permit dissident Democrats and even some Republican legislators to participate in the caucus, Lamar's role in the nominations diminished, however. Consequently, Barksdale nearly captured the nomination on the first ballot; Singleton ran a close second and Walthall a distant third. Through thirty-five ballots and six nights of caucusing, supporters of the three leading contenders fought for their candidate. Then, on the seventh night, Walthall withdrew his name. By prior arrangement with Lamar, W. S. Featherstone of Holly Springs (a hotbed of anti-Lamar and Greenback sentiment) immediately nominated James Z. George. The irony of Featherstone nominating a "hard money Democrat" struck many at the convention, but

35. Quoting L. Q. C. Lamar to Edward Donaldson Clark, December 26, 1879, but see, too, Edward C. Walthall to Clark, December 22, 1879, all in Clark Collection. Columbus *Patron of Husbandry,* October 25, 1879; Jackson *Weekly Clarion,* June 11, 1879, January 14, 1880; Jackson *Comet,* January 4, 1880. On the currency situation, see Irwin Unger, *The Greenback Era: A Social and Political History of American Finance, 1865–1879* (Princeton, 1964), 337–38, 377–78.

George's entrance as a candidate influenced the body only after Barksdale withdrew from the race, sending his support to George, who won the nomination.[36] After the caucus the press continued to criticize Lamar for his stand on financial questions, but believed the selection of George a fair compromise for both factions of the party. Yet appearances that the internecine struggle between the agrarian and Lamar wings of the party had ended were short-lived. Events between 1881 and 1883 proved that the ranks of dissidents, especially those with agrarian support, were growing.

In 1881 Benjamin E. King, a former Democrat, headed a fusion ticket composed of Greenbackers, black Republicans, and Democratic bolters. Ominous talk of a return to Radical power united regular Democrats against their former brother, who had, they said, unleashed his Republican conspirators to commit acts of "extravagance, corruption, disorder, and violence." Repeatedly during the campaign the Democratic nominee for governor, Robert Lowry, employed race-baiting rhetoric to chastise his opponent and to remind voters of the link between dissident whites and African Americans: "As the stream could not rise above its source, neither can the candidate rise above his constituency." To regular Democrats the financial issues raised by Greenbackers mattered less than the specter of white and black men united in politics. By Lamar's own recounting of the election, regular Democrats used "repression, intimidation, and other . . . illegal devices" to defeat King. The campaign of violence kept 68 percent of registered blacks from voting.[37]

Building on the lesson of King's defeat, James R. Chalmers attempted another dissident campaign in 1882, and through his run for the second district seat in Congress, discovered another approach to upsetting the regular Democratic party. Although blacks comprised roughly 50 percent of the registered population in the district, he consciously avoided soliciting their votes. Already gerrymandered out of a seat in Congress by the Lamar wing, Chalmers attempted to capture a position from Lamar's home district by running against Van Manning, an associate of the senator. Simply by confronting the Lamar wing of the party, Chalmers garnered agrarian

36. Quoting Edward C. Walthall to Edward Donaldson Clark, January 27, 1880, but see, too, Walthall to Clark, January 23, 1880, in Clark Collection. Jackson *Weekly Clarion,* January 14, 21, 28, 1880.

37. Lowry quoted in Miller, "'Let Us Die to Make Men Free,'" 259, but see also 247–72; Lamar quoted in Kirwan, *Revolt of the Rednecks,* 8. See Willie D. Halsell, "Democratic Dissensions in Mississippi, 1878–1882," *Journal of Mississippi History,* II (1940), 135. On King's alliance with the Republican party, see John Roy Lynch, *Reminiscences of an Active Life: The Autobiography of John Roy Lynch,* ed. John Hope Franklin (Chicago, 1970), 256. King polled thirty-one thousand votes to Lowry's forty-eight thousand.

support, but farmers likely would have more avidly championed his cause had he proposed an alternative economic program.[38] Instead of emphasizing inflationary currency policies, Chalmers sought to lure white farmers to his side by challenging the alliance of Democrats and black Republicans, which fell under the control of James Hill, John R. Lynch, and Blanche K. Bruce, all black members of the national patronage machine. His purpose was simple. He would beat Democrats at their own game, linking the Lamar wing to black Republicanism through his own adamant rejection of black support. When approached by Chalmers, the recently installed Chester A. Arthur administration, weary of dealing with the black wing of the party, agreed to shift responsibility for patronage from the state's three black Republicans. He even opened the party's coffers to the dissident Democrat. Immediately, Chalmers named leading white Republicans to positions as postmaster, federal attorney, and federal supervisor of elections. George McKee, a white Republican and former congressman, approved the tactic. For some time, he had resented the Lamar-Bruce arrangement that allowed the former a say in naming black Republicans to minor offices. "Bruce & Lamar," McKee posited, "humbug the different administrations and keep up negro rule in the Rep[ublican] party in order that fear of negro rule in the State may keep men in the Dem[ocratic] party." By openly appealing to white Republicans and agrarian Democrats, Chalmers pioneered the tactic that later-day dissident politicians would attempt—he courted white agrarians and dissidents but ignored black voters. Chalmers' strategy of uniting "out" groups in each party might have worked had not the Democratic party committed vote fraud.[39]

Chalmers' defeat served as an augur of the rough treatment to come for politicians who attempted to unite with Greenbackers and Independents. It testified as well to the persistence of the political culture of racism. The fact that Chalmers sought to damage the Lamar wing without seeking black voters especially boded ill for dissidents. For the tactic was a confession

38. Miller, "'Let Us Die to Make Men Free,'" 287–336. Willie D. Halsell's "James R. Chalmers and 'Mahoneism' in Mississippi," *Journal of Southern History,* X (1944), 37–58, remains the best account of the Chalmers affair.

39. Quoting George C. McKee to William E. Chandler, July 6, 1882, in Willie D. Halsell, ed., "Republican Factionalism in Mississippi, 1882–1884," *Journal of Southern History,* VII (1941), 93–94. See, too, Halsell, "Democratic Dissensions in Mississippi," 123–35, 255–61; Lynch, *Reminiscences of an Active Life,* 255–61. On the deal struck between Lamar and Bruce, see L. Q. C. Lamar to Edward Donaldson Clark, March 15, 1877, in Clark Collection. On vote fraud in 1882 see Greene C. Chandler to B. H. Brewster, October 20, December 22, 1882; J. L. Morphis to Brewster, August 21, 1882, all in DJ (2); Halsell, "James R. Chalmers and 'Mahoneism,'" 45–58.

that even white dissidents viewed the racial assumptions of Mississippi political culture as relevant. Henry C. Niles, a white Republican, denounced the Democratic party's exploitation of the black wing of his party. As long as Democrats used it as a tool to whip up animosity toward dissenters, he said, "the negro [will be] on top—the '*race issue*' will be the cry in every contest—and we will be the sufferers." More plainly, the Crystal Springs *Monitor* announced: "The issue is paramount in Southern politics. It cannot be concealed, it must be admitted that the white people are determined to keep the negro beneath them socially, and to use him for their own supremacy in the political world." Driving home the demand for party loyalty and linking dissent to the activity of unvirtuous voters, regular Democrats liked to remind whites that "every man who wishes to see white supremacy and Democratic rule continued in Mississippi, should go to the polls." [40] Between 1876 and 1896 the Democrats, using the race issue to ensure party solidarity, converted attacks on the commercial order and its protectors into the work of "Black Republicans," turning dissenters, however far they removed themselves from black voters, into foes of white supremacy.[41]

Agrarian influence in Mississippi politics remained real, despite the abuse of dissidents that occurred in the 1880s. Even as regular Democrats whipped Chalmers and King at the polls, farmers and their friends assumed seats in the legislature and passed laws designed to check the authority of the commercial order. Two of the most significant laws dealt with the regulation of railroads and the leasing of convicts to private citizens and corporations; agrarians also sought to redress their grievances in the constitutional convention of 1890 and the Populist party.

Of the agents of the commercial order that farmers identified as inimi-

40. Henry C. Niles to William E. Chandler, November 25, 1882, quoted in Halsell, ed., "Republican Factionalism in Mississippi," 97–98; Crystal Springs *Monitor,* September 25, 1882; Macon *Mississippi Sun,* October 31, 1884. See as well Senator George's remarks connecting race loyalty to party loyalty found in Grenada *Sentinel,* October 20, 1886. On the difficulty of combating the regular Democratic party, see Goodwyn, *The Populist Moment,* Chapt. 1. For accounts of Democratic reactions to Greenback-Independent fusion in Copiah County, see *Senate Reports,* 38th Cong., 1st Sess., No. 512, pp. xxvii–lxxxii, and Crystal Springs *Meteor,* February 10, 17, October 13, 1883.

41. Suppression of Democratic dissenters took other forms as well. In 1885, to stop Putnam Darden's bid for the governor's office, regular Democrats required participants in the nominating process to prove that they had voted the straight ticket in the preceding election. Carthage *Carthaginian,* July 11, 18, 1885; Jackson *Weekly Clarion,* February 25, 1885; Agnew Diary, November 3, 1885.

cal to their interests, railroad companies, which received tax exemptions, held large parcels of land, and monopolized the transportation of cotton, troubled agrarians almost as much as merchants. Equally galling to farmers was the cooperation railroads received from state and local governments. Railroad companies resembled the antebellum banking industry. They threatened the liberty of the people by procuring special privileges. Frank Burkitt, soon to become a Populist leader in Mississippi, honed his political skills in the 1880s decrying the corrupting influence of railroads, especially the Memphis, Birmingham, and Atlantic. In the 1870s the MB&A undertook an aggressive campaign to convince local governments to support its completion with public money. But more than a decade after receiving several thousand dollars from the Democratic-controlled Choctaw County government, Burkitt's home county, organizers of the line skipped over Choctaw, leaving it without a return on its investment. Statewide, farmers and their allies registered similar complaints and added to them criticism of railroads for pricing small shippers out of business.[42] Responding to the protests the legislature considered founding a state board to referee relations between railroads and farmers.

In 1884, after previously failing to establish a railroad commission, both houses concurred on creating a board to settle citizens' disputes with shippers. According to the law, the governor would appoint three commissioners at a salary of $2,500 a year. Charged chiefly with hearing complaints, railroad commissioners, especially after the High Court of Errors and Appeals emasculated the enforcement powers originally assigned them, spent their time recommending depot and track repairs. Opposition to the law emanated from railroad officials and the state's New South prophets who feared the "obnoxious measures" proposed would, by lowering rates and drowning private enterprise in a sea of regulation, prevent railroads from expanding. The ruin of the commercial order was destined to follow. But once the law passed, even the Natchez *Daily Democrat and Courier*, which had first opposed it, recognized the weakness of the commission and professed suddenly to believe it might save shippers from high rates. Predictably, the commission achieved no great fame as a protector of shippers. Within two years of its creation, agrarians characterized the commission as an agency of corporate power: extravagantly paid commissioners served at the pleasure of the governor, not the people, and felt obligated to make him happy. And shipping rates remained high. Confronted with criticism of the commission as a do-nothing board and with complaints against the peni-

42. Kirwan, *Revolt of the Rednecks*, 55.

tentiary system, legislators enlarged the commissions' duties, making it a Board of Control to supervise Mississippi convicts.[43]

The addition of duties overseeing state prisoners coincided with mounting agrarian interest in abolishing the convict lease system, a system against which farm advocates and middle-class reformers united in 1886. While the keepers of the New South order looked upon convict leasing as inhumane, agrarians believed that it permitted the few to reap great profits at the expense of the many. In 1886, reports circulated that in order to sign over state convicts to the Gulf and Ship Island Railroad former Attorney General Thomas C. Catchings secretly cancelled between sixty and eighty thousand dollars in debt owed the state by the former leaseholders Hamilton and Hoskins. Hamilton and Hoskins represented to agrarians the evils of the commercial order, and the state condoned their activities by granting them the right to lease prisoners and then forgiving their debts. By all accounts Hamilton and Hoskins had poorly managed the penitentiary and neglected to build, as prescribed by the terms of their lease, a central housing unit at Jackson. They and other sublessees, however, successfully lined their pockets with large profits. News of Catchings' generous treatment of the lessees and reports of others' profiteering circulated, enraging agrarians further. The Grange leader and Redeemer-era state treasurer, Colonel W. L. Hemingway, using convicts he leased from the state, reportedly cleared 110 acres of prime Delta land for ten dollars per acre; a Leflore County planter cleared 150 acres at five dollars per acre; and a Washington County planter, state regulators calculated, produced hundreds of bales of cotton at a rate of seventy-five cents per hundred pounds. A sublessee in Madison County paid only fifteen cents a day for each convict he employed.[44]

Agrarians counted the Gulf and Ship Island Railroad Company the worst abuser of its privileges by far. Not only did the company use convict labor to extend the hurtful commercial order, it treated prisoners with great cruelty, the latter fact more troubling to middle-class reformers than to agrar-

43. Quoting Natchez *Daily Democrat and Courier,* March 30, 1887, but see, too, April 12, 1887. On the passage of the law, see Jackson *New Mississippian,* March 25, May 6, 1884, April 28, 1885; Jackson *Weekly Clarion,* November 24, 1886. On customers' complaints about rates, see A. L. Rives to Robert Lowry, February 25, 1882, in RG 27, MDAH; Raymond *Hinds County Gazette* quoted in Jackson *Weekly Clarion,* December 18, 1878. On the railroad commission, see Daniel C. Vogt, "Problems of Government Regulation: The Mississippi Railroad Commission, 1884–1956" (Ph.D. dissertation, University of Southern Mississippi, 1980), Chapts. 1 and 2.

44. Grenada *Gazette,* July 20, 1888; Jackson *Weekly Clarion,* December 15, 1886; Steve Sullivan, "Prison Without Walls: A History of the Mississippi State Penal System" Typescript, MDAH, 105; *Mississippi House Journal,* 1888, p. 19.

ians. A legislative investigation in 1887 echoed the agrarians' critique of the lease system and accused lessees of possessing a "thirst for gain" that supplanted feelings of humanity. Comparing the treatment accorded convicts to the treatment of slaves, the committee posited that the practice "simply restores a state of servitude worse than slavery, in this, that it is without any of the safe-guards resulting from ownership of the slave." Their assessment was accurate. Between 1880 and 1885 nearly 10.97 percent of black convicts and 5.3 percent of whites died; the latter rate doubled the percentage of deaths recorded in Midwestern prisons. The comparative figures included in the legislative committee's report awakened interest in alternative methods of housing prisoners, which prompted the state eventually to found three prison farms in central Mississippi. After the Board of Control gained supervisory powers over convicts, but before the constitutional ban on the leasing of state prisoners in 1890 (the actual prohibition went into effect four years later), the death rate fluctuated but generally declined between 1886 (9.08 percent) and 1893 (5 percent). Even though the prohibition against leasing state convicts did not extend to the leasing of county prisoners, and even though the mistreatment of county chain gangs and state penal farm residents continued, agrarians were pleased with the changes. The evils associated with the state granting special privileges to keepers of the commercial order had ended and the issue of prison reform had been formally addressed to agrarians' satisfaction by the constitutional convention.[45]

Throughout the 1880s agrarians persistently looked to a constitutional convention for redress of their grievances against the commercial order. Unlike middle-class reformers, who expected a convention to disfranchise the degenerate, agrarians viewed a new constitution as an opportunity to restrain corporate authority. Agrarians, in fact, loathed disfranchisement plans that had been bandied about since 1876 as they suspected that poor or illiterate whites would be subjected to restriction as well as blacks. They preferred instead to eliminate the offices of lieutenant gov-

45. Quoting *Mississippi House Journal,* 1888, pp. 3, 16, 25–35. On convict leasing in Madison County, see Lessee Accounts, November 26, 1883, Hearn Family Papers. On the lease and farm systems, see Carthage *Carthaginian,* February 14, 1885; Jackson *Weekly Clarion,* February 10, 1886, February 28, 1889, August 18, 1886, quoting Vicksburg *Post.* See Ruby E. Cooley, "A History of the Mississippi Penal Farm Sytem, 1890–1935: Punishment, Politics, and Profit in Penal Affairs" (M.A. thesis, University of Southern Mississippi, 1981), 47, 50; Sullivan, "Prison Without Walls," 119–20. On treatment of prisoners on the farms, see Joe Baddy to A. J. McLaurin, June 14, 1896, in RG 27, MDAH; on county's leasing prisoners, see Alex Lichtenstein, "Good Roads and Chain Gangs in the Progressive South: 'The Negro Convict is a Slave,'" *Journal of Southern History,* LIX (1993), 85–110.

ernor and superintendent of education, make the judiciary elective, limit governors to one term in office, deprive corporations of tax exemptions, and recalculate the method of appropriating state funds among the counties. Implicit in agrarians' demands for a convention was the fervent hope that the balance of political and economic power would be shifted away from a select few and restored to people deserving of liberty and virtue in a just social order.[46] They derived little pleasure from the constitution that resulted, however, though they forced the convention to adopt some of the measures they favored.

More than any other reform, rewriting the formula used to determine state appropriations motivated farmers to embrace the idea of a constitutional convention. Since 1868 when, according to Frank Burkitt, Ames and "his dirty crew" had written into law a method of appropriations based on the number of qualified electors in each county, black majority counties had received a disproportionate share of state funds. Farmers in the thinly populated counties of the northeast contended that since regular Democrats' machinations denied blacks the full benefits of citizenship (free access to the ballot and educational institutions), the counties in which they lived should have their take of state funds reduced and their legislative representation diminished. They pointed to the fact that in 1890 forty white majority counties elected only fifty-two members of the state house and twenty-one members of the senate, while thirty-four black majority counties sent sixty-eight representatives to the lower house and twenty-five to the upper. According to Frank Burkitt's calculations, three white males in Yazoo County elected four representatives, while sixteen hundred white males in Itawamba County elected only one.[47] A variety of remedies that addressed what representatives of white majority counties considered inequities in the system of appropriations made their way into the convention, and delegates wrote into law a compromise version. As approved, white majority counties exchanged thirteen new seats in the legislature, some of which had been carved from black counties, for accepting franchise qualifications (for illiterates); black majority counties retained their predominant influence in the senate, which received sole authority over revenue acts. Black counties also saw established a state electoral college, thereby canceling the one-man-one-vote tradition that permitted agrarians to disrupt statewide races.

46. On agrarians' demands, see Ackerman *Choctaw Plaindealer,* April 4, 1890; Carthage *Carthaginian,* June 27, 1890; Grenada *Gazette,* August 9, 1889; Jackson *Weekly Clarion-Ledger,* February 23, 28, 1889. See, too, the Farmers' Alliance Memorial in Regan Papers; letter signed "Conservative" in Raymond *Hinds County Gazette,* April 26, 1890.

47. Clark, "The Mississippi Constitutional Convention of 1890," 77–78.

By and large, agrarians supported the compromise appropriations and suffrage measures, but white politicians from the Delta bridled at the thought of losing leverage in the legislature. Actually, the convention's use of the 1880 census to calculate racial majorities overlooked changes in population distribution, permitting black majority counties to continue electing more representatives to the house than did white majority counties.[48] Regarding appropriations and apportionment, then, agrarians might be counted losers.

They fared little better in other matters decided by the convention. Funding for schools, for example, continued to favor black majority counties as the state appropriated money based on the number of educable children, black and white, in each county. Literacy qualifications and poll taxes for the suffrage, designed by middle-class reformers to eliminate from the political process the ignorant and venal also harmed agrarians, but the inclusion of an "understanding clause" soothed most farmers' feelings as it ensured that they would continue to vote. Other agrarians considered their achievement in the area of suffrage more stunning than it was in practice. The elimination of black voters promised by literacy qualifications and the prejudicial application of the understanding clause, they thought, removed the prospect of oppression of white dissenters since they could no longer be labeled foes of a white man's democracy. But as they found out in the political canvasses of the 1890s, the use of race as a stalking-horse proceeded. The only unqualified successes that agrarians achieved in the convention involved the taxation of corporations and the election of judges.[49]

By the early 1890s, having failed in the legislature and the constitutional convention to restore Jacksonian concepts of liberty and virtue to Mississippi politics, agrarians refocused their attention on economic matters. Specifically, they embraced (though reluctantly at first) the subtreasury plan advocated by the Alliance. Unlike previous attempts to unseat the commercial order by diluting the authority of the government and politicians, the subtreasury depended on the intrusion of the government into the economy. Its proposal divided agrarians. The plan called for the federal gov-

48. Albert Kirwan, "Apportionment in the Mississippi Constitution of 1890," *Journal of Southern History,* XIV (1948), 235–36; Kirwan, *Revolt of the Rednecks,* 82–83. Clark, "The Mississippi Constitutional Convention of 1890," 87, 93. On opposition to the franchise law as passed, see "Letter to the Editor of the *Subsoiler and Democrat,*" October 19, 1891, in Reynolds Papers: the law was "wholly insufficient as a measure to secure any governmental principle and as mere devices to secure white supremacy, only temperary [*sic*] in duration and practicality."

49. *Journal of the Proceedings of the Constitutional Convention, 1890,* 612.

ernment to erect warehouses where farmers could store crops until prices reached a satisfactory level. Provisions of the subtreasury system allowed farmers to borrow 80 percent of staple crops' local market value and to pay a 2 percent fee for storage. After selling their crops, farmers would repay the subtreasury the actual sum borrowed and retain the profits. Through the establishment of subtreasury warehouses, farmers hoped to obtain currency, avoid the application of the crop-lien law, and break their dependence on credit. In 1891, two years after its proposal, the Farmers' Alliance, still professing allegiance to the Democratic party, began applying the subtreasury as a yardstick to measure politicians' support for the countryside. According to Frank Burkitt, the Alliance wished to reform the Democratic party from within in order to preserve the political culture of racism. He found, however, that high-ranking Democrats doubted his sincerity. Both of the state's U.S. senators, George and Walthall, opposed the measure, as did other party leaders. Leaping at the opportunity provided by George's refusal to embrace the plan, Barksdale and Burkitt headed a campaign to elect subtreasury men to the state house in 1891, intending that agrarian legislators would remove George from his Senate seat. Even though the Alliance elected a number of members, they mustered insufficient votes to unseat George.[50]

Through the legislative elections of 1891 the Democratic elite's unmoving stand on the subtreasury reminded agrarians of their entrenched authority. Disgusted but confident that the commercial order's protectors in politics could be beaten, the most adventurous agrarians rushed into the newly formed Populist party. Led by Burkitt, the party made inroads in Democratic strongholds in the eastern half of the state, especially in the North-Central Hills, but as a third party seeking to unite with the white wing of the Republican party, Populists faced the full wrath of their Democratic rivals. Besides representing to Democrats a threat to the commercial order, they resembled Chalmers in his bid to disrupt white supremacy. References to Populist–black Republican collusion, however, denied the reality of agrarian exclusion of African Americans from their vision of an egalitarian social order, except as an underclass. (Indeed, in one instance white farmers embarked on a murderous rampage in the Delta to quiet black farmers who possessed a more egalitarian vision than did they.) Portrayed as a sorehead determined to resurrect "Black Republicanism," Burkitt especially suffered

50. On the 1891 election for legislative offices, see Kirwan, *Revolt of the Rednecks,* 89–91. See, too, a report of Burkitt's speech on the third party in Macon *Mississippi Sun,* February 20, 1891. Not all Alliance men favored the subtreasury; some looked upon it as granting an unconstitutional power to the federal government; see Grenada *Sentinel,* March 13, 1891.

Democratic denunciations. He responded in private to such charges by announcing that he had been "born a plebian [*sic*]" and preferred "to suffer with my people than to eat from the flesh pots of Egypt. Every impulse of nature revolts at the treatment the money power has visited upon the laboring people of the country for the past twenty-five years and every beat of my heart is in sympathy with the wealth producers of the land." Continuing, he added, "The Democratic party has ceased to hear them cry for relief and I cannot follow it further."[51] For almost three years agrarians, through the Populist party, harassed their Democratic rivals with such critiques of the political and economic inequities of the commercial order.

In 1892, however, despite a concerted push to elect congressmen, they fared poorly. None of the seven congressional districts recorded a Populist vote of more than 38 percent, and most recorded totals of about 20 percent. Two years later, when congressional seats again came open, the total vote for Populist candidates declined by 21 percent.[52] The Populist campaign turned toward disaster as quickly as it had begun. The last hurrah for Mississippi Populists occurred in Burkitt's 1895 bid for governor, an election he lost by some twenty-five thousand out of sixty thousand votes cast. Divisions among farmers opened by the subtreasury perhaps accounted for his weak showing, as did the emergence of free silver in Populist rhetoric. Most importantly, intimidation and the political culture of racism quelled the enthusiasm previously felt by many agrarians. As they had in 1882, Democratic leaders courted African-American voters to halt the fusion of Populists and white Republicans, affixing to Populists, at the same time, accusations that they wanted to revive black Republican rule. Most Mississippians, of course, were unaware of any such deals between Democrats and the black wing of the Republican party, but they plainly understood the threat of "Black Republican" resurgence that Democrats described.

51. Quoting Frank Burkitt to Walter A. Barker, July 21, 1892, but see, too, [?] Barker to John M. Stone, July 27, 1892, all in RG 27, MDAH. On Burkitt as a demagogue, see Jackson *Weekly Clarion-Ledger,* July 26, 1888; Grenada *Sentinel,* October 22, 1892. The *Sentinel*'s criticism of Burkitt as a demagogue and mere sorehead testifies to the divisiveness of the Populist party; the Grenada newspaper was the Alliance organ in the county. On the reluctance of farmers to join the Populist party, see Eric Anderson, "The Populist and Capitalist America: The Case of Edgecombe County, North Carolina," in *Race, Class, and Politics in Southern History: Essays in Honor of Robert F. Durden,* ed. Jeffery J. Crow, Paul D. Escott, and Charles L. Flynn, Jr. (Baton Rouge, 1989), 109. On the massacre of black farmers, see William F. Holmes, "The Leflore County Massacre and the Demise of the Colored Farmers' Alliance," *Phylon,* XXXVIII (1973), 267–69, 273–74.

52. For returns of 1892 and 1894 congressional elections, see Carthage *Carthaginian,* November 30, 1894. On the 1892 election, see Carthage *Carthaginian,* March 3, 1892.

Even knowledgeable party members missed the irony of Democratic rhetoric. James McCarthy praised Burkitt's gubernatorial foe, Anselm J. McLaurin, for preserving white supremacy in Mississippi: "The rest of the country may be given over to Negro rule and Republican highway robbers, but all Mississippi, God bless her, will always remain true to Democracy, Good Government, and White supremacy." [53] As Chalmers and the other dissident Democrats had discovered, Populists learned too that combating the political culture of racism was foolhardy, especially if the challengers neglected to pursue black support.

The acceleration of free-silver agitation in 1896 heralded the end of the Populist revolt, not because Populists became distracted with an issue irrelevant to their vision of agrarian capitalism but because the Democratic party rededicated itself to free silver and cheated agrarians of the one issue that separated them from the industrial-commercial wing of the party. The free and unlimited coinage of silver had always been one of farmers' demands, and in the mid-1890s silver men, according to a Scott County resident, became "as thick as fiddlers are said to be in that country where perpetual summer exist [sic] and overcoats are never needed." [54] Most Mississippi Democrats, despite party leadership, had supported free silver since the 1870s, and they used the occasion of the presidential election to remind agrarians of their faithful embrace of the issue. Although the introduction of free silver into the 1896 presidential campaign temporarily en-

53. Quoting James S. McCarthy to Anselm J. McLaurin, November 7, 1895, in RG 27, MDAH. On the essential sameness of Democrats and Populists, especially in regard to their views of race and silver, see Charles L. Flynn, Jr., "Procrustean Bedfellows and Populists: An Alternative Hypothesis," in *Race, Class, and Politics in Southern History: Essays in Honor of Robert F. Durden*, eds. Jeffery J. Crow, Paul D. Escott, and Charles L. Flynn, Jr. (Baton Rouge, 1989), 83, 97–99; Barton C. Shaw, *The Wool-Hat Boys: Georgia's Populist Party* (Baton Rouge, 1984), 85–86; Michael Goldfield, "The Color of Politics in the United States: White Supremacy as the Main Explanation for the Peculiarities of American Politics from Colonial Times to the Present," in *The Bounds of Race: Perspectives on Hegemony and Resistance*, ed. Dominick LaCapra (Ithaca, 1991), 129. On the use of race to detract from Populist support, especially after the election of 1892, see Grenada *Sentinel*, June 27, 1894; Natchez *Evening Banner*, December 2, 1892. On the continuation of the agreement between the Democratic party elite and black Republican leadership, see R. S. Haynie to Anselm J. McLaurin, April 14, 1897, in RG 27, MDAH; on the fusion of Democratic dissenters and Populists, see D. T. Pitts to John M. Stone, November 6, 1891, in RG 27, MDAH.

54. Quoting J. L. Powder to Anselm J. McLaurin, April 13, 1896, RG 27, MDAH; Goodwyn, *The Populist Moment*, 125–73, uses the term *shadow movement* to describe the free silver cause. On efforts to persuade farmers that free and unlimited coinage would devalue currency and thus harm producers, see Solomon S. Calhoon, "Address on Silver" (MS in Calhoon Papers), unpaginated.

couraged agrarians to believe they at last had an issue with which they could win, the split in the ranks of free silverites, precipitated by the appearance of William Jennings Bryan on the tickets of both the Democratic and Populist parties, killed Populism across the South.

Not all Mississippi Democrats were saddened by the 1896 election results that returned a Republican to the White House. The Democratic elite, particularly members of that small coterie residing in the Delta, celebrated Bryan's defeat and the death of Populism. The "revolutionary talk" that had animated political conversations since 1891 ceased. As Henry Waring Ball observed, "I never thought to see southern men rejoicing at a Republican victory, but it has come to pass. I have had my hand almost shaken off today. And now how the little fence corner country newspapers are going to howl and weep and swear and cuss us!" [55]

Howling and weeping, even swearing and cursing, the Democratic party could withstand; attempts to disrupt the party's command of state politics it would not tolerate. Although the road to establishing dominance had been a long one, by 1896 the party could proclaim its supremacy over all contenders. Methods used to suppress Populists in the 1890s differed little from the treatment reserved for Chalmers in 1882. Any deviation from the Democratic faith resulted in the political death of dissenters.[56] But the agrarians of the 1880s and early 1890s had at least tried to install again in society a sense of homogeneity based on egalitarian notions derived from the Jacksonian era. Like their antebellum heirs, they envisioned a world in which self-sufficient producers also raised crops and livestock for the market and thus controlled the flow of wealth and power, liberty and virtue into the countryside.

Their acceptance of racial theories that undergirded the social ethic and their preference for seeing black labor at work in others' cotton fields, however, impinged upon their egalitarian vision of a republic of producers and blinded them to the fact that blacks supported the agrarian cause. To distinguish white yeomen from the underclass, they endorsed instead the excesses of the political culture of racism. In doing so, they condemned them-

55. Quoting Ball Diary, November 24, 1896.

56. Populists discovered that their break with the Democratic party ended their political careers. The chair of the Democratic Executive Committee in Leake County, for instance, considered R. L. Wallace unfit to hold the office of circuit clerk because he had voted Populist in the congressional election of 1892; George W. Gates derisively referred to J. L. Calcote as an "Ex Popolite Sheriff." See Gates to Anselm J. McLaurin, n.d., 1895; O. A. Luckett, Jr. to John M. Stone, October 30, 1895, all in RG 27, MDAH.

selves to the treatment with which African Americans had been familiar since 1868. Agrarians' concepts of a cooperative and just economy and their notions of liberty and virtue for whites harkened back to the late antebellum period. Their own class-consciousness testified to the heterogeneity of the commercial order, as well as to the order's permanence and the irrelevance of their interpretation of history.

CHAPTER 9

A POSTSCRIPT: THE WORLD THE REDNECKS MADE

Two versions of homogeneity clashed in the late nineteenth century. Middle-class reformers, who embraced the economic benefits of modernity, trembled at the social consequences of industrial-commercial development; black and white Mississippians left behind by the commercial order's advance particularly concerned them. Restoring to society the sense of white cultural homogeneity that had existed in the antebellum period led them to press to the periphery of political culture all blacks and any whites who refused to endorse their vision of a New South. According to the beneficiaries of the commercial order, ignoring those deemed too inferior to possess liberty and virtue and offering marginal white men in the social order an underclass upon whose back they might stand fostered the reformation of a homogeneous world reminiscent of the Old South. Agrarians articulated a different version of homogeneity. Unlike the middle class, which made for itself a place in the commercial order, agrarians believed that they ate the bad fruit of corporate capitalism; penury and dependence on merchants for their sustenance characterized their position. The makers and keepers of the New South despised farmers for failing to retain their place in the social order, and because of their own careless disregard for diversified production and the tenacious power of the crop-lien law, farmers at times despised themselves. To restore tillers of the earth to their rightful place in society, agrarian reformers proposed reviving the political culture of the Jacksonian period and thus to invigorate all white men with an equal chance at securing personal political and economic liberty.

Even after the defeat of Populism in the mid-1890s agrarians continued to shape political culture in Mississippi, though their influence diminished. Demagogic politicians (the so-called "rednecks" who assumed seats of power in the early twentieth century) consciously paid homage to their agrarian predecessors by denouncing privileged power and proclaiming themselves the sons of farmers and protectors of white liberty. Yet where the agrarians of the 1880s and 1890s decried the commercial order, the rednecks treated modernity more gently. Depicting in their rhetoric a society torn between "haves" and "have-nots," they sought as well to sustain the commercial order. In redneck rhetoric the division between the white middle class and white farmers could be overlooked as long as each class compromised its vision of a homogeneous world to accommodate the other and concentrated on the importance of the one aspect of the social ethic that both groups shared: the theories of race that undergirded concepts of white liberty and virtue. Just as in the antebellum period, when concerns about maintaining white cultural homogeneity doused the fiery debate over payment of state debts, the rednecks (without forswearing attacks on privileged power) vaulted to prominence in twentieth-century political culture the notion that white liberty and virtue depended foremost upon the presence of an underclass of brutish folk too degenerate to ascend to citizenship.

The outbreak of race- and class-inspired violence that occurred at the height of the Populist movement provided the milieu in which rednecks rose to infamy. The perpetrators of violence, known as whitecappers (mostly small landowners living in the Piney Woods: "pine top toughs," according to one contemporary), unleashed a carnival of terror against their traditional enemy, African Americans, as well as representatives of the commercial order. Millowners, merchants, and blacks exemplified to whitecappers the antithesis of the good republic; if they could be removed from the state, or at least whipped into submission, long-standing concepts of liberty and virtue might be restored.[1] The union of African-American labor and millowners especially disturbed agrarians because their cooperation bound the degenerate and the makers of the commercial order, a combination guaranteed to reduce white cultivators' authority in the social order. W. T. Rawlins, himself a victim of whitecap threats, discerned the purpose of the vigilantes: "It was entirely a farmers['] organization [that made the threats] for the purpose of protecting themselves against thieving negroes also for the purpose of controlling the labor of the county for the farmers." According to Rawlins, whitecappers perceived their status in the

1. Quoted in William F. Holmes, "Whitecapping in Mississippi: Agrarian Violence in the Populist Era," *Mid America,* LX (1973), 141, 144–45. Holmes argues that Populism was "the enlightened side of agrarian protest, whitecapping the dark side."

social order as endangered by the presence of free black labor, particularly when blacks worked in industry, and intended to make African Americans a submissive people by denying them access to employment in mills and threatening merchants with harm if they extended blacks credit.[2] Unable to secure work as tenants or mill hands, blacks would be forced to pick cotton as seasonal labor, providing small white farmers not only pickers but ample reason to doubt black professions to being liberty-loving and virtuous.

Lumber mill owners and planters, as the chief employers of black labor and owners of large tracts of land, garnered the attention of whitecappers, too. In 1893 John Lemoit and John P. Foxworth of Columbia watched whitecappers drive tenants from their plantations. Lemoit inferred that the whitecappers believed "if we are deprived of labor we will then be forced to sell." The Chicago owners of Norwood and Butterfield (Lincoln County manufacturers of longleaf yellow pine) lost black laborers to whitecap violence. In January, 1893, vigilantes visited workers at night, warning them to terminate their employment or face the full wrath of night riders. Norwood and Butterfield's Mississippi representatives correctly surmised that the company enraged whitecappers because it held vast parcels of land and hired black laborers. Encouraged by the millowners' pleas to protect business interests, Governor Stone posted rewards ranging from $100 to $350 for the capture of whitecappers, and the company paid an additional reward when six confessed brigands stood trial. Norwood and Butterfield's troubles, however, persisted after the arrests and prosecutions. At the close of the year, when farmers looked to sign sharecroppers to contracts, the mill experienced a mysterious series of fires. One destroyed the company's engine house, and another damaged a locomotive.[3]

For roughly five years whitecappers burned barns, stores, and mills in their dual critique of black liberty and the commercial order. The intervention of Governor Stone and the lengthy prison sentences handed convicted whitecappers contributed to the end of the violence, which ceased just as the agrarian revolt collapsed. Whitecappers, however, had not failed to make a lasting impression on their victims. Black mill laborers at Ellisville, nothing more than "pore negros" according to P. K. Meshack, be-

2. W. T. Rawlins to John M. Stone, October 29, 1893, but see, too, D. C. McInnis to Stone, August 15, 1893, all in RG 27, MDAH.

3. Quoting John Lemoit to John M. Stone, February 15, 1893; but see, too, Norwood and Butterfield Company to Stone, January 11, December 12, 1893; Joseph H. Neville to Stone, June 24, 1893; R. M. Wilkerson to Stone, March 27, August 28, 1893, all in RG 27, MDAH. William T. Walthall Diary, July 6, 1892 (in Walthall Papers).

lieved that peace and justice awaited their race only in Africa. "The Whole Reason for the Negros wants to leave, is because theare is so much mobing[.] Lynching are among them till it forces the Negros to wants to go some wheare to prevent such things." The steady retraction of equal protection under the law discouraged blacks from regarding their citizenship in Mississippi as real.[4]

In the midst of the whitecapper reign of abuse, James K. Vardaman, a Delta attorney, first emerged as a player in Mississippi politics. Like James Chalmers, he donned the guise of Democratic party critic and foe of black liberty. Recognizing the racial animosity inherent in the political culture, Vardaman intended to woo farmers uncommitted to the Populist party, as well as middle-class reformers, by using race and the Populist critique of Democratic party hegemony to fuel his 1895 bid for the gubernatorial nomination. During his campaign Vardaman gleefully exposed the machinations of the Democratic party, which, he said, exploited black voters to carry the nomination and election for Anselm J. McLaurin, legatee of the New Departure school. The disfranchisement of blacks promised in the 1890 constitution worked against whomever regular Democrats determined to mistreat. While plain folk struggled against party rules to gain representation in conventions and on tickets, he charged, leading Democrats perpetuated the secret arrangement pioneered by the Lamar wing of the party. Their habit of manipulating black votes to out count dissident whites fomented agrarian loathing for the party, and Varadman spurred farmers to reject the party so that they might proclaim themselves self-respecting citizens no longer willing to brook the arrangement.[5] According to T. J. Ford, Vardaman spoke truthfully about the intentions of the Democratic party: "We have been calculating on the negro vote which is inclined to the straight Democratic [ticket] because of our course in breaking up the whitecaps. When Vardaman was here, he made a most imprudent speech using such expression[s] as these. 'To educate a negro is to spoil a good field hand.'" Vardaman's strategy of driving whites away from the ordained candidate of the Democratic party floundered, however. For Populist contenders employed a similar strategy, denying him his obvious constituency. To many

4. Quoting P. K. Meshack to John M. Stone, August 24, 1895; but see, too, A. E. Perkins to Stone, October 30, 1892, all in RG 27, MDAH. In addition to the restrictions sanctioned by the Constitution of 1890 and whitecap depredations, the state began strictly enforcing Jim Crow rules in public facilities. See, for example, J. M. Buchanan to John M. Stone, November 18, 1891, in RG 27, MDAH, on the segregation of inmates at the East Mississippi Insane Asylum.

5. Kirwan, *Revolt of the Rednecks,* 107–109.

Mississippians Vardaman appeared to be just another rogue politician in a season of rogues.[6]

Vardaman's failure to obtain an office in 1895 fueled his resolve to capture the gubernatorial nomination four years later, but as an officer of the Mississippi National Guard fighting in Cuba, he posed only a minor threat to the Democratic elite's control of the nomination. Nevertheless, he undertook a letter-writing campaign to muster support among Mississippi journalists. As the newspaper editor Henry Waring Ball observed, his cheerleading came too late; party leadership had already anointed Andrew W. Longino as McLaurin's successor. In fact, ring control of the election ensured Vardaman's defeat in the nominations as local leaders, most notably in Hinds and Carroll counties, mobilized solid black support for Longino.[7]

As long as faithful Democrats prescribed party action and nominations, Vardaman and his allies were cut off from political office. Yet in 1902 the passage of a primary election law, which effectively ended clique control of nominations and conventions, lifted Vardaman's hopes. (Since the 1870s some counties had used primary elections to nominate candidates for local offices, and the Populists had taken up the cry for electoral reform in the 1890s. The appearance of blacks at the voting booth in 1895 and 1899 proved to the emerging redneck faction that the Constitution of 1890 fell short of removing blacks from a position of influence in state politics.) Rednecks contended that the 1902 primary law, providing as it did for the popular election of all state officers and county-level party convention delegates, ejected blacks once and for all from the voting process and allowed challengers of Democratic orthodoxy to make a direct appeal to the people. Adopting a rule that counties had previously used to determine voter eligibility, the law required that citizens establish an identity with the party for two years before participating in a primary. A 1903 ruling by the Democratic executive committee prohibited blacks from voting in the party's primary elections, signaling the demise of black voting strength in Mississippi.[8] Heralded as a great reform that restored liberty to the people, the

6. Quoting T. J. Ford to John M. Stone, September 24, 1895, in RG 27, MDAH. McLaurin believed that Vardaman's attempt to capture the non-Populist rural vote backfired. "Vardaman and his friends by their attacks upon me have disgusted the people of the state and are benefitting me wherever it is known," he said. See Anselm J. McLaurin to A. M. Kimbrough, June 24, 1895, in A. M. Kimbrough Family Papers, MDAH.

7. Kirwan, *Revolt of the Rednecks*, 110–21; Ball Diary, February 1, 11, 1899.

8. Edmund F. Noel, "Mississippi Primary Election Laws," Mississippi Historical Society *Publications*, VIII (1904), 261; Kirwan, *Revolt of the Rednecks*, 125–27. See, too, Agnew Diary, July 24, 1891, August 2, 1899. On oppressive features of the primary system, a system designed to produce "a straight Democratic nomination," see Carthage *Carthaginian*, July 12, 1895.

law removed the layers of control over nominations and elections that the Democratic party had enjoyed since 1877. It opened the way for politicians like Vardaman to take their cases to the people and to eschew party executive committees. Old-line politicians, including James McCool (the Canton, Aberdeen, and Nashville Railroad lawyer), found themselves facing a bevy of office seekers determined to portray regular Democrats as oppressors of the people. McCool thought about dropping out of a legislative race in 1906 to avoid the vitriol emanating from his opponent. His son encouraged him to quit the legislature, for the cost of the canvass, both financially and psychologically, exceeded the value of defending oneself against charges made by the political and moral pygmies who had burst upon the political scene.[9]

Besides opening Democratic party politics to those who might formerly have been forced to bolt the party, the primary law demanded that candidates seek the support of the people. The direct intrusion of the people into the nomination process infused the politics of the early twentieth century with a measure of race-baiting not known since 1874. Rednecks' utilization of overtly racist rhetoric and class-conscious characterizations of their Democratic foes distinguished them from other party contenders. But the rednecks also needed the support of Mississippi's respectable bourgeoisie. Curiously, then, Vardaman and his redneck allies endorsed reforms previously advocated by the benefactors of the commercial order, including penitentiary reform, the establishment of a uniform system of textbooks in public schools, statewide prohibition, and the development of good dirt roads, all of which passed the legislature after the rednecks captured state government in 1903.[10] Even though he embraced aspects of middle-class reform, Vardaman achieved his office primarily because he attracted agrarians through the use of class-conscious rhetoric. Not only did he campaign on a racist platform, he promised to reform the commercial order by increasing corporate taxes and checking the distribution of special privileges to defenders of the order.

Toward that end, he focused on the state university, a supposed bastion of privilege that was in fact mired in disciplinary problems. The highly pub-

9. Kirwan, *Revolt of the Rednecks,* 132. Jason McCool to James McCool, October 20, 1906, McCool Family Papers. On his father's contemplated withdrawal from the race, the young McCool posited "I think it is the best for it will take so much money and an iron constitution to go through with it[,] and after all in case of success there is nothing to it but a little honor."

10. George Coleman Osborn, *James Kimble Vardaman: Southern Commoner* (Jackson, 1981), 39; William F. Holmes, *The Great White Chief: James Kimble Vardaman* (Baton Rouge, 1970), 160–65; Kirwan, *Revolt of the Rednecks,* 162–75, 188.

licized difficulties that the university had controlling social fraternities garnered the attention of the newly elected governor and the state house of representatives. At one of Vardaman's first meetings with the Board of Trustees he, according to one observer, "seemed impressed that something was wrong, but wholly unable to designate what it was. . . . The spirit of change combined with a want of information seemed dangerous." Although a majority of the house investigating committee empaneled by Vardaman demurred at criticizing the university, a minority report written by the governor's legislative vanguard labeled the entire university rotten. "Secret societies" exercised an unhealthy influence and relegated poor boys to a second-class citizenship at the university. Hoping to expel fraternities from campus, the minority proclaimed that "the rich and the poor, when they enter her door, must have an equal chance in the great battle of life." [11] Vardaman, however, was slow to upset the university system, though he refused to permit Chancellor Robert B. Fulton to accept a Carnegie Foundation grant to build a university library and eventually appointed a number of his friends to the university's governing board. Then, in 1905, he changed tactics, firing the entire faculty on the chance that he could replace obstreperous opponents. But the purge failed. Too few candidates expressed interest in teaching at the university, forcing Vardaman to rehire most of the faculty, except Fulton (whose brother-in-law, John Sharp Williams, led the anti-Vardaman faction of the party) and several other of his foes.[12]

Considering Vardaman's mixing of class-conscious attacks on special privilege and his race-baiting rhetoric, Jehu Amaziah Orr thought the future of the state grave. "I look upon the future," he said, "with painful apprehension. The Politicians are playing with fire." Other informed and conscientious Mississippians feared the rise of the rednecks, too; after all, they believed, Vardaman's persistent swearing to repeal the Fourteenth and Fifteenth amendments spawned a renewed outbreak of whitecapping (and prompted the federal government to promise a reduction in the state's congressional representation if the rednecks succeeded). Henry Waring Ball also looked upon the situation in Mississippi with a sense of shame. In 1903, after the lynching of an African American accused of attacking a young

11. Quoting R. H. Thompson to Jehu Amaziah Orr, June 10, 1904, in Orr Papers; *Mississippi House Journal*, 1904, pp. 346–47, cited in Holmes, *The Great White Chief*, 169.

12. Early in his administration, Vardaman also warred against other institutions of higher learning. He closed the State Normal College (a black school at Holly Springs), reduced the salaries of academic professors at Alcorn A and M, increased salaries of vocational instructors at the black agricultural and mechanical college, and closed several academic programs at the A and M college at Starkville. See Sansing, *Making Haste Slowly*, 77–79.

white girl, Ball went to see the body hanging from a telephone pole: "It was quite a gala occasion, and as soon as the corpse was cut down all the crowd betook themselves to the park to see a game of baseball. Lord Lord! I am 20 degrees out of my latitude." [13] The irony of rednecks utilizing an instrument of modernity to state their affection for traditional social relations elicited no response from Ball. But in their own despicable way the lynchers offered symbolic evidence of their view of the commercial order: when it served their purposes, particularly if it could be used to limit blacks' claims to citizenship, they readily embraced it.

The easy violence bred by Vardaman's racist rhetoric and his portrayal of wealthy white Mississippians as enemies of poor whites frightened society's respectable members. Like Orr, the Episcopal minister Charles Galloway understood the consequences of Vardaman's pandering to "class prejudice." The chief cause of "the alarming growth of the mob spirit is the small politics of our day—the easy stock-in-trade of the little demagogue." While the little demagogues might in reality have an affection for the commercial order, they cynically juxtaposed class-conscious rhetoric (to lure agrarians to their side) and race-baiting rhetoric (to testify that they rejected political revolution or the overthrow of the commercial order). Populists, in part, had previously tried the strategy, but the rednecks achieved success where the Populists failed because they defended the racial division of society more vigorously than they attacked the commercial order.[14] Skillfully, they espoused a social ethic derived from the middle class and agrarian reform movements, but relied most heavily for their version of a good republic on the element that the movements shared: the idea that white liberty and virtue depended upon the preservation of a black underclass. Under the redneck regimes of the early twentieth century, concepts of the social ethic equated white skin, regardless of its possessors' economic achievement, with liberty and virtue.

13. Quoting Ball Diary, June 5, 1903. See, too, Osborn, *James Kimble Vardaman,* 39. It should be noted that despite his role in precipitating the rebirth of whitecapping, Vardaman helped to quell it as he feared that attacks on the commercial order harmed Mississippi's economy. See A. U. Montgomery to James K. Vardaman, July 28, 1906; a series of letters/reports signed by "A. J. H.," a Pinkerton detective hired by the governor to investigate whitecapping incidents; A. J. H. to Vardaman, March 20, March 3, April 11, April 15, May 2, July 8, 1904, all in RG 27, MDAH.

14. Quoting Charles B. Galloway, "Some Thoughts on Lynching," *South Atlantic Quarterly,* V (October, 1906), 352, rpr. in A. H. Stone Collection. But see also Edgar Gardner Murphy, "Shall the Fourteenth Amendment Be Enforced," *North American Review,* CLXXX (1905), 109–33; Clarence Poe, "Lynching: A Southern View," *Atlantic Monthly,* XCIII (1904), 155–65.

Never mind the changes that had occurred in postbellum Mississippi (the rise of professional men, the advent of industry, the removal of farmers from their once-cherished position of authority and wealth), white citizens continued to look upon the presence of a black underclass as evidence of their own command of liberty and virtue. As had their forefathers in the 1850s, twentieth-century whites created, in the words of James Silver, a "closed society" through which the maintenance of white cultural homogeneity took precedence over all other concerns. Although whites might divide over the roles of industry and agriculture, sustained political discourse focused on blacks' place in the political culture of the South. By the twentieth century white Mississippians understood that any advocate of too thoroughgoing a revolution against the commercial order or traditional values would be branded, in J. W. Biggs's phrase, "a Black bastrd [*sic*]" and "a home made flop." In 1904, at the height of a second outbreak of whitecap violence, Mary Church Terrell, honorary president of the National Association of Colored Women, posited that "lynching is the aftermath of slavery."[15] Had she wished, she might have added that the entire postbellum social ethic, with its overarching defense of white cultural homogeneity, drew upon antebellum theories of race and white southerners' fears that emancipation had forever made impossible the unchallenged assertion of white supremacy. Such was the inheritance left twentieth-century Mississippians by the makers of the political culture of the nineteenth century.

15. Quoting Mary Church Terrell, "Lynching from a Negro's Point of View," *North American Review,* CLXXVIII (1904), 856; J. W. Biggs to John Stone, November 28, 1892, in RG 27, MDAH. See James W. Silver, *Mississippi: The Closed Society* (New York, 1964), especially Intro. and Chapt. 1.

Bibliography

PRIMARY SOURCES

Manuscripts

Amistad Research Center, New Orleans.

American Missionary Association. Papers. Microfilm.

Baker Library, Harvard University, Cambridge.

R. G. Dun and Company. Mercantile Agency Credit Ledgers. Dun Collection. Copiah, Jones, Harrison, Leake, Lowndes, Marshall, Noxubee, Panola, Pontotoc, Warren, Washington, Wilkinson Counties, Mississippi.

Cook Memorial Library, University of Southern Mississippi, Hattiesburg.

Hardy, William H. and Hattie Lott. Papers.

Illinois Central Railroad Company Archives, Newberry Library, Chicago.

Chicago, St. Louis, and New Orleans Railroad Company. Papers.

Map Collection.

Mississippi Central Railroad Company. Papers.

New Orleans, St. Louis, and Chicago Railroad Company. Papers.

Photograph Collection.

Louisiana and Lower Mississippi Valley Collection, Hill Memorial Library, Louisiana State University, Baton Rouge.

Knight, Thomas. Papers.

Percy, Leroy. Papers.

Ware, Catherine Ann and Eleanor. Papers.

Mississippi Department of Archives and History, Jackson.

Adams, Simeon Roe, and Family. Papers.

Alcorn, James L., and Family. Collection.

Alexander, Robert B. Diary and Account Ledger.

Aldridge Family Letters.

Ames, Adelbert. Papers.

Archer-Finlay-Moore. Collection.

Ball, Henry Waring. Diary.

Barnes Family. Papers.

Booth, Roswell Valentine. Journal.

Brantley, A. H. Scrapbook.

Brookdale Farm Record. Typescript on microfilm.

Brumby and Smith Family. Papers.

Calhoon, Solomon S. Papers.

Campbell, Josiah A. P. and Robert. Papers.
Catchings, Dr. Philip Marshall. Collection.
Claiborne, James Francis Hamtrack. Papers. Microfilm.
Clark, Kate Freeman. Collection. Microfilm.
Cook, Mrs. Jared Reese. Diary. Typescript.
Darden Family. Papers. Typescript.
Dunn, Matthew A., and Family. Papers.
Evans, R. A. Papers.
Fewell, John W. Papers.
Fontaine, Charles D., and Family. Papers.
Forbes, Alden Spooner. Diary. Typescript.
Fox, Nathan. Papers.
Fox, Tryphena Holder. Collection. Typescript.
Golladay, George S. Papers.
Gordon, Robert and James. Diaries. Typescript.
Green, William M. Papers.
Griffith, B. W. and Rondo A. Westbrook. Papers.
Harper, Annie E. Manuscript.
Hearn, David Russell, and Family. Papers.
Henry, Patrick. Papers.
Hilgard, Eugene W. Papers.
Humphreys, George Wilson, and Family. Papers.
Humphries, W. W. Estate Plantation Account Book. Microfiche.
Jonas, S. A. Papers.
Jones-Smith Plantation Journal.
Kearney, Belle. "Patrician Days of Madison County."
Killona Plantation Journals, 1836–86. Microfilm.
Kimbrough, A. M., and Family. Papers.
Leverich, Charles P. Papers.
Lightsey, Joseph B. Diary.
Lippincott, Leon S. "History of the Mississippi State Medical Association." 1931. Typescript.
Lockhart-Weir Family. Papers.
Lyon, James A. Journal. Typescript.
Matthews, James and Samuel. Letters. Typescript.
McCardle, William H. Papers.
McCool Family. Papers.
McCorkle, Samuel. Papers.
McNabb, Eliza R. Letters. Typescript.
McRae, John J. Papers.
Meek, Samuel M. Papers.
Middleton Family. Papers.
Miller, Letitia D. "Recollections."

Mississippi Mills Collection.
Nicholson, Flavellus G. Diary-Journal.
Nicholson, Samuel T. Papers.
The 1916 Year Book of the United States Brewers' Association.
Parrott, Johnny. Diary.
Patrons of Husbandry. Mississippi State Grange. Papers.
Port Gibson Bank. Papers.
Regan, Charles K. Papers.
Reynolds, J. E. Papers.
Rollins, Mrs. Roy. Papers.
Smith, Benjamin Lafayette. "Autobiography."
Somerville, Nellie Nugent. Papers. Microfilm.
Stone, Alfred Holt. Collection.
Stone, John Marshall. Papers.
Stone, William A. Papers.
Stuart, Oscar J. E., and Family. Papers.
Subject File Collection. "Reconstruction."
Sullivan, Steve. "Prison Without Walls: A History of the Mississippi State Penal System."
Sykes, Columbus. Papers.
Timberlake, William Poindexter. Papers.
U.S. Army. Officers and Soldiers Miscellany.
Wade, Walter. Plantation Diaries. Microfilm.
Wailes, B. L. C. Diaries. Microfiche.
Walthall, William T. Papers.
Ward, Benjamin F., and Family. Papers.
Weston, Henry, and Family. Papers.
Whitehurst, Mary. Papers.
Wright Family. Papers.
Yerger, Lafayette P. Papers.

Mitchell Memorial Library, Mississippi State University, Starkville.

Baskin Family. Papers.
Carter, Brad. Papers.
Hobbs Family. Papers
Trotter, Sallie Stone. Ledgers. Midway Grange Account Books.

Southern Historical Collection, University of North Carolina, Chapel Hill.

Agnew, Samuel A. Diary. Microfilm.
Alcorn, James Lusk, and Family. Papers.
Bateman, Mary E. Diary.
Broidrick, Annie Laurie. "A Recollection of Thirty Years Ago." Typescript.
Bullock, John and Charles Eaton Hamilton. Papers.
Claiborne, James Francis Hamtrack. Papers.
Crutcher-Shannon Family. Papers.

Dixon, Harry St. John. Papers.
Fowler, Joseph S. Papers.
Gale and Polk Family. Papers.
Harrington, P. C. Papers.
Harrison, James T. Papers.
Henry, Gustavus A. Papers.
Holcombe, William Henry. Books.
Howell, Robert Phillip. "Memoirs."
Johnson, John Lipscomb. Papers.
King, Thomas Butler. Papers.
Lamar, Lucius Quintus Cincinnatus. Papers. Typescript.
Lee, Stephen Dill. Papers.
Lovell, William Storrow. Plantation Journals.
Maury, James F. Diary, 1861.
Metcalfe, James Wistar. Papers.
Niles, Jason. Diary.
Norton-Chilton-Dameron Family. Papers.
Pattison, William J. Papers.
Orr, Jehu Amaziah. Papers.
Quitman Family. Papers.
Roach and Eggleston Family. Papers.
Rust, J. R. Papers.
Scales, Cordelia Lewis. Letters. Typescript.
Worthington, Amanda Dougherty. Papers.
Wright and Herring Family. Papers.

Special Collections, University of Chicago, Chicago.
Douglas, Stephen A. Papers.

Special Collections, University of Mississippi, Oxford.
Lamar, Lucius Quintus Cincinnatus. Collection.
Walthall, Edward Cary. Collection.
West, A. M. Collection.

William R. Perkins Library, Duke University, Durham.
Champion, Sidney. Papers.
Dantzler, Absalom F. Papers.
Davies, Maria Dyer. Papers.
Dimitry, John Bull Smith, Papers.
Downey, Samuel Smith. Papers.
Kelly, John N. Papers.
McDowell, James, II. Papers.
McLaurin, Duncan. Papers.
Meek, Alexander Beaufor and Samuel Mills. Journals.
Reynolds, Lafayette P. Papers.
Shoemaker, Isaac. Diary, 1864.

Vester, Benjamin H. Papers.
Weaver, Phillip J. Papers.
Webber, Thomas E. Diary.
Wilson, Robert. Papers.

Official Papers

Mississippi Department of Archives and History, Jackson.
Record Group 27, Governors' Papers.
Record Group 28, Records of the Secretary of State.

National Archives, Washington, D.C.
Manuscript Census, Schedule I: Free Population, 1840, 1850, 1860. Copiah, Harrison (1840), Jasper, Jones, Leake, Lowndes, Marshall, Noxubee, Panola, Pontotoc, Warren, Washington (except 1860), Wilkinson Counties, Mississippi. Microfilm.
Manuscript Census, Schedule II: Agriculture, 1850, 1860. Copiah, Harrison, Jasper, Jones, Leake, Lowndes, Marshall, Noxubee, Panola, Pontotoc, Warren, Washington (except 1860), Wilkinson Counties, Mississippi. Microfilm.
Manuscript Census, Schedule III: Slave Population, 1850, 1860. Copiah, Harrison, Jasper, Jones, Leake, Lowndes, Marshall, Noxubee, Panola, Pontotoc, Warren, Washington (except 1860), Wilkinson Counties, Mississippi. Microfilm.
Records of the Assistant Commissioner for the State of Mississippi, Bureau of Refugees, Freedmen, and Abandoned Lands. Microfilm.
Source-Chronological File, Northern and Southern Districts of Mississippi, General Records of the Department of Justice, Record Group 60. Microfilm.

Printed Government Documents

Mississippi

The Annotated Code of the General Statute Laws of the State of Mississippi. Nashville, 1892.
Code of Mississippi: Being an Analytical Compilation of the Public and General Statutes of the Territory and State from 1789 to 1840. Jackson, 1848.
Journal of the Convention of the State of Mississippi and the Act Calling the Same with the Constitution of the United States and Washington's Farewell Address. Jackson, 1851.
Journal of the State Convention, and Ordinances and Resolutions Adopted January, 1861, with an Appendix. Jackson, 1861.
Journal of the Proceedings and Debates in the Constitutional Convention of the State of Mississippi, August, 1865. Jackson, 1865.
Journal of the Proceedings in the Constitutional Convention of the State of Mississippi, 1868. Jackson, 1871.
Journal of the Proceedings of the Constitutional Convention of the State of

Mississippi Begun at the City of Jackson on August 12, 1890 and Concluded November 1, 1890. Jackson, 1890.

Laws of the State of Mississippi. Title and place vary, 1824–1903.

Mississippi House Journal, 1852; October Term, 1865; October Term, 1866; 1873; 1888.

Mississippi Reports: Reports of Cases Argued and Determined in the High Court of Errors and Appeals for the State of Mississippi. Vol. XXV of 254 vols. Boston, 1854.

Mississippi Senate Journal, 1840; 1841; 1843; October Term, 1865; October Term, 1866.

Report of the Auditor of Public Accounts, 1881. Jackson, 1881.

Report of the Mississippi State Board of Health. Title and place vary, 1878–1917.

The Revised Code of the Statute Laws of the State of Mississippi of a Public and General Nature. . . . Jackson, 1871.

The Revised Code of the Statute Laws of the State of Mississippi of a Public and General Nature. . . . Jackson, 1880.

The Statutes of the State of Mississippi of a Public and General Nature. . . . New Orleans, 1840.

United States

Congressional Globe. 31st Cong., 1st Sess; 31st Cong., 2nd Sess; 32nd Cong., 1st Sess; 32nd Cong., 2nd Sess.

Congressional Record. 51st Cong., 2nd Sess.

House Document. 22nd Cong., 1st Sess., No. 263.

House Miscellaneous Documents. 40th Cong., 3rd Sess., No 53.

———. 43rd Cong., 2nd Sess., No. 53.

House Reports. 42nd Cong., 2nd Sess., No. 22. Vols. XI, XII.

———. 43rd Cong., 2nd Sess., No. 265.

———. 39th Cong., 1st. Sess. No. 30, Pt. 3.

Mississippi in 1875: Report of the Select Committee to Inquire into the Mississippi Election of 1875, with the Testimony and Documentary Evidence. 2 vols. Washington, D.C., 1876.

Senate Executive Documents. 39th Cong., 1st Sess., No. 2.

Senate Miscellaneous Documents. 50th Cong., 1st Sess., No. 166.

Senate Reports. 38th Cong., 1st Sess., No. 512; 44th Cong., 1st Sess., No. 527; 48th Cong., 1st Sess., No. 512.

U.S. Bureau of the Census. *Agriculture of the United States, 1860: Compiled from the Original Returns of the Eighth Census*. 1864.

———. *Compendium of the Eleventh Census, 1890: Part I, Population*. 1892.

———. *Compendium of the Enumeration of the Inhabitants . . . from the Returns of the Sixth Census*. . . . 1841.

———. *Compendium of the Ninth Census, June 1, 1870*. 1872.

———. *Eleventh Decennial Census of the United States, 1890: Volume I, Population*. 1892.

———. *Mortality Statistics of the Seventh Census of the United States, 1850.* 1855.
———. *Population of the United States in 1860: Compiled from the Original Returns of the Eighth Census.* 1864.
———. *Report on Manufacturing Industries in the United States at the Eleventh Census, 1890: Part I, Totals for States and Industries.* 1895.
———. *Report on the Forests of North America (Exclusive of Mexico): 1880.* Vol. IX. Washington, D.C., 1884.
———. *Report on the Manufacturing of the United States at the Tenth Census, June 1, 1880, Embracing General Statistics.* 1883.
———. *Report on the Mortality and Vital Statistics of the United States as Returned at the Tenth Census.* 1885.
———. *Report on the Production of Agriculture as Returned at the Tenth Census.* 1883.
———. *Report on the Statistics of Agriculture of the United States at the Eleventh Census, 1890.* 1895.
———. *Seventh Census of the United States, 1850.* 1853.
———. *Statistics of the Population of the United States at the Tenth Census.* 1883.
———. *The Statistics of the Population of the United States . . . Compiled from the Original Returns of the Ninth Census.* Vol. I. 1872.
———. *Statistics of the United States (Including Mortality, Property, Etc.) in 1860.* 1866.
———. *The Statistics of Wealth and Industry of the United States . . . Compiled from the Original Returns of the Ninth Census.* Vol. III. 1872.
———. *Tenth Census of the United States, 1880: Population.* 1882.
———. *Thirteenth Census, 1910: Volume II, Population 1910, Reports by States with Statistics for Cities and Other Civil Divisions.* 1912.
———. *Twelfth Census, 1900: Agriculture, Part 1: Farms, Live Stock, and Animal Products.* 1902.
———. *Twelfth Census, 1900: Agriculture, Part 2: Crops and Irrigation.* 1902.
———. *Twelfth Census, 1900: Manufactures, Part II: States and Territories.* 1902.
———. *Twelfth Census, 1900: Population, Part I.* 1901.
U.S. Department of Agriculture. *Dietary Studies with Reference to Food of the Negro in Alabama, 1895–1896.* 1897.
———. Forest Service. *A Forest Atlas of the South.* 1969.
———. *Report of the Secretary of Agriculture, 1893.* 1894.
U.S. Department of the Interior. *Report of the Secretary of Interior.* Various places, 1830–60.
U.S. Department of the Treasury. *Report of the Internal Commerce of the United States: Part II of Commerce and Navigation: The Commercial, Industrial, Transportation, and Other Industries of the Southern States.* 1886.

U.S. Patent Office. *Report of the Commissioner of Patents for the Year 1850.* 1850.

———. *Report of the Commissioner of Patents for the Year 1853.* 1853.

———. *Report of the Commissioner of Patents for the Year 1858.* 1858.

U.S. War Department. *The War of the Rebellion: A Compilation of the Official Records of the Union and Confederate Armies.* 130 vols. Washington, D.C., 1880–1901.

TRAVELERS' ACCOUNTS, MEMOIRS, COMMENTARIES, AND PUBLISHED CORRESPONDENCE

Adams, Nehemiah. *A South-Side View of Slavery: Or Three Months at the South, in 1854.* Boston, 1854.

Alcorn, James L. *Views of the Honorable James L. Alcorn on the Political Situation of Mississippi.* Friar's Point, Miss., 1867.

Allen, William H. "Shadows of Steamboat Life." *Knickerbocker Magazine,* XL (August, 1852), 123–59.

Ames, Blanche, comp. *Chronicles from the Nineteenth Century: Family Letters of Blanche Butler and Adelbert Ames.* Vol. II of 2 vols. Clinton, Mass., 1957.

Aughey, John. *The Iron Furnace: Or Slavery and Secession.* Philadelphia, 1863.

Bailey, T. J. *Prohibition in Mississippi: Or Anti-Liquor Legislation from Territorial Days, with Its Results in the Counties.* Jackson, 1917.

Baird, Robert. *View of the Valley of the Mississippi: Or the Emigrants and Traveller's Guide to the West. . . .* Philadelphia, 1832.

Baldwin, Joseph G. *The Flush Times in Alabama and Mississippi.* 1853; rpr. Americus, Ga., 1898.

Banks, Charles. *Negro Bankers of Mississippi.* Cheyney, Penn., 1908.

Barinetti, Charles. *A Voyage to Mexico and Havana: Including Some General Observations on the United States.* New York, 1841.

Beaumont, Mrs. B[etty]. *Twelve Years of My Life: An Autobiography.* Philadelphia, 1887.

Boyd, Samuel S. *Speech of the Honorable Samuel S. Boyd Delivered at the Great Union Festival Held at Jackson, Mississippi the 16th Day of October, 1851.* Natchez, 1851.

Bullock, William. *Sketch of a Journey Through the Western States of North America . . . in 1827.* London, 1827.

Burwell, A. *Dramshops, Industry and Taxes: Address to the People of Mississippi.* New York, 1875.

Chandler, Greene Callier. *Journal and Speeches of Green Callier Chandler.* Privately published, Memphis, 1955.

Claiborne, J. F. H. "A Trip Through the Piney Woods." Mississippi Historical Society *Publications,* IX (1906).

———. *Life and Correspondence of John A. Quitman, Major-General, U.S.A. and Governor of the State of Mississippi.* 2 vols. New York, 1860.

Cluskey, M. W., ed. *Speeches, Messages, and Other Writings of the Honorable*

Albert G. Brown, a Senator in Congress from the State of Mississippi. Philadelphia, 1859.

Cobb, Joseph B. [A Southron]. "The True Issue Between Parties in the South, Union or Disunion." *The American Whig,* n.s., XXXVI (1851), 587–602.

"Cotton and Cotton Planters." *De Bow's Review,* III (1847), 1–20.

Crist, Lynda Lasswell, ed. *The Papers of Jefferson Davis, 1849–1852.* Vol. IV. Baton Rouge, 1983.

Darden, John P. *The Secret of Success, or Family Affairs: A Memoir in One Volume by a Mississippian.* Cincinnati, 1853.

Davis, Reuben. *Recollections of Mississippi and Mississippians.* Boston, 1891.

De Bow, J. D. B. "Some Thoughts on Political Economy and Government." *De Bow's Review,* IX (1850), 257–271.

Dickens, Charles. *American Notes for General Circulation.* Leipzig, 1842.

Directory and Shipping Guide of Lumber Mills and Lumber Dealers in the United States and Canada. Chicago, 1884.

Ellet, Charles, Jr. *The Mississippi and Ohio Rivers. . . .* Philadelphia, 1853.

Estes, David C., ed. *A New Collection of Thomas Bangs Thorpe's Sketches of the Old Southwest.* Baton Rouge, 1989.

Estes, Matthew. *A Defense of Negro Slavery: As It Exists in the United States.* Montgomery, 1846.

Everest, Robert. *A Journey Through the United States and Part of Canada.* London, 1855.

Fitzhugh, George. *Sociology for the South: Or the Failure of Free Society.* Richmond, 1854.

Flynt, Timothy. *Recollections of the Last Ten Years.* Boston, 1826.

Fox, John A. *A National Duty: Mississippi River Flood Problems: How the Floods Can Be Prevented.* Washington, D.C., 1914.

Frankenfield, H. C. *The Floods of the Spring of 1903 in the Mississippi Watershed.* Washington, D.C., 1904.

Fulkerson, Horace Smith. *The Negro; As He Was; As He Is; As He Will Be.* Vicksburg, 1887.

Galloway, Charles B. *Handbook of Prohibition: Specially Designed for Circulation in the State of Mississippi.* N.p., 1886.

Glenn, D. C. "Mississippi." *De Bow's Review,* VII (1849), 38–44.

Golovin, Ivan. *Stars and Stripes: Or American Impressions.* London, 1856.

Goodspeed Brothers. *Biographical and Historical Memoirs of Mississippi . . . and a Record of the Lives of Many of the Most Worthy and Illustrious Families and Individuals.* 2 vols. Chicago, 1891.

Gould, E. W. *Fifty Years on the Mississippi: Or Gould's History of River Navigation.* 1899; rpr. Columbus, Oh., 1951.

Graf, Leroy P., and Ralph W. Haskins, eds. *The Papers of Andrew Johnson, 1858–1860.* Vol. III. Knoxville, 1972.

Handy, Alexander H. *A Parallel Between the Great Revolution in England in*

1688 and the American Revolution of 1860–1861. Meridian, Miss., 1864.

Hennessy, Una Pope, ed. *The Aristocratic Journey: Being the Outspoken Letters of Mrs. Basil Hall Written During a Fourteen Months' Sojourn in America, 1827–1828. New York, 1931.*

Howard, H. R., comp. *The History of Virgil A. Stewart and His Adventure in Capturing and Exposing the Great "Western Land Pirate" and His Gang in Connexion with the Evidence*. New York, 1836.

Humphries, A. A., and H. L. Abbot. *Report upon the Physics and Hydraulics of the Mississippi River . . . Based upon Surveys and Investigations*. Philadelphia, 1861.

Lamar, L. Q. C., *et al.* "Ought the Negro to be Disfranchised?" *North American Review*, LXXVIII (1879), 231–38.

Letter of Lucius Q. C. Lamar in Reply to Honorable P. F. Liddell of Carollton, Mississippi. N.p., n.d.

Lynch, John Roy. *Reminiscences of an Active Life: The Autobiography of John Roy Lynch*. Edited by John Hope Franklin. Chicago, 1970.

Mayes, Edward. *L. Q. C. Lamar: His Life, Times and Speeches, 1825–1893*. Nashville, 1896.

McCain, William David, and Charlotte Capers, eds. *Memoirs of Henry Tillinghast Ireys: Papers of the Washington County Historical Society, 1910–1919*. Jackson, 1954.

McGehee, Miles H. "How Shall Cotton Maintain Remunerating Prices?" *De Bow's Review*, VII (1849), 73–75.

McKibben, Davison Burns, ed. "Extract of a Letter from a Gentleman in Clinton, Mississippi to a Gentleman in Lynchburg, Virginia, Dated the 5th of July, 1835." *Journal of Negro History*, XXXIV (1949), 91–94.

McLaughlin, Andrew C. "Mississippi and the Negro Question." *Atlantic Monthly*, LXX (1892), 828–37.

Millsaps, R. W. "History of Banking in Mississippi." *Sound Currency*, X (March, 1903), 16–48.

Mississippi Boy Convicts. Jackson, 1911.

A Mississippi Planter. "Production and Manufacture of Cotton." *De Bow's Review*, VIII (1850), 99–101.

Mitchell, Samuel Augustus. *Mitchell's Traveller's Guide Through the United States. . . .* Philadelphia, 1836.

Morgan, Albert T. *Yazoo: Or on the Picket Line of Freedom in the South: A Personal Narrative*. 1884; rpr. New York, 1986.

Murphy, Edgar Gardner. "Shall the Fourteenth Amendment Be Enforced." *North American Review*, CLXXX (1905), 109–33.

"Negro Agrarianism." *De Bow's Review*, After the War Series, V (February, 1868), 134–138.

Orr, J. A. "A Trip from Houston to Jackson, Mississippi, in 1845." Mississippi Historical Society *Publications*, IX (1906), 173–78.

Parsons, C. G. *Inside View of Slavery: Or a Tour Among the Planters.* Boston, 1855.

Patton, W. H. "History of the Prohibition Movement in Mississippi." Mississippi Historical Society *Publications,* X (1909), 181–202.

Phillips, M. W. "Duty of Cotton Planters," *De Bow's Review,* VII (1849), 410–412.

Poe, Clarence. "Lynching: A Southern View." *Atlantic Monthly,* XCIII (1904); 155–65.

Pulszkey, Francis, and Theresa Pulszkey. *White, Red, Black: Sketches of American Society in the United States During the Visit of Their Guests.* New York, 1853.

Rawick, George, ed. *The American Slave: A Composite Autobiography, Supplement.* Vols. VI and VII of 41 vols. Westport, Conn., 1977.

Reid, Whitelaw. *After the War: A Southern Tour, May 11, 1865 to May, 1866.* Cincinnati, 1866.

Rogers, George. *Memoranda of the Experiences, Labors, and Travels of a Universalist Preacher.* Cincinnati, 1845.

Rowland, Dunbar. *Jefferson Davis, Constitutionalist: His Letters, Papers, and Speeches.* Vol. II of 2 vols. Jackson, 1923.

Seal, Albert Garrel, ed. "Letters from the South: A Mississippian's Defense of Slavery." *Journal of Mississippi History,* II (1940), 212–31.

Shackleford, Thomas. *Proceedings of the Citizens of Madison County, Mississippi and Livingston, in July 1835, in Relation to the Trial and Punishment of Several Individuals Implicated in a Contemplated Insurrection in the State.* Jackson, 1836.

Smedes, Susan Dabney. *Memorials of a Southern Planter.* Baltimore, 1888.

Somers, Robert. *The Southern States Since the War, 1870–1871.* 1871; rpr. University, Ala., 1965.

Somerville, Nellie Nugent. *Moral Leadership: The True Basis of Woman Suffrage.* Greenville, n.d.

A Southwestern Planter. "True Remedy for the Embarrassment of Cotton Planters of the South and Southwest." *De Bow's Review,* I (1846), 434–36.

Sparks, W. H. *The Memories of Fifty Years . . . Chiefly Spent in the Southwest.* 4th ed. Philadelphia, 1882.

Starling, William. *The Floods of the Mississippi River . . . with a Particular Account of the Great Flood of 1897.* New York, 1897.

Terrell, Mary Church. "Lynching from a Negro's Point of View." *North American Review,* CLXXVIII (1904), 853–68.

Tracy, S. M. *Mississippi as It Is: A Handbook of Facts for Immigrants.* Jackson, 1895.

Trowbridge, J. T. *A Picture of the Desolated States: And the Work of Restoration, 1865–1868.* Hartford, 1868.

Van Buren, A. De Puy. *Jottings of a Year's Sojourn in the South . . . and Reminiscences of Distinguished Men.* 1859; rpr. Louisville, 1960.

Wailes, B. L. C. *Report on the Agriculture and Geology of Mississippi: Embracing a Sketch of the Social and Natural History of the State.* Jackson, 1854.

Wall, E. G. *Handbook of the State of Mississippi.* Jackson, 1882.

———. *The State of Mississippi: Resources, Condition and Wants. . . .* Jackson, 1879.

Weems, Mrs. Albert G. "Work of the United Daughters of the Confederacy." Mississippi Historical Society *Publications,* IV (1901), 73–78.

Woodward, D. W. *Negro Progress in a Mississippi Town: Being a Study of Conditions in Jackson, Mississippi.* Cheyney, Penn., 1908.

CONTEMPORARY PUBLICATIONS RELATING TO BUSINESS, EDUCATION, AND PROFESSIONAL SOCIETIES

Annual Report of the President and Directors of the Mississippi Central Railroad Company to the Stockholders, for the Year Ending August 31, 1867. New Albany, Ind., 1867.

Cobb, Charles. *American Railway Guide and Pocket Companion for the United States.* New York, 1851.

Directory by States and Counties of More Than Eight Thousand of the Students and Graduates of Eastman, Poughkeepsie, New York: Part Two, Southern and Gulf States. N.p., 1908.

Directory for the City of Mobile, 1859. Mobile, 1859.

Illinois Central Railroad Company. *One Hundred Cities and Towns Wanting Industries . . . on the Lines of the Illinois Central Railroad and Yazoo and Mississippi Valley Railroad.* Chicago, n.d.

Illinois Central Railroad Company. *Railroad Lands for Sale Owned by the Yazoo and Mississippi Valley Railroad Company in the Famous Yazoo Valley of Mississippi.* N.p., 1896.

Kimball and James' Business Directory, for the Mississippi Valley, 1844. Cincinnati, 1844.

Larnder, Dionysius. *Railway Economy: A Treatise on the New Art of Transport, Its Movement, Prospects, and Relations . . . in America.* New York, 1850.

Lewis' Southern Directory, 1871 and 1872. N.p., n.d.

Maloney's 1907 Jackson City Directory. N.p., n.d.

Manual of the Public Schools of Hattiesburg, Mississippi, 1910–1911. Hattiesburg, n.d.

Mississippi Women's Christian Temperance Union: Report of the Thirtieth Annual Convention, Held in Tupelo, Mississippi, October 11th to 14th, 1914. Jackson, 1914.

Mississippi Women's Christian Temperance Union: Report of the Thirty First Annual Convention, Held in Europa, Mississippi, October 23rd to 26th, 1915. N.p., n.d.

Ninth Annual Report of the President and Directors of the Mississippi and Tennessee Railroad. . . . Memphis, 1865.

Poor, Henry V. *Manual of the Railroads of the United States, 1890*. New York, 1890.

———. *Manual of the Railroads of the United States, 1900*. New York, 1900.

———. *Manual of the Railroads of the United States, 1910*. New York, 1910.

Proceedings of the Mississippi Bankers' Association: Twenty-Fifth Annual Convention, West Point, Mississippi, May 20–21, 1913. Jackson, 1913.

Proceedings of the Mississippi Bankers' Association: Twenty-Sixth Annual Convention: Vicksburg, May 5–6, 1914. N.p., n.d.

Proceedings of the Mississippi Bar Association at its Sixth Annual Meeting Held January 6, 1891. Jackson, 1892.

Report of the Second Annual Meeting of the Mississippi State Bar Association Held at Vicksburg, Mississippi, May 7th, 8th, and 9th, 1907. N.p., n.d.

Sixth Annual Report of the President and Directors of the Mississippi and Tennessee Railroad. . . . Memphis, 1859.

The Southern Business Directory and General Commercial Advertiser. Vol. I of 2 vols. Charleston, S.C., 1854.

Transactions of the Mississippi State Medical Association at the Fifth Annual Session Held at Holly Springs April 3rd and 4th, 1872, with Constitution and By-Laws and Roll of Members. Columbus, Miss., 1872.

Transactions of the Twenty-Fourth Annual Session of the Mississippi State Medical Association Held at Meridian April 16th and 17th, 1891. Jackson, 1891.

Transactions of the Twenty-Seventh Annual Session of the Mississippi State Medical Association Held at Jackson April 4th, 5th, and 6th, 1894, with Rolls of Members. Jackson, 1894.

Yazoo and Mississippi Valley Company: Laws and Documents. Vol. I of 2 vols. N.p., n.d.

CONTEMPORARY PERIODICALS

De Bow's Review, 1847–60.

De Bow's Review, After the War Series, 1865–72.

Rural Carolinian, 1870–73.

Mississippi Medical Monthly, 1891–94.

NEWSPAPERS

Ackerman *Choctaw Plaindealer,* 1888, 1890, 1894, 1897

Batesville *Weekly Panolian,* 1902

Carthage *Carthaginian,* 1885–95

Crystal Springs *Meteor,* 1883, 1885, 1889

Crystal Springs *Monitor,* 1882–83

Columbus *Patron of Husbandry,* 1879

Columbus *Southern Sentinel,* 1866–67

Forest *Weekly Register,* 1869–73

Grenada *Gazette,* 1888, 1889

Grenada *Sentinel,* 1882–94

Hazelhurst *Copiah Signal,* 1882–90
Jackson *Comet,* 1880
Jackson *Daily Clarion,* 1868, 1875
Jackson *Evening News,* 1898–99
Jackson *Mississippian,* 1840–59
Jackson *Mississippian and State Gazette,* 1851–59
Jackson *New Mississippian,* 1883–86, 1889, 1890
Jackson *Weekly Clarion,* 1873–90
Jackson *Weekly Clarion-Ledger,* 1884, 1886, 1888–90
Jackson *Weekly Mississippian,* 1860
Lexington *Union,* 1840–41
Lexington *Whig Republican,* 1840
Liberty *Advocate,* 1845
Macon *Mississippi Sun,* 1884, 1888, 1891
Macon *New South,* 1881
Meridian *Mississippi White Ribbon,* 1888–90
Natchez *Daily Courier,* 1866
Natchez *Daily Democrat,* 1875
Natchez *Daily Democrat and Courier,* 1877, 1887
Natchez *Evening Banner,* 1892
Natchez *Mississippi Free Trader,* 1843–51
Natchez *Mississippi Free Trader and Natchez Gazette,* 1849–51
Natchez *Weekly Democrat,* 1868
Raymond *Hinds County Gazette,* 1850–51, 1884, 1886, 1889–90
Vicksburg *Daily Whig,* 1840–58
Vicksburg *Evening Banner,* 1887
Vicksburg *Tri-Weekly Whig,* 1840–55
Vicksburg *Weekly Whig,* 1844–60
Woodville *Republican,* 1840–43

SECONDARY SOURCES

Published Articles and Essays

Alston, Lee J., and Robert Higgs. "Contractual Mix in Southern Agriculture Since the Civil War: Facts, Hypothesis, and Tests." *Journal of Economic History,* XLII (1982), 327–53.

Anderson, Mrs. W. A. "A Chapter in the Yellow Fever Epidemic of 1878." Mississippi Historical Society *Publications,* X (1909), 223–36.

Appleby, Joyce. "Modernization Theory and the Formation of Modern Social Theories in England and America." *Comparative Studies in Society and History,* XX (1978), 259–85.

Arsenault, Raymond. "The End of the Long Hot Summer: The Air Conditioner and Southern Culture." *Journal of Southern History,* L (1984), 597–628.

Barney, William L. "Patterns of Crisis: Alabama White Families and Rural Change, 1850–1870." *Sociology and Social Research,* LXIII (1979), 524–43.

Battalio, Raymond C., and John Kagel. "The Structure of Antebellum Southern Agriculture: South Carolina, a Case Study." *Agricultural History,* XLIV (1970), 25–37.

Baxter, Robert J. "Cattle Raising in Early Mississippi: Reminiscences." *Mississippi Folklore Register,* X (1976), 1–23.

Blumin, Stuart M. "The Hypothesis of Middle-Class Formation in Nineteenth Century America: A Critique and Some Proposals." *American Historical Review,* XC (1985), 302–38.

Bond, Bradley G. "Edward C. Walthall and the 1880 Senatorial Nomination: Politics of Balance in the Redeemer Era." *Journal of Mississippi History,* L (1988), 1–20.

———. "Habits of Foodstuff and Market Production: A Look at Mississippi." *Journal of Mississippi History,* LVI (August, 1994), 211–31.

Braden, W. H. "Reconstruction in Lee County." Mississippi Historical Society *Publications,* X (1909), 135–46.

Brough, Charles Hillman. "History of Taxation in Mississippi." Mississippi Historical Society *Publications,* II (1899), 113–24.

Brown, Marice C. "Early Pharmaceutics in the Deep South." *Mississippi Folklore Register,* VIII (1974), 232–40.

Campbell, E. G. "Indebted Railroads: A Problem of Reconstruction." *Journal of Southern History,* VI (1940), 167–88.

Campbell, J. A. P. "Union and Planter's Bank Bonds." Mississippi Historical Society *Publications,* IV (1901), 493–98.

Coclanis, Peter A. "Bookkeeping in the Eighteenth-Century South: Evidence from Newspapers Advertisements." *South Carolina Historical Magazine,* XCI (1990), 23–31.

Coleman, E. C., Jr. "Reconstruction in Attala County." Mississippi Historical Society *Publications,* X (1911), 147–64.

Coleman, James P. "The Origin of the Constitution of 1890." *Journal of Mississippi History,* XIX (1957), 69–92.

Cooper, William J., Jr. "The Cotton Crisis in the Antebellum South: Another Look." *Agricultural History,* XLIX (1975), 381–391.

DeCanio, Stephen. "Cotton 'Overproduction' in Late Nineteenth-Century Southern Agriculture." *Journal of Economic History,* XXXIII (1973), 608–33.

Diggins, John Patrick. "Comrades and Citizens: New Mythologies in American Historiography." *American Historical Review,* XC (1985), 614–38.

Drake, Winbourne, M. "The Mississippi Reconstruction Convention of 1865." *Journal of Mississippi History,* XXI (1959), 225–56.

Ellis, David Maldwyn. "The Forfeiture of Railroad Land Grants, 1867–1894." *Mississippi Valley Historical Review,* XXXIII (1946), 27–60.

Evans, W. A. "Steamboats on the Upper Tombigbee in the Early Days." *Journal of Mississippi History,* IV (1942), 216–24.

Faulkner, William. "Mississippi." In *Essays, Speeches, and Public Letters,* edited by James B. Meriwether. London, 1967.

Fischer, David Hackett. "Climate and History: Priorities for Research." *Journal of Interdisciplinary History,* X (1980), 821–30.

Ford, Lacy K. "Rednecks and Merchants: Economic Development and Social Tensions in the South Carolina Upcountry, 1865–1900." *Journal of American History,* LXXI (1984), 294–318.

———. "Yeoman Farmers in the South Carolina Upcountry: Changing Production Patterns in the Late Antebellum Era." *Agricultural History,* LX (1986), 17–37.

Gallman, Robert E. "Self-Sufficiency in the Cotton Economy of the Antebellum South." *Agricultural History,* XLIV (1970), 5–23.

Genovese, Eugene. "Yeomen Farmers in a Slaveholders' Democracy." *Agricultural History,* XLIX (1975), 331–42.

Goldfield, Michael. "The Color of Politics in the United States: White Supremacy as the Main Explanation for the Peculiarities of American Politics from Colonial Times to the Present." In *The Bounds of Race: Perspectives on Hegemony and Resistance,* edited by Dominick LaCapra. Ithaca, 1991.

Gonzales, John Edmond. "Henry Stuart Foote: A Forgotten Unionist of the Forties." *Southern Quarterly,* I (1963), 129–39.

Guice, John D. W. "Cattle Raisers of the Old Southwest: A Reinterpretation." *Western Historical Quarterly,* VIII (1977), 167–87.

Hahn, Steven. "The Yeomanry of the Non-plantation South: Upper Piedmont Georgia, 1850–1860." In *Class, Conflict, and Consensus: Antebellum Southern Community Studies,* edited by Orville Vernon Burton and Robert C. McMath. Westport, Conn., 1982.

Halsell, Willie D. "Democratic Dissensions in Mississippi, 1878–1882." *Journal of Mississippi History,* II (1940), 123–35.

———. "James R. Chalmers and 'Mahoneism' in Mississippi." *Journal of Southern History,* X (1944), 37–58.

———, ed. "Republican Factionalism in Mississippi, 1882–1884." *Journal of Southern History,* VII (1941), 84–101.

Harrison, Robert W. "Levee Building in Mississippi Before the Civil War." *Journal of Mississippi History,* XII (1950), 63–97.

Haygood, Tamara Miner. "Cows, Ticks, and Disease: A Medical Interpretation of the Southern Cattle Industry." *Journal of Southern History,* LII (1986), 551–64.

Hearon, Cleo. "Mississippi and the Compromise of 1850." Mississippi Historical Society *Publications,* XIV (1914), 7–230.

Hickman, Nollie W. "The Lumber Industry in South Mississippi, 1890–1915." *Journal of Mississippi History,* XX (1958), 211–23.

Hilliard, Sam Bowers. "Hog Meat and Cornpone: Food Habits in the Antebellum South." *Proceedings of the American Philosophical Society,* CXIII (1969), 1–13.

Hodge, Jo Dent. "The Lumber Industry in Laurel, Mississippi, at the Turn of the Nineteenth Century." *Journal of Mississippi History,* XXV (1973), 361–79.

Holman, Hamilton. "Democratic Senate Leadership and the Compromise of 1850." *Mississippi Valley Historical Review,* XLI (1954), 403–18.

Holmes, William F. "The Leflore County Massacre and the Demise of the Colored Farmers' Alliance." *Phylon,* XXXVIII (1973), 267–74.

———. "Whitecapping in Mississippi: Agrarian Violence in the Populist Era." *Mid America,* LX (1973), 134–48.

Hughes, John S. "Labeling and Treating Black Mental Illness in Alabama, 1861–1910." *Journal of Southern History,* LVIII (1992), 435–60.

Humphrey, George D. "Public Education for Whites in Mississippi." *Journal of Mississippi History,* III (1941), 26–36.

Hutchinson, William K., and Samuel H. Williamson. "The Self-Sufficiency of the Antebellum South: Estimates of the Food Supply." *Journal of Economic History,* XXXI (1971), 591–612.

Johnson, Charles Ripley. "Railroad Legislation and Building in Mississippi, 1830–1840." *Journal of Mississippi History,* IV (1942), 195–206.

Katz, Michael B., Michael J. Doucet, and Mark J. Stern. "Migration and the Social Order in Erie County, New York, 1855." *Journal of Interdisciplinary History,* VIII (1978), 669–701.

Kellar, Herbert A., ed. "A Journey Through the South in 1836: Diary of James D. Davidson." *Journal of Southern History,* I (1935), 345–77.

Kelly, Arthell, and Robert C. Spillman, "Sequence Occupancy of the Piney Woods in Southeastern Mississippi, 1805–1976." *Mississippi Geographer,* IV (1976), 25–40.

Kirwan, Albert. "Apportionment in the Mississippi Constitution of 1890." *Journal of Southern History,* XIV (1948), 234–46.

Koeniger, A. Cash. "Climate and Southern Distinctiveness." *Journal of Southern History,* LIV (1988), 21–44.

Leftwich, George. "Reconstruction in Monroe County." Mississippi Historical Society *Publications,* IX (1906), 53–84.

Legan, Marshall Scott. "Mississippi and the Yellow Fever Epidemic of 1878–1879." *Journal of Mississippi History,* XXXIII (1971), 199–217.

———. "A Nineteenth-Century Treatment of Yellow Fever." *Mississippi Folklore Register,* VI (1972), 91–93.

Lichtenstein, Alex. "Good Roads and Chain Gangs in the Progressive South: 'The Negro Convict is a Slave.'" *Journal of Southern History,* LIX (1993), 85–110.

McCardell, John. "John A. Quitman and the Compromise of 1850." *Journal of Mississippi History,* XXXVII (1975), 239–66.

McCorkle, James L., Jr. "Nineteenth Century Beginnings of the Commercial Vegetable Industry in Mississippi." *Journal of Mississippi History,* XXX (1968), 260–74.

McDonald, Forest, and Grady McWhiney. "The Antebellum Southern Herdsman: A Reinterpretation." *Journal of Southern History,* XLI (1975), 147–68.

———. "The South from Self-Sufficiency to Peonage: An Interpretation." *American Historical Review,* LXXXV (1980), 1095–118.

McGuire, Robert, and Robert Higgs. "Cotton, Corn, and Risk in the Nineteenth Century: Another View." *Explorations in Economic History,* XIV (1977), 167–182.

McKee, James W., Jr. "William Barksdale and the Congressional Election of 1853 in Mississippi." *Journal of Mississippi History,* XXXIV (1972), 129–58.

McKibben, Davison Burns. "Negro Slave Insurrections in Mississippi, 1800–1865." *Journal of Negro History,* XXXIV (1949), 73–90.

Martin, J. M. "True History of Incorporation of the Industrial Institute and College." Mississippi Historical Society *Publications,* Centenary Series, IV (1921), 277–80.

Merrill, Michael. "Cash is Good to Eat: Self-Sufficiency and Exchange in the Rural Economy of the United States." *Radical History Review,* IV (1977), 42–66.

Miles, Edwin A. "The Mississippi Slave Insurrection Scare of 1835." *Journal of Negro History,* XLII (1957), 48–60.

Noel, Edmund F. "Mississippi Primary Election Laws." Mississippi Historical Society *Publications,* VIII (1904), 253–92.

Orr, Ellen. "The Bottle Tree." *Mississippi Folklore Register,* III (1969), 109–11.

Owens, Harry P. "Steamboat Landings on the Yazoo and Tallahatchie Rivers (1875–1882)." *Journal of Mississippi History,* XLVII (1985), 266–83.

Ownby, Ted. "The Defeated Generation at Work: White Farmers in the Deep South, 1865–1890." *Southern Studies,* XXIII (1984), 325–47.

Price, Beulah, M. D'Olive. "The Dog-Trot Log Cabin: A Development in American Folk Architecture." *Mississippi Folklore Register,* IV (1970), 92–93.

———. "The Legendary Panther of the Forks of Hatchie." *Mississippi Folklore Register,* V (1971), 15–18.

Puckett, E. F. "Reconstruction in Monroe County." Mississippi Historical Society *Publications,* XI (1910), 103–62.

Ransom, Roger, and Richard Sutch. "Debt Peonage in the Cotton South After the Civil War." *Journal of Economic History,* XXXII (1972), 641–69.

———. "The Ex-Slave in the Post-Bellum South: A Study of the Economic Impact of Racism in a Market Environment." *Journal of Economic History,* XXXIII (1973), 131–48.

———. "The Impact of the Civil War and of Emancipation on Southern Agriculture." *Explorations in Economic History,* XII (1975), 1–28.

———. "The 'Lock-In' Mechanism and Overproduction of Cotton in the Postbellum South." *Agricultural History,* IL (1975), 405–25.

Reid, Joseph D., Jr. "Sharecropping as an Understandable Market Response: The Post-Bellum South." *Journal of Economic History,* XXXIII (1973), 106–30.

———. "Sharecropping in History and Theory." *Agricultural History,* XLIX (1975), 426–40.

———. "White Land, Black Labor, and Agricultural Stagnation: The Causes and Effects of Sharecropping in the Postbellum South." *Explorations in Economic History,* XVI (1979), 31–55.

Roland, Charles P. "The Ever-Vanishing South." *Journal of Southern History,* XLVIII (1982), 3–20.

Ross, Dorothy. "The Liberal Tradition Revisited and the Republican Tradition Addressed." In *New Directions in American Intellectual History,* edited by John Higham and Paul Conkin. Baltimore, 1979.

Rothstein, Morton. "The Antebellum South as a Dual Economy: A Tentative Hypothesis." *Agricultural History,* XLI (1967), 373–82.

Schmitz, Mark D. "Farm Interdependence in the Antebellum Sugar Sector." *Agricultural History,* LII (1978), 93–103.

Shalhope, Robert. "Race, Class, Slavery, and the American Southern Mind." *Journal of Southern History,* XXXVII (1971), 557–75.

———. "Thomas Jefferson's Republicanism and Antebellum Southern Thought." *Journal of Southern History,* XLII (1976), 529–56.

———. "Toward a Republican Synthesis: The Emergence of an Understanding of Republicanism in American Historiography." *William and Mary Quarterly,* 3rd ser., XXIX (1972), 49–80.

Shammas, Carole. "How Self-Sufficient Was Early America?" *Journal of Interdisciplinary History,* XIII (1982), 247–72.

Shingleton, Royce. "The Republic of Porkdom." *Proceedings of the American Philosophical Society,* CLXII (1968), 407–10.

———. "The Utility of Leisure: Game as a Source of Food in the Old South." *Mississippi Quarterly,* XXV (1972), 429–46.

Skates, John Ray. "The Early Years." In *Hattiesburg: A Pictorial History,* edited by Kenneth G. McCarty. Jackson, 1982.

Smith, John David. "More Than Slaves Less Than Freedmen: The 'Share Wages' Labor System During Reconstruction." *Civil War History,* XXVI (1980), 256–66.

Snyder, Perry A. "Remedies of the Pineywoods Pioneers." *Mississippi Folklore Register,* VII (1973), 11–14.

Thompson, R. H. "Suffrage in Mississippi." Mississippi Historical Society *Publications,* I (1898), 25–49.

Thorne, Mildred. "A Population Study of an Iowa County in 1850." *Iowa Journal of History,* LVII (1959), 331–54.

Turner, Mrs. Arthur. "Turkey Drives: South Mississippi, Greene County." *Mississippi Folklore Register,* III (1969), 31–32.

Vickers, Ovid S. "The Stratton Booger." *Mississippi Folklore Register,* IV (1970), 92–93.

Weiman, David F. "Farmers and the Market in Antebellum America: A View from the Georgia Upcountry." *Journal of Economic History,* XLVII (1987), 627–47.

Witty, Fred M. "Reconstruction in Carroll and Montgomery Counties." Mississippi Historical Society *Publications,* X (1909), 115–34.

Woodman, Harold. "Economic Reconstruction and the Rise of the New South, 1865–1900." In *Interpreting Southern History: Historiographical Essays in Honor of Sanford W. Higginbotham,* edited by John Boles and Evelyn Thomas Nolen. Baton Rouge, 1987.

Wright, Galvin, and Howard Kunreuther. "Cotton, Corn and Risk in the Nineteenth Century." *Journal of Economic History,* XXV (1975), 526–551.

Books

Allen, Michael. *Western Rivermen, 1763–1861: Ohio and Mississippi Boatmen and the Myth of the Alligator Horse.* Baton Rouge, 1990.

Appleby, Joyce. *Capitalism and a New Social Order: The Republic Vision of the 1790s.* New York, 1985.

———. *Liberalism and Republicanism in the Historical Imagination.* Cambridge, Mass., 1992.

Ashkenazi, Elliott. *The Business of Jews in Louisiana, 1840–1875.* Tuscaloosa, 1988.

Ayers, Edward L. *The Promise of the New South: Life After Reconstruction.* New York, 1992.

Bailyn, Bernard. *Ideological Origins of the American Revolution.* Cambridge, Mass., 1967.

Barney, William L. *The Secessionist Impulse: Alabama and Mississippi in 1860.* Princeton, 1974.

Barron, Hal S. *Those Who Stayed Behind: Rural Society in Nineteenth-Century New England.* New York, 1979.

Bettersworth, John. *Confederate Mississippi: The People and Policies of a Cotton State in Wartime.* Baton Rouge, 1943.

Brandfon, Robert L. *Cotton Kingdom of the New South: A History of the Yazoo Mississippi Delta from Reconstruction to the Twentieth Century.* Cambridge, Mass., 1967.

Brown, Richard D. *Modernization: The Transformation of American Life, 1600–1865.* New York, 1976.

Burnham, W. Dean. *Presidential Ballots, 1836–1892.* Baltimore, 1955.

Burton, Orville Vernon. *In My Father's House Are Many Mansions: Family and Community in Edgefield, South Carolina.* Chapel Hill, 1985.

Cain, Cyril Edward, ed. *Four Centuries on the Pascagoula: History and Genealogy of the Pascagoula River Country.* 2 vols. 1962; rpr. Spartanburg, 1983.

Cash, W. J. *The Mind of the South.* 1941; rpr. New York, 1969.

Cecil-Fronsman, Bill. *Common Whites: Class and Culture in Antebellum North Carolina.* Lexington, Ky., 1992.

Clark, Christopher. *The Roots of Rural Capitalism: Western Massachusetts, 1780–1860.* Ithaca, 1990.

Clark, Thomas D. *Pills, Petticoats, and Plows: The Southern Country Store.* Indianapolis, 1944.

Clark, Thomas D., and John D. Guice. *The Old Southwest, 1795–1830.* Albuquerque, 1989.

Cobb, James C. *The Most Southern Place on Earth: The Mississippi Delta and the Roots of Southern Identity.* New York, 1992.

Coclanis, Peter. *Shadow of a Dream: Life and Death in the South Carolina Low-country.* New York, 1989.

Coker, William L. *Repudiation and Reaction: Tilghman M. Tucker and the Mississippi Bond Question.* Floral Park, Fla., 1969.

Cole, Arthur Harrison. *Wholesale Commodity Prices in the United States, 1700–1861: A Statistical Supplement: Actual Wholesale Prices of Various Commodities.* Cambridge, Mass., 1938.

Coleman, J. P. *Choctaw County Chronicles: A History of Choctaw County, 1830–1973.* Ackerman, Miss., 1973.

Cooper, William J., Jr. *Liberty and Slavery: Southern Politics to 1860.* New York, 1983.

———. *The South and the Politics of Slavery, 1828–1856.* Baton Rouge, 1979.

Cowdrey, Albert E. *This Land, This South: An Environmental History.* Lexington, Ky., 1983.

Cronon, William. *Changes in the Land: Indians, Colonists, and the Ecological History of New England.* New York, 1983.

Crow, Jeffery J., Paul D. Escott, and Charles L. Flynn, Jr. *Race, Class, and Politics in Southern History: Essays in Honor of Robert F. Durden.* Baton Rouge, 1989.

Diggins, John Patrick. *The Lost Soul of American Politics.* New York, 1984.

Doyle, Don Harrison. *The Social Order in a Frontier Community, Jacksonville, Illinois, 1825–1870.* Urbana, Ill., 1978.

Dubay, Robert W. *John Jones Pettus, Mississippi Fire-Eater: His Life and Times, 1813–1867.* Jackson, 1975.

Duffy, John. *The Sanitarians: A History of American Public Health.* Urbana, Ill., 1990.

Durden, Robert F. *The Climax of Populism: The Election of 1896.* Lexington, Ky., 1965.

Eisenstadt, S. N. *Modernization: Protest and Change.* Englewood Cliffs, N.J., 1966.

Ellis, John H. *Yellow Fever and Public Health in the New South.* Lexington, Ky., 1992.

Faulkner, William. *Absalom, Absalom!* 1936; rpr. New York, 1964.

———. *The Hamlet.* 1931; rpr. New York, 1964.

Faust, Drew Gilpin. *James Henry Hammond and the Old South: A Design for Mastery.* Baton Rouge, 1982.

Fitzgerald, Michael. *The Union League Movement in the Deep South.* Baton Rouge, 1989.

Flynn, Charles L., Jr. *White Land, Black Labor: Caste and Class in Late Nineteenth-Century Georgia.* Baton Rouge, 1983.

Fogel, Robert William, and Stanley L. Engerman. *Time on the Cross: Evidence and Methods: A Supplement.* Boston, 1974.

Foner, Eric. *Free Soil, Free Labor, Free Men: The Ideology of the Republican Party Before the Civil War.* New York, 1970.

Ford, Lacy K., Jr. *Origins of Southern Radicalism: The South Carolina Upcountry, 1800–1860.* New York, 1988.

Formisano, Ronald P. *The Transformation of Political Culture: Massachusetts Parties, 1790s–1840s.* New York, 1983.

Franklin, John Hope. *The Militant South, 1800–1861.* Cambridge, Mass., 1956.

Garner, James Wilford. *Reconstruction in Mississippi.* New York, 1901.

Gaston, Paul. *The New South Creed: A Study in Southern Mythmaking.* New York, 1970.

Genovese, Eugene. *The Political Economy of Slavery: Studies in the Economy and Society of the Slave South.* New York, 1965.

Goodwyn, Lawrence. *The Populist Moment: A Short History of the Agrarian Revolt in America.* New York, 1978.

Gray, Lewis. *History of Agriculture in the Southern United States to 1860.* 2 vols. Washington, D.C., 1933.

Gutmann, Myron P., *et al. Staying Put or Moving On? Ethnicity, Migration, and Persistence in Nineteenth-Century Texas.* Austin, 1990.

Hahn, Steven. *The Roots of Southern Populism: Yeoman Farmers and the Transformation of the Georgia Upcountry, 1850–1890.* New York, 1983.

Hahn, Steven, and Jonathan Prude, eds. *The Countryside in the Age of Capitalist Transformation: Essays in the Social History of Rural America.* Chapel Hill, 1985.

Hardeman, Nicholas. *Shucks, Shocks, and Hominy Blocks: Corn as a Way of Life in Pioneer America.* Baton Rouge, 1981.

Harris, J. William. *Plain Folk and Gentry in a Slave Society: White Liberty and Black Slavery in Augusta's Hinterlands.* Middletown, Conn., 1985.

Harris, William C. *Day of the Carpetbagger: Republican Reconstruction in Mississippi.* Baton Rouge, 1979.

———. *Presidential Reconstruction in Mississippi.* Baton Rouge, 1967.

Hawk. Emory Q. *Economic History of the South.* New York, 1934.

Haywood, Robert C. *Victorian West: Class and Culture in Kansas Cattle Towns.* Lawrence, Kan., 1991.

Hickman, Nollie W. *Mississippi Harvest: Lumbering in the Longleaf Pine Belt, 1840–1915.* Montgomery, 1962.

Hilliard, Sam Bowers. *Atlas of Antebellum Southern Agriculture.* Baton Rouge, 1984.

———. *Hog Meat and Hoecake: Food Supply in the Old South, 1840–1860.* Edwardsville, Ill., 1972.

Holmes, William F. *The Great White Chief: James Kimble Vardaman.* Baton Rouge, 1970.

Holt, Michael F. *The Political Crisis of the 1850s.* New York, 1978.

Howe, Daniel Walker. *The Political Culture of the American Whigs.* Chicago, 1979.

Humphreys, Benjamin G. *Floods and Levees of the Mississippi River.* Washington, D.C., 1914.

Humphreys, Margaret. *Yellow Fever and the South.* New Brunswick, N.J., 1992.

Hyman, Michael R. *The Anti-Redeemers: Hill Country Political Dissenters in the Lower South from Redemption to Populism.* Baton Rouge, 1990.

Jaynes, Gerald David. *Branches Without Roots: Genesis of the Black Working Class in the American South, 1862–1882.* New York, 1986.

Jordan, Winthrop D. *Tumult and Silence at Second Creek: An Inquiry into a Slave Conspiracy.* Baton Rouge, 1993.

Kammen, Michael. *Spheres of Liberty: Changing Perceptions of Liberty in American Culture.* Madison, 1986.

Kenzer, Robert C. *Kinship and Neighborhood in a North Carolina Community: Orange County, North Carolina, 1849–1881.* Knoxville, 1987.

Kirwan, Albert D. *Revolt of the Rednecks: Mississippi Politics, 1876–1925.* 1951; rpr. New York, 1965.

Kousser, J. Morgan. *The Shaping of Southern Politics: Suffrage Restriction and the Establishment of the One-Party South, 1880–1910.* New Haven, 1974.

Loewen, James W. *The Mississippi Chinese: Between Black and White.* Cambridge, Mass., 1971.

Lonn, Ella. *Salt as a Factor in the Confederacy.* University, Ala., 1965.

May, Robert E. *John A. Quitman: Old South Crusader.* Baton Rouge, 1985.

McCormick, Richard P. *The Second American Party System: Party Formation in the Jacksonian Era.* Chapel Hill, 1960.

McCoy, Drew R. *The Elusive Republic: Political Economy in Jeffersonian America.* New York, 1980.

———. *The Last of the Fathers: James Madison and the Republican Legacy.* Cambridge, England, 1989.

McMillen, Neil R. *Dark Journey: Black Mississippians in the Age of Jim Crow.* Urbana, Ill., 1989.

McWhiney, Grady. *Cracker Culture: Celtic Ways in the Old South.* Tuscaloosa, 1988.

McWhiney, Grady, and Perry D. Jamieson. *Attack and Die: Civil War Military Tactics and the Southern Heritage.* University, Ala., 1982.

Miles, Edwin A. *Jacksonian Democracy in Mississippi.* Chapel Hill, 1960.

Mississippi: A Guide to the Magnolia State: Compiled and Written by the Fed-

eral Writers' Project of the Works Progress Administration. New York, 1938.

Moore, John Hebron. *Andrew Brown and Cypress Lumbering in the Old Southwest.* Baton Rouge, 1967.

———. *The Emergence of the Cotton Kingdom in the Old Southwest: Mississippi, 1770–1860.* Baton Rouge, 1988.

Morgan, Edmund S. *American Slavery, American Freedom: The Ordeal of Colonial Virginia.* New York, 1975.

Murphy, James B. *L. Q. C. Lamar: Pragmatic Patriot.* Baton Rouge, 1973.

Naipaul, V. S. *A Turn in the South.* New York, 1989.

North, Douglas. *The Economic Growth of the United States, 1790–1860.* 1961; rpr. New York, 1966.

Oakes, James. *The Ruling Race: A History of American Slaveholders.* New York, 1982.

O'Brien, Gail Williams. *The Legal Fraternity and the Making of a New South Community, 1848–1882.* Athens, 1986.

Odum, Howard. *An American Epoch: Southern Portraiture in the National Picture.* New York, 1930.

Osborn, George Coleman. *James Kimble Vardaman: Southern Commoner.* Jackson, 1981.

Ownby, Ted. *Subduing Satan: Religion, Recreation, and Manhood in the Rural South, 1865–1920.* Chapel Hill, 1990.

Palmer, Bruce. *"Man Over Money": The Southern Populist Critique of American Capitalism.* Chapel Hill, 1980.

Penick, James Lal, Jr. *The Great Western Land Pirate: John A. Murrell in Legend and History.* Columbia, Mo., 1981.

Percy, William Alexander. *Lanterns on the Levee: Recollections of a Planter's Son.* 1941; rpr. Baton Rouge, 1973.

Pereyra, Lillian A. *James Lusk Alcorn: Persistent Whig.* Baton Rouge, 1966.

Perman, Michael. *The Road to Redemption: Southern Politics, 1869–1879.* Chapel Hill, 1984.

Phillips, Ulrich Bonnell. *Life and Labor in the Old South.* 1929; rpr. New York, 1937.

Pocock, J. G. A. *The Machiavellian Moment.* Princeton, 1975.

———. *Virtue, Commerce, and History: Essays on Political Thought and History, Chiefly in the Eighteenth Century.* Cambridge, England, 1985.

Polakoff, Keith Ian. *The Election of 1876 and the End of Reconstruction.* Baton Rouge, 1973.

Polk, Noel, ed. *Mississippi's Piney Woods: A Human Perspective.* Jackson, 1986.

Pollack, Norman. *The Humane Economy: Populism, Capitalism, and Democracy.* New Brunswick, N.J., 1990.

Powell, Lawrence N. *New Masters: Northern Planters During the Civil War and Reconstruction.* New Haven, 1980.

Quan, Robert Seto, and Julian B. Roebuck. *Lotus Among the Magnolias: The Mississippi Chinese.* Jackson, 1982.

Rable, George. *But There Was No Peace: The Role of Violence in the Politics of Reconstruction.* Athens, 1984.
Rainwater, Percy Lee. *Mississippi: Storm Center of Secession, 1856–1861.* Baton Rouge, 1938.
Ranck, James Byrne. *Albert Gallatin Brown: Radical Southern Nationalist.* New York, 1937.
Ransom, Roger, and Richard Sutch. *One Kind of Freedom: The Economic Consequences of Emancipation.* New York, 1977.
Reidy, Joseph P. *From Slavery to Agrarian Capitalism in the Cotton Plantation South: Central Georgia, 1800–1880.* Chapel Hill, 1992.
Roark, James L. *Masters Without Slaves: Southern Planters in the Civil War and Reconstruction.* New York, 1977.
Rodabaugh, John E. *Steamboats on the Upper Tombigbee.* Hamilton, Miss., 1985.
Rowland, Dunbar. *Military History of Mississippi, 1803–1898.* 1908; rpr. Spartanburg, 1978.
Sansing, David G. *Making Haste Slowly: The Troubled History of Higher Education in Mississippi.* Jackson, 1990.
Schweikart, Larry. *Banking in the American South from the Age of Jackson to Reconstruction.* Baton Rouge, 1987.
Sellers, Charles. *The Market Revolution: Jacksonian America, 1815–1846.* New York, 1991.
Shaw, Barton C. *The Wool-Hat Boys: Georgia's Populist Party.* Baton Rouge, 1984.
Shore, Laurence. *Southern Capitalists: The Ideological Leadership of an Elite, 1832–1885.* Chapel Hill, 1986.
Silver, James W. *Mississippi: The Closed Society.* New York, 1964.
Simpson, Brooks D. *Let Us Have Peace: Ulysses S. Grant and the Politics of War and Reconstruction, 1861–1868.* Chapel Hill, 1991.
Smith, Frank E. *The Yazoo River.* New York, 1954.
Stover, John F. *History of the Illinois Central Railroad.* New York, 1975.
———. *The Railroads of the South, 1865–1900: A Study in Finance and Control.* Chapel Hill, 1955.
Strode, Hudson. *Jefferson Davis, American Patriot, 1808–1861.* Vol. I of 2 vols. New York, 1955.
Summers, Mark W. *Railroads, Reconstruction, and the Gospel of Prosperity: Aid Under the Radical Republicans, 1865–1877.* Princeton, 1984.
Thornton, J. Mills, III. *Politics and Power in a Slave Society: Alabama, 1800–1860.* Baton Rouge, 1978.
Trelease, Allen. *White Terror: The Ku Klux Klan Conspiracy and Southern Reconstruction.* Westport, Conn., 1971.
Unger, Irwin. *The Greenback Era: A Social and Political History of American Finance, 1865–1879.* Princeton, 1964.

Warren, George F., and Frank A. Pearson. *Prices.* New York, 1933.

Warren, Robert Penn. *All the King's Men.* 1946; rpr. San Diego, 1982.

Watkins, James L. *King Cotton: A Historical and Statistical Review, 1790 to 1908.* New York, 1908.

Wayne, Michael. *The Reshaping of Plantation Society: The Natchez District, 1860–1880.* Baton Rouge, 1983.

Weaver, Herbert. *Mississippi Farmers, 1850–1860.* Nashville, 1945.

Weber, Max. *The Protestant Ethic and the Spirit of Capitalism.* Translated by Talcott Parsons. New York, 1958.

Wharton, Vernon Lane. *The Negro in Mississippi, 1865–1890.* 1947; rpr. New York, 1965.

Williams, Wirt A., ed. *History of Bolivar County, Mississippi: Compiled by Florence Warfield Sillers and Members of the Mississippi Delta Chapter, Daughters of the American Revolution and the County History Committee.* Jackson, 1948.

Windham, Kathryn Tucker. *Count Those Buzzards! Stamp Those Grey Mules.* N.p., 1979.

Wood, Gordon S. *The Creation of the American Republic, 1776–1787.* 1969; rpr. New York, 1972.

Woodman, Harold. *King Cotton and His Retainers: Financing and Marketing the Cotton Crop of the South, 1800–1915.* Lexington, Ky., 1968.

Woodward, C. Vann. *Origins of the New South, 1877–1913.* Baton Rouge, 1951.

Wright, Gavin. *The Political Economy of the Cotton South: Households, Markets, and Wealth in the Nineteenth Century South.* New York, 1978.

Wyatt-Brown, Bertram. *Honor and Violence in the Old South.* New York, 1986.

Theses and Dissertations

Breese, Donald H. "Politics in the Lower South During Presidential Reconstruction, April to November, 1865." Ph.D. dissertation, University of California, Los Angeles, 1963.

Clark, Eric Charles. "The Mississippi Constitutional Convention of 1890: A Political Analysis." M.A. thesis, University of Mississippi, 1975.

Cobb, James C. "'Deepest South,': The Mississippi Delta and the Riddle of Regional Identity." Paper Delivered at the Fifty-Sixth Annual Meeting of the Southern Historical Association, November 1, 1990, New Orleans, Louisiana.

Coker, William Leon. "Cotton and Faith: A Social and Political View of Mississippi Wartime Finance, 1861–1865." Ph.D. dissertation, University of Oklahoma, 1973.

Cooley, Ruby E. "A History of the Mississippi Penal Farm System, 1890–1935: Punishment, Politics, and Profit in Penal Affairs." M.A. thesis, University of Southern Mississippi, 1981.

Cranford, Sammy O. "The Fernwood, Columbia, and Gulf: A Railroad in the

Piney Woods of South Mississippi." Ph.D. dissertation, Mississippi State University, 1983.

Cresswell, Stephen Edward. "Resistance and Enforcement: The United States Department of Justice, 1873–1893." Ph.D. dissertation, University of Virginia, 1986.

Currie, James Tyson. "Vicksburg, 1863–1876: The Promise and the Reality of Reconstruction on the Mississippi." Ph.D. dissertation, University of Virginia, 1976.

Davis, William Graham. "Attacking the 'Matchless Evil': Temperance and Prohibition in Mississippi, 1817–1908." Ph.D. dissertation, Mississippi State University, 1975.

Easom, Percy. "Public School Legislation in Mississippi, 1860 to 1930." Ph.D. dissertation, George Peabody College for Teachers, 1937.

Ferguson, James Sharborough. "Agrarianism in Mississippi, 1871–1900: A Study in Non-Conformity." Ph.D. dissertation, University of North Carolina, 1952.

Foust, James D. "The Yeoman Farmer and Westward Expansion of U.S. Cotton Production," Ph.D. dissertation, University of North Carolina, 1967.

Hardin, Paul Douglas. "Edward Cary Walthall: A Mississippi Conservative." M.A. thesis, Duke University, 1940.

Legan, Marshall Scott. "The Evolution of Public Health Services in Mississippi, 1865–1910." Ph.D. dissertation, University of Mississippi, 1968.

Miller, Clarke Leonard. "'Let Us Die to Make Men Free': Political Terrorism in Post-Reconstruction Mississippi, 1877–1896." Ph.D. dissertation, University of Minnesota, 1983.

Moore, Ross. "Social and Economic Conditions in Mississippi During Reconstruction." Ph.D. dissertation, Duke University, 1938.

Salamon, Lester Milton. "Protest, Politics, and Modernization in the American South: Mississippi as a 'Developing Society.'" Ph.D. dissertation, Harvard University, 1971.

Vogt, Daniel C. "Problems of Government Regulation: The Mississippi Railroad Commission, 1884–1956." Ph.D. dissertation, University of Southern Mississippi, 1980.

Weems, Robert Cicero, Jr. "The Bank of the State of Mississippi: A Pioneer Bank of the Old Southwest, 1809–1844." Ph.D. dissertation, Columbia University, 1952.

Young, David Nathaniel. "The Mississippi Whigs, 1834–1860." Ph.D. dissertation, University of Alabama, 1968.

Index